ALL THE LIGHT HERE COMES FROM ABOVE:

The Life and Legacy of Edward Hitchcock

by Robert T. McMaster

UNQUOMONK PRESS
Williamsburg, Massachusetts
U. S. A.

ALL THE LIGHT HERE
COMES FROM ABOVE:
The Life and Legacy of
Edward Hitchcock

Printed in the United States of America.

www.EdwardHitchcock.com

ISBN 978-0-9856944-9-4

Published by Unquomonk Press
Williamsburg, Massachusetts 01096 USA

Dedicated to

Robert L. Herbert

1929-2020

Dr. Robert L. Herbert, art historian and Professor Emeritus at Mount Holyoke College, passed away just a few days before this book went to press. Dr. Herbert was the preeminent Hitchcock scholar of our time, an inspiration to me and to many other scholars and writers.

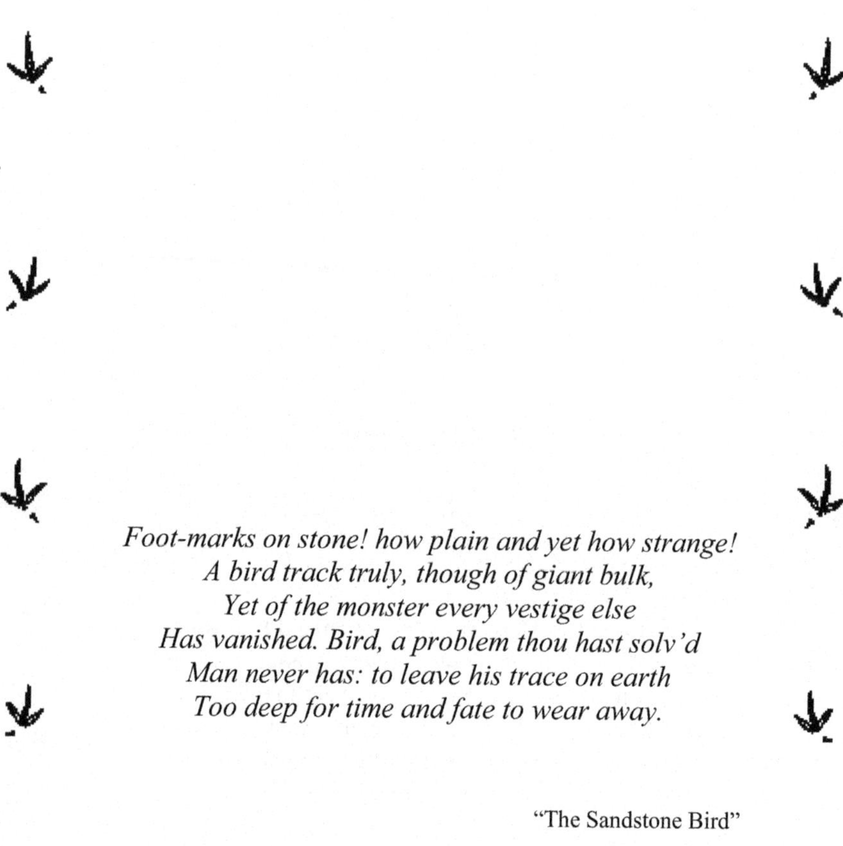

Foot-marks on stone! how plain and yet how strange!
A bird track truly, though of giant bulk,
Yet of the monster every vestige else
Has vanished. Bird, a problem thou hast solv'd
Man never has: to leave his trace on earth
Too deep for time and fate to wear away.

"The Sandstone Bird"

Contents

AMHERST 1826-1844

THE PRESIDENCY 1845-1854

RETIREMENT 1854-1864

RETROSPECTIVE

Introduction

I was barely ten years old when, on a winter's day, my father took me to visit the Pratt Museum of Natural History at Amherst College in Amherst, Massachusetts. We were the only visitors, and I walked about awestruck by what I saw: bones, skulls, and skeletons of all manner of creatures large and small, including an enormous mammoth and a dazzling exhibit of rocks and minerals. We then descended to the basement, groping about in the dark to find a light switch. And there we found tracks in stone—curious and enigmatic to that little boy—and capable of evoking all sorts of questions, though I do not recall either signs or docents to provide answers. Those remarkable artifacts, I learned, were the life work of someone named Edward Hitchcock. Even at that tender age, I was surprised to see such an extraordinary collection exhibited so poorly and obscurely.

Fast forward a half century. I walk into the recently opened Beneski Museum of Natural History, a handsome edifice of brick, steel, and glass. Just inside the entrance I pause, look up, and gaze on that mammoth, no doubt the same creature I had observed in the dimly lit gallery long ago. It is magnificent and cannot fail to evoke questions in the minds of every child, young or old, who enters. Thankfully, the climate and lighting are ideal in this gleaming new home, as is the signage. A docent is giving a tour to a group of school children not far from where I stand. At last, I think, Edward Hitchcock has received the recognition he deserves. His remarkable collections are now displayed to great advantage, for all to see, to enjoy, to understand.

Since that day, I have not stopped thinking about, reading about, and studying Edward Hitchcock—poet, playwright, pastor, preacher, professor, paleontologist, president, and *pater familias*. The more I have learned of the man, the more convinced I am that there is a story yet to be told—many stories, in truth. For his legacy, one that even today in the minds of many begins and ends with those tracks in stone, actually extends far beyond them.

Edward Hitchcock was a man supremely grounded in place and time. He lived nearly his entire life—three score and ten years as he would say—within fifteen miles of that museum in Amherst, Massachusetts. He knew the countryside from Deerfield to Conway to Amherst better than any of his contemporaries, better perhaps than anyone since. Later in life he would venture farther afield—to New York, Virginia, the Midwest, and once to Europe. But even when at home his vision was not limited—he did not wear blinders like one of the horses in his barn. He traveled very widely, in a manner of speaking, thanks to books, mostly borrowed, and not idly skimmed but devoured. Nor did his geographical limitations reduce his influence, for even in his time, newspapers and periodicals—literary, scientific, and religious—were proliferating. His words in print—close to five million in all—appeared and no doubt were read by thousands around the world.

Without question Hitchcock's greatest influence was in the field of paleontology. Those tracks, bones, and skeletons came to life in his imagination and were committed to paper with equal verisimilitude. But he also made contributions of great import in the broader field of geology. No, he was not a visionary like Charles Lyell or Louis Agassiz or Charles Darwin. He was, however, an observer, a thinker, an accumulator of data, who at several important points in the nineteenth century weighed in on the grand debates about earth's past with great effect. Edward Hitchcock thirsted for contact with his fellow scientists, and was thus a key contributor in the early days of the *American Journal of Science and Arts* and a founder of the Association of American Geologists and Naturalists, soon to be renamed the American Association for the Advancement of Science, the preeminent professional organization of American scientists to this day.

Hitchcock was an educator with a lifelong desire to teach and a determination to do so in whatever way was most effective. He used demonstrations, experiments, models, posters, murals, field trips, and all manner of what might today be called "hands-on" instructional methods with his students at Amherst College. He had little technology at his command—even photography had barely developed until the last years of his life. But he knew the value of employing every means available to bring a subject to life for his students. And while he was devoted to science education, he was equally impassioned about agricultural education. He argued strenuously for the creation of a state agricultural college in Massachusetts, and his support of that idea had a good deal to do with the establishment of Massachusetts Agricultural College in Amherst—known today as the University of Massachusetts—just three years after his death.

Edward Hitchcock's entire college teaching career was spent instructing young men. But he was equally committed to the education of women and played a pivotal role in the development of two female seminaries, as they were then termed, one in Amherst that did not survive, one in nearby South Hadley—Mount Holyoke College—that did survive and thrived.

In 1844 the prospects for Amherst College looked very bleak. Enrollment was declining, faculty and student morale were abysmal, the college's finances meager. When the day came that the trustees of Amherst College called on Edward Hitchcock to become the third president of that institution, he at first demurred. He was convinced that he was poorly suited to the post and the last person who could rescue the institution from almost certain demise. But he eventually accepted the position, however reluctantly, and from the very day of his inauguration, the clouds over the college parted and the sun began to shine once more on that "consecrated eminence."

As to the Reverend Edward Hitchcock, he was a deeply spiritual man who strove throughout his adult life to do what was good and right in the eyes of his Lord. He was an evangelical Christian who held the Bible to be inspired and literally true, who believed that there was no hope for any man or woman but through Jesus Christ. He was a skilled preacher who, long after giving up his one parish, was called on regularly to preach. He spoke out on many of the great moral issues of his time—slavery, war, the mistreatment of the American Indian. His faith drove him as a preacher, as a teacher, as a parent, as a man. But it caused him great consternation as a scientist, seeing the simple truths of the Bible challenged. And it caused him great spiritual malaise when he came to realize that he was himself devoted to the pursuit of worldly prizes, even as he warned his parishioners against such temptations.

Despite his many achievements in science, religion, and education, Edward Hitchcock was a troubled man. As a preacher he often employed the metaphor of a human being as a ship adrift on a vast and perilous ocean. If we apply that metaphor to the man himself, we must conclude that his was a most unseaworthy ship, tossed about by an angry sea and in peril of crashing on the rocks or sinking beneath the waves at any moment. Fortunate indeed was Edward Hitchcock to have Orra White Hitchcock as his wife and "coadjutor" for over forty years. She was his anchor, his rudder, his keel. Without her steadying hand, her constancy, her faithfulness, his career would have had a very different trajectory, his life would likely have been shortened by decades, his soul buried in self-doubt and guilt. That ship would most certainly have foundered on the rocks.

In *All the Light Here Comes from Above—The Life and Legacy of Edward Hitchcock* I have tried to do justice to this man, to recognize the many facets of his personality, of his career, of his legacy. I have tried to avoid reducing him to lowest terms—a scientist, for instance, who could not accept scientific truth—or a Christian at war with his religious principles—or a flawed personality that could not shake the belief that his body was on the verge of expiring at any minute. For every weakness in his body or spirit, he possessed a matching and countervailing strength. In nearly every pursuit he undertook in his long life, he excelled despite many powerful demons.

I have depended heavily on Edward Hitchcock's own words for my research. Fortunately, most of his unpublished writings—sermons, notes, letters, diaries, etc.—have been preserved in the Amherst College Archives and Special Collections in Amherst, Massachusetts, and in the collections of the Pocumtuck Valley Memorial Association and Historic Deerfield in Deerfield, Massachusetts. He has left an enormous paper trail, considering he lived long before word processors, typewriters, even fountain pens. Spelling and grammatical variations are common in the writings of Edward Hitchcock. In most cases I have transcribed those variations exactly as they appear in the original, without the notation "*sic*" used by some authors. Thus when Edward writes of "bowlders" or "vallies" or "millenium," I have shown those words exactly as written. The only exceptions are the few occasions when a change seemed necessary to make the meaning clear.

Rather than clutter the text with hundreds of footnotes, I have listed my sources under "Notes and References" (beginning on page 371) including notes by page number followed by sources specific to each chapter. Most of the direct quotations cited may be found by searching one of the transcriptions which are accessible online (see page 373).

Among the most valuable of Hitchcock's unpublished manuscripts for my research have been his personal writings recorded over thirty-five years that he titled "Private Notes." They were not a diary in the strict sense. They were kept, he explained in the first entry, for the sake of his children, that they might better understand him and his life when he was gone. Entries were made very irregularly, sometimes as infrequently as two or three times a year. Over a five-year period in the 1830s he made no entries. Late in life there is a two-year gap, although in that case it appears pages were lost or intentionally removed. I will refer to these hereafter as his "notes."

At the beginning of each chapter I have allowed my imagination some license, depicting a scene, sometimes with dialogue, from the life of Edward Hitchcock and other family members. While these vignettes are to some degree fictional, they are based on real events and I believe accurately depict Edward, Orra, Justin, their families, their contemporaries, and the times in which they lived. It is my hope that they will help twenty-first century readers better to conjure up the true spirit of Edward Hitchcock.

Prologue

Amherst, Massachusetts, December 16, 1844

Darkness had already descended on the snow-covered landscape as a single figure made his way haltingly up the rutted path toward College Hill, drawing a heavy black cloak around him with one hand while grasping a bail-handled oil lamp with the other. To his right rose the brick edifice of North College, entirely dark but for candlelight flickering in the rooms of the few students who chose to remain over the vacation period between the first and second terms.

At the crest of the hill the figure turned into the curved pathway that led to a stately Georgian structure, the residence of the president of Amherst College. A dim glow shone through the windows of the first floor. Just as he approached the front door, it opened—he was expected. He was directed to a seat by the fireplace in the drafty vestibule.

In the musty, dimly lit library a few steps away, four bearded men sat around a long chestnut table, sheaves of papers stacked before them. Present were George Grennell, Alfred Foster, Samuel Williston, and Lucius Boltwood, all members of the Board of Trustees appointed to this committee. The mood was solemn, befitting the darkness of the occasion, for all four men knew too well that the fate of Amherst College was in their hands.

For those who had known the college throughout its nearly quarter century, the circumstances in which they found themselves must have had a surreal quality. How quickly the young institution had grown after its opening in 1821, and how well it had been received by students, faculty, and the community around it. For years there had been only glowing reports of students exceling, graduating, many of them going on to the ministry or to missionary work, for the college was dedicated to educating young men "of hopeful piety" for a religious vocation. Financially the college had never been flush, but thanks to the generosity of many individuals it had managed to do reasonably well for more than a decade.

Then, in 1835, everything began to go wrong. Fueled by a national recession, the school's enrollment declined. At the same time gifts from its many supporters dropped as well. This two-edged sword cut to the bone of the young institution. The college's second President, Reverend Heman Humphrey, had done his best under trying circumstances, but even he had begun to despair. The social cohesion of the institution also had suffered, with conflicts erupting frequently between students and faculty, sometimes at public events. Even some of the college's own alumni spoke ill of their alma mater, spreading the alarm that the end was near.

President Humphrey had tendered his resignation just six months earlier, probably aware that his departure was deemed necessary by many board members. Immediately the Board of Trustees had circulated the intelligence that they were seeking applicants for the Presidency. They made at least three offers in three months, all of which were declined. No one it seemed wanted to take the helm of a sinking ship.

In the fall term when enrollment hit rock bottom, the message was clear. Unless the trustees took dramatic action to save it, Amherst College would soon be facing dissolution. The Board of Trustees at this time included men of wisdom and strength, men who dearly loved the college and would not allow it to fail without doing their utmost to save it. One of those men was Reverend Joseph Vaill. Vaill acted as a go-between for the board and the faculty as they sought agreement on a plan to save the college. It had been brought to the Board only days earlier and approved. It was up to this committee to work out the details, the most important of which was finding a new leader for the institution in these most trying circumstances.

What the college needed in a president was a man known and respected by all, students, faculty, and the larger community. He must be someone whose devotion to the college was complete, one who could instill confidence in the institution and bring old friends, students, alumni, and donors, back into the fold. In short, he must be capable of rebuilding Amherst College from the rubble it had become. All agreed, there was only one man who filled those requirements, and he was the man waiting nervously in the anteroom.

After some minutes of further deliberations, the men huddled in the library fell silent. Lucius Boltwood rose from his chair and walked to the door, then opened it.

"Professor Hitchcock, will you please come in, sir?"

Today, nearly two centuries after that fateful December evening, the choice of Edward Hitchcock as third president of Amherst College seems like an obvious one. But without the advantage of a crystal ball to gaze into the future, it was not an easy decision, certainly not for Edward Hitchcock himself. Doubts most likely lurked in the minds and hearts of some board members as well.

Hitchcock's scientific credentials were stellar. He had undertaken the job of State Geologist in 1830, had completed two extensive geological surveys of the state, and written three lengthy, widely praised reports on those surveys. His survey and reports had become models that dozens of other states were now replicating. His research on the fossil footmarks of the Connecticut Valley was nothing short of revolutionary for paleontology, for understanding the history of life on the planet. Publishing his findings had taken courage—he had had his critics. But by 1844 nearly all those critics had been silenced. He was preeminent in the field of geology in America, and highly regarded by scientists abroad as well.

As a professor, Edward Hitchcock was well liked by his students, his teaching methods exhibiting the same devotion and unstinting energy as his research. In the chemistry laboratory he had a flair for the theatrical, one might even say the pyrotechnical. He taught botany as well, marching his charges over hill and dale in search of a rare orchid or fern. His geology lectures were informed largely by his research, and he developed a curriculum of his own design. His textbook, *Elementary Geology,* had drawn wide acclaim from his colleagues and peers. It was already in its fifth edition.

Reverend Edward Hitchcock was known far and wide as a man of deep conviction and strictly orthodox Christian views, a man of impeccable moral stature. While his career as a pastor had been short, he continued to preach and to publish in the religious press. His sermons were epic and frequently requested by ministers and parishioners near and far. As a friend and neighbor, Edward Hitchcock was admired in Amherst for his warmth, his compassion, his concern for all, students, colleagues, neighbors. He was known as a devoted husband and father as well.

With all this admiration and respect to buoy him, one might expect Edward Hitchcock would have been honored at the proposal presented to him on that day. But despite all his talents, all his honors, all the recognition he enjoyed as a teacher, a scientist, a preacher, a man, he was deeply troubled by the offer of the presidency of Amherst College. It was a post he had never sought, that he had never wished for, that he felt ill-prepared to fill.

Why was he so strongly disinclined to accept this highest of academic honors? One consideration was his lack of an earned degree. How, he asked himself, could one who had never earned a degree lead an academic institution like Amherst College? And there was his writing, his research. He would be unable to carry them on as President, of that he was certain.

But most worrisome of all was his health. The truth was that Edward Hitchcock, for the last fifteen years or more, had been convinced that he was plunging into dissolution. Every bout of illness he feared would be his last. He wrote as much again and again in his own notes, as if reminding himself. He confessed his fears repeatedly to his wife. He even told his children regularly that he would not be with them much longer.

He had also shared his worries with his colleagues, faculty, board members, and with President Humphrey. All of them were aware that this was a man whose body was fragile and whose spirit was tenuous as well. How could they not have wondered if such a wounded soul was the one Amherst College needed to revive its own spiritual malaise?

This was the perilous balance in which hung the lives of both Edward Hitchcock and Amherst College on that December evening in 1844.

DEERFIELD 1779-1820

Figure 1. Western Massachusetts in Edward Hitchcock's time. The original Hampshire County incorporated in 1662 extended from the Vermont and New Hampshire borders to the Connecticut border. It was subsequently divided into three counties, with Franklin County to the north (1811) and Hampden County to the south (1812).

View of Pocumtuck

1 The Hatter of Deerfield

"There is nothing in the history of a boy that is worth recording."

November 25, 1779

The bells of the meetinghouse in Deerfield, Massachusetts, pealed brightly on a crisp autumn morning in 1779. The tintinnabulations could be heard the full length of "The Street," the broad thoroughfare that bisected the village center. They could be heard in its dozens of shops—saddler, smithy, broom-maker, shoemaker—and in every shingled or clapboarded home along the way. So too could the chorus be heard in the weathered barns beyond the shops and residences, barns where workers labored, stacking hay to feed cows, horses, sheep, and oxen—and in low, dark sheds where the meat of freshly slaughtered hogs was being salted, then stored away in oaken barrels against the long, cold winter to come.

Still farther did that clanging chorus carry across the broad valley where the season's wheat, rye, and corn crops had been reduced now to mere stubble, where farmers busy dressing their gardens or tending their livestock paused from their labors for a moment to listen. To the east the clangor echoed off the steep shoulders of the Sugarloafs—Wequamps as the native peoples called them—their stunted, wind-wizened oaks already cloaked in early winter snow. To the west the chiming carried across the river once called Pocumtuck, rolling to the base of the Sunsick Hills more than a mile distant.

The occasion of all that bell ringing was a marriage ceremony in the white clapboarded meetinghouse. When at last the bells fell silent, a small wedding party stood at the church doors. As the bride spoke with some family members, the groom turned and approached the Reverend Jonathan Ashley who stood apart, grim-faced, his dark, sunken eyes cast downward.

"Mr. Ashley."

The old pastor nodded, his gaze rising to meet the groom's but briefly. "Sir."

There was an awkward pause. Finally the groom spoke again. "Thank you, Mr. Ashley, for your kindness, to myself and to Miss Hoyt...er...Mrs. Hitchcock."

After another pause, the old minister spoke. "Godspeed to you, sir, and to Mrs. Hitchcock," he said glumly.

The groom acknowledged the well-wishes with a bow, then turned away and without another word rejoined his bride, leaving the Reverend Ashley standing apart, alone.

For the Reverend Jonathan Ashley, now seventy years of age, this would be the last wedding performed in his nearly half a century at Deerfield. His constancy as a minister had earned him the admiration of most of the townspeople. But the Reverend Ashley was a Tory, a supporter of the King of England. His political views had carved a deep rift between him and many of his parishioners who were Whigs and bitterly opposed to the King. It was a rift that would never be mended. Reverend Ashley would die a few months later, a lonely, embittered old man, a lesson on mixing religion and politics that his successors would be wise to take to heart.

Both bride and groom on that November day were well known to nearly all Deerfield's residents. Miss Mercy Hoyt, the twenty-four-year-old bride, was the daughter of David and Silence Hoyt, a member of one of Deerfield's most prominent families. The first Hoyt arrived in Deerfield from Windsor, Connecticut, in 1682. Mercy's great-grandfather, David Hoit, and her grandfather, Jonathan Hoit, both were captured in the infamous raid of February

1704, when several hundred soldiers from Canada, both French and native American, crept into the sleeping village, killed dozens of townspeople, captured over one hundred others, then transported them north toward Canada. Jonathan Hoit was eventually released; his father died en route. Seven decades later, the Hoyt family still occupied the "Old Indian House" in the center of town, the same dwelling in which seven of their forebears were living on that fateful night. Three were killed, the others taken to Canada. Mercy's father, who fought bravely in the French and Indian War, was now keeper of one of the village's public houses and a "maker of wigs and foretops."

Of the personal qualities of the bride we know very little. One reference published decades after her death described her as "a woman of active mind and marked character," another as "...a high-bred New England woman, one of those perfect creations of divine skill by which the development of our race is guaranteed, a woman of quick intelligence, pure heart, and exquisite sensibility." Genealogies of that period often rambled on and on about fathers and sons, their physical attributes, moral character, education, career, accomplishments, honors. Mothers and daughters, on the other hand, received little mention beyond the husband's name, unmarried daughters still less. In *Reminiscences*, Mercy's son Edward had much to say about his father, yet made only one mention of his mother, suggesting that his health problems were "...hereditary on my mother's side..." Based on what we do know about her younger brothers, David, Epaphras, and Elihu, we may assume that Mercy was intelligent and received some basic education.

The twenty-seven-year-old groom, Justin Hitchcock—hatter, fifer, sing-master—was less familiar to many of the town's residents, for he had only recently arrived in Deerfield. Nevertheless, he had quickly gained the respect and admiration of nearly all. We know a great deal of the life of Justin Hitchcock thanks to an extraordinary memoir, "Remarks and Observations by Justin Hitchcock," subtitled with typical self-effacement, "A Sort of Autobiography." Here he recorded the events of his life, his memories, and reflections from 1780 to 1799.

Early in his musings Justin warns his reader not to expect much of interest: "There is nothing in the history of a boy that is worth recording." And yet what follows is an illuminating account of daily life in eighteenth century New England—from clothing to farming, from politics to religion—as well as a family genealogy, a history of the early years of the nation, and an almanac of all manner of natural phenomena from canker worms to hurricanes, from eclipses to meteors.

We learn that Justin was born in Springfield, Massachusetts, in 1752. In 1756 his parents, Luke and Lucy Hitchcock, removed from Springfield to Granville, a tiny farming community in the Berkshire foothills where they managed to eke out a living on their 100-acre farm, raising cattle, growing wheat and rye, and maple sugaring. Life was not all hard work for the Hitchcocks of Granville. "Our family were fond of music," Justin recalled.

> My Father and Mother could sing, my brother Charles played well on a violin. I was very fond of Music when young tho I made awkward work of it at first and never got my insight of the rules before I went from my Fathers. Being fond of singing I picked off a book of Music in square or diamond notes…

Neither of Justin's parents had much formal schooling and so they were determined that their children should have the benefit of the best education available in Granville, a single room schoolhouse just a mile from their home. Justin described two of his teachers:

> One, Mr. Doer Smith, kept the school, and he was a proper tyrant. He kept a stick by him, long enough to reach every boy in the school. Although he improved his advantage, so that we all feared him, few if any felt any affection for him, and the consequence was that we learned slowly.

Justin much preferred the methods of Mr. Smith's successor, Mr. Harvey, who "…used a very different method with us, and instead of going to school as a task, we now went as a pleasure." But Justin was not satisfied with following his father's chosen work:

> Our business was husbandry and we had a great deal of driving plough to be don. This was a business I never liked. My Brother Merick showed more ambition as a good plough boy than I and I was willing to have him praised up as a teamster if I could thereby be freed from my turn of driving. I had an inclination to learn a trade.

To that end, Justin took an apprenticeship with a family friend and expert hatmaker, Moses Church, of Springfield. The terms of that arrangement were spelled out in detail in a document of indenture dated May 5, 1766. In his memoir Justin describes with remarkable frankness his life during the seven years of his apprenticeship in Springfield. His pastimes included hunting and fishing, as well as a few other less admirable pursuits common to young men of that time, partying, cardplaying, gambling, imbibing, inhaling snuff, and playing pranks on friends and unwitting citizens in the streets and back alleys. "…I was so much with parties especially in the evenings," he wrote, "that I could scarcely find the money enough to bear the expense…" Much to his credit, young Justin also found time to read.

> My Father recomended to me to spend my leisure time in reading and I following his advice in some measure and I read the history of England and other books but particularly dramatic pieces and some novels notwithstanding

> the great arg[ument] maid against the latter yet I think my reading them has never don me harm but that if I know anything of what is proper in the stile of writing I am partly indebted to this kind of reading as the language of these books is generally good.

Justin's love of music led him to join a singing group when he was nineteen, but the choirmaster, a Mr. J. Stickney, offered little encouragement to him or his fellow choristers: "The Master told us we could not learn and it was best not to try…" Nevertheless, Justin began composing music during those years. Singing and songwriting would play an important role in his later life, even in his military career.

In June of 1773 Justin completed his seven-year apprenticeship, the only apprentice of Mr. Church ever to do so. He served a few months as a journeyman for his mentor, but soon was ready for more independence. He wrote, "Now began a new era in my existence [when I] launched forth into the world and must take care of myself." He decided he would practice his trade in a promising new venue:

> I went to Deerfield in May this year notwithstanding my attachment to Springfield. I found it to be more for my interest to live at Deerfield for here I kept but little company but at Springfield it cost me to much.

Deerfield, Massachusetts, lay at the confluence of two of New England's great rivers, the Connecticut and the Deerfield, and it was that very position that made this place fertile ground for agriculture. At regular intervals the waters rose and flooded the adjacent lowlands, depositing a new layer of minerals with each inundation, yielding some of the richest soils in all of New England. The Pocumtucks, a tribe of the Abenaki nation, first inhabited that land, perhaps arriving shortly after the retreat of the last glacier. They were generally a peaceful people who cleared the land, grew crops, hunted and fished for several thousands of years. But in the 1660s, faced with incursions by larger tribes from the north and west, they went to war against the intruders, a war they lost. The survivors integrated into the conquering forces and in a matter of a few years, the Pocumtucks were no more. The rich farmlands they once occupied were visited briefly by other tribes, but for the most part were abandoned.

Enter the English. In 1664 the General Court of the Bay Colony in Boston, to compensate the people of the town of Dedham for lands that had been misappropriated, awarded the town the rights to settle a large tract of land in the Connecticut Valley. That tract included the former home of the Pocumtucks. Most of the beneficiaries never settled their land; probably few even visited to view their property. Parcel by parcel, the land was divided and sold, mostly to farmers from towns farther south along the river, Hatfield, Hadley, Northampton, men who likely had more of an appreciation for the potential value of the land.

But the position of the new settlement of Deerfield, on the westernmost frontier and relatively isolated from neighboring villages, made it a frequent target of attack by natives who feared the incursion of the English here and elsewhere in western and northern New England. Deerfield thus became a site of hostilities in 1675, 1689, 1704, 1722, and 1756. In the notorious raid of 1704, forty-four residents were killed and over one hundred carried away.

Despite the uncertainties and the bloodshed of the "Indian Wars," the town thrived. Its wealth was founded mainly on agriculture, with the rich soils proving ideal for cultivation of wheat, rye, corn, and tobacco. So successful was farming in the community that many landowners became very wealthy.

Deerfield was a small community, and Justin likely came to know Mercy Hoyt before long. They spent sufficient time as a couple among other young folk of Deerfield to feel the pressure of social expectations, as suggested by this undated note:

> In my last hours of reflection I often think of the says of people, that it is not good for us to keep company so long together. So often in my own mind [I] resolve that whenever I am going to spend an evening with you that I will lay a restraint on some passions by not allowing myself to urge some things which might have a tendency to lead on to _____. [The handwritten text here is obscured, perhaps by the writer, the recipient, or another family member at a later time.] I am sensible I am naturely inclined to every thing that is bad full of lust and passion. But hope I have some power to govern them—I have thought that if we shall disappoint some people by not fulfilling their prophecy consequent on so long keeping company. It might be some satisfaction to us if not cause of Pride. [At this point he must have realized he was rambling] It is well the paper is just wrote out for tis hard to make any more nonsensical folly.

If the idea of a permanent affiliation had already been contemplated by the young couple, circumstances of a different sort soon would intervene. Barely seventy-five miles to the east, trouble was brewing, the long-endured strictures imposed by "our Sovereign Lord George ye third" on his American colonies, had finally become unbearable. A town meeting was held in Deerfield on the evening of April 20, 1775, to appropriate funds for a small force of men to be organized under the leadership of Lieutenant Joseph Stebbins in the event that war should erupt with England. Sheldon recounts the occasion dramatically:

> It is evident from the record of this meeting that the report of the "shot heard round the world," fired the day before, had not yet reached Deerfield. Our fathers were faithfully providing for a contingency which had already occurred. At the very moment these wise precautions were being taken, the resounding

> hoof-beats of the galloping horse, and the hoarse call "To arms!" of the excited rider, were rapidly moving westward. The people could hardly have left the schoolhouse on the common, where they met, before the foaming steed with bloody flanks, bearing the dusty courier, was in their midst. "Gage has fired upon the people! Minute men to the rescue! Now is the time, Cambridge the place!" and the twain are off again like a meteor. Then there was hurrying to and fro, and arming in hot haste, and before the hours of the day were numbered fifty minute men were on their way to the scene of bloodshed, to join the band of patriots already encircling Gage in its toils. In their haste they were badly supplied for the service. One of them writes, "after I had got from home I found myself destitute of so necessary an article as a blanket."

That ill-prepared soldier was none other than Justin Hitchcock. "I went with Minutemen from Deerfield as a fifer—I also carried a gun," he wrote. "When we marched into Cambridge Common I beheld more men than I have ever seen together before…" But Justin's first military adventure would be brief. While tensions remained high in Boston, his unit saw no action.

> After we had been there a week or more it was said that a lot had been cast to see who should return home and who should be enlisted for eight months. I was told that my lot was to stay. I then hired on Smith of Sudbury to take my place for ten Dollar.

Back in Deerfield, the young hatter's trade was faltering. He moved briefly to Wethersfield, Connecticut, in 1775, setting up shop with a man named Smith. But the partnership apparently did not go well. By 1776 he had returned to Deerfield for good and restarted his trade—and his courtship of Miss Mercy Hoyt.

Figure 2. The Hitchcock House, Deerfield, Mass., birthplace of Edward Hitchcock, today

In summer of 1777, Lieutenant Stebbins's militia was mobilized again, this time to join Colonial forces fighting General Burgoyne's army near Saratoga, Justin Hitchcock among them. Barely a day on their way, Justin learned of the death of his father. The fifty-four-year-old man had contracted smallpox and died in New Lebanon, New York, reportedly on his way home from Crown Point where he fought with other volunteers from his hometown against General Burgoyne. A few days later the Deerfield contingent fought with others to defeat Burgoyne. Justin makes no further mention of his role, if any, at the Battle of Saratoga. He may have been attending to his father's affairs.

With his military obligations behind him, Justin made a series of decisions aimed at securing himself a favorable position in Deerfield and with his young lady friend. His hatmaking business was on the upswing. He had in 1775 established a singing school, much to the delight of many townspeople. "I was rather bashful and difident but I succeeded so as to get the singing considerably revived which had almost run out before." Soon Justin and Mercy began thinking seriously about their future. On April 3, 1778, he composed a letter to David and Silence Hoit asking their consent to marry their daughter. The following spring he began construction of a house on a one-acre parcel on the Albany road near the center of Deerfield.

In just four years, Justin Hitchcock, a farmer's son from a hardscrabble hill town, a man with limited formal education, had made a home among the well-heeled, well-educated patricians of Deerfield. His status seemed to be secured once and for all when in March 1779, he was chosen Town Clerk by the Tories: "I was now 27 years old and as I attended public worship and led in the singing there I thought the Tories might have some hope of gaining me to their party by this mark of distinction." They soon learned that the earnest young man's political inclinations were not fungible.

Eight months later Justin Hitchcock and Mercy Hoyt were joined in holy matrimony. Inauspicious would not be too strong a word to describe the time chosen by the young couple to consecrate their vows. In his letter to Mercy's parents Justin described it as a period when "our public affairs are in so unhappy a situation." He was referring, of course, to the progress—or lack thereof—in the war with England. Presiding over the ceremony was the church pastor, the Reverend Jonathan Ashley. It would be Reverend Ashley's last wedding, possibly one of the last official acts of his nearly half-century ecclesiastical career. His demise was symptomatic of the political crosscurrents that were tearing at the fabric of American society. It remained to be seen how those tides would turn. On them was borne the fate of an incipient nation and of a young couple setting out on a new life together.

Sugarloaf Mountain by Orra White Hitchcock

2 Justin and Mercy

"There was time sufficient afterwards to regret this hasty foolish bargain."

Deerfield, May 15, 1780

"Gentlemen, if you please," shouted Eliphalet Dickinson, rapping the gavel heavily on the table in the meetinghouse. Dickinson was Deerfield's town moderator and thus responsible for presiding over town meetings.

"The ballots having been counted, the results are as follows: Mr. Lyman, 21 votes..." A buzz spread through the audience. "Mr. Dickinson, 43 votes." Again a murmur rose among the townspeople. "And thirdly, Mr. Hitchcock, 85 votes." Silence. "Mr. Hitchcock, sir, you are hereby declared to be the clerk of the town of Deerfield in this, the one-thousand-seven-hundred-eightieth year of Our Lord."

Justin Hitchcock, seated in the front row, nodded to the moderator. His brother-in-law, David Hoyt, seated next to him, smiled and patted his back in congratulations.

The moderator continued. "If there be no other matters before the meeting, let us proceed to the final order of business, the first reading of the proposed constitution of the state of Massachusetts." Dickinson gestured to a tall stack of loosely bound printed pages placed in the middle of the table before him. "Mr. Hitchcock."

"Sir?" replied the newly elected town clerk.

"Mr. Hitchcock, I believe you have been chosen by this body as the new town clerk, have you not?"

Justin nodded.

"Mr. Hitchcock, your first duty in that post is the reading of the proposed constitution. Pray proceed."

Justin got to his feet and stepped forward to a position behind the moderator's table. He looked up at the townspeople who seemed to be waiting patiently for him to begin.

"Commence, sir, with the first reading."

"The first reading, sir?"

"Yes, Mr. Hitchcock, the first reading. The General Court requires that the document be read, three times, at three meetings...by the clerk." He nodded to the sheaf of papers on the table.

Justin Hitchcock smiled weakly, looked up at his fellow townspeople, then to his brother-in-law, before picking up the first page. Slowly he began:

"We, the people of Massachusetts, acknowledging, with grateful hearts, the goodness of the great Legislator of the universe..."

Immediately after the wedding, the bride and groom moved into the first floor of the newly constructed house on the Albany road in Deerfield. "We lived for some time without any other in the family," wrote Justin, adding that their first winter together was "extremely severe and a vast quantity of snow lay on the ground."

Fortunately, the Hitchcock home was well situated for the young couple, within sight of the Hoyt homestead and the Deerfield meetinghouse, and but a few minutes' walk from most of the town's shops and other places of business. Mercy's services were no doubt called on daily by her family. She had five younger siblings ranging in age from eight to twenty-two, all still living with their parents a short distance away. In addition she had two half-siblings by her father's first marriage, Persis and Jonathan, each with little ones who likely benefited from her services as well. Justin worked hard at his trade out of a shop next door to their home while also carrying out his duties as Town Clerk.

Despite the long, cold winter, a spirit of optimism pervaded Deerfield, and the entire Massachusetts Bay Colony, in the first half of 1780. Only a few months earlier, a constitutional convention led by Samuel and John Adams had met in Cambridge to formulate a state constitution. That document was remarkable for its declaration of individual rights, establishment of three branches of government, separation of powers, and system of checks and balances. It became a model for many other state constitutions as well as the federal constitution that was adopted in Philadelphia seven years later.

In Deerfield as in every other city and town in the Massachusetts Bay colony, the proposed state constitution had to be presented and read aloud to the citizens at Town Meeting, and read not just once or twice, but three times, before a vote could be taken. Young Justin Hitchcock had just been elected Town Clerk for the second year, and so the task fell to him to do the reading. This must have been no mean feat; the document ran to fifty-five pages and more than 12,000 words.

The war, on the other hand, had taken a turn for the worse. After a series of victories for the Continental Army between 1775 and 1777, British forces seemed to be gaining the upper hand. In early 1779 the British occupied Georgia. The severity of that winter hampered the war effort as well. Wrote Justin, "…the American Army ware in danger of perishing for want on account of the difficulty of transporting provisions to them. The roads were so blocked up with snow." Then the summer of 1780 saw a series of humiliating losses for the colonies, including the British capture of Charleston, South Carolina, the defeat of General Gates's force at Camden, South Carolina, the defection of General Benedict Arnold, and numerous mutinies from the Continental Army.

Almost from the start, the Hitchcocks struggled financially. Justin was a craftsman who specialized in hats—fine hats, elegant hats, hats of castor (beaver), musquash (muskrat), and felt, hats decorated with looping ribbons, with buckles, with ruffles or feathers. His felt hats usually sold for about sixty pence, fur hats for a pound. Nearly all transactions were recorded in pounds, shillings, and pence, although after 1790 dollars appear in a few instances in his account book. Most of the hatter's customers were from Deerfield or surrounding towns although he shipped one hat by coach to Putney, Vermont, and sold a hat to a man from Longmeadow, Massachusetts. He also provided related services such as repairing or altering hats and gloves, coloring fabric and yarn, and smithing belt buckles. Payment was sometimes made in cash, but more often involved barter for various goods or services needed by his trade or in his home: ashes, tallow, wood, "a barrel of early cyder," or "keeping a heifer nine weeks." In payment for a felt hat in August 1793, Justin noted that a Mr. Edward Upham had agreed to "schooling one of my boys."

While Justin's trade was successful as far as it went, it is also clear from his account book that hatmaking was not in itself a sufficient livelihood. Besides making and selling hats, he also provided a range of other services to his

Figure 3. Winter in Deerfield

customers: chopping wood, mowing gardens, gathering corn, picking apples, or "a half days work making hay." For several years Justin worked with a partner, but he was "...a very talkative unstable man and some of his proceedings gave me uneasiness," wrote Justin. They soon parted company. Justin then purchased a small building with two rooms not far from his house with the intention of moving it to his land for a shop. But he rushed headlong into the transaction without proper consideration and paid far too high a price. He admitted, "There was time sufficient afterwards to regret this hasty foolish bargain." This would prove only one factor in his accumulating financial troubles. A few years later he agreed to rent some farmland from a neighbor, land he intended to work for additional income. But he fell into arrears on the rent and eventually was sued by the owner. To pay his debt, he found it necessary to sell a cow, no small sacrifice in those times.

The couple's financial woes in that period were due in part to their own errors, but in equal measure to factors beyond their control. The currency then authorized by the Continental Congress was being used to finance the war, yet it had no intrinsic value, no legal standing. As the war dragged on, many citizens saw their cash devalued. Some had to give up their homes and land to pay their debts. Tradesmen and shopkeepers like Justin became middlemen in a chain of debt, owing some, owed by others. He would have been humiliated to read the words of his youngest son, Edward, written some seventy years later, referring to the "...comparative poverty of my early condition." Debts incurred early in the couples' marriage," wrote Edward, "hung like an incubus upon him nearly all his life..."

By 1781 the fortunes of the colonies began to improve. With the defeat of British General Cornwallis and his army, Britain began to seek a way out of the war. Wrote Justin, "...petitions were presented to the King to allow us our independence and the House of Commons had a majority in favour of peace with us which was agreed to the next winter, although the definitive Treaty was not signed till the year after." The war naturally enough was a life changing experience for the young hatter:

> Thus indeed this long and arduous struggle which continued almost eight years. I was at an age when the whole conflict was likely to interest me and was impressed with it so much as to have the events as they took place fixed in my memory and it is not likely that the like or those of vastly greater importance will ever engage my attention to such a degree again.

Justin then expounded at length on the possible reasons for the success of the colonies in the war. The British, he argued, had a low opinion of the will of the colonies to fight a war or of their means to do so. Furthermore, they believed they could choke off the colonies economically. What they did not weigh seriously enough was the immense cost of maintaining their forces from a distance of 3000 miles. And then there was the brutality of the British forces:

> ...[N]o savages ever treated prisoners of war with more cool determined cruelty than they treated our prisoners confined in New York in the winter of 1777, besides their burning so many of our populous towns, Casco Bay, Norfolk in Virginia, Esopus, Fairfield, Danbury, New London, served to inflame the minds of our people and was a wanton and very impolitic mode of warfare...

Finally, Justin added one more cause for the victory of the Americans over the British forces: "I may add as one cause why we did not sink under our difficulties and become subdued was the prudence perseverance and skill of our worthy commander in chief in the years 1776 and 1777." His entry in "Remarks," made in 1799 on the news of the death of General Washington, is clearly a measure of the importance of that man in the life of the hatter of Deerfield:

> On the 14th of December this year Genl Washington died...He came the nearest to perfection in my opinion of any man I ever heard of. The loss of such a Man was deeply lamented throughout the United States such was my respect and attachment to him (tho I never saw him) that the sound of his name excited emotions that I cannot describe. It sounds like that of a Father and friend. Historians will do justice to his character which I cannot.

Adulation for George Washington was nearly universal in Massachusetts then and continued long after the general's death. Over the next decade, the citizens of Deerfield, like those of many other Massachusetts cities and towns, formed a Washington Benevolence Society, dedicated to remembering and commemorating the esteemed general and President. Deerfield's chapter sponsored a celebration each summer in Washington's honor, an event that became an opportunity for expressing one's Federalist political sentiments and raising not a few tankards of ale for decades to come.

As the nation's prospects improved toward the war's end, so did those of the Hitchcocks of Deerfield. Their first child, a girl, was born in January 1781. They named her Charissa after one of Mercy's sisters who had died of dysentery at the age of fifteen months. Over the next dozen years, they were blessed with four more children. Justin's memoir documents the births of the first four:

> On the 13th of January 1781 born and was baptized by Mr Reed of Warwick occasionally preaching here. We called her name Charissa…
>
> This year I had a son born whom we called Henry. He was born on the 6th day of November 1783. He was baptized the next sabbath by Mr Newton of Greenfield.
>
> On the 3rd day of November this year [1785] I had another son born and was baptized the next sabbath by Mr Newton of Greenfield. We called his name Charles.
>
> On the 16th of January this year [1789] I had a Daughter born and on the eighteenth she was baptized by Rev. Mr Newton of Greenfield. We called her Emilia.

As to why the baptisms of Henry, Charles, and Emilia were not performed by the minister of the Deerfield church, it may have been due in part to the lack of a permanent pastor in Deerfield in those years. It may also have had to do with family connections; by 1783 Justin's brother, Merrick, had moved to

Figure 4. George Washington at Valley Forge

Greenfield with his wife, children, their sister Lucy, and the widow of another Hitchcock brother, Charles. The "Rev. Mr. Newton" was pastor of the First Church of Greenfield, the church that Merrick and his family attended. There may also have been certain issues of a theological nature that others thought unimportant, but that Justin Hitchcock could not overlook.

Justin's parents had not been particularly devout. True, they attended Sunday services regularly. Justin's father took careful notes of the sermons each week so that his mother, who was deaf, could read them later. But it fell on young Justin to nudge his family into more regular devotions and practices: "I always attended public worship and a pious woman living in the family perswaded me to ask a blessing at the table and afterward to pray in the family."

During the years of his apprenticeship, Justin's interest in matters of faith flagged. He admits to reading "but little of religious books before I came of age." But a few years later, when he was in his early twenties, he had become "…more seriously impressed upon religious subjects…" Around the age of twenty-four he underwent something of a spiritual renewal, publicly confessing his faith. A few months later he took another important step, joining the church.

> I was induced to do it in a great measure from a serious consideration of the words of Christ Mark 8th 38. If Christ had a cause in the world and I pretended to hope for salvation through him I felt satisfied that I ought to make it known by obeying his command. I therefore Joined the Church in November the last year 1778.

He would continue as an active member of that congregation for the remainder of his life, serving as deacon from 1798 until his death in 1822.

While Justin Hitchcock and Reverend Ashley were poles apart politically, they were in accord on matters spiritual. Following Ashley's death in 1780, the Deerfield church was led for six years by interim pastors. Some of the difficulty of that period may have stemmed from a growing divide between parishioners like Justin who were strict Calvinists and those harboring new and unorthodox views. Some called themselves Unitarians, causing their orthodox brethren to hurl epithets such as "infidel" or "atheist" at them like darts at a dartboard in Mr. Hoyt's tavern.

Unitarianism was already well established in Europe, particularly in eastern Europe and in Britain, when it was introduced in America. It was in Boston that the first American Unitarian Societies were established in the 1770s and 1780s. Deerfield may have been especially ripe for the spread of Unitarianism. According to town historian George Sheldon, it was the French and Indian War and the American Revolution that forged in Deerfield's hardy residents a spirit of independence and self-reliance.

> And if they made the wilderness blossom as the rose, they also set free thought in the high places among them, and set adrift on the sunless sea of oblivion, barks freighted with the enfeebling superstitions and harassing fears which had been their heritage; and the eternal backward set of the current carried these away forever.

Perhaps of equal importance in the rise of liberal theologies in Deerfield was a reaction to the "The Great Awakening" of the mid-eighteenth century that had its epicenter only fifteen miles away in Northampton. Some believers were dubious of the revivals that were so common in those times and the motives of the evangelical preachers such as Jonathan Edwards, George Whitefield, and David Brainerd. Even some orthodox Christians found certain elements of that brand of Calvinism troublesome, particularly original sin, election, and perseverance of the saints. Increasingly, Justin Hitchcock found himself at odds with his fellow parishioners in Deerfield.

Figure 5. Reverend Jonathan Edwards (1703-1758)

As to Mercy Hitchcock's religious inclinations, her parents were members in good standing of the Deerfield church as were her siblings. But regarding their personal beliefs, there is little evidence to be found. Two brothers, Epaphras and Elihu, became well-known as authors and public figures, but not in the realm of religion. One measure of a family's spiritual credentials in those times was the appointment of the men of the family as deacons. During the nineteenth century, at least four Hitchcocks held the post of deacon for decades, including Justin, his sons Charles and Henry, and Henry's son Nathaniel. By contrast, no Hoyt ever held the position of deacon in Deerfield in that century. But the religious beliefs of Mercy's husband were very well known, and they were entirely antithetical to those of the Unitarians in his midst. Late in life, when the overthrow of the Deerfield church by Unitarian notions was complete, Justin would pen a heartfelt missive on Christian doctrine, taking issue with the liberalism of Reverend Willard and most of the citizenry of Deerfield.

While Justin Hitchcock may have been at odds spiritually in Deerfield, his political sentiments were shared with virtually every man in the town—women, of course, having no vote and few opinions on such matters, at least not that their husbands and fathers paid any heed to. During the war Justin had been an avowed Whig, but now foremost among the sentiments of him and most of his fellow townspeople was support for a strong central government for the new nation. This was the era before the adoption of the U. S. Constitution, when the states were only loosely united under the Articles of Confederation. The central government under those articles was weak, and its weakness had a good deal to do with the economic woes of Deerfield, of Massachusetts, and of the nation.

Figure 6. Deerfield town historian George Sheldon, (1818-1916)

Justin Hitchcock and many of his neighbors were quick to answer the call to defend the government of Massachusetts when, in August 1786, "The coals of discontent tho partially buryied kindled afresh this year and burst into a flame." An angry mob of some 1200 men attempted to prevent the sitting of the state Supreme Court in Springfield. They were led by a farmer from Pelham named Daniel Shays. Justin and some forty other men from Deerfield traveled to Springfield where they joined other forces and faced down the mob. That winter another insurrection was fomented by the same group and promptly quelled. Justin Hitchcock and his fellow townsmen were firm believers in the new government, the government that many had fought for just a decade earlier.

On May 24, 1793, Mercy bore another child, a boy. They named him Edward. Curiously, Justin makes no mention of Edward, their last child, in his memoir. The five Hitchcock children grew up in the same house on the Albany road that their parents had occupied from the day they were married, fourteen years earlier. It was a small house for such a large family and money was scarce: "As to myself I had sometimes dark prospects as to obtaining a support for my growing family," wrote Justin in 1789, "…And sometimes I found it very difficult to get grain and wood."

But what the Hitchcock children lacked in luxuries they made up for in other riches. On the Hoyt side in 1795 they had twelve aunts and uncles and over twenty cousins living right in Deerfield, ranging in age from one to thirty-three. On the Hitchcock side they had several aunts and uncles and another six or more cousins living in nearby Greenfield. Besides enjoying the many benefits of a large extended family, the Hitchcock children were spiritually well-endowed. Having been raised in a family that was not particularly devout, Justin was determined to do better by his own children:

> It will be proper to observe that when I began to live in a family of my own I began to put in practice a resolution I had formed before and that was to attend

> to morning and evening prayers in the family. And if my advice is worth nothing I can freely advise all young men to do the same. They will find less difficulty in performing this duty at the commencement of their family state than they will ever after...

Despite Justin's devoutness, life in the Hitchcock household was far from dour or cheerless. Justin was a musician and he and Mercy raised their children to love and appreciate music. Their eldest son Charles followed in his father's footsteps musically, serving as choirmaster of the church and leading singing groups in Deerfield throughout his life.

The Hitchcocks' last child seems to have presented particular disciplinary challenges for Justin and Mercy. George Sheldon writes of Mercy Hitchcock, "[Edward] was the torment of her life." That he was temperamental and prone to tirades as a boy is confirmed by Edward himself. Late in life he described himself as a boy possessed of "unusual obstinacy and self will." Edward related one example: "…I remember crying so loud one night on being put to bed the people in the street came in to see what the matter was. This did me good because it made me ashamed of myself." He attributed these traits to his father: "I do not think [he] held the reins quite tight enough over me." But he then relates two incidents in his boyhood when his transgressions were dealt with severely, one by his father, one by his uncle:

> I had wandered away one sabbath into the meadows. [My father] followed me and I recollect to this day how sharply the switches of a stick in his hand were laid upon me and though it roused my wrath it opened my eyes and in a measure broke my will. I recollect also on another occasion when I was ugly towards my mother her brother chased me through the snow and when I was tumbled into a drift he pelted it into my face till I thought I should not be able to breathe again. But it subdued me and made me see my vileness.

It is not clear whether Mercy shared her husband's views on discipline or spiritual training of their flock. But education was a subject on which the couple were in full agreement, as were the citizens of Deerfield as a whole. In 1787 the town adopted a new plan for schools, designating six districts, and opening a new school in the center of town. It was a small, simple building with one room accommodating about thirty students. The first teacher was a Mr. Freegrace Reynolds, a graduate of Yale and a licensed minister. In addition to his salary he was to be provided a room in the village and firewood. It was in that school that the formal education of the Hitchcock children began. But a system of one room schoolhouses, while admirable, would not long suffice for the scholars of Deerfield. Within a decade a new and ambitious project would be undertaken that would forever mark the town and its citizenry as forward-thinking exemplars for public education in the young nation.

The original Deerfield Academy building

3 A New Academy

"Thou shalt be commended according to thy wisdom."

Deerfield, January 7, 1804

The rumble of heavy boots on the wooden floors of the Academy's second floor resounded down the narrow hallway as some forty scholars, all boys, burst into the recitation room. Preceptor John Hubbard stood, his back to the class, examining with some satisfaction a series of algebra problems he had inscribed on the chalk board.

"Gentlemen," he began as the students settled into their narrow wooden benches, "your attention is directed to a few numerical challenges from yesterday's lesson. Pray begin...in silence." He was possessed of a self-congratulatory smile, a certainty that these would prove sufficiently challenging to guarantee the maintenance of good order among the sometimes boisterous entourage, at least for a few minutes.

At a desk near the back of the room he spotted an unfamiliar face, a boy with black hair and intense dark eyes, peering into a book. The preceptor stepped slowly along the aisle until he stood towering above the lad.

"And you would be..." he said sternly.

The boy looked up briefly. "Edward Hitchcock." Then his eye returned to his book.

"Sir," replied Hubbard. The boy nodded. "Sir," the preceptor repeated.

The boy looked up again, confused. "Sir."

"Edward—Hitchcock—Sir," spoke the preceptor, sounding each word distinctly.

"Edward Hitchcock, Sir," replied the boy at last.

The preceptor looked sternly on the boy. "Master Hitchcock, you seem to have misunderstood the instructions." He placed one finger on the small slate on the desk, then nodded toward the problems on the board. "You are instructed to solve the equations...for x. I trust you understand." The boy looked up at the distant blackboard but did not reply, still clutching the book in his hand.

Hubbard reached down and lifted the book from the boy's hand, opened it, and gazed at the title page. "Spherical Trigonometry," he read with a frown. "Hmmm...unlikely reading for a boy of your age. Please explain why you are in possession of such an advanced work."

"To determine the orbits of the planets...and the moon...and comets," answered the boy. Hubbard fixed a stern gaze on the boy until he added, "Sir."

"Hmmm...I see. Well, perhaps it would help if you were to learn algebra first, I doubt not."

"Oh, I learned algebra...when I was eight...Sir."

"When you were eight? Well, perhaps it is time for you to refresh your learning." And he tapped the slate loudly.

The boy picked up the slate and a piece of chalk and, without looking up, replied, "Yes...Sir."

Early in the life of the new nation, public education became a rallying cry. It was, asserted many of the leading figures in America at the time, a "pillar of republican society." National figures including Thomas Jefferson and Benjamin Rush argued that only by providing free education for all could a free nation sustain itself. Jefferson proposed a three-tier system of public education: free elementary schools in every town, regional academies for older students, and state colleges for the most promising students. Despite their efforts, public education was slow to spread through the states.

Massachusetts was a leader in this trend. In Deerfield at least six district schoolhouses were established in 1787. But the citizens of Deerfield were not

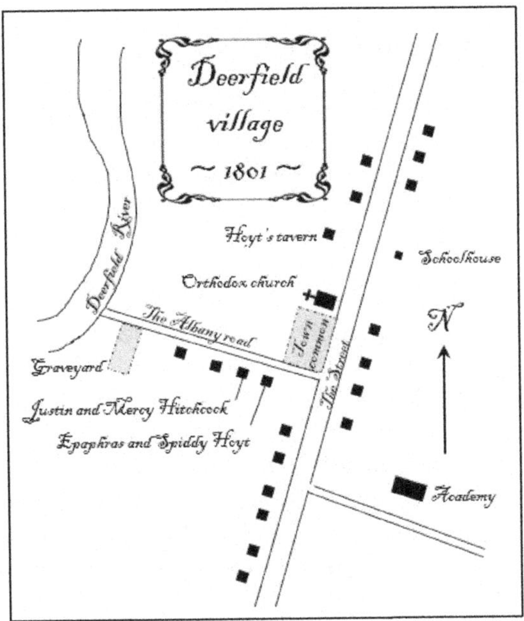

Figure 7. Deerfield village circa 1801

content with this system of district schools. In 1797 a group of men gathered for the purpose of establishing an academy of higher learning in the town. They petitioned Governor Samuel Adams who, on March 1 of that year, approved the petition and passed it on to the state legislature. Shortly thereafter the Academy received its charter, permitting the trustees to raise funds, "…for the sole trust & purpose of supporting an Academy in said Town of Deerfield, for the promotion of Piety, Religion & Morality, & for the Education of Youth in the liberal Arts & Sciences, & all other useful Learning..." With those words the state legislature in 1797 gave official sanction to the new school at Deerfield. Vigorous fundraising could now begin, and within a year a new edifice had risen that would become Deerfield Academy.

The first of January, 1799, was a day of double celebration in Deerfield. Not only was it the first day of the new year, it also marked the official opening of Deerfield Academy. The proceedings began with a sermon in the meetinghouse by Reverend Joseph Lyman who gave eloquent expression to the lofty goals of the new institution in a sermon, *The Advantages and Praises of Wisdom*, citing Proverbs 12:8: "A man shall be commended according to his wisdom." He then expounded on the subject of wisdom:

> Wisdom is the principal thing, therefore get wisdom, and with all thy getting, get understanding. Exalt her, and she shall promote thee; she shall bring thee to honour when thou dost embrace her. She shall give to thine head an ornament of grace; a crown of glory shall she deliver to thee. Thou shalt be commended according to thy wisdom.

Reverend Lyman concluded with a charge to his audience:

> ...[M]ay this respectable assembly, who now worship God in this house of prayer, and honor the cause of literature, by their presence, at the consecration of the Academy, to the purposes of knowledge and virtue, duly, appreciate their privileges, in this land of liberty, of light, and of christian knowledge. May they cultivate their own minds with wisdom and virtue.

Even before the Academy opened its doors, the Board of Trustees adopted a lengthy set of rules to guide them, the preceptor, and their students. Among those rules was a declaration of the Academy's admissions policy: "Youth, of both sexes, provided they are found, in a degree, capable of reading and writing, may be admitted into the Academy." Instruction would be provided for all in "reading, writing, and English grammar"; an extra fee would be levied for instruction in "other branches of Literature" that included Latin, Greek, and the Ornamental Arts. Tuition was low, but students were also expected to bring firewood to heat the Academy building. One preceptor wrote to a friend about the new school in 1799:

> The Academy is an elegant Edifice, having, on the lower floor, four rooms, one for the English school, one for the Latin and Greek School, the Preceptor's room, and a room for the Museum and Library. The upper room, being all in one, is used for examinations, and exhibitions.

The assemblage then adjourned to the new Academy building where Mr. Enos Bronson, a recent graduate of Yale, was inducted as the first preceptor. The following day, the first quarter began. While many of the students were from Deerfield and surrounding towns, many others came from farther afield including several dozen from Connecticut, Vermont, and New York State. Among the students who attended that first year were Charissa and Henry Hitchcock. Charles began the following year, Edward in 1804, Emilia in 1805. So far as the early records indicate, the four older children attended for only one or two terms. Edward, on the other hand, attended six winter terms varying in length from two to five months, from January 1804 to May 1809.

Why were the tenures of Edward's siblings at the Academy so brief? Charissa was already eighteen when the Academy opened. She married a classmate, Jonathan Swett, in 1803. No explanation is found as to why Emilia's schooling at the Academy ended after only two quarters. It is clear, however, that financial considerations played a role in cutting short the education of Edward's two older brothers. Both left school at age sixteen or so after just one or two quarters to work on a neighbor's farm to help their father pay off his debts. In a letter to Edward late in life, Charles Hitchcock wrote in a reflective moment, "... my going out when 16 years old to work by the season more or less till I was 19 years old to pay our good Father's debts is not a service of regret to me but I think of it to this hour with satisfaction."

Both Charles and Henry would devote their lives to farming. But what about Edward? Why did he not follow a similar path? He worked alongside his brothers for a time over several summers, but as he recalled late in life,

> I had acquired a strong relish for scientific pursuits, and I seized upon every moment I could secure—especially rainy days and evenings—for those studies. I was treated very leniently by my father and brother, who probably did not know what to do with me, but saw plainly that I should not become distinguished as a farmer.

At the Academy, Edward clearly thrived. Not only did he excel in his regular studies, he also found time for extracurricular involvements as well, as noted in *Reminiscences*:

> My literary taste was also greatly encouraged by a few companions in Deerfield with whom I united in a society, whose weekly meetings we kept up for years, which had a department for debate, and another for philosophical discussion. I always regarded this as one of the most important means of mental discipline that I ever enjoyed.

Edward's notes suggest that as a young man he possessed a strong vein of independence.

> I think that my earliest history exhibited a good deal of peculiarity and not a little of idiosyncrasy of character. I was never content to follow in the beaten track but was always seeking out some side path. After I got interested in the study of science this trait of character was more fully developed and it had not a little to do with my success.

He admitted to having little use for "ordinary amusement and recreations": "I never learned how to dance or to play cards and never I think attended a ball or more than once or twice till I got into a profession sat down to dinner or supper at a public house." Besides his precocious intellectual abilities, young Edward had a particularly strong mechanical aptitude. His father had a shop full of tools that Edward put to frequent use:

> ...I early attempted to set up some machines such as saw mills and planetariums—a whirling table—wooden quadrants—an annulary sphere—a globe etc. etc. They were poorly made and must have been so with such tools. For years I had a strong passion for such occupations and spent much time upon them. I do not think that I ever excelled in delicate mechanical work. But in coarse work I did something. It was while yet little more than a boy that I superintended the framing of two buildings of considerable size although I had

> never worked with a carpenter a day. But working by the square rule I had complete success.

Edward well may have possessed a "strong relish" for science from an early age, but the earliest of his writings that survive reveal a literary appetite of a different sort. At sixteen he penned a poem, "A Poetical Sketch of Democracy in the County of Hampshire 1809," that mocked many of the political elders of Hampshire County. Although the cover of the handwritten manuscript is inscribed, "Probably the first intellectual effort of President Edward Hitchcock which was made public," there is no record of its publication. Perhaps he recited it at an exhibition at the Academy.

The poem contains thirty-eight stanzas varying in length from four to twenty lines each. The poet even provides footnotes explaining some references or providing verification of several accusations included in the poem. In the opening stanza Edward states the object of his "humble rhyme":

> He undertakes a tedious task
> Who would democracy unmask
> To dark designs find out a clue
> And turn them inside out to view
> Yet as the world is growing older
> Their Demagogues grow somewhat bolder
> Their Conduct which we've seen of late
> Affords a rule to calculate
> Then let us sketch in humble rhyme
> Some of the evils of the time
> None need to fear our doggerel Ditty
> Will much provoke their rage or pity.

Hitchcock proceeds to skewer dozens of Hampshire County politicians. Of Solomon Smead, Chief Justice of the Hampshire Sessions Court, he writes,

> Some years ago he turn'd his coat
> The reason why we don't find out
> T'is likely tho, the real cause
> Was thirst for popular applause…

A Col. Burt, comes in for a different sort of taunt:

> Of Col. Burt not much is said
> That's very good or very bad
> He after all appears so slender
> As to remain of doubtful gender

Of a legislator from nearby Pelham he writes,

> Pelham that virtuous society
> So full of Democratic Piety
> Have sent we did not say a Monkey
> No that were rong his name is Conkey.

He attributes some political skullduggery of the times to intemperance:

> Midst many a cause we mention some
> But none have equal force with rum
> Unless what equally makes frisky
> As Cyder Brandy gin and Whiskey

Near the end of the poem he issues a warning to those who have escaped his vitriolic verse:

> The legislators which we knew
> We've tried to paint in colors true
> If there is some not mentioned here
> When known—we'll Touch they need not fear.

Although he promised to spare no one, all Edward's barbs were directed toward members of the Democratic-Republicans, the party of President Jefferson; not a single Federalist candidate was similarly skewered. The Federalist party had its origin during Washington's presidency. Its guiding principle was the value of a strong central government. The Democratic-Republicans, on the other hand, were skeptical of the central government and favored retaining power in the states and local communities.

Why this apparent political bias in a sixteen-year-old? Strong family, community, as well as regional influences were no doubt all at play. His father was a Federalist, an ardent supporter of George Washington who had answered the call to defend the state court in Springfield during Shays's Rebellion. Justin's brother-in-law, Epaphras Hoyt, was also a Federalist. In fact the town of Deerfield was overwhelmingly Federalist: according to the *Greenfield Gazette*, Deerfield voted for the Federalist candidate for governor in 1809 by a margin of 272 to 9. Hampshire County as a whole leaned Federalist as well, although some of its small outlying communities were staunchly Democratic-Republican. Two of the county's largest newspapers at the time, the *Greenfield Gazette* and the *Hampshire Gazette*, were both unapologetically Federalist.

In the last few stanzas of "A Poetical Sketch" Edward gives voice to the deep worries in the nation regarding Napoleon's advances in Europe. Since 1795, Napoleon had dispatched his armies across the continent, rolling over one independent nation after another with both speed and brutality. In the eyes of some American politicians of that time, President Jefferson and his supporters, the Democratic-Republicans, were attempting to appease the tyrant, an allegation that young Edward seems to take to heart:

> Yet now like any tame spectator
> We see them view the great Dictator
> Whom heav'n in wrath on earth has sent
> T'inflict its heavy punishment
> Who strongly to such power has crept
> And from the Earth all freedom swept
> And when the nation is distressed
> By arbitrary laws oppress'd
> Their fears receive a full dismission
> Are passive now and all submission.

It would be several years before Edward's next political missives would appear in print, but they would address many of the same themes: admiration for George Washington and the Federalist party, doubts about the motives of the Democratic-Republicans, Thomas Jefferson and James Madison, and fear that Napoleon's next target of conquest might be the young American nation.

The society that so influenced Edward's intellectual development in Deerfield was known as the Literary Adelphi. Few records of the group have survived, but its early members likely included Edward, several of his cousins, and his close friend Jackson Dickinson. The Greek word "adelphi" means brothers, and the membership of the society was exclusively male, perhaps in deference to the Academy's rules about mingling of the sexes. They met weekly for discussions and debates. Distinguished guests were often invited to deliver orations. Edward was called on to deliver addresses to the Adelphi, one in August 1813. Another a year later he entitled "An introductory address delivered before the 'Society of literary Adelphi,' at their seventh anniversary, August 8th 1814." These were long, rambling orations on politics, philosophy, and religion.

That summer Edward also presented to the group a "dramatic production." The Adelphi were impressed with the work and determined to offer a public performance. But several of the key roles in the play were women. Fortunately, in 1813 a parallel organization had been formed, the Young Ladies' Literary Society. We know more about this organization than about its male counterpart; a lengthy constitution was drawn up and signed by several dozen young women of Deerfield. Among the signatories was Edward's sister, Emilia Hitchcock. Another was a young woman who through a combination of charm, intellect, and religious zeal, would come to play a vital role both in Edward's play and in his life. Her name was Orra White.

The Comet of 1811

4 The Great Almanack Debate

"You have got the comet's tail in your stomach."

Deerfield, September 1811

"Edward," called a voice from beneath the giant elm tree. It was early on a September evening and a hush hung over the village. "Edward—are you up there?"

"Yes, Uncle," came the reply from amid a tangle of branches high up in the old tree.

In a few moments Epaphras Hoyt had climbed, grunting and straining, till he was seated on a large limb beside his nephew. "I have the telescope set up, son. Are you not going to assist me as you promised?"

There was no reply.

"I thought you were interested in being my astronomical aide-de-camp during the eclipse. Have you changed your mind?"

Again no reply.

"Is something troubling you, Nephew?"

"No, sir, not something...someone." The strident rattle of katydids was beginning to rise all around them.

"Ah," replied Epaphras. "Your father?"

"Yes, Uncle." Edward squirmed, his voice cracking with emotion. "He wants me to apprentice with Mr. Jones, to learn smithing."

"And you are not so inclined, would be my guess."

There was no response at first. The boy cradled his chin on his hand, as if trying to prop up his spirits. "If ever there were a trade for which I am poorly suited, blacksmith would be that trade."

"It is a perfectly admirable, respectable profession, Nephew. Remember, your father undertook an apprenticeship when he was about your age. He has often spoken of it, how it made him what he is."

"I want to do more, Uncle," replied Edward. "I do not plan to spend my life shoeing horses and oxen, or fashioning nails and hooks and hinges."

"Well, then, how do you plan to make a living, may I enquire?"

"I want to...I suppose I mean...to be a...a blessing for my people...for my nation...for liberty."

"Another General Washington, then?" said Epaphras in a mocking tone. As soon as he spoke the words he regretted it and hastened to correct them. "Listen to me, son. Your goals are admirable, and you have many, many talents. But you need to expand your knowledge, your experience, your education. You..."

"How can I do that? We have no more money to spend on my education. Father says..."

"Yes, yes, I understand. But listen to me. I have a proposition. I will teach you...or rather you and I will together explore the world of knowledge, from the tiniest particles to the great universe beyond. How about that? Would you like that?"

"Well, yes, sir...but...but what about Father?"

"Let me worry about him. I will have a heart-to-heart with your mother. My sister and I are usually of one mind. And she always knows the way to your father's heart."

Edward nodded. "Thank you, Uncle Ep."

"Now, if I may coax you down from your perilous perch, I have something to show you...in the telescope...I do not mean to exaggerate, son, but this could be something quite important...quite large...dare I say... astronomical!"

It may be argued that the Almighty conspired to promote the scientific interests of young Edward Hitchcock both in the Firmament and on earth. In heavenly realms, two extraordinary events occurred within days in September 1811, sufficient to inspire both his curiosity and his intellectual zeal. One was a solar eclipse, the first to occur in thirty-three years in Deerfield. The second was the appearance of a comet the likes of which no one then alive could recall. It became known as the Great Comet of 1811 and even today it holds a prominent place in astronomical history, for it remained visible for some 267 days, a record not to be broken until the appearance of the Hale-Bopp Comet in 1996.

Both events might have passed unnoticed, however, had it not been for another fortunate conjunction in the life of Edward Hitchcock. Epaphras Hoyt was Mercy Hitchcock's brother. He was, in fact, the second Epaphras of that generation of Hoyts. The first, born to David and Mercy Hoyt in 1751, passed away on December 28, 1765. Just three days later, a boy was born to Silence, David's second wife. Named to honor his late half-brother, he would come to be known by his nieces and nephews as Uncle Ep.

Like most Deerfield children of that era, Epaphras Hoyt the latter attended but a few years in the village school, a twenty-two-foot square one room structure. Beyond that he was self-educated, yet he would distinguish himself as a military man, politician, teacher, and scholar. He joined the Massachusetts Militia as a young man, eventually rising to the rank of Major General. He was

Figure 8. Major General Epaphras Hoyt (1765-1850), uncle of Edward Hitchcock

offered an appointment as Commander in the United States Army by President George Washington in 1798, a position he declined. He went on active duty with the Massachusetts Militia in 1812 although his unit never saw combat. Epaphras held a range of civic positions in Deerfield from postmaster to justice of the peace to Register of Deeds of Franklin County. In 1820 he was chosen a delegate to the state Constitutional Convention. He taught military science at Deerfield Academy for several years. And he published books, treatises, and papers on military science, astronomy, and history. He is best known outside of the military for *Antiquarian Researches*, a history of Deerfield and its adjacent territory.

Epaphras married Experience Harvey, also known as Spiddy, in 1792. In 1801 the couple purchased the house next door to the Hitchcock family on the Albany road. Soon it became clear that Epaphras Hoyt and his nephew, Edward Hitchcock, now neighbors, shared a special bond both of blood and of interests. Epaphras proved to be an inspirational tutor. Edward credits him with instilling his "taste for science" and, in particular, astronomy. According to one account the pair did much of their work perched on a limb of a large elm tree in the Hoyts's yard:

> It is related that the General and his nephew were in the habit of fleeing, to escape the disturbance from the children and the swash of Aunt Spiddy's mop on the floor, to a seat among the branches of this even then giant tree, to study their most profound problems…

One of the earliest astronomical endeavors of Edward and Uncle Ep was the determination of the longitude of Deerfield. Lines of longitude stretch from pole to pole. The prime meridian, designated 0° longitude, passes through Greenwich, England. Other meridians are defined by their angular displacement east or west of the prime meridian. In that time the most reliable method for determining one's longitude was astronomical: measure the angle between various heavenly bodies such as the moon and a nearby star. Note the local time. Then consult an almanac to determine the exact time in Greenwich when that angle could be observed. A comparison of the times at Greenwich and Deerfield could then be used to calculate the longitude of Deerfield. If, for example, the time difference was 4 hours, 50 minutes, 36 seconds, that equals two-tenths of a day; hence, Deerfield is approximately 72.5° West Longitude. According to the calculations of Edward and Uncle Ep, the longitude of the church in the center of Deerfield was 72° 39', barely two miles off the actual longitude.

A paper entitled "Astronomical observations made near the centre of the village of Deerfield, Massachusetts" appeared in the *Memoirs of the American Academy of Arts and Science* in 1815. It included observations on the total solar eclipse of September 17, 1811, azimuths for Sirius from September 1811 to February 1812, as well as observations regarding the latitude and longitude of Deerfield for autumn of 1811. Its author was Epaphras Hoyt, but it seems likely that some of the work was done by his young assistant.

The pair kept nightly vigils during the months when the Comet of 1811 was visible. This was clearly a life altering experience for the eighteen-year-old. Among other things he came to realize the importance for astronomers, navigators, and farmers of accurate astronomical data. And it appears that he threw himself into this new interest with all his energies. As he would recall many years later, "I gave myself to this labor so assiduously that my health failed, and I well remember that when my physician was consulted he said, 'I see what your difficulty is; you have got the comet's tail in your stomach.'"

THE
COUNTRY ALMANACK,
FOR THE YEAR OF OUR LORD
1816:
And Year of the World according to Scripture,
5778.
Being Leap Year, and 40th of American Independence.
Fitted to North Latitude 42° 32½′ and Longitude 72° 41′ West from Greenwich; being a point NEAR THE CENTRE OF NEW-ENGLAND.
Constructed on a new and improved plan.
Containing more than an ordinary number of ASTRONOMICAL CALCULATIONS, and other Instructive, Useful, and Entertaining matter.

Greenfield—Printed by Denio & Phelps.
And sold by them at their Bookstore, and by other Booksellers and Traders in the State.
Price 9 Dols. per Gross—37½ Cts. Doz.—12½ Cts. Single.

Figure 9. The cover of Hitchcock's *Country Almanack* for 1816 with a woodcut by Orra White

Despite his maladies, Edward soon directed his energies to a new and related project, publication of an almanac for the farmers of Deerfield. Almanacs were a well-established institution in America in those times and their form and content likely were already familiar to Edward. They were small, booklet sized, usually with twenty-four or thirty-six pages. Most included calendars, weather predictions, some astronomy and astrology. Many offered folk remedies for a variety of ailments, hints for happy living, and practical advice. Ornate poetry often appeared side by side with folksy aphorisms.

He began work on his almanac in 1812. Soon America found itself once again at war with Britain. Edward decided to delay publication of his first edition for fear it would provide aid to the enemy. But in December 1813, identifying himself only by the initials "E.H.", he published the first edition.

Just below the title appears a poem written by Erasmus Darwin, grandfather of Charles Darwin, in 1791, that suggests that Edward Hitchcock's almanac would be a reflection of his astronomical inclinations:

> Roll on ye stars! exult in youthful prime,
> Mark with bright curves the printless steps of time;
> Near and more near your beamy cars approach,

> And lessening orbs on lessening orbs encroach;
> Star after star from heaven's high arch shall rush,
> Suns sink on suns, and systems systems crush…

After a three-page introduction, the editor presents astronomical information for each month. "Solar Calculations" includes times of sunrise and sunset, the sun's declination, southings (angle south of the celestial equator) of prominent stars, elevation, and positions of the sun and other planets for each day of the month. In "Lunar Calculations" dates and times of each phase of the moon appear followed by times of its rising and setting, as well as its position by sign of the Zodiac for each day of the month. One column on each calendar page is devoted to important astronomical events: the Moon's apogee, Jupiter's opposition, the times of immersion and emersion of the Jovian moons. Sprinkled among the heavenly happenings are important dates in history such as for January 1814, under "Solar Calculations":

> Jan. 4 Sir I. Newton born, 1643
> Jan. 14 Peace rat. by Congress, 1784
> Jan. 21 Louis XVI beheaded, 1793

Weather forecasts, perhaps more properly termed weather expectations, are sometimes provided in that same column under "Lunar Calculations":

> Jan. 11 Now…good weather for sledding.
> Jan. 22 Look out for a very severe snowstorm about this time.

Listings of astronomical and historical events are often interrupted by amusing predictions of a different sort:

> Jan. 1 Look out for a number of domestic storms about this time; but which upon the whole will be productive of more happiness than misery; for by their means many pairs will be put asunder whom nature never intended should have been united.
>
> Jan. 24 Some political twistings and turnings will appear about this time, which in the end will prove highly beneficial to the country.

Following the calendars, the editor presents what he must have regarded as essential information for the farmers of Deerfield: locations and dates of court sessions, college vacation schedules, and postal rates.

Finally, perhaps just to fill the remaining space, appear similes ("Love is like an Indian's birch canoe. If anyone unacquainted with it endeavors to step into it, he may be sure to get a ducking."), maxims ("Envy not the appearance of happiness in any man, for thou knowest not his secret griefs."), a recipe for cider wine, and useful instructions such as how to forecast the weather from a spider's web and how to determine the age of an ox or cow.

A line of poetry by Alexander Pope appears at the end of the month of February in the first edition that seems to presage Hitchcock's stance toward religion and science:

> Nature and nature's laws lay hid in night:
> God said, "Let Newton be," and all was light.

Hitchcock published *The Country Almanack* annually from 1814 to 1818. The astronomical data were all his own and nearly all the editorial content of each issue was original.

Epaphras no doubt introduced Edward to the *Nautical Almanac*, an annual publication that listed the exact locations of the stars and planets as well as their distances from each other, the Sun, and the Moon. The original *Nautical Almanac* had been published in London since 1767. It was used by ships' captains and navigators around the world to determine their longitude and thus measure their easterly or westerly progress across the oceans of the world. Beginning in about 1810 an American version was published by an entrepreneur named Edmund M. Blunt. It was a licensed copy of the British publication, but with modifications for use in North America. Sailors of those days depended on the accuracy of the astronomical data provided by the *Nautical Almanac* as evidenced by this statement that appeared a dozen times in each issue, on the first page for every month: "Ten dollars will be paid on the discovery of an error in the figures."

When Edward compared his astronomical data with those of Blunt's edition of the *Nautical Almanac*, he found errors, many errors. He felt an obligation to point these out to the editor, and thus began a remarkable episode in the life of one young man and in the history of astronomy and navigation that came to be known as "The Great Almanack Debate." It had a certain Biblical quality to it, reminiscent of the tale of David and Goliath, with Edmund M. Blunt, world-renowned publisher and entrepreneur, as Goliath, young Edward Hitchcock of Deerfield, Massachusetts, as David.

Edward's first letter to Blunt in early 1814 began, "In your edition of the Nautical Almanac for the year 1814 I have discovered the following error." He proceeded to point out two small errors, one the inversion of two digits in one table, the other a misuse of the symbols for Mercury and Venus, errors that would likely have had no serious consequences for navigators. The last paragraph of this letter began,

JANUARY *begins on Thursday, hath* 31 *days.*

"Think'st thou there are no serpents in the world
"But those who slide along the grassy sod?
"There are who in the path of social life
"Do sting the soul."

***SOLAR* CALCULATIONS, &c.**

D.	Sun.	Mer.	Ven.	Mars.	Jup.	Sat.	Hers.
1	9 11	9 28	8 24	2 9	8 26	11 2	8 17
7	9 17	10 6	9 1	2 9	8 27	11 3	8 18
13	9 23	10 10	9 9	2 8	8 29	11 3	8 18
19	9 29	10 8	9 16	2 9	9 0	11 4	8 18
25	10 5	10 1	9 24	2 9	9 1	11 5	8 19

M.D.	W.D.	*Calendar, Notable events, &c.*	Sun rises	Sun sets	S.S.	7*s Sou.	Moon South
1	Th.	Circumcision.	7 32	4 28	4	8 49	6 50
2	F.	*Let a man*	7 32	4 28	4	8 44	7 45
3	Sat.	Affair at Princeton, 1777.	7 31	4 29	5	8 40	8 57
4	Sun	2d. Sund. aft. Christmas.	7 31	4 29	5	8 36	9 37
5	M.	*do his best.*	7 30	4 30	6	8 31	10 59
6	Tu.	Epiphany.	7 30	4 30	6	8 27	11 45
7	W.	*and the world*	7 29	4 31	6	8 23	ev. 49
8	Th.	*may do*	7 28	4 32	7	8 19	1 49
9	F.	*its worst.*	7 27	4 33	7	8 14	2 43
10	Sat.	*A good cause*	7 26	4 34	8	8 10	3 31
11	Sun	1st. Sund. aft. Epiph.	7 25	4 35	8	8 6	4 15
12	M.	*makes a*	7 24	4 36	9	8 1	4 54
13	Tu.	*courageous heart.*	7 23	4 37	9	7 57	5 34
14	W.	Peace rat. by Cong. 1784	7 22	4 38	9	7 53	6 14
15	Th.	*They that*	7 21	4 39	10	7 48	6 56
16	F.	*fear an*	7 20	4 40	10	7 44	7 40
17	Sat.	Bat. Cowpens.	7 19	4 41	10	7 40	8 26
18	Sun	Septuages. Sund.	7 18	4 42	11	7 36	9 16
19	M.	*overthrow, are*	7 17	4 43	11	7 31	10 8
20	Tu.	*half conquered.*	7 16	4 44	11	7 27	10 59
21	W.	*The deepest waters*	7 15	4 45	12	7 23	11 52
22	Th.	Winchest. def. 1813.	7 14	4 46	12	7 19	morn.
23	F.	*move silently, the hottest*	7 13	4 47	12	7 14	0 44
24	Sat.	*fires have the smallest*	7 12	4 48	12	7 10	1 34
25	Sun	Sexa. Sund. Conv. St. Paul.	7 11	4 49	13	7 6	2 22
26	M.	*flame, and*	7 10	4 50	13	7 2	3 7
27	Tu.	*spheres have the*	7 9	4 51	13	6 58	3 53
28	W.	*swiftest motion.*	7 8	4 52	13	6 54	4 40
29	Th.	*yet move*	7 7	4 53	13	6 50	5 28
30	F.	*without*	7 6	4 54	14	6 45	6 21
31	Sat.	*noise.*	7 5	4 55	14	6 41	7 17

JANUARY. *first month,* 1818. Winter.

Time of the Planets' Southing. &c.

D.	Mer. H. M.	Ven. H. M.	Mars. H. M.	Jup. H. M.	Sat. H. M.	Hers. H. M.	Sun's Semid.
1	1 16	22 47	9 40	22 53	3 52	22 14	16 18
13	1 10	23 0	8 44	22 12	2 44	21 25	16 17
25	23 31	23 15	7 57	21 32	1 58	20 35	16 16

***LUNAR* CALCULATIONS, &c.**

New Moon 6th day, 6 h. 46 m. even.
First Quarter 14th day, 1 h. 54 m. morn.
Full Moon 22d day, 5 h. 36 m. morn.
Last Quarter 29th day 11 h. 52 m. morn.

M.D.	W.D.	*Weather, Aspects, &c.*	Moo age.	Moo. place.	Moo. r & s	Diary.
1	Th.	Sun nearest Earth.	24	reins	1 5	
2	F.	*Prepare for*	25	secrets	2 21	
3	Sat.	Jup. Ven. in Cont.	26	secrets	3 37	
4	Sun.	Moo. Hers. conj.	27	thighs	4 57	
5	M.	Moo. Jup. conj.	28	thighs	6 12	
6	Tu.	Moo. Ven. conj.	0	knees	sets.	
7	W.	Moo. runs low.	1	knees	5 19	
8	Th.	Moo. Merc. conj.	2	legs	6 35	
9	F.	*winter in*	3	legs	7 51	
10	Sat.	Moo. Sat. conj.	4	feet	9 0	
11	Sun.	*earnest.*	5	feet	10 4	
12	M.	*N. E. storm,*	6	head	11 7	
13	Tu.	*and very*	7	head	morn.	
14	W.	Mars Stat.	8	head	0 9	
15	Th.	*cold.*	9	neck	1 9	
16	F.	Moo. Apogee.	10	neck	2 13	
17	Sat.	Moo. Mars conj.	11	arms	3 16	
18	Sun.		12	arms	4 17	
19	M.	Moo. runs high.	13	arms	5 18	
20	Tu.	Sun Ent. Aquarius.	14	breast	6 14	
21	W.	*Bleak N. W.*	15	breast	rises	
22	Th.	*winds*	16	heart	4 56	
23	F.	Merc. Inf. conj.	17	heart	6 5	
24	Sat.	*Warmer*	18	bowels	7 16	
25	Sun.	*and threatening*	19	bowels	8 26	
26	M.	*a thaw.*	20	bowels	9 35	
27	Tu.	*Rain*	21	reins	10 46	
28	W.	*and hail.*	22	reins	11 59	
29	Th.	*Sudden*	23	secrets	morn.	
30	F.	*change*	24	secrets	1 14	
31	Sat.	*to cold.*	25	thighs	2 31	

Figure 10. Astronomical charts for January from Hitchcock's *Country Almanack* for 1818

Now on the first page of every month of your edition I observe your promise that ten dollars will be paid on the discovery of an error. Confiding in your character as a gentleman and believing that justice will be done me, Mr. Edmund M. Blunt, Esq., I am Sir respectfully your humble servant.

Thus far the tone was polite, the focus limited to a few minor details of Blunt's work. But the scope of their dispute soon would escalate dramatically, as would the rhetorical temperature. Several months having passed without a reply from Blunt, Hitchcock composed a second letter. It listed twelve more errors in the 1814 edition of the *Nautical Almanac*. Unlike the minor flaws pointed out previously, these errors, he argued, were critical to the use of the tables for navigation and could lead to catastrophe on the high seas.

Just a few days after that letter, on April 20, 1814, Blunt finally penned a response to the young upstart. If Hitchcock expected a gracious reply, he must have been disappointed. Blunt argued that the errors Hitchcock cited related to the moons of Jupiter which were not visible from the deck of a ship and hence of limited navigational use. "Nothing is wanting on my part, to make it correct." Further, he refused to honor his pledge of a reward, arguing that he, like all humans, was fallible.

Not surprisingly, Blunt's reply did not satisfy Hitchcock. He would likely have carried the issue further, but in May another health crisis befell him, one of life changing proportions, the near total loss of his eyesight, probably a result of mumps earlier in life. For someone with an all-consuming passion for astronomy, the blow could not have been more devastating.

For nearly two years Edward's pursuit of his scientific inclinations was thwarted by his disability. Edmund Blunt probably began to feel that he had vanquished his nemesis, or at least outlasted him, regarding those alleged errors in his almanacs. But he had only been granted a reprieve. In October 1816, more than two years after his last letter, Edward penned another to Blunt:

> Since I received your letter of the twentieth April 1814 I have been so much engaged that I have not found time to write an answer. But having now a convenient opportunity to send by M. W. Cooley of N. York, I have concluded to address you again on the subject of your edition of the Nautical Almanac…I thank you for the copies of the Almanack you sent me though I had obtained some for the same years previously. I must mention however that in the copy for 1815 which you sent me all the calculations for August were for August 1814.

We can only imagine the reaction of Blunt. Not only had his adversary been revived, but his ardor was augmented. Blunt had stated in a previous letter that he had made some corrections. But Hitchcock was not convinced:

> With regard to the correction of the areas mentioned in your letter I have not noted any except one which was evidently altered with a pen. And how could errors be corrected after the copies were distributed through the union and many of them sold?

Blunt's torment still was not finished as Hitchcock's next paragraph began: "I shall now proceed to point out some errors in the Almanack for 1816 and 1817." Edward's letter ended with a warning: "I shall expect an answer to this—but if you do not consider this additional bit worthy of notice and I do not hear from you soon the public may from me and you from the public. From your humble servant EH."

Another year passed. Once again we can imagine Blunt resting confident that his albatross had taken flight. Hitchcock's health repaired, he was now preceptor of Deerfield Academy. Yet in October 1817 he found time to send a letter to the editors of a new periodical, the *American Monthly Magazine and*

Critical Review, in New York. The letter appeared in the December issue of the magazine and began:

> To Astronomers and Navigators: Considering the great care used in calculating the Nautical Almanack, I had been accustomed to rely upon it with almost implicit confidence; but having for several years past, made use of Blunt's American edition of that work, I have noticed several errors in it.

He proceeded to list sixteen errors in the *Nautical Almanac*, some in the London edition, others in Blunt's edition, including the years 1814, 1816, 1817, and 1818. The last paragraph read,

> These errors are offered to astronomers and navigators, without comment. I would only observe, that Mr. Blunt 'pledges his reputation it (the Nautical Almanack) shall not in one instance deviate from the English Edition;' and offers a reward of 'ten dollars' for the discovery of an error. He has been written to several times on the subject; but his answers were evasive and unsatisfactory.

The publication of the debate apparently motivated Blunt to make a reply through the same journal in the January 1818 issue. He attributed an inversion of a page number to the printer. The substitution of "immersion" for "emersion" he admitted but claimed it was corrected before the edition was printed. To Hitchcock's statement of an error in the signs for Virgo and Scorpio, Blunt argued that the two signs were easily confused: "There is such a similarity between the two characters to offer some excuse for this neglect." Blunt may have had a point:

♍ ♏

Of a series of errors Hitchcock cites in "Chronological Cycles," "Ember Days," and "Moveable Feasts," Blunt was, well, blunt: "This declaration of Mr. Hitchcock at once exposes him. It is not true; before three respectable persons I have compared my edition with the English, and find it corresponds in every particular." He then also mounted an ad hominem attack on his critic and, it would seem, all astronomers:

> The pages he refers to are used generally by Astronomers, and although I would willingly bestow every reasonable attention to make those pages correct… I would rather ten errors should escape me there, than one by which the mariner should be deceived. I am led to this remark by his shameful neglect, in the examination of that Almanack, and shall point out errors which I have corrected in my edition, of more importance to the mariner than all the services he ever rendered that useful class of society.

BLUNT'S
Edition of the Nautical Almanac, for 1816
Ten dollars will be paid on discovery of an error in the figures.

Figure 11. Edmund M. Blunt (1770-1862); below, the notice of a reward to be paid for the discovery of an error in Blunt's *Nautical Almanac*.

In his reply a month later, Hitchcock cited several dozen additional errors, then appeared to address his adversary's new line of attack: "…since the errors are in a part of the Almanack most important to navigators, it is of consequence that those in the copy of 1818, should be made public in season for seamen to make the corrections…"

But the crowning blow of this assault on the credibility of the *Nautical Almanac* was yet to come. Undeterred by Blunt's denials and accusations, Hitchcock wrote another letter to the *American Monthly Magazine* in July listing no fewer than sixty-five errors in the recent editions of the publication, ending with a warning: "Whenever I may chance to notice any errors of magnitude in a work of such vital importance as the Nautical Almanac, I shall consider myself bound to offer them for publication, whether they be made by A, B, or C." A month later, Esq. Blunt seemed to admit he had met his match:

> GENTLEMEN, The communication from the pen of Mr. Hitchcock, relative to errors in my edition of the Nautical Almanac, deserves notice, and he is entitled to much credit for his perseverance… Mr. H. has examined my edition for 1819, and discovered THIRTY-FIVE ERRORS, all which I have corrected with the pen, in the copies on hand, and beg him to accept my thanks for the information, whatever may be his motive.…Mr. H. will be pleased to

> continue his labours, and contribute all in his power to that perfection which guides the mariner through the pathless ocean, and relieves the solicitude of a respectable class of society, which it is a duty incumbent on every man to aid. With great respect, The public's obedient servant, EDMUND M. BLUNT.

Thus ended "The Great Almanack Debate." The now twenty-five-year-old Edward had carried the day. Whether Edmund M. Blunt had truly seen the errors of his ways or was suffering from loss of revenue due to the young man's criticisms, we cannot know. For Edward Hitchcock, however, the resolution must have given great satisfaction both as a young scientist and a debater. Had he received the promised ten dollar reward for each error found in the *National Almanack* he would have been a wealthy man, even by Deerfield standards. But a far greater reward awaited him.

Barely a month after Blunt's final response, a stunning announcement was made by Yale College. It appeared in the same journal that hosted the debate: "At the annual Commencement of Yale College, New-Haven, Con. On the 9th of September, the Honorary Degree of Master of Arts was conferred on Mr. Edward Hitchcock of Deerfield, Massachusetts." That this honor was both unexpected and overwhelming to the recipient is attested to by this letter from Edward to Yale Professor Benjamin Silliman a few weeks later:

> The unexpected conferring of a degree upon me by your college awakens within me the liveliest feelings of gratitude and I have much reason for supposing that you Sir have not been inactive in my favour. Having been completely frustrated in every effort to pass regularly through a college by weakness of sight and of constitution I had relinquished the idea of ever acquiring the honors of any, much less of one so eminent as Yale. I fear I shall never be able to make any adequate return for this high favour: but I hope at least that a thankful heart will not fail me. Very respectfully yours, Edward Hitchcock

Thanks both to the errors of Edmund M. Blunt and the beneficence of Yale College, the name Edward Hitchcock was now known far beyond the boundaries of Deerfield, Massachusetts.

Josephine and Napoleon

5 Bonaparte's Downfall

"For such an one to attempt a tragedy on so difficult a subject may seem folly."

Deerfield, August 1814

"I call this special meeting to order," began twenty-year-old John Hoyt, president of the Literary Adelphi Society. The group of a dozen young men had gathered as was their custom outside the meetinghouse in the shade of an immense sycamore tree. But this evening there were guests.

"We are honored to welcome to our meeting this day several members of the Young Ladies' Literary Society—Miss Johnson, Miss White, Miss Cooley. And now Mr. Williams has asked your forbearance to discuss a subject of pressing importance that will explain the presence of our distaff guests. Sir?"

"Err, uhh," began William Williams. "I...it is in regard to a dramatic creation...of our worthy friend here, Mr. Hitchcock." He held a sheaf of papers in one shaky hand as he spoke.

"Yes," interjected Mr. Hoyt, recognizing the manuscript that had been handed among the members over the last two weeks. "We have all seen it and perhaps read it through." There then proceeded a good deal of banter as some

members confessed to having merely skimmed the lengthy work, others to reading it not at all.

"Miss Cooley?"

"I read every line, Mr. President," replied the young woman breathily. "I found it ever so moving, quite thrilling." She blushed at her emotional outburst.

At which point Jackson Dickinson rose, smiling broadly. "Dearest friends, I wish to make a proposition, if I may." All eyes were on the young man who had a way with words and a certain presence that commanded everyone's attention. "What say you all..." He paused, looking about wide-eyed at his fellow Adelphians and guests for dramatic effect. "...to a production...by our two Societies...of Mr. Hitchcock's play?"

There ensued several minutes of animated discussion. Miss Johnson spoke up then. "But we have no actors among us, Mr. Dickinson, not even any aspiring Thespians, sir."

"True," replied Mr. Dickinson, "but are we not all lovers of literature? Of the refined arts? Are we not all prepared to heed the call of our tragedic muse? What our friend has produced here, under the most trying circumstances of degraded health and vision...is a masterpiece. Should we not deem it of the greatest importance to present his oeuvre to the world, for its approbation?"

Again a hubbub commenced. Finally the president spoke up. "Mr. Hitchcock, sir. This work is yours to do with as you see fit. How are you disposed on this question?"

Edward Hitchcock stood, all diffidence and humility, his thin frame noticeably unsteady. He spoke slowly and softly. "I am honored, gentlemen and ladies, that you should consider my humble product worthy of such an audacious plan. Alas, modesty and my fragile constitution would argue strongly against your proposal."

Sighs of regret could be heard, particularly from the female members. Finally, one of them, a Miss White, rose and addressed the group.

"Mr. President, having read the manuscript in its entirety, I should like to express my wish that these two societies might jointly undertake the production of 'The Emancipation of Europe, or The Downfall of Bonaparte,' by the most capable Mr. Hitchcock." She turned and acknowledged the author with a polite smile and a bow. Cheers went up from all quarters.

Edward breathed a heavy sigh of resignation. "Well, then, if Miss White...and the rest of this esteemed assemblage wishes, let it be so." Again cheers were raised all around. But Edward continued. "I have in truth given the matter some thought, even though I believed it unwise, and would like to make a few humble suggestions. In the role of Napoleon, Mr. Williams—he has the necessary depth of character, a certain fierceness of spirit. As Emperor Alexander I would nominate myself—we share I believe bonds both of heart and of soul. And in the role of Marie Louise I can imagine none finer than our very dear friend, Miss Orra White."

When the thirteen colonies rose up against their oppressor, King George III, in 1775, they had from the start the sympathy of France. Early in the American Revolution, a small contingent of French soldiers joined the colonial forces, among them the redoubtable Marquis de Lafayette. Perhaps of even greater importance was the willingness of the French to supply the colonial forces with supplies, guns, and ammunition. According to one estimate, nearly three-quarters of the weapons used by the Continental Army against Burgoyne in the pivotal Battle of Saratoga were of French origin. Some historians would argue in later times that the American war for independence would have been lost without the assistance of France.

Barely a decade later, when a popular uprising began in France against another oppressive monarch, King Louis XVI, Americans watched with more than a little interest. But the excesses and brutality of the revolution in France horrified most Americans, particularly as the reign of one brute was replaced by others, first by the Jacobins, and then by General Napoleon Bonaparte who with the French army's support overthrew the elected government in 1799 and appointed himself Emperor in 1804.

Even before Napoleon's overthrow, France was engaged in military operations on every border. By 1799 it had overrun and subdued Belgium, Holland, Switzerland, Austria, and Italy. Napoleon already had his sights set on Britain, but he realized that England's superior naval forces could not be overcome. With the sale of Louisiana to the United States, France's coffers were full and it was able to renew its military aggressions, setting its sights ultimately on Russia and Great Britain. By 1812 France dominated nearly all of Europe, from Italy and Spain north to Switzerland, Germany, and Holland. It also had alliances with Norway, Denmark, Prussia, and the Austrian Empire. Standing against Napoleon were Great Britain, Russia, Sweden, and Portugal.

Americans watched what was happening in Europe with alarm. Weapons and ammunition were provided by the United States to both British and Russian forces in hopes of strengthening opposition to the French army. Great Britain had the advantage of mastery of the seas, and they were anxious to preserve that advantage at all costs. They imposed blockades on American ships they thought were damaging their war effort; and they began boarding American naval vessels and conscripting American sailors against their will. President Jefferson, in retaliation for British naval activities, pushed through Congress the infamous Embargo Act, prohibiting British ships from entering American waters. Eventually antagonism between Britain and the United States reached a critical level; in 1812 Congress declared war on Britain.

Thus it was that many Americans, particularly Federalists such as Edward Hitchcock, believed that, by declaring war against Britain, America was sympathizing with Napoleon. They feared that France's armies, after overrunning Europe, would turn next to subjugate Britain, then America.

In two letters to the *Franklin Herald* in Greenfield, Hitchcock gave voice to some of those fears. In the first, entitled "The Appeal," dated August 11, 1812, he struck an ominous tone, calling on the elected leaders of the New England states to take a stand against the war with Britain:

> At this gloomy crisis, in this day of darkness for America and for liberty—when the civilized world totters on the brink of dissolution—when this country is rushing with infatuated madness into the calamities and devastations of war—when the cankering influence of the political Upas of Europe is fast extending on these late peaceful and happy shores—and when the last republic on earth, the only refuge of pure liberty below heaven, is fast yielding to the mighty sweep of despotism; in such an hour of gloom, the people of New England whose souls have not been contaminated by that gangrene of freedom, French influence, as the last resort of their hopes, appeal to those whom they have elected, for their patriotism and talents, to high and responsible offices in these States.

Furthermore, he predicted that the American war with Britain would only assist Napoleon:

> The people have also been told, that altho' this war is unnecessary, unjust, and ruinous, yet it is their duty to unite in its prosecution, and to endeavor to carry it on with the utmost vigor. What! are they to lift their hands to aid the assassin in plunging a dagger to their hearts? Shall they assist to render nerveless the only arm which can save them from the grasp of despotism? No: the people of New England will not voluntarily aid in linking the chains of Bonaparte about their necks.

In the second letter, dated November 18, 1812, he drew an analogy between the change of the seasons and the decline and fall of American democracy:

> Half a century has not yet elapsed since the American Republic emerged from oppression, and first attracted the attention of mankind. But already has she passed her zenith. Her summer is gone, and her autumn has commenced. Soon, it is to be feared, will the winter of oppression close the scene of America's freedom. Soon will the keen blasts of tyranny prostrate the fair tree of our country's liberty, and strip it of its verdure...As the meteor of night marks a bright path in the heavens, and for a short time engages the attention of mankind, but soon fades on its course and drops into darkness, for the American Republic, having traced for a few years a splendid course on the pages of history, now grows dim, and soon will sink to rise no more.

In an undated essay entitled "Genius and Application" that may never have appeared in print, he used Switzerland as an example of the possible fate of America. How was that nation subjugated?

> Not by the point of the bayonet, not by open force, but by a system of intrigue…French emissaries were spread…throughout the whole of Switzerland. These by their insidious exertions excited party spirit and jealousies among the people and king like dead weights in the operation of government. At length the influence of the unfounded insinuations of their emissaries extended so far that the party in favor of France acquired the ascendancy in the national councils. Alliances with France were then formed and the grossest insults from her were received with impunity.

It was with this kind of political insinuation, argued Hitchcock, that Presidents Jefferson and Madison were aiding France's interests in the United States. It was a far-fetched scenario that was often imputed by Federalists who believed the nation had been kidnapped by the Democratic-Republicans.

The depth of Hitchcock's despair over the plight of the nation is evinced in his long essay, "On a Separation of the United States." Likely written in 1814, it asserted the urgency of the New England states separating from the other states. The immediate issue was the war with Britain; but he revealed a deep cynicism as to the motives of Jefferson, Madison, and the Democratic-Republican Party in general, and misgivings regarding the differences between the northern states and southern states. If the northern states do not secede now, he argued, war will surely ensue, perhaps within a decade. So far as is known, the essay was never published; but it may have been presented to the Adelphi.

Thankfully, circumstances would spare the nation from such fearmongering. The war with Britain took a heavy toll on the United States, it is true, with the burning of Washington and the loss of thousands of American lives. Eventually, however, the two adversaries reached an agreement with the signing of the Treaty of Ghent in 1814. As to Napoleon, whatever visions of conquest he harbored were dashed, first by the disastrous campaign against Russia in 1811 and 1812, and finally by his defeat at the hands of the British and Belgian armies at Waterloo in 1815.

Public esteem for the late General George Washington, particularly in the New England states, seemed to grow stronger with time. Ten years after his death many cities and towns celebrated Washington's memory on or about the fourth of July. The Washington Benevolent Society of Deerfield held its celebration on July 6, 1813. It began in late afternoon on the common with hundreds of townspeople in attendance. According to one newspaper account, there was a substantial collation of "ham, beef, lamb, crackers, bread, cheese etc.," that had to be depleted lest it go to waste…not to mention "an exhilerating supply of brandy, spirits, & wine."

By evening the women and children had gone home but a crowd of boisterous men lingered at Hoyt's tavern, honoring General Washington most vociferously. Amidst swirls of pipe smoke and peals of laughter, Elihu Hoyt stood and slammed his pewter tankard on the table top. When the uproar had subsided, he raised the tankard and threw back his head:

> Gentlemen, at this time I wish to offer a toast to the 37th anniversary of the day on which our fathers declared us independent: may the spirit which roused those patriots to assert and maintain their rights, continue to animate the children of Washington, to the latest posterity.

Shouts and cheers erupted once again. Then another member, a rotund, bald-headed fellow, rose at the rear.

> To the memory of our great patriot and leader George Washington—the rock on which the storms of democracy, and the lightning and thunder of Jacobinism, have in vain spent their rage; may we strive to imitate his great virtues.

There followed more than a dozen additional toasts—to Massachusetts Governor Strong—to the Russian Emperor Alexander—to the Union of the States—to the Free Sons of Massachusetts—to her "sister" states, New Hampshire, Rhode Island, New York, Vermont, and Connecticut—to "our gallant little Navy"—to the Militia of Massachusetts—to the army of the United States.

Finally Mr. Hoyt calmed the crowd again. "Gentlemen, there remains one more toast to be offered, and as I am informed a few brief comments by one of our native sons." A hush came over the crowd as the lank figure of Edward Hitchcock rose from a seat at the side, stepped forward, and stood unsmiling beside his uncle.

> I rise to propose a sentiment relating to the future success of the Russians over the tyrant of Europe; but as the subject is peculiarly interesting, I beg leave to make a few preliminary observations.

Perhaps Elihu Hoyt was unaware that his nephew, even at age twenty, was not in the habit of delivering brief comments. His oration ran to nearly forty-five minutes, which given the lateness of the hour and the well stuffed and lubricated audience, was perhaps a bit long. But by the end, those who were still awake and listening rose in unison and cheered the young man's inspired narrative and ringing tribute to the heroism of the Russian army against Napoleon. It may well have been young Hitchcock's first public oration, the first of many he would make over the coming forty years.

By spring of 1814 Edward's path in life, at least for the near future, seemed clear. He had just published the first edition of his *Country Almanack*. He was preparing two manuscripts on geology that he planned to submit to a Boston based journal, the *North American Review*. He was crafting several addresses to present before the Adelphi on philosophy, religion, and politics. If all went well, he harbored hopes of entering Harvard College in the fall to study astronomy and mathematics. Then fate intervened.

> A slight epidemic disease attacked me not severe enough to prevent my attention to study: but on opening my Majora one morning my eyes were so much affected that I was obliged to close it. As the disorder passed off, I supposed my sight would recover its strength: but from that day to the present I have never spent an hour in reading without suffering severely from pain in my eyes: and for a year or more such was their weakness that I was compelled to abandon almost entirely my classical studies. All my plans for life—my high hopes of distinction among men of science were thus blasted in a moment.

He had taken such pleasure and interest in his astronomical studies—no more. He had harbored dreams of attending Harvard—hopes now dashed. "Darkness that might be felt rested upon my prospects," he would recall many years later. Yet the sudden impairment of his vision and the constant pain did not seem to diminish his activity; on the contrary, his physical impairments seemed to drive him forward with even more determination.

Much of the news that appeared in the *Franklin Herald* that spring pertained to the progress of the war with Britain. But the May 24, 1814, issue carried this headline: "LATE AND IMPORTANT INTELLIGENCE: Confirmation of the defeat of Bonaparte—the capture of Paris by the allies—and the breaking off the Negociations at Chatillon." Napoleon's army had been severely weakened by a series of defeats in Russia and Poland in 1812 and 1813 and had retreated to France. Britain and her European allies—Prussia, Austria, Sweden, Russia, Spain, and Portugal—seized the opportunity to surround the French forces and pressure Napoleon to surrender. On April 6, 1814, he abdicated unconditionally and was banished to the island of Elba. All of Europe celebrated their freedom from Napoleon's tyrannical rule. Americans celebrated as well, not only on behalf of the republics of Europe, but for their own safety. Of course, history records that Napoleon would eventually escape Elba and return for a time to France, but his ultimate demise would occur in the Belgian city of Waterloo, a name that would become eponymous with ignominious defeat.

For Edward the downfall of Napoleon represented a critical turn in the affairs of mankind. Within days of learning the news he had scrawled out a manuscript of over 100 pages, a play entitled *Emancipation of Europe, or The Downfall of Bonaparte: A Tragedy*. The setting was Paris, the time shortly after the French army's invasion of Russia. Most plays of that time were in three acts or "unities," but the playwright asked his audience's forgiveness that the "unities are violated"–his play would run on to five acts and some 35,000 words. He also alluded to his infirmities: "...whatever be [the play's] fate, the alleviation it has afforded in many a dejected hour, is ample compensation for the labor bestowed upon it."

The main characters were Emperor Napoleon, his wife Marie Louise, his military leaders Marshal Ney and General Lescourt, his foreign minister Talleyrand, King Louis XVIII, and Allied leaders including Alexander of Russia and Lord Wellington of Great Britain. Little subtlety or nuance is evinced in these characters. Napoleon is portrayed as a mercurial tyrant, quick to issue orders and ruthless toward any who resist them. His generals are sycophants, only too ready to do his bidding. The Allied leaders are all upright, honest, refined men. In other words, this was a morality play of sorts, conceived to satisfy a Deerfield audience. Perhaps the playwright betrayed his parochialism too baldly: "His Frenchmen talked not like Frenchmen but like eager Deerfield boys, discussing the news of the day in blank verse!" wrote one reviewer. But he wrote from his own experience, filling the work with allusions to geology, natural history, and especially astronomy–sun and moon, stars and planets, comets and meteors.

In May, shortly after his twenty-first birthday, Hitchcock joined the Deerfield church, and undertook a program of religious studies on his own. He began a thorough reading of the Bible. In one year's time, he wrote later in life, he read the Holy Scriptures in their entirety. Soon he returned to his many writing projects. He completed the play and offered it to his friends of the Literary Adelphi, and to the Young Ladies' Literary Society, for their consideration.

In short, it seems, the temporary loss of his eyesight, the event that had seemed to put an end to all Edward Hitchcock's hopes and dreams, proved to be but a minor setback. The only real casualty had been his plans for Harvard. And yet would it not have been possible for him to enter Harvard still, perhaps a term or two later? In 1815 his uncle wrote him a letter of introduction to a member of the Harvard faculty asking that Edward be permitted to view the college's "philosophical apparatus," by which was meant their telescopes. So perhaps he considered reapplying. True, it might have proved too much for a young man of diminished capacity, but perhaps there were other influences that turned him away from Cambridge. The expense, for one; he knew it would have been a very considerable strain on his family's finances. And then there was his faith. Harvard, after all, was well known by that time as the center of Unitarianism in America. Perhaps Hitchcock had begun to feel a certain theological repulsion against the college that made much easier the decision not to attend.

The fall of 1814 found Edward Hitchcock preparing the next edition of his almanac, sending off completed manuscripts on geological subjects, and, of course, there was the play. The production of a play was an entirely new undertaking for the Literary Adelphi, but they threw themselves into the task with great energy and devotion.

Miss Orra White, Edward's choice for the role of Napoleon's wife, a native of nearby Amherst, was the daughter Jarib and Ruth Sherman White. Her father was a successful businessman and proprietor of a large housewares store in Amherst. The couple had eight children, but only Orra and three brothers, Jay, Bela, and George, lived to adulthood. Orra was an intelligent and talented child and her parents provided her with what was probably at the time the best education a young girl could receive. At age ten she was sent to a boarding school in South Hadley for perhaps five years. After that she attended a female seminary in Boston for at least one year.

From an early age Orra had a particular fondness for the decorative arts, but she also showed exceptional aptitude in the sciences and mathematics. At age seventeen, she was hired as one of the first preceptresses at Deerfield Academy. During her years in Deerfield, she became involved in the town's cultural organizations including the Young Ladies' Literary Society. Her years in Deerfield afforded her many opportunities to meet other well educated young people of both sexes and she forged many close friendships, including one with Edward Hitchcock, who was quick to recognize her many talents and graces which won her a key role in his play. On her departure with the closing of the Academy in 1819, Orra was hired as preceptress at Amherst Academy.

The performance took place on the evening of Friday, December 2, 1814, in the Deerfield meetinghouse. A brief item in the next edition of the *Franklin Herald* seemed to offer encouragement if not outright praise for the work:

> We were gratified, that the reception this juvenile attempt at the Thespian art met with, from a numerous and respectable auditory, was honorable as well to the author as to the society by which it was "got up." It evinces a literary emulation, which we wish to see more widely diffused, and which, perhaps, more than any other principle, is designed to ameliorate the state of society in our country, and ensure the stability of our public institutions—We heartily wish the most brilliant success to this rural society, in their laudable pursuit.

In his notes Hitchcock wrote of the play and that period of his life,

> ...I was then in a state of deep dejection having by a failure of eyes and health had all my plans cut off and I printed this in the hopes that it might lead some one to extend to me a helping hand. God be thanked that it was not written well enough to attract the attention of the managers of the theater: for destitute as I then was of a saving knowledge of religion had I been drawn into that vortex I fear I should never have been reserved.

Many years later he would write of *Downfall*, "It should not have been published," although adding that the play, "was loudly called for by the rural population before whom it was acted with much success." But he thought enough of his effort to have a few copies printed and to send one to the Russian playwright, Alexi Eustaphieve, who was living in Boston at the time. Edward's cover letter seems intended to lower the expectations of his esteemed reader:

> I herewith send you a tragedy which I hope you will do me the honor to accept. I feel much diffidence in presenting to your inspection a piece written under so many disadvantages...I know that it will appear presumptuous for a person like myself just past my teens, not assisted by a liberal education, unacquainted with the deep windings of the human character, who have scarcely seen a theatrical performance and of course know not how to touch those delicate things which will produce a good stage effect, and whom a locality of situation and a want of means prevent from obtaining an accurate knowledge of European politics, for such an one to attempt a tragedy on so difficult a subject may seem folly.

How was his letter and his gift received? Cordially, to be sure:

> Your tragedy was delivered into my hands by the friend to whose care it was entrusted. For the handsome manner in which you have accompanied its offer as well as for the offer itself, and the gratification I experienced in perusing the piece, I offer you my sincere thanks and acknowledgments. I also congratulate you on the successful effort which in various parts of the drama are too obvious to be overlooked...The beauties which display themselves throughout the whole are of the first order, emanating from the true inspiration of genius, and glorying with all the ardour of youth. They are all your own, and can never be alienated.

But the playwright then goes on to a frank critique of the work:

> The defects...are such as you have yourself anticipated...They come... from a young too exuberant fancy which is a good fault, but generally they proceed from the subject itself. Great and at the same time familiar events, passing as it were before our eyes...are the most difficult, ungracious and unsuitable subjects for drama, that can possibly be selected.... My first opinion is that under any other title but the present, as a mere poem in fragments, not offered to the tragic muse it would make an excellent composition, dismembered from all those objections which I have taken the liberty of suggesting.

So ended Edward Hitchcock's incipient career as a playwright. So ended as well, it would appear, his interest in and taste for political discourse.

Yale College, 1840

6 Season of Love

"Three years of my life have passed like a winged dream."

Deerfield, May 1819

The Reverend Samuel Willard sat at his desk, worrying over the final details of the sermon he would deliver that Sunday. He was fastidious in his writing, constantly rereading and revising, which made the composition of two discourses each week a most protracted endeavor. He was in the midst of scratching out a whole paragraph of text with a steel pen when a soft rap sounded on the door.

"Yes—come in," he grumbled without looking up, still vigorously wielding his pen.

The door opened slowly, but the visitor stood quietly without, awaiting acknowledgment. Still sputtering, the pastor made one more swipe with his pen before looking up. "Ah, Mr. Hitchcock."

"Pardon me, sir. May I have a word?" asked Edward.

"Of course," replied the pastor. "Come—sit," he added, pointing to a rush-seated chair that held a precarious pile of books.

"Oh no, Pastor. I...I needn't take up much of your time. I am certain you have many obligations to attend."

The pastor nodded. Still standing, Edward fidgeted with his cap that he held before him with both hands.

"Sir?" prompted the pastor. "Is it about this week's prayer meeting?"

"Well, Reverend Willard, yes. Or rather..." He paused, clearly uncomfortable with what he had to say. "I am afraid, Pastor, that I will be unable to attend...this week...or for the foreseeable future."

"Oh?"

"I am leaving, sir, in the morning, for New Haven."

"Really. What, not enough attractions here in Deerfield to hold you?" Perhaps it was meant as a lighthearted comment, but Edward was certain he detected resentment in the pastor's tone, the slight tightening of his lips, a trace of redness in his face. "Pursuing your science, then, I trust?"

"No, sir, pursuing my religious studies."

The pastor's brow furrowed with worry. At New Haven was Yale, and at Yale were men of deep orthodox views, views the Reverend could not countenance.

"Are you certain, Mr. Hitchcock, that this...this removal is wise?"

Edward nodded. He was suddenly in urgent need of taking his leave without offending the pastor any more than he knew he already had. "I wish to thank you, Reverend, Sir, for all your ministrations on my behalf. I must be on my way."

But the pastor was not finished. "I have many things to say to you, Mr. Hitchcock...about your faith...our faith...but clearly you cannot bear them now."

The remark stunned Edward. He exited the study and the parsonage quickly, then hastened homeward. As he crossed the common, he was muttering to himself those words he wished he had said back in the parson's study had he been more courageous, more forthright: "I have sat twelve years under your ministry," he was saying to himself. "I have been two years your student in divinity." "Two years," he repeated aloud, smiling at the heavens, his head shaking with emotion. "Two years—two years and yet there remain 'many things in your system which I cannot bear'?" He stopped, his gaze rising to the distant church steeple, and he spoke now loudly, forcefully, with uncharacteristic emotion: "Is your faith so complicated, so convoluted, that after all this time you are still unable to explain it to me?"

The next morning Edward departed by stage for New Haven. As the stage rocked and rumbled along the dusty road from Deerfield to Springfield, he gazed absently at the Connecticut River just visible in the distance. At last everything was clear, even for one with poor vision: his spiritual life, his intellectual life, and his career path all had been suddenly and utterly transformed.

Edward Hitchcock's harrowing experience in 1814—the sudden loss of his vision, doubts for a time of any recovery whatsoever, then a slow, very gradual improvement, but accompanied by withering pain and fatigue—had seemed to put an end to all the young man's hopes and dreams. It nevertheless appeared to have a bright side—perhaps two bright sides. First, it had spurred him to renewed and invigorated intellectual activity—his play, his *Almanack*, his first scientific papers—all those followed the crisis within a few months. But there was still another field of endeavor that was stimulated rather than frustrated by his fragile constitution: a renewed interest in and full-throttled pursuit of religious truth.

Ever since Edward was old enough to remember, Unitarianism had been on the ascendancy in Deerfield. Unitarianism had its roots in the Protestant Reformation of the sixteenth century. It was a belief system that eschewed some of the basic principles of Christianity, most notably the Holy Trinity: Father, Son, and Holy Ghost. But the tenets of this sect went well beyond the Trinity. It recognized the importance of reason in interpreting Holy Scriptures and emphasized a scholarly approach to faith. Each believer must study and constantly reexamine his belief system and his relationship with God.

The arrival of Reverend Samuel Willard in 1807 was nothing short of a spiritual earthquake for the town of Deerfield. Willard was unapologetically Unitarian, having trained at Harvard. The debate over his ordination was in itself an ordeal for the town, lasting some two months. In the end Willard was selected by a clear majority of the church members, including Justin Hitchcock.

Despite the one-sided result, the installation of Samuel Willard as pastor of the Deerfield meetinghouse left a deep fissure in the town—literally. Within seven months of his selection, a petition was circulated calling for the separation of the southern part of the town. It was not only religious differences that triggered this division; Deerfield had been from its creation a large, ungainly township. Issues about maintaining schools, meetinghouses, and roads in the outlying districts were also involved. The process took several years, but by 1810 Deerfield had been officially divided, the southerly portion being incorporated into the town of Whately.

Among the many citizens of Unitarian inclination in Deerfield was Epaphras Hoyt. It seems that besides cultivating Edward Hitchcock's astronomical interests, Uncle Ep was largely responsible for promoting in his nephew a "disrelish" for the orthodox Christianity of Edward's father. Some fifteen years later, Hitchcock would write of his uncle's teaching:

> ...he was extremely sceptical in regard to religious subjects having little more regard for Christianity than an avowed Deist. Although I now perceive that he was extremely superficial upon religious subjects...his frequent lectures against orthodox religion made too deep an impression on my youthful mind puffed up with my supposed attainments in science. I never however became

> quite as sceptical as my instructor: but embraced the Unitarian views which had for some years been gradually gaining ground in my native place and which were highly recommended by the gravity of deportment and highly respectable character of the clergyman who was labouring there to disseminate these views.

Hitchcock's religious views were not well formed at this point:

> Probably…if asked I never could have told definitely what were my views of religious truth: for I had never seriously examined the subject. I knew enough however to perceive that Unitarian principles and practice were much less repulsive and difficult than orthodox…I therefore was ready to advocate Unitarianism—though not infrequently doubting whether it were true…

His personal religious studies commenced with the Bible. "I began with Genesis and went through to the end of Revelation in about a year constantly offering up prayers that were at least sincere for guidance and wisdom and a disposition to receive every truth contained in the bible however repugnant to my prejudices." This was no small feat for one with limited vision. In the process, he wrote that he discovered "the leading truths of evangelical religion though my prejudices and pride resisted their reception for a long time and I received them only after a severe struggle." And here he added, "Some of the most offensive [truths] as election and the perseverance of the saints were not admitted fully into my creed until even after I began to preach."

During this period he also employed what might be described as an empirical approach to religion, observing the lives of people around him and drawing conclusions. What he found convinced him still further of the rightness of orthodox Calvinism and a fundamental weakness in Unitarianism. His orthodox acquaintances, he found, had far greater love for their fellow man than the Unitarians he had come to know.

In 1815 Hitchcock's first small efforts at scientific writing appeared in print. In that year Boston journalist Nathan Hale (nephew of the Revolutionary War hero of the same name) and a group of writers, politicians, and scientists founded the young nation's first literary magazine, the *North American Review*. Its scope was broad, including items of literary, historical, political, and scientific interest. Two brief communications from Hitchcock appeared in the third number of the *Review*, dated September 1815. They were introduced with this letter to the editor:

> SIR, I send you some account of the works now going on at the Lead mine in Southampton; and also of the Basaltick Columns in South Hadley, which may serve to call the attention of the publick to two objects well worth visiting.

> There are persons living in the vicinity who can and ought to give you a better account of them: this is at your service in the mean time. E. H.

The Southampton lead mine and the "Basaltick Columns"—Hitchcock later dubbed them "Titan's Pier" and "Titan's Piazza"—were well known to locals at the time. Perhaps Hale found them of particular interest as he was a native of nearby Westhampton. Both would be subjects of detailed study and discussion in Hitchcock's geological survey of Massachusetts two decades later. And while these two scientific productions were small, they represented the first cautious steps of Edward Hitchcock onto the stage of scientific discourse in America, a stage on which he would ere long become a major actor.

In May 1816, the young Hitchcock pursued his religious studies still further, including Hebrew and "Evidences of Christianity," under the tutelage of the Reverend Willard. That he made this decision is somewhat surprising, for he must have known from the start that Willard's spiritual principles ran entirely counter to his own.

Figure 12. Titan's Piazza on Mt. Holyoke, subject of one of Hitchcock's earliest scientific publications

In August of that year, Edward was appointed preceptor at Deerfield Academy. Though he had no teaching experience, the trustees, most of whom had known him from birth, must have recognized the young man's potential. And though he held no college degree which was usual for a preceptor at the time, perhaps his record of publications had already impressed them. At Deerfield he quickly became well known and admired. He taught astronomy, mathematics, and natural philosophy to his students, and gave public lectures in the evenings.

Shortly after his appointment, Hitchcock suffered another personal blow of a different kind. A lifelong friend, Jackson Dickinson, died at the age of twenty-five, leaving a wife, Harriet, and a two-month-old daughter, Mary. On his deathbed Jackson had confessed his faith in Christ to Edward, and that was the final instrument of Edward's conversion. In his notes Hitchcock wrote,

> In particular he [God] called me to witness the death of a companion and bosom friend who in health was even more loose in his religious views than myself

> but who on his death bed avowed his belief in the truth of orthodoxy. Perhaps I yielded my heart to the Saviour if ever I have done in the very evening in which he died.

So moved was Hitchcock that he wrote a poem for his friend in which he expressed a deep sense of loss, but concluded with an expression of hope that religion could become the instrument of man's salvation.

Hitchcock had been active in the Literary Adelphi Society since his days as an Academy student. Several members of that group, most of whom were orthodox in their beliefs, proposed to meet on Wednesday evenings for prayer and religious reflection. When they informed Reverend Willard of their plan, the pastor chose to join the group. According to Edward's recollection, Willard actually took over the group in an effort to enforce his own ideological and theological inclinations on them.

Orra White, who was a preceptress at the Academy, at some point became one of Edward's spiritual confidantes. Whether she was a member of that Wednesday evening group is not clear, but she had very definite religious convictions of her own that strongly influenced Edward. As he wrote in his notes some years later: "It was [Orra's] conversion and subsequent consistent conduct that first disarmed my skepticism and was a powerful means of leading me to embrace the same precious faith and hopes."

Edward Hitchcock's tenure as preceptor of Deerfield Academy was not to be long, perhaps as brief as two years. All indications suggest that he was well liked by the students and the trustees. He had made some welcome additions and innovations to the curriculum, particularly in the sciences. He designed and constructed several instruments to aid in his teaching of astronomy including a torquetum, a device used to predict eclipses. But times were hard for the academy. Enrollment was declining; it would close its doors temporarily in 1819. It is possible that Edward was dismissed due to financial difficulties, but the departure seems to have been on good terms.

His final address to the students of the academy is a handwritten document dated October 1817. But it has two or three alternate endings and additions that suggest that his planned departure may have been delayed several times, most likely no later than August 1818. In the address he offers encouragement to his young charges. But the emotional tone differs sharply from most of his writings to that time:

> I am unwilling this term should be closed without making a few observations. Duty might impell me to this but my feelings also prompt to it. We are so constituted thank heaven that we insensibly become attached to those with

> whom we have lived a considerable time, particularly if their conduct has been mild and interesting. These attachments frequently produce much pain at separation. The cords of friendship and habit are not to be broken without an effort. We cannot avoid feeling a peculiar interest for those with whom we have been connected as it were in the same family even for a few months…

He next offers some advice to his students, while at the same time giving voice to regrets of his own changed circumstances. Life, he tells them, is full of difficulties and discouragements. Our fondest plans are often thwarted. "Do not be discouraged if those very objects on which you now place your chief support and from which you derive your chief enjoyment should become the objects of your aversion." Here he apologizes for his inability to do more for his charges, blaming this failure on his poor health.

> Perhaps too I may from the same cause have sometimes appeared unsocial and reserved…If ever the time come when day after day month after month and year after year you shall feel the slow gnawings of disease—the nerveless arm, the feeble pulse, and the trembling knee you will then and not till then know how to judge of my feelings. I sincerely hope such a time may never arrive.

He then reflects on his own tenure:

> Like many of you I now must bid adieu to these walls and this I cannot do without emotion. For here three years of my life have passed like a winged dream…I commenced instruction in this place under peculiar difficulties being unassisted by a public education and laboring under a weakness of constitution and of right that made me almost despair of success. I feel grateful for all the favours I have received and thankful to that Providence which has been so gracious to me to this time. I must now again launch forth over the ocean of the world. Whither I shall steer or what will [be] the issue of my voyage I know not.

When at last he concludes his address, it is most interesting that he speaks not just for himself:

> In these sentiments and feelings Miss White desires to join with me: and we beg you to accept our hearty thanks for the gratification we received in instructing those who have had disposition and ability to advance in knowledge. So brittle is the thread of human life that many of you we may never meet again on earth. But be assured our best wishes attend you wherever you go and our solicitude for you goes forth from our hearts…for your welfare…We have done. We bid you farewell!

Miss White would stay on a few months beyond Hitchcock's departure, yet their wishes and dispositions, at least in his mind, appeared to be as one. Deerfield town historian George Sheldon observed that in the early years of Deerfield Academy, many a preceptress eventually married a preceptor (or in two instances trustees) of the institution. And that tradition, he suggested, would soon play out again:

> During all the years he labored here as preceptor, Mr. Hitchcock had an able assistant in Miss Orra White. She, too, could calculate eclipses, and she calculated to, and did, eclipse from her unsophisticated superior all the shining lights of his native town. When leaving this institution in 1819,—having before him the example of the trustee who enticed away the first preceptress,—Mr. Hitchcock made no scruple of engaging Miss Orra to go with him as his assistant for life.

In 1817 Hitchcock began exchanging letters with Benjamin Silliman, Professor of Chemistry and Natural History at Yale. The initial letters pertained to geology and mineralogy. Edward had by then accumulated quite a collection of mineral specimens obtained from all over western Massachusetts which he was anxious to describe to Silliman. In addition he shared his observations on the geology of the Connecticut River Valley, a subject that interested Silliman. He credited two acquaintances with assisting these efforts, Dr. Stephen W. Williams of Deerfield, Edward's cousin who shared his interest in mineralogy, and Miss White, who drew maps and other illustrations to accompany his writing. He also intimated to Silliman that he wished to share his geological findings with some scientific society.

In a reply dated October 17, 1817, Silliman revealed some plans of his own that proved to be of great interest to Hitchcock: "I would however mention to you in confidence that a project is in contemplation for the publication of a scientific journal to consist entirely of original American pieces…Should this thing be matured I expect to have something to do with it & should be very happy to have your work appear in the first No."

Silliman was referring to the *American Journal of Science and Arts*. Under his editorship, the first issue was published in April 1818. Two articles by Edward appeared in subsequent issues later that year. The first, "Remarks on the Geology of the Connecticut Valley," included one of the first detailed geological maps of the region, executed by the hand of Miss Orra White. The second, "On a Singular Disruption of the Ground," described some unusual effects of frost he had observed in the bed of the Deerfield River. It was also illustrated by Miss White. The journal would become the primary avenue for the dissemination of Edward's scientific findings; more than sixty articles under his name would appear in it over the next forty-five years.

In spring 1818, Hitchcock made his first visit to Yale where he attended Professor Silliman's lectures. It is clear that the pair got along well from the outset. Hitchcock admired and respected Silliman's scientific acumen, his teaching skill, and his views on religion. Silliman was most impressed by Hitchcock's intellect and ambition. He must have been impressed, for only four months later Edward was awarded his honorary degree from Yale, thanks in large measure to Silliman's efforts.

Figure 13.
Professor Benjamin Silliman (1779-1864) of Yale

Edward Hitchcock was never one to confine his interests and pursuits, no matter how pressing his other responsibilities or how degraded his health. During his preceptorship at Deerfield, he studied and wrote constantly. Even as he prepared additional scientific papers for Silliman's journal, and worked on the calculations for the next edition of his *Almanack* and studied theology under the tutelage of Reverend Willard, he also undertook two writing projects of a philosophical and religious nature.

By this time he had developed a business relationship with John Denio and Ansel Phelps of Greenfield, printers and publishers of the *Franklin Herald* and of Edward's almanacs. A series of four articles on the topic of profaneness written by Hitchcock (although signed simply "E.") appeared in consecutive issues in June 1816, in an ongoing feature entitled "The Weekly Monitor." In fall 1817 he undertook a more ambitious project, a series of thirty articles entitled "The Moral Telescope." The first six ran in a competing and short-lived newspaper, the *Franklin Federalist.* On the termination of that publication, Denio and Phelps picked up the series in the *Franklin Herald.* In the first article to appear in the *Herald* in January 1818, the author explained the purpose of the column:

> ...[T]o give an account of the appearances seen in a certain glass, which exhibits the conduct and thoughts of men in all situations, both public and private. This glass, or Moral Telescope, as it may properly be called, is possessed by two ladies, called Reason and Experience, who offered their assistance in directing it to proper objects and explaining the meaning of appearances.

In "The Moral Telescope" Hitchcock addressed the many varieties of misconduct to be observed among the general citizenry. In one he targeted idle, indecent conversation on trivial topics full of "slander, envy, and malice." In another he warned of fads and fashions in foods as well as other vices such as "snuff, tobacco, tea and ardent spirits." Prejudice in its many forms was also addressed, including prejudice against religion and "prejudice of place." Of the latter he stated, "Whoever forms an opinion of a man from the place in which he was educated, is prejudiced. Even in Sodom there was one righteous man." Two other vices did not escape examination in his telescope. "Of all my enemies, none are more powerful, willful, and hateful than Pride and Passion. They so insinuate themselves into every avenue of the human heart, that they too often alas, succeed in barring my entrance."

The religious sentiments expressed in the "Moral Telescope" are vague. Nowhere is there mention of God, of faith, of sin, of the Judgment Day, rarely any reference to the scriptures. Nevertheless, they do reveal a dawning awareness of several questions that would be central to his later spiritual thinking. To one question, How do we reconcile our religious principles with the dictates of reason and experience? he offered this response:

> I here asked Reason, how far her powers were to be used in regard to revelation. "In the first place," said she, "I examine with the keenest scrutiny, whether the volume presented to me as a revelation from heaven be indeed so. And having decided this in the affirmative, I next examine that book with caution to see what doctrines and precepts it contains. If a doctrine be directly contrary to my plainest dictates, I am bound not to receive it. But if it be only above my comprehension and not opposed to the laws of nature, I must adopt it. It is no objection to a doctrine that it is mysterious, since a great part of physical and moral events are so. But you will find many among men, who reject every truth that is beyond their comprehension; not considering that their powers are limited by very narrow bounds and that in a revelation from the DEITY, we ought naturally to expect many things beyond the reach of human capacity."

Similarly, Hitchcock confronted what would be another lifelong challenge to his character:

> On the contrary, if we perceive a man in public, loud in his professions of purity, full of zeal against vice, rigidly exact in his moral principles, forward to proclaim his own good deeds and in his censures against the slightest faults; yet in his private practice, loose and irregular, seldom examining his own heart, puffed up with an idea of his goodness, indifferent to the cause of truth, and guilty of the very faults he condemns in others; then it is, we suspect there is something rotten at the core. But does not this last description apply to more of us than the former! and do not many of us deceive ourselves, supposing the will of God to be our main-spring of action, when in fact, it is the applause of man?

> If such be not the case, why are we so deeply affected with the censure of the world when we know God to be our friend?

Encouraged by his warm reception at Yale the previous year, Hitchcock in January 1819 wrote to Silliman of his departure from Deerfield Academy and of his interest in pursuing theology. He expressed the desire to return to New Haven and sit in on classes of Silliman and several other faculty members. "Pray, sir," he asked Silliman, "do the laws of your College permit access to your lectures to one who is not an alumnus of it?" The answer must have been yes, for that spring he returned to New Haven and took up residence there for the better part of nine months.

If Harvard at that time was decidedly Unitarian in its religious sentiments, Yale College was just as decidedly Orthodox. How could it have been otherwise? After all, Timothy Dwight, then president of Yale, was the grandson of Jonathan Edwards, the most illustrious and influential American Calvinist of his time and himself a Yale alumnus. Calvinism was still very much alive in New Haven and elsewhere in the northeastern states, but it was by 1815 under siege, in part from the influence of Harvard and the production of newly ordained ministers with decidedly liberal views. But it suffered also from adverse public reaction to its more extreme views and apparent contradictions.

Among the Yale faculty could be found a number of theologians and ministers who, while avowedly Orthodox, sought ways to soften its harsher notions and proscriptions. But in the process, they would strive to avoid alienating their orthodox forebears and believers. In other words, some would say, they wished to have their theological cake and eat it too!

One prominent theologian at Yale who wrestled with this enigma was the Reverend Eleazar Fitch. Born in Connecticut in 1791, Fitch graduated from Yale in 1810, then attended Andover Theological Seminary in Massachusetts. In 1817 he returned to his alma mater as Professor of Divine Theology, a post he held for over forty years. Fitch was a Calvinist of a most traditional stripe, a charismatic teacher and preacher of whom a colleague wrote, "Dr. Fitch was a mingling of the metaphysician and the poet."

Hitchcock's time in New Haven was devoted largely to his attendance at lectures, especially those of Professor Fitch. It was a time when he was confronted by his own prejudices against Calvinism and those who embraced its tenets. In his notes, Hitchcock wrote:

> ...I went to New Haven most resolutely opposed to Orthodox intolerance, and to certain doctrines which I supposed belong to the Orthodox creed. Judge then of my agreeable surprise when I found that my views in all important respects coincided with those of the Orthodox and my still greater surprise to find much less of intolerance and bigotry than among Unitarians.

Hitchcock's notes provide few details of those months spent in New Haven. But Professor Fitch's influence is apparent in Edward's later writings. Fitch argued for a "strict" Calvinism but he found ways to soften its impact. To the Calvinist tenet of original sin, he countered that no sin could occur until the individual became aware of right and wrong and chose voluntarily to go astray. To the matter of election that some saw as evidence that God created sin, he countered that man through his own free will created sin. These were issues Edward was already wrestling with. As to the controversial Calvinist tenet of infant punishment, Fitch would admit that it was a difficult question:

> I left that point undecided, because I was not satisfied that the sacred writers, in speaking of the race, meant to decide it for me: and I was willing to leave the decision with him, who is the Arbiter of right in his kingdom. I am still willing to leave it there.

That argument was one that Edward Hitchcock would later employ with his own parishioners: one day all will be explained—one day, in heaven. But the issue of infant death, which probably seemed like an abstract formulation at that time, would become all too real and personal a few years hence.

On a Sabbath morning in June 1819, at the invitation of the minister of a church in West Haven, Hitchcock delivered his first sermon using as his scriptural text Matthew 11:28, "Come unto me, all ye that labour and are heavy laden, and I will give you rest." In his notes he reflects on the experience:

> Felt much solicitude diffidence and weakness in this first effort in the pulpit: but have much reason to be grateful that utterance was given me. And if my efforts did not advance I hope that they did not retard the cause of my redeemer. I feel fearful that my lungs never will permit me to preach long should I live to complete my studies but with God all things are possible.

During the period of his New Haven residency, Hitchcock must have made frequent return trips to Deerfield as evidenced by two letters to Miss White that testify to the increasing intimacy of their relationship. The first may have been written while Orra was still in Deerfield, or perhaps when she was visiting there after she had moved back to Amherst. The postscript suggests this may not have been the first such encounter:

> Friday Evening, May 21 [1819]
>
> Lovely is the evening. Fair is the soft-eyed queen of night. Sweet is the whipapoor will's song in the woods. Mild is the zephyr of spring. 'Tis the

> season of love. Then let us meet my friend where the eye of suspicion cannot perceive us. But no more of poetry—What say you Orra to professing to wish to make Charissa Dickinson a visit this evening. Friend John understands the plot. He will speak of Charissa—you can say you have scarcely called upon her since you came to Deerfield. He will then invite you to go this evening. I will meet you sat at H. D.'s—Yours—E.
>
> P. S. Do not be in fear of another all night interview.

A few months later, Edward wrote Orra once again, anxious to arrange another "interview." Orra on this occasion must have been planning to visit in Deerfield with her friend, Harriet Dickinson, widow of Jackson Dickinson. Eliphalet and Mary Dickinson were Jackson's parents:

> September 6th [1819]
>
> Do you think Orra, if you should go up to Harriet's towards night we could make it so muddy, dark and rainy this evening that it would be impossible for you to get back to night? If such should be your belief I assure you I should be very happy to be placed in the same predicament (after Mr. Eliphalet and wife have gone to bed) or in other words "I'll be with you bye and bye." E.
>
> P. S. How soon the quarter will be out!

On his return to Deerfield in January 1820, Edward seemed to have acquired a new voice, a new vocation. Almost immediately he began receiving invitations to preach in churches up and down the Connecticut Valley. "Pulpit supply" was the common practice of churches to hire a preacher to deliver a sermon in the absence of the pastor on a Sunday. Such arrangements were normally made by the pastor himself. If the visiting preacher was pastor of another church, he might be compensated by a reciprocal arrangement in the near future. When the visiting preacher was unaffiliated, a small stipend would be awarded.

Edward Hitchcock was by this time well known in the Valley for his rhetorical skills. While a tad longwinded, he was eloquent and his intellectual qualifications were beyond dispute. As to his spiritual merits, he may have been somewhat of an unknown, but his reputation must quickly have spread as a man of strict orthodox views and an appreciation for the perfection of Divine Revelation. With but a few months of theological training at Yale and no degree, he nevertheless became in great demand on Sabbaths near and far.

Hitchcock began his career as an itinerant preacher in February 1820, delivering some fifteen different sermons on more than fifty occasions in that year on subjects ranging from sin to death to judgment. Most of the churches were within twenty miles or so of Deerfield, but he often traveled considerably farther on a few occasions, including Brattleboro, Vermont; Saratoga Springs, New York; and Waterbury, Connecticut. He delivered three sermons in Amherst that year, four at the meetinghouse in Deerfield, ten in the several parishes in Brattleboro.

He also preached on at least seven occasions in 1820 at the meetinghouse in Conway, Massachusetts, just five miles from Deerfield. The pastor, the Reverend John Emerson, was seventy-five years of age and in poor health. He and his parishioners may have taken a liking to the young preacher or found his theological stance particularly consonant with their own; but it is also possible that Edward recognized in Conway a long-term employment opportunity and thus made himself available whenever his services were required.

The following year found Hitchcock's services in even greater demand. His calls to the Conway church were so frequent that in February 1821 he found lodging in that town. Also in that month he traveled to Waterbury, delivered a sermon, then penned a letter to Orra that speaks volumes of their relationship and of his emotional condition. Orra's father had died in Amherst only three weeks earlier, no doubt the "distressing scene" alluded to.

> My friend dearer than ever,
>
> I never had a more uncomfortable and perplexing journey…how grateful should I be to my father in heaven for his preservations!...Since the distressing scene which you have lately you are hourly in my waking and dreaming thoughts. And indeed why should your heart be wounded without wounding mine?…Do remember me in your prayers. Mine for you are sincere but I fear they are not the prayers of "the righteous." I depend more upon your prayers for my success in the ministry than upon my own. Believe me affectionately and sympathetically the same. E.

Even then Orra must have realized that her friend was prone to episodes of deep despair over his health and the state of his soul. She must have accepted these fluctuations of mood, the frequent predictions of imminent death, without reservations, as the price to be paid for allying herself with Edward Hitchcock.

In May 1821, Reverend Emerson announced his intention to resign from his full-time duties. On May 31, Edward Hitchcock and Orra White were joined in holy matrimony in Amherst. A few days later, they arrived in Conway, where Edward had been appointed junior pastor.

CONWAY 1821-1825

A Conway farm

7 Preaching in the Wilderness

"Who is sufficient for these things?"

Conway, October 1821

"Oh, Edward, is it not the most beguilingly beautiful of all God's works?" Orra Hitchcock was referring to the autumnal splendors spread before them as the newlyweds stood atop Cricket Hill. "A feast for the eyes as well as the soul."

But Edward was distracted, studying the contents of two splint reed baskets he had set on a tree stump.

"Peziza, Merulius, Agaricus, Boletus, Amanita—at least four, possibly five species of Agaricus, I would judge. Oh, and Clavaria as well. Many a botanist would count this a respectable harvest for a week's labors over miles of New England woods and fields. Yet here, within sight of our home, we have it all...for barely a morning's effort. Autumnal splendors indeed."

Orra smiled. "His bounties are everywhere, are they not, my husband?"

But Edward was transfixed. He was holding a loupe to his left eye and peering intently at one of the specimens. "I cannot determine whether this be one plant with a single pileus that is deeply invaginated or many plants in a large cluster."

Orra stepped forward, took hold of the specimen, and pulled it very carefully from Edward's grasp. He looked up surprised. "Edward," she said, gazing warmly into his eyes, "it fills me with gratitude to see you so well these days."

"Yes, well, there is nothing better for a fragile constitution than fresh air and a little fungal foraging. It relieves the indolent spirit and invigorates the internal organs." Orra smiled and nodded. "And I look forward to compiling a list of our discoveries. I do believe Professor Silliman would consider publishing it in his excellent journal...once our work is complete, of course."

He looked lovingly at Orra. "And your extraordinary talents, my dear, will most certainly bring these specimens to life, even the drab, colorless ones. It will be a delight to all who..." But as he was speaking he witnessed the color leaving his wife's face and he halted abruptly in mid-sentence. "Is something the matter? You suddenly look quite pallid."

"Oh, nothing, really, Edward. Just a slight touch of the vapours..." She grasped his arm. "I need to rest—just for a moment—if you please."

Edward took both her hands and helped her to be seated on a patch of dry moss. He knelt down facing his wife and examined her with a furrowed brow. "What is it, Orra?"

"Oh, nothing, Edward, really. Just one of those little episodes that a woman has from time to time."

Already he could see the color returning to her countenance.

"Dear me, you did give me a start there for a moment. Well, now, let us sit here for a while and simply gaze upon that grand palette of the Almighty." A few moments went by without a word. "Well, I suppose we should be starting homeward. I yet have much work to do on this Sunday's discourses. But perhaps we may return on Monday, or Tuesday, to continue our labors."

Orra smiled and nodded. "There is nothing I would love more, Edward." He smiled. Then she continued. "But I fear my days of clambering over hill and dale may be over, at least for a time."

"But my dear, you just said there was nothing you would love more."

"Yes, I did say just that. But alas events may soon occur that will make it impossible, at least for a time."

"Events? Dearest Orra, what sort of events are you talking about?"

In April 1769, the Reverend John Emerson visited Conway, Massachusetts, for the first time. A recent graduate of divinity school, he was under consideration for pastor of the Conway church and had been invited to preach that Sabbath. There was as yet no church building. Many years later he would recall that day, of feeling like "John preaching in the wilderness," with only "ye light of heaven" for illumination. Compared to his hometown, Malden, Massachusetts, or to Cambridge where he had preached just a week earlier, Conway must have seemed at the very limits of civilization. Nevertheless he accepted the call, and a few weeks later moved to far away Conway with his wife to take up the position he would hold for the remainder of his life, over a half century.

Conway, Massachusetts, lay nestled among the eastern foothills of the Berkshires, known in that time as the Hoosac Mountains. Three rivers and many smaller streams coursed among those hills, producing narrow strips of fertile bottomland which could be planted for crops. But forest still covered most of the hills, dense, vigorous forests of chestnut, maple, birch, and oak. Even before the War of Independence, some of that high terrain had been cleared, not for crops as the soils were poor, but as pasture for cattle, horses, and sheep.

The next two decades witnessed a near doubling of Conway's population—by 1790 it was the third largest town in western Massachusetts, exceeded only by West Springfield and Westfield. Reverend Emerson's once remote outpost had become a commercial hub of the region, due in large measure to the rugged landscape. The steep terrain and the rushing streams supported dozens of small mills—sawmills, grist mills, fulling mills, flaxseed oil mills, peppermint oil mills, and many more. The fields yielded crops of rye, corn, wheat, even tobacco. And the pastures teemed with livestock, much of which was driven to markets in Boston, Albany, Hartford, and New Haven.

Conway was a large town in area as well as in population, encompassing some thirty-nine square miles, nearly all of which by 1800 was inhabited. While the town was a single corporate entity, it consisted of more than a dozen neighborhoods—Pumpkin Hollow, Burkeville, Baptist Hill, Fields Hill, Cricket Hill, Hardscrabble, Southpart, Dry Hill, Chapel Falls, Poland, Bear River, Shirkshire, Broomshire, Hoosac. At least a dozen schoolhouses were situated at key crossroads around the town in 1800; by 1830 they numbered sixteen.

Reverend Emerson was an orthodox Christian and his church would remain the sole house of worship in the town until the Baptist society erected an edifice in 1790. His diary suggests that he was sometimes discouraged at the lack of earnestness and piety among his congregation, but he must have taken heart from the fact that Unitarianism, the bane of orthodox Christians, while on the rise elsewhere in New England, never made inroads in Conway. Politically, most of the citizens of Conway, like those of neighboring Deerfield, were Federalists, although more than a few members of the opposition Democratic-Republican party could be found here.

By the winter of 1821 Reverend Emerson's health was declining and he proposed to the church membership that they hire an assistant pastor to lighten his workload. Over the previous year he had turned repeatedly to Edward Hitchcock of Deerfield to supply the pulpit in his stead, and Mr. Hitchcock quickly became a strong contender for the position.

Events then followed in rapid succession. On May 28, 1821, at a church meeting, a committee was formed "to select an ecclesiastical Council for the ordination of Mr. Edward Hitchcock to the pastoral office over the Congregational Church and society in this town." Three weeks later, on June 20, the candidate was interviewed:

> After ascertaining the regular church membership of Mr. Hitchcock, and his license to preach the gospel, council proceeded to examine him as to his experimental, practical, and doctrinal religion, and his views in entering into the gospel ministry and being fully satisfied with qualifications, voted unanimously that we approve Mr. Hitchcock and that we proceed to his ordination tomorrow at 11 O.C. A. M.

The ordination took place in the meetinghouse the next morning at eleven o'clock as planned .

Meanwhile in Amherst on May 31, Edward Hitchcock and Orra White were joined in holy matrimony. Within weeks of Edward's ordination, they had gathered together their few possessions, loaded them in a small, rude wagon, and made their way to Conway. Several routes were then available to travel from Deerfield to Conway, none of them easy. One was a steep and harrowing ascent over Field's Hill, the second a winding path along the Mill River with several precarious river crossings, the third a climb over rocky terrain north of the Deerfield River to Bardwell's Ferry, a crossing that could be difficult when the river was roaring down through a narrow gorge. Whichever route the Hitchcocks followed, they must have felt a great sense of relief when at last they found themselves in the bosom of the Conway hills. We can only imagine the couple's joy and satisfaction when they gazed out on their new town, admired its waving fields of corn, wheat, and rye, its humming mills, its embracing and enfolding hills, its prosperous hustle and bustle. But they could ill afford to indulge such reveries for long.

ORDAINED

At Conway, on the 21st ult. Rev. Edward Hitchcock, associate Pastor with the Rev. John Emerson, of the Congregational Church and Society in that town. Rev Josiah Spaulding, of Buckland, offered the introductory prayer, Sermon, by Professor Dewy, of Williams College, from II Tim iv; 2. "Preach the word." Consecrating prayer by Rev. Moses Miller, of Heath, address to the Church and people by the Rev. senior Pastor, Charge by the Rev. Rufus Wells, of Whately, Fellowship of the Churches by Rev. Thomas Shepard, of Ashfield, and the concluding Prayer, by Rev. Daniel A. Clark, of Amherst.

Figure 14. Announcement of Edward Hitchcock's ordination in the *Franklin Herald*

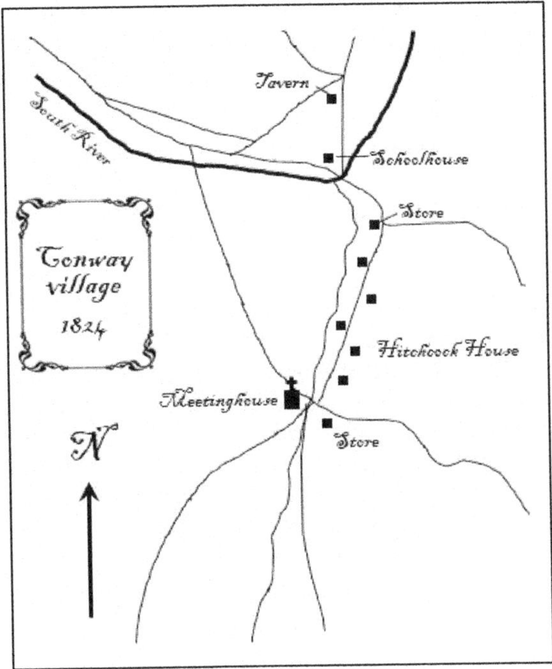

Figure 15. Map of Conway circa 1824

They had a new home to settle into, and the junior pastor had two sermons to deliver on the next Sabbath.

"Gather yourselves together that I may tell you that which shall befall you in the last days." With those words of the prophet Jacob from the book of Genesis, the new pastor of the tiny Congregational church in Conway, Massachusetts, began his sermon on Sunday, June 24, 1821. The congregation was no doubt larger than usual on that day, the atmosphere charged with anticipation.

We can only guess at some of the emotions stirring among the parishioners on that morning. Excitement: Imagine, welcoming a new pastor to our church for the first time in half a century! Curiosity: What kind of pastor will he be? Unease: What must he think of us—our piety, our faithfulness—our generosity?

In some respects Edward Hitchcock had been an unlikely candidate for the pastorate. His theological studies at Yale had lasted but a few months—he had earned no divinity degree. True, he was born and raised just down the road in Deerfield—and he had distinguished himself at an early age for his scientific acumen. But in matters spiritual, was he fully qualified for this position?

One consideration may well have tipped the scales in his favor: his preaching ability. In the year and a half since returning from New Haven, he had been called more than eighty times to supply pulpits up and down the Connecticut River Valley, including some two dozen times in this very sanctuary—the best possible testimony to the young man's credentials, spiritual as well as rhetorical.

The reverend proceeded with his Sabbath discourse, entitled "A Glance at the Future":

> The events of the past week my brethren remind us that we have entered into a relation to one another whose solemnity and interest and consequences the records of eternity can alone develop. And now standing on the threshold of so momentous and responsible an office you will permit me to pause for a few moments and casting an eye along the stream of time and viewing ourselves as minister and people carried down this stream you will indulge me in endeavoring to point out some of the scenes through which we may pass and some of the scenes through which we must pass.

Over the next forty-five minutes, Reverend Hitchcock considered the promises and the perils that lay before the church. In his concluding remarks, he reminded his parishioners, as he would in nearly every sermon over the next four years, of the terrors and triumphs of the Judgment Day.

It was perhaps his great fortune—or God's will—that on that first Sunday the new pastor's view "along the stream of time" was not particularly clear. If it had been, he might have been distressed at the prospect: a brief tenure marked by poor health, self-doubt, despondency, and tragedy. His new post would quickly become his cross to bear.

In that day's afternoon discourse, Reverend Hitchcock delivered a sermon, "Preaching the Gospel," with a markedly different tone from the first. He used as his text a passage from the fourth chapter of Paul's second letter to Timothy: "I charge thee therefore before God and the Lord Jesus Christ who shall judge the quick and the dead at his appearing and his Kingdom: Preach the word, be instant in season, out of season; reprove rebuke exhort—with all long-suffering and doctrine."

Preaching the Gospel, he argued, was the most fundamental duty of a minister to his congregation. Furthermore, he emphasized, it was not for him to pick and choose what to preach:

> If a minister of the Gospel intentionally year after year passes over any part of the Gospel, he has not preached the gospel and especially if he omits any of the essential doctrines or precepts thereof he has probably helped more souls to

> perdition than to salvation and has injured more deeply the cause of religion than he could have done had he been an open champion for infidelity.

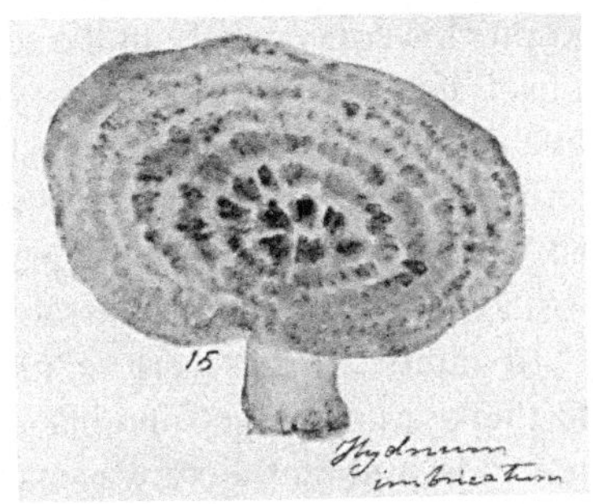

Figure 16.
Hydnum imbricatum, drawing by Orra White Hitchcock.

A good sermon must not be hurriedly or casually prepared, he added. "The preacher of the Gospel [should] not bring before his people loose undigested discourses—but such as evince study and care." It was just such carefully crafted discourses that the young pastor intended to deliver to his parishioners, not just one a week but at least twice every Sunday.

At this point Reverend Hitchcock adopted a distinctly defensive tone as he enumerated the duties of a pastor and—dear parishioners please note—some reasonable limitations. "Were my own experience required I should say that four days constant study are necessary for me to compose two sermons even in a decent style and manner," he stated.

> A man may throw together in a short time many pious and correct observations—but to select for a sermon a single point—and to bring every argument and remark to bear upon this point—and at the same time not to fall short of or exceed the standard of God's word—to select the most appropriate passages from the scripture and to put the whole into such language as shall overwhelm by its energy and delight—by its smoothness—to do all this must be the work of time and close reflection.

He then warned that too many demands could sometimes be placed on a minister. "In regard to the practice of giving sermons on funeral occasions we believe it to be an unreasonable requirement—and one with which the gospel minister cannot in general comply consistently with the faithful performance of his other duties." As to home visitations which he referred to as "parochial visits," Reverend Hitchcock was blunt: "These ought not to be neglected and therefore in the first place such visits should be short."

Repeatedly during this sermon he reminded his parishioners of the fragility of his health. And near the end he seemed to be attempting to lower expectations:

> The duties are so multitudinous and arduous—our zeal is so far below what it should be—our bodily constitutions are often so debilitated and our sins are so manifold that we are too apt to rest in a very imperfect performance. Even the indefatigable Paul in view of the magnitude of his labors was forced to exclaim, Who is sufficient for these things?

Despite his concerns about the scope of his new post, Reverend Hitchcock threw himself into his pastoral duties with a work ethic that John Calvin himself would have applauded. Besides the task of composing two sermons every week, there were the obligatory "parochial visits" with each family of the parish, no small task in such a town which was, as he wrote Benjamin Silliman, "perhaps the most extensive parish in Massachusetts to oversee, it being in extent 12 miles by 7." In addition there were regular evening prayer meetings that often required the preparation of yet another discourse. In that same letter, furthermore, he seemed to hint that there was a spiritual movement taking place in the church, a religious revival that "imposes severe duties."

Some of the new pastor's initiatives appear to have expanded on the normal duties of his predecessor. In a sermon only a few weeks after his ordination, he proposed the establishment of a Sunday school, something the church had not previously provided. Such a school, he argued with great emotion, would have a lasting effect on the children of the church and a direct bearing on the fate of their souls. That autumn he was instrumental in the establishment of the town's first library. The following year he would introduce yet another educational innovation, a summer church school.

For her part, Orra Hitchcock was also "much occupied" during her first few months in Conway. Naturally, there were many household tasks to be done, but at the same time she was unstinting in her artistic pursuits. Only a few days after their marriage and before Edward's installation, probably before they had even moved to Conway, they began a joint undertaking of both a scientific and artistic nature, the perfect way to celebrate the union of these two souls. We might even consider it their honeymoon.

The object of this new endeavor was the humble mushroom—or fungus. In those times fungi were usually lumped in the plant kingdom. They were, after all, organisms rooted in the earth like plants. The fact that they eschewed sunlight and displayed none of the features of plants—leaves, flowers, fruits, seeds—made this association awkward, but it was common practice in botany, even into the twentieth century. Edward had accumulated a most impressive collection of minerals as well as an herbarium of flowering plants and ferns. He dearly wished to add to his collections specimens of the fungi. But most did not lend themselves to pressing; many fungi within hours of collecting were reduced to an unpleasant mass of gelatinous ooze. What he needed were the skills of an artist to capture the glories of the fungi. And now he had just such an artist to fulfil his requirements. As he wrote to Benjamin Silliman, "I am getting paintings executed of many of the Fungi because they cannot be preserved except in pickle."

From June to early October of 1821 Edward and Orra wandered the fields, forests, and farms around Conway in search of fungi, Orra drawing and painting, Edward recording his observations. The greatest diversity of fungi could be found in the forests—"wet woods" and "dry woods" were the most frequent habitat notations on their collections—where they grew "on wet leaves," "on rotten wood," or, sometimes, "on bare ground." Many showed clear affinities for decaying wood of particular species, most commonly birch, hemlock, oak, or beech. Conway's farms were also a rich source for the foragers, where specimens could be found growing in open fields, on horse dung, or, in one instance, "out of a crack in an old building."

As to the organisms themselves, Edward recorded detailed notes on each specimen, notes he entitled "Remarks on Fungi Painted 1821." He observed first the "pileus" or cap, whether it be smooth, wrinkled, bossed, warty, shaggy, lobed, grooved, striated, wrinkled, translucent, or umbilicate (having a depression in the middle), fleshy, jelly-like, or juicy. Many stems he described as simple and unbranched, others as divided into smaller stems not unlike the branches of a tree, their caps imbricate or overlapping. Of a particular bolete fungus he wrote, "…I counted 475 ramifications and no less number of pilei."

Most mushrooms bear their spores in tiny pores or thin, membranous gills. Hitchcock often described the spores as whitish, yellowish, or bluish. Of one specimen, *Sphaeria bulbosa*, he wrote, "Resembles an old dry stick and I should not have suspected it was a plant had I not often knocked off the pollen." In a later version he substituted "a white powder" for "pollen," perhaps recognizing the distinction between the pollen of flowering plants and the spores of fungi.

The caps or pilei of the mushrooms ranged in color from white to brown to yellow or red; of No. 74, *Boletus*, he wrote that the cap turned green when broken. It is curious that in his *Remarks* Hitchcock rarely made mention of color—he described cap color for only about 15 of 120 specimens. Perhaps he found Orra's tiny paintings, many of which blazed with deep oranges and vibrant reds, captured those colors much better than could mere words.

Many of Edward's descriptions consisted of but a few words or phrases, such as "No. 21 Clavaria—on wet rotten logs—Nat. size—June." Still others were considerably more detailed:

> No. 43. Agaricus—On the ground in the [dry] woods July—instead of a common ring there is an inverted pileus which is laciniate—lobed and gilled like the principal pileus the gills of which run into those of the lower pileus. The under side of this lower pileus is of the same color and texture as the upper one—both being smooth. Nat. size—in dry woods—July.

Hitchcock was well aware of the taxonomic challenges presented by the fungi. Clearly the 120 or so specimens they had collected and cataloged represented far fewer distinct species. *Agaricus* he found to be a particularly difficult genus to sort out; he attributed fifty-two specimens to that genus but was able to identify only one to species. About a specimen of *Agaricus* he wrote, "this and the next No. are probably varieties of No. 8 which is more abundant and grows all summer." His "Remarks" include authorities for many specimens.

Thirteen are attributed to South African native Christiaan Hendrick Persoon, two to the English naturalist James Sowerby. The only reference cited is Rees's *Cyclopedia of the Arts, Sciences, and Literature*. He had acquired that volume at great expense only a few months earlier and it was likely the only reference book he owned at that time.

The labels in Orra's album include more than twenty Latin binomials not found in Edward's "Remarks." Some have obviously been added after or in place of the original label. For example, specimen No. 104 appears to have been originally labeled *Geoglossum hirsutum*, then *Clavaria.* Those names were subsequently covered with white paint and the name *Sphaeria polymorpha* Pers. added above.

Every specimen was numbered in Edward's "Remarks" to correspond with Orra's drawings and paintings. He also recorded the scale of each illustration, usually indicating "natural size," occasionally "half natural size" or "a third natural size" for larger specimens. The month in which each specimen was collected or observed was also recorded, providing us with a timeline for the collecting phase of the project: twenty-five in June of 1821, thirty-nine in July, fifteen in August, thirty-six in September, one in October, and one in spring 1822. Seven of the 120 specimens are not fungi at all; three are mosses, four are lichens.

Orra drew the specimens in ink or in pencil, some no doubt right in the field, others at home shortly after collection lest their characteristics be obscured by the process of decay. She may have added the lively, incandescent colors later, perhaps using her notes to assist her memory and guide her brush.

The arrangement of the drawings seems to have been based as much on Orra's artistic sensibilities as on taxonomic considerations. The drawings on each plate have been carefully arranged with just enough white space to set them off from surrounding illustrations. Large, brightly colored specimens are balanced on most plates with a number of smaller, less striking images. The naturalist or taxonomist may wish that the genera were grouped together for purposes of comparison, but the eye of the artist framed these specimens according to a taxonomy all its own.

The finished product resides today in the Smith College Special Collections, a gift of Edward and Orra's youngest daughter, Emily Hitchcock Terry. It is a small but exquisite album constructed of twenty sheets of 6 5/8 inch x 8 inch artist's paper sewn together. It includes approximately 100 paintings, most with the specimen number and the Latin genus. For nearly thirty the complete binomial (genus and species) is provided such as *Peziza scutellata* and *Clavaria coralloides*.

In May 1822, the Hitchcocks sent the album to Professor John Torrey of New York, perhaps the foremost American botanist of that era, along with some

Figure 17. Left, title page, below, one of twenty pages of watercolors from "Fungi, Selecti Picti" by Orra White Hitchcock, 1821

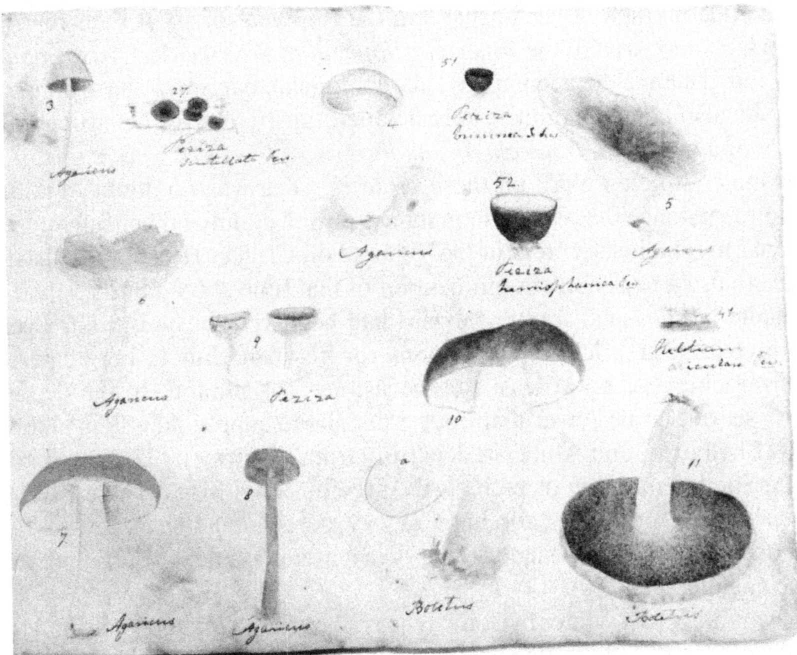

thirty-nine of the specimens. A letter from Hitchcock to Torrey in November of the same year suggests that the album and list were returned with many annotations. Unfortunately, the annotated version of the list has been lost. The binomials that were absent in "Remarks" but later added to the album were likely provided by Dr. Torrey.

In August 1821, even as the project was in progress, Edward wrote to Benjamin Silliman proposing that the two produce a geologic map of western Massachusetts that would include a list of lichens, mosses, and fungi. That joint project was never completed, but all thirty-five species identified in Conway were eventually included in two subsequent Hitchcock publications, *Catalogue of Plants Growing Without Cultivation in the Vicinity of Amherst* (1828), and *Report on the Geology of Massachusetts* (1833).

Whether the Hitchcocks ever intended the album itself for publication we do not know. It did eventually find its way into print in a beautiful volume edited by art historian Robert L. Herbert in 2011. Thus, two centuries after its creation, Orra Hitchcock's remarkable little album of fungi survives both as a work of art and as a representation of the complementary relationship that would make Edward and Orra White Hitchcock a successful team in art, in science, and in life.

Besides "Fungi, Selecti Picti," Orra contributed her artistic skills to two other scientific undertakings of her husband in the first year or so of their marriage, both of which appeared in the *American Journal of Science and Arts.* She drew and colored the map to accompany his geological paper on the Connecticut Valley. She also created an intricately detailed illustration for his article on the discovery of a new fern, *Botrychium simplex*.

As she completed work on these projects, Orra was no doubt mindful of another circumstance that would soon intervene and command her full attention, the "event" to which she refers in the vignette on Cricket Hill. For the pastor's wife was, to use a common circumlocution of that time, "in a family way."

Despite his physical frailty, Edward had been very busy as well. Even as he was preparing and delivering sermons for his own church, he preached in neighboring churches on at least five occasions that autumn. In the depths of winter he set out on no fewer than four Sabbaths to supply pulpits in Ashfield, Whately, Shelburne, and Amherst, departing from Conway by horse and buggy early of a Sunday morning or perhaps the previous day. Most of those sermons had been written originally for his Conway parish, but the many revisions marked on the manuscripts suggest that he spent a good deal of time preparing for these engagements.

The couple's first winter in Conway was likely challenging, snow and bitter cold arriving early in the hills and lingering late. By January, Orra was in the sixth month of her pregnancy. In February Edward's father, Justin, passed away in Deerfield. But spring finally did arrive, and with it the hearts of the young couple were doubly gladdened, for on the fifth day of May 1822, Orra gave birth to a baby boy. They named him Edward.

Camp Meeting, 1850

8 Revivals and Declensions

"Christians, go into your closets!"

Conway, October 1823

An unusually large number of children were in attendance at the Conway meetinghouse for the Sabbath morning service. The harvest was complete and those young people who might have been engaged in work on their parents' farms, even on the Sabbath, were likely urged, perhaps required, to attend this service which would be of particular relevance to the youth of the church.

Long ago, Reverend Hitchcock explained in his sermon, God took vengeance on Jerusalem, destroying the city and killing thousands of its residents. But before he did this, he warned the good Christians of Jerusalem, men, women, and children, to flee. Only the good children fled, however, and the bad children were all killed when the city was destroyed. "The little children who thus went away from Jerusalem were scattered all over the world: and John knowing that he should never preach to them anymore wrote them a letter to persuade them to be good children and continue such so long as they should live. I write you today for this same purpose."

The preacher paused here, his gaze rising from the papers before him, coming to rest first on a chubby girl with golden curls seated in the first row of pews, then on a tall, lanky boy standing stiffly at the rear. The sanctuary was silent, every eye on the stern figure in the pulpit.

First, he reminded them of their Sabbath teachers over the previous summer. "You little know how much they have done for you. Every Sabbath they have attended to hear you recite and make you understand the Bible and persuade you to be good children." He urged them to remember and take to heart what they had learned: "...if you forget all you have learned and do not listen to what they have taught you how sorry you will be for it and how you will weep for it when you come to die, enough to break your heart!"

Next he warned them against keeping bad company with those who steal fruit, who read bad books, or who fail to honor the Sabbath. "But such people do not love God and God does not love them and he will punish them dreadfully ere long." And lying: "If any of you then have told a lie or deceived any body and have never confessed it to them and asked their pardon depend on it you are in danger of being cast into the lake of fire and brimstone."

He urged his young parishioners, above all, to obey their parents. "Now as they are older than you are can you doubt but that they are better able to determine what is good for you and what is fruitful to you than you are?" Here he quoted from the thirtieth chapter of Proverbs: "The eye that mocketh at his father and despiseth to obey his mother, the ravens of the valley shall pick it out and the young eagles shall eat it."

By now the little girl in the front row was whimpering, her mother holding her and consoling her. Even the tall lanky boy at the rear seemed uneasy, his eyes lowered as he wrestled with a loose thread on his shirtsleeve. But the pastor was not finished. For at last he reminded his young parishioners of their mortality: "More than half the children that are born die before they are twelve years old—and it is not at all unlikely that you may be among the number." Then he added, "If you seek God early he will love you and bless you and make you happy in this world and the next. But if you neglect him in youth he will neglect you when you grow up and leave you when you die to sink down with devils and wicked men... The Bible tells us that there will be a worm that will gnaw them and a fire that will burn them through all eternity. Whosoever goes to hell will never come away from it. And yet little children you will certainly go there when you die if you do not love God and Christ and one another."

As the parishioners stepped out of the meetinghouse into the chill October morning, many a parent shook the pastor's hand vigorously and thanked him, as did a few of the children. Others, however, including the chubby girl from the front row and the lanky older boy at the rear, slipped away to escape the church, its pastor, and those discomforting images of one's eyes being plucked out by eagles, one's body gnawed by worms, one's ears assailed by the cries of bad boys and girls as they descended into a lake of fire and brimstone.

Barely six weeks into his pastorate in Conway, Reverend Hitchcock was optimistic about the state of religion in his new town. "A revival of religion appears to be commencing among us," he wrote Benjamin Silliman on August 6, 1821, "and this imposes severe duties." A few months later he devoted an entire Sabbath, both morning and afternoon discourses, to the subject of religious revivals. In "History of Revivals," he began with "a brief history of the special outpourings of the Spirit of God in all ages of the church," recounting events from Old Testament times to New Testament times, from Ancient Greece to Europe of the sixteenth, seventeenth, and eighteenth centuries, to Boston to Northampton to Hatfield and to Deerfield since the "Great Awakening." Then he brought his parishioners up to date, observing that, "Probably no period of our history was ever so much distinguished by the extraordinary influences of the Spirit as the present…" He concluded with a warning of the often fleeting state of religious fervor following revivals:

> While we cannot but rejoice to see some beginning that new race that will give them the final everlasting victory over sin and sorrow how distressing to see others as the work is drawing to a close gradually losing their interest in the subject and settling back into the iron slumber of impenitence and unregeneracy.

In the afternoon discourse he ruminated on some of the effects of revivals, and offered yet another warning:

> My hearers we well know that Christ has been specially present with us in this institution for weeks and what lesson does the history of revivals teach us?...Must it be Christian brethren that our Divine Master who is now so specially present with this people will soon leave us? Must we be left to go back to the world and to crucify this Redeemer afresh—and must so many of the dear mortal souls in this place be left to perish?

A year later, the Holy Spirit seemed still to be very much alive in his parish. "I do not yet give up the idea of taking a geological tour this autumn, but it must depend upon the state of my health & the state of religion among us," he wrote to Benjamin Silliman in September 1822, "for when the Lord appears to be preparing a harvest of souls we reapers must gather them in."

Was the new pastor himself responsible for this revival of religion in Conway? Hitchcock would never accede to such a notion, attributing all to the influence of the Holy Spirit. Nevertheless there can be no doubt that Edward Hitchcock's rhetorical skills were exceptional and may well have played a key role in the revival of religion in Conway.

Over the course of his lifetime, Edward Hitchcock probably wrote more than 300 sermons. About 250 have survived, most as handwritten manuscripts on which he listed the location and date of each delivery. A few were delivered only once, but most were delivered again and again, often after considerable revision. For example, he preached "Consideration" at least fourteen times between 1823 and 1844, "Sinners Dreaming" at least nineteen times from 1824 to 1848. "Moral Sublimity" topped the list with twenty-one deliveries between 1847 and 1861. Surviving records indicate that he preached on some 950 occasions between 1819 and 1862.

The sermons of Edward Hitchcock provide remarkable insights into the man: his preaching style, his spiritual life, his social conscience. They underscore his unswerving belief in science as a means to confirm rather than contradict the truths of revelation. They reveal some of the political crosscurrents buffeting a young America barely a half century after its founding. And they expose a pervasive tension throughout Hitchcock's life between a desire to serve God and a passion for worldly stature and success.

Hitchcock's sermons are works of rhetorical art, meticulously crafted, much as a sculptor winnows away at marble or granite, shaped into powerful works of oratory, sometimes soaring and beautiful, often frightening and foreboding. Even today, nearly two centuries after their creation, a reader can almost hear the pastor's voice echoing off the stark walls of that tiny sanctuary. But his delivery was not theatrical. The impact of his sermons derived more from his sincerity and depth of conviction than histrionics. Many years later he would write of sermons he heard while traveling in Europe, "…[W]hy is it that most of these ministers must use such a holy swell in their speech? Why not speak plainly and directly?"

Edward Hitchcock was intimately familiar with the King James Version of the Bible, and he often employed the formal English of that translation—ye, thee, thy, thou, doeth, saith, hither, thither, etc.—in his sermons. In a sermon delivered in February 1823 on the occasion of the death of a parishioner, he pleads with the congregation to consider the state of their own souls:

> Approach then his coffin…Approach and tremble at the end which awaits you if [you] have no Jesus on whom to lean in a dying hour. Approach ye afflicted mourners!…Approach ye whose souls are bound up in pursuit of wealth…Approach ye who are seeking the praise of men more than the praise of God…Approach ye who are pursuing forbidden pleasures thou glutton—thou drunkard—thou adulterer—thou bacchanalian—approach and remember that death stands ready to cut you down also: and that hell is waiting to receive you except you abandon your polluted and debasing idols.

Many of Hitchcock's favorite biblical phrases and expressions crop up repeatedly in his sermons. Some are agricultural. The souls of your parishioners

Figure 18. *Botrychium simplex*, drawing by Orra White Hitchcock, 1823

will be ripe for the harvesting, he advises a newly ordained minister: "Grasp the sickle with a courageous and a hopeful heart and…thrust it among the ready grain." The hearts of men have many spots and blemishes, he declares, just as the "tares will grow together with the wheat," a reference to a common garden weed in the Holy Land. Some are nautical. He says of unrepentant men, "O let them…fly to the cross of Christ—let them cling to this as the shipwrecked sailor clings to the rocks resolving if they must perish to perish there." Some expressions may elicit a chuckle from readers today, although they may not have been intended to amuse. How often it is, he observes, that a man recently reformed and repentant returns to a life of sin, "like the dog to his vomit—like the sow that was washed to her wallowing in the mire!"

Naturally Hitchcock's sermons abound with references to science and nature. For his discourse on Thanksgiving Day 1821, entitled "Works of God," he enumerates—literally—God's creation. He begins, of course, with man, God's greatest work: "110,000 millions of immortal souls: my heavens! Can you form any conception of such a multitude? And yet hearer you and I shall see them all at the day of judgment." He proceeds then to descend the tree of life by number: from mammals (some 562 species) to birds (nearly 300 species) to amphibians (400 species) to fish (more than 1000) to insects (at least 20,000 species) to plants (44,000 species), adding even minerals (600 species). In another sermon he draws elaborate analogies between the qualities of minerals and humans. Quartz, for example, might be compared to the semitransparent character of some men:

> Objects may be perceived through it but not distinctly. We often meet with such characters. We admire their general conduct and it seems as if they were but slightly out of the way. Nevertheless they are always more or less cloudy. There is a want of definiteness and cleanness in their principles and of decision in their conduct—you cannot be sure where you will find them when great moral questions are to be decided.

Astronomy was Edward's earliest scientific passion, and his admiration for the heavens shines through his sermons like the very stars in the firmament. In "Meditation Part I" he writes,

> Consider the sun how glorious in his course, the moon how beautiful in her silver glory, the stars how changing in their evening splendour! Ten thousand worlds are rolling nightly over our heads moving with a velocity we cannot conceive yet all is harmonious no clashing no interference no confusion. And yet how simple the laws by which they are guided.

What is known of the theology of Edward Hitchcock? He was by his own admission a follower of French theologian John Calvin who emphasized the personal relationship between a believer and his God, repentance for one's sins, and renewal of one's heart in order to achieve salvation. Western Massachusetts in the 1730s and 1740s had become the epicenter of "The Great Awakening," a rebirth of Christian fundamentalism, thanks in large measure to the preaching and writing of Reverend Jonathan Edwards of Northampton. From the 1730s on, revivals of religion became common in many Massachusetts cities and towns. Prompted by a charismatic preacher in a church pulpit, on a village green, or in a farmer's field, sinners repented publicly, threw themselves to the ground begging for their immortal souls, then arose as if born anew.

By the 1820s Calvinism had its competitors in the region, most notably Unitarianism. Nevertheless, Hitchcock's theology lay solidly in the religious mainstream of Massachusetts and Connecticut of that time. The fundamental tenets of Calvinism were central to nearly every sermon of Edward Hitchcock, and they stood in marked contrast to the "Unitarian notions" that were on the ascendancy in Deerfield and throughout New England. They included doctrines such as infallibility of scripture, depravity of man, justification by faith, repentance, and salvation.

"The knowledge derived from the scriptures," he wrote, "is infallible and immutable." And while approving the application of reason to the scriptures, he warned his parishioners lest reason should lead them to doubt the word of God: "No folly can be greater than to cavil at any thing contained in the bible." If careful, prayerful study of a passage of scripture should leave you still in doubt as to its meaning, your course is simple: "Wait for the solution of your difficulties till you enter eternity."

"All men are dead in trespasses and sins and by nature children of wrath," he declared. Among his most often quoted lines of scripture was Paul's description of humankind, Gentile and Jew alike, in Romans 3:10: "They are all gone aside…they are altogether become filthy; there is none that doeth good, no not one."

Does our salvation depend on morality, piety, good works? "No," answered Hitchcock emphatically, "It is by faith alone and not by works." Does this imply that a man justified by faith in Christ is free to live in sin? God forbid! he replies. Faith in God, in Christ the Redeemer, leads to good conduct. "Their holiness is the effect, not the cause, of their being elected."

Men's souls are immortal and destined to live on after the body has died, either in eternal glory or in eternal damnation. Said Reverend Hitchcock in a sermon entitled "Repentance," "O that the voice of the archangel and the trump of God might be sounded in this assembly to call you to repentance ere it sound over your graves to call you to the judgment." The only avenue to salvation for humankind is faith in the Redeemer, Christ Jesus.

When he spoke of the Judgment Day—and he spoke of it often—Hitchcock was not merely recounting some dark and distressing words from antiquity, but a constant, pressing, frightening reality which he described as if he had been there himself:

> We shall not attempt to paint before you the terrors and solemnities of that day—the burning universe—the opening graves—the shout of the archangel—the Son of man coming in the clouds with power and great glory—the tribunal of God rising on the ruins of the world—God himself ascending the judgment seat—the book of life opening wherein is registered the character and the fate of every individual—the universe of beings crowding with trembling solicitude around their Judge—nor the joy on the one side or the agony painted in the countenances of those on the other side as this Judge separates the righteous from the wicked…the day is at hand when you will sleep no more unless you can sleep in a lake of fire and brimstone, unless you can sleep amid the gnawings of the undying worm, unless you can sleep in the wine press of the fierceness and wrath of Almighty God.

One message Hitchcock stressed in nearly every sermon was that of religious practice, what he referred to as the "ordinances of religion," including prayer, attendance on the Sabbath, reading the scriptures, loving thy neighbor, and Holy Communion.

"Christians, go into your closets!" he admonished his hearers again and again, using "closet" in the Biblical sense, a private place for prayer and meditation. "Private fervent effectual prayer," he wrote, is the most fundamental practice of a true Christian. "Therefore if he loves God above everything besides, he will delightfully and habitually pray unto Him in public, in the family, and above all, in his closet."

The fourth commandment, he asserted, was perfectly clear: "Remember the Sabbath day to keep it holy." Furthermore, he regularly reminded his flock, "Irregular and only occasional attendance may be the ruin of your souls."

As to the scriptures, he reminded his parishioners: "If a man has not certain stated times, for instance, in which to pray in his family and in his closet and to read the scriptures and to examine himself and to attend public and social worship, he cannot grow in grace."

Of course the Christian is required to emulate Jesus in every way, especially with brotherly love. For as the Apostle said, "If a man say I love God and hateth his brother he is a liar."

The Lord's Supper was an ordinance fundamental to Christianity. Through it Christians are nourished symbolically by the body and the blood of Jesus Christ. In a sermon preceding communion he uses the text of I Corinthians 28: "But let a man examine himself, and so let him eat of that bread and drink of that cup." Hitchcock often reminded his parishioners of the importance of approaching the Lord's table with the proper state of mind, humility, awareness of one's depravity, a willingness to give oneself to God's will.

Perhaps more than any other theme, Reverend Hitchcock's sermons stressed the importance to a Christian of following the ways of God rather than the ways of man. As he often phrased it, we must not become enamored with "the riches honors and pleasures of the world...ye cannot serve God and Mammon."

This theme may well have rankled many of his parishioners who were much attracted by those worldly amenities. Conway, Massachusetts, after all, was a prosperous town in those years. Even when most of the nation was recovering from a deep recession, this town bristled with commercial as well as agricultural activity, and signs of prosperity were everywhere to be found. Conspicuous across the landscape were the many large farms with broad agricultural fields in the rich bottomlands below, rolling pastureland crisscrossed with stone walls on the hills beyond.

The town's farmers were justifiably proud of their holdings, and if the pastor's words can be taken literally, they boasted of them often and loudly. One symbol of a man's success in the town in that period was his "equippage," a term referring to wagons, carriages, and teams of horses employed to carry a well-to-do farmer and his family about on the many miles of roads in the town. Reverend Charles S. Pease, in his 1917 town history, reported that the wife of Dr. Samuel Ware, one of the town's first doctors, commented that the roads were of such good quality in 1770 that "there might someday be chaises in this town." And chaises there were very soon. In fact, Reverend Emerson is said to have contracted with local wagon maker Robert Hamilton for the construction of the first carriage in Franklin County and, according to Reverend Pease, the first constructed in America. Whether that assertion is true, it seems clear that Conway's farmers, merchants, and businessmen took great pride in their "equippage."

Such pride of ownership seems to have incurred the particular opprobrium of the new pastor. For all the sins and evils which he might have found objectionable in a New England town, it was excessive attachment to worldly effects that most often attracted Reverend Hitchcock's scorn.

In January 1822, the first Sabbath of the new year, his parishioners were forewarned early in the discourse entitled "Neglect of Precious Opportunities" that they were about to be chastised. "Such an important season as this ought not then to pass by without pausing and looking into our hearts and back upon our lives and forward upon the days to come." Apparently New Year's resolutions were common even then, for the pastor warns, "Yet with the greater part of us the farm, the money, and the merchandise or the honors and pleasures of the world so absorb our thoughts that our resolutions prove mere empty words and scarcely do we think of them again until we find that this year is gone." In an 1823 sermon, "Examination of the Scriptures," he bemoans the fact that while nearly every home in the town has a Bible,

> Many who have it in their house suffer it to lie day after day and week after week unopened and unthought of while they eagerly enquire of every one who will show them any earthly good—any better mode of carrying on the farm or managing the money and the merchandise.

In an 1825 sermon he presses the point still further, arguing that "...should Christ come among them they would pay more attention to the farm, the money, the merchandise, the dress, or the equippage than to him."

In the last paragraph of a sermon entitled "Sinners Dreaming" delivered first in June 1823, in Conway, Reverend Hitchcock put the matter into an eternal context:

> And let those who have lived even to middle age and whose dreams of worldly greatness and happiness have not been broken...be urged to burst away from the murderous delusions. Your dream is almost at an end. You may hug and worship that farm, that money, that house, that equippage, and that reputation a little longer. But the bubble will soon burst. Death will break you away from these fond idols and you will be confronted with that God who has said, "thou shalt have no other gods before me—ye cannot serve God and Mammon." And that meeting depend upon it will put an end to all your earthly dreams. The alternative is now before you...to yield your hearts to God or to be his enemy through all eternity. Choose then before God shall choose for you.

That sermon, it should be noted, was one of Hitchcock's most popular—he delivered it on some nineteen occasions after the first in his own church. Perhaps such a message was just what churchgoers wished to hear in those times—or perhaps it was a message their pastors believed they *needed* to hear.

One curiosity regarding the sermons of Edward Hitchcock is the almost complete absence of discussion of the stories of the Creation and the Flood in

Genesis. These were subjects very much on the minds of orthodox theologians of his day. The nascent science of geology was beginning to foster doubts in some quarters regarding those stories and we know that Hitchcock had very definite opinions on the subject, yet he rarely shared them with his congregation. Nowhere in all his surviving sermons does he address the Genesis story of creation with more than a few brief sentences.

In January 1823 he did deliver a discourse to his Conway parishioners entitled "Noachian Deluge" in which he discussed at some length the story of Noah and the flood. Barely a month later in a sermon on idolatry, he returned to the subject briefly. As far as his church sermons were concerned, that was the extent of his attention to that story. Perhaps he felt uneasy about calling too much attention to the opinions of those he regarded as "infidel scientists." The less his flock knew of such things, he may have believed, the better.

Those very subjects and the growing conflict between science and religion must have been much on his mind, however, when he was invited to deliver a "discourse" at the Berkshire Medical Institution in Pittsfield in September 1823. It was a propitious occasion, the inaugural meeting of the Lyceum of Natural History. A number of colleagues and acquaintances were present including Professor Chester Dewey of Williams College, Dr. David Hunt of Northampton, Dr. Jacob Porter of Plainfield, and very likely Hitchcock's cousin, Dr. Stephen West Williams, of Deerfield. Hitchcock chose as his topic, "Utility of Natural History." It would be a tour de force, longer than two Sabbath sermons, and it contained the first coherent presentation of his views regarding science and religion.

Hitchcock chose as his "motto" for the discourse a verse from 1 Kings referring to Solomon: "And he spake of trees, from the cedar tree that is in Lebanon, even unto the hyssop that springeth out of the wall: he spake also of beasts, and of fowl, and of creeping things, and of fishes." He then enumerated the benefits of the study of natural history, benefits to science and medicine, as well as to the physical and mental health of the student. He next turned to the relationship of science to religion, a subject that occupied at least half of the discourse.

The only detailed account of the Creation in the Bible is in the book of Genesis, Chapter 1 and the first few verses of Chapter 2. Here are found the familiar words:

> In the beginning God created the heaven and the earth. And the earth was without form, and void; and darkness was upon the face of the deep. And the Spirit of God moved upon the face of the waters. And God said, Let there be light: and there was light. And God saw the light, that it was good: and God divided the light from the darkness.

Here too we read of the creation of the land and the sea, of the stars in the firmament, of living things, and of course, of humankind, all in those first six days. In the second chapter we learn of the Garden of Eden, and the first man and woman, Adam and Eve. A few chapters later, a mere six generations (very long generations), comes the Genesis account of Noah and the flood, the inundation of the entire earth, and the destruction of all living things except those, man and beast alike, saved in the Ark. This story can be found, with variations, in a number of other books of the Bible. Some biblical scholars have determined that based on scriptural accounts, the earth was created some 4000 years before Christ.

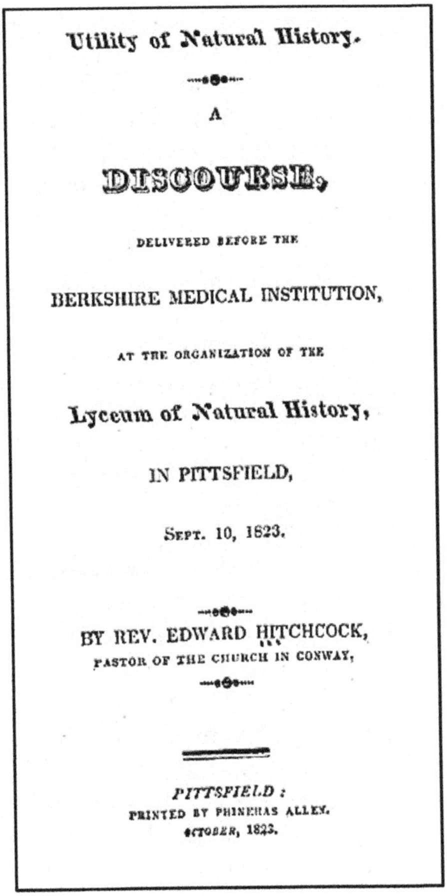

Utility of Natural History.

A

DISCOURSE,

DELIVERED BEFORE THE

BERKSHIRE MEDICAL INSTITUTION,

AT THE ORGANIZATION OF THE

Lyceum of Natural History,

IN PITTSFIELD,

SEPT. 10, 1823.

BY REV. EDWARD HITCHCOCK,

PASTOR OF THE CHURCH IN CONWAY,

PITTSFIELD:
PRINTED BY PHINEHAS ALLEN.
OCTOBER, 1823.

Figure 19. *Utility of Natural History: A Discourse*, 1823

Geologists of the early nineteenth century found ample cause to question Genesis. That the earth was far older than this seemed obvious to many scientists, including Edward Hitchcock. Charles Lyell, the eminent English geologist, famously estimated the ages of some sedimentary rock formations by observation of contemporary sedimentation rates. Paleontologists made similar observations on the rate of mineralization of plant and animal remains to estimate the age of some fossils. Such evidence suggested that the rocks in the earth's crust were hundreds of thousands, even millions of years in the making.

Was the Genesis account of the Creation in error? Many biblical scholars before and during Hitchcock's time defended it, arguing that the Hebrew word "yom," translated in the English of the King James Version as "day," could be interpreted to mean almost any time interval. Thus the six "days" of creation could easily have meant a period of hundreds, thousands, millions, even billions of days. This would allow ample time for the geological processes to carry on, for sediments to be laid down, mountains built up, organic remains converted to rock, etc. Edward Hitchcock had heard lengthy discussions of these explanations of creation and the flood from his mentors at Yale in 1819 and no doubt read it in the works of eminent geologists such as James Hutton, Robert Hooke, and Abraham Gottlob Werner.

As to Noah's flood, geologists had unearthed ample evidence of an ancient deluge, possibly numerous floods, any one of which might have been the subject of the biblical story. And that evidence could be found on all the continents. Much of the evidence for a "diluvium" had to do with the movement of rocks and boulders, some of immense size, that geologists like Hitchcock were more than willing to attribute to a flood or floods. Reverend Hitchcock made this very argument to his parishioners in "Noachian Deluge."

> We have proof of it all around us in our everyday excursions. Whence came these numerous worn and rounded masses of stone which are scattered over the tops of our highest hills and mountains? Surely no river could have conveyed them thither. Nothing will account for their situation but an universal deluge. Let the unbeliever then remember that as he passes over our hills the very stones cry out against him.

Indeed, those very stones did cry out loudly to Edward Hitchcock a few years later, but they would lead him to a quite different conclusion.

Hitchcock's discourse clearly was well received in Pittsfield that day. Shortly afterwards, the Lyceum published it and Hitchcock was elected a Vice President of the young society. The address was well publicized, locally in the *Franklin Herald* and the *Pittsfield Sun*, as well as in the *New England Farmer*, a Boston weekly. An anonymous writer in the *New York Statesman* wrote of the Hitchcock's discourse, "His speculations on the various geological theories are both learned and rational, defending the Mosaic account of the creation and of the deluge." A review in the *North American Review* in December 1823, suggested that the address was a call to scholars and students to get out into nature:

> Let the emaciated, dyspeptical votary of literature shoulder his mineralogical hammer, or buckle on his botanical apparatus, and sally out daily to explore the domains of nature, and he will soon be able to perform as valiant exploits as any one of his forefathers in writing folios. The author is a little poetical on this topic, but there is force in his words, and wisdom in his counsels.

A very telling remark of Reverend Hitchcock comes near the conclusion of his discourse when he warns his audience to be wary of idle theories.

> The marked extravagance of former theories of the earth adopted by geologists, such as those of Burnet, Woodward, Hutton, Winston and the whole school of Hutchinson, have produced a strong prejudice against everything on the same subject. But the present constellation of European geologists are men of a very different stamp—men whose grand object is the collection of facts, and who

are extremely cautious of hypothesis; adopting none, except such as seem absolutely necessary to explain appearances.

Hitchcock himself was the consummate "collector of facts." And yet certain facts would later in life lead him to some startling new hypotheses.

Most of Hitchcock's sermons dealt with the fundamentals of orthodox Protestantism: sin, repentance, atonement, and so on. Morality was also a common theme, most often addressed with a litany of the vilest sins of humankind, such as in this passage from I Corinthians: "Be not deceived: neither fornicators nor idolaters nor adulterers nor effeminate nor abusers of themselves with mankind, nor thieves nor covetous, nor drunkards, nor revilers nor extortioners shall inherit the kingdom of God."

A modern-day reader of these sermons may be surprised at how relatively infrequent are references to the Christian's duty to his fellow man in society at large, what would come to be known as the "social gospel." In all his sermons, there are fewer than a dozen that deal at length with such topics. Rare though they are, they nevertheless reveal a man with an acute social conscience who was unstinting in calling out those responsible for society's greatest crimes against humanity: slavery, war, intemperance, and the mistreatment of the American Indian.

Edward Hitchcock grew up in Deerfield, Massachusetts, a town where slaves were common up until the time of the American Revolution. His mother was raised in a Deerfield household with at least two slaves. Antislavery sentiment was strong in the Bay State by the 1820s, despite the Commonwealth's growing economic dependence on cotton and tobacco

Figure 20. "Diluvial hillocks" woodcut by Orra White Hitchcock, 1841

produced by slave labor in the South. Many defenders of slavery in those times, including some clergy, argued that slavery was not a sin, citing examples of holy men in the Bible who owned slaves. How interesting it is then to read "Religious Condition of the United States," delivered in Greenfield in 1820, in Shelburne in 1821, and in Conway in 1822. Here he cites an unexpected scriptural basis for his antislavery views:

> But the eighth commandment, thou shalt not steal, cannot in conscience be passed over by any professed preacher of morality or religion while he knows himself to be a member of that nation which contains within its bosom more than a million of human beings that have been stolen and enslaved. This is a fact, my hearers, that ought to freeze the blood of this nation. The existence of slavery in a land of tyranny is to be expected—in a land of monarchy it might be endured but in a free country it is intolerable—it is an abomination of desolations standing where it ought not. Its enormity will never be known until we stand as a nation around that tribunal in heaven where the blood of these poor murdered beings will be demanded at our hands—For the mighty ocean of their blood will go before us to judgment and for every drop of it will there be poured out in equal measure of God's wrath… as individuals we are not chargeable with this sin—but as members of this nation can we say that we are free from the blood of these innocent men?

As a young man Hitchcock had at times sounded hawkish on the subject of war, such as in his 1814 address before the Literary Adelphi when he called on New Englanders to prepare to go to war with the southern states. But in a sermon entitled "Wars," first delivered in April 1823, he quotes the Epistle of James: "From whence come wars and fightings among you? Come they not hence, even of your lusts that war in your members?" He goes on to speak of the glorification of war:

> There has been a false tinseled splendor thrown about war and its true character has been too long concealed under softening and sounding epithets. When its true character is known when its deceitful accompaniments shall be stripped away it will stand forth the king of monsters, the scourge of scourges, the abomination of desolations.

Hitchcock was a lifelong teetotaler, and the dangers of alcohol and its associated sins were frequent topics in his sermons. In his sermon entitled "Idolatry" delivered in April 1823, he strikes what would be a frequent theme on the subject of temperance:

> The intemperate drunkard makes a god of the intoxicating cup and sacrifices to this without scruple his health, his reputation, the comfort of his friends, and finally his life...Approach ye who are pursuing forbidden pleasures thou glutton thou dip and strike, thou adulterer thou bacchanalian—approach and remember

that death stands ready to cut you down also: and that hell is waiting to receive you except you abandon your polluted and debasing idols.

In "Prosperity the Ruin of Mankind," first delivered in Conway in 1824, he speaks forcefully about the mistreatment of the native peoples of North America:

> Our prosperity has led us to trample on the rights of the Indian. Ninety nine hundredths of this country, originally all his, had been in one way or another wrested from him…the army of the United States were employed to force the red man from his native soil and drive him at the point of the bayonet into the wilds of the far west. There with a crushed and an agonized spirit, and hopeless of justice or mercy from man, has he been lifting up his cry to God while we have been gloating over his inheritance…(God) has never yet failed to punish national sins with national judgments."

He would return to these social causes—slavery, war, temperance, and the mistreatment of the American Indian—again and again later in his preaching career.

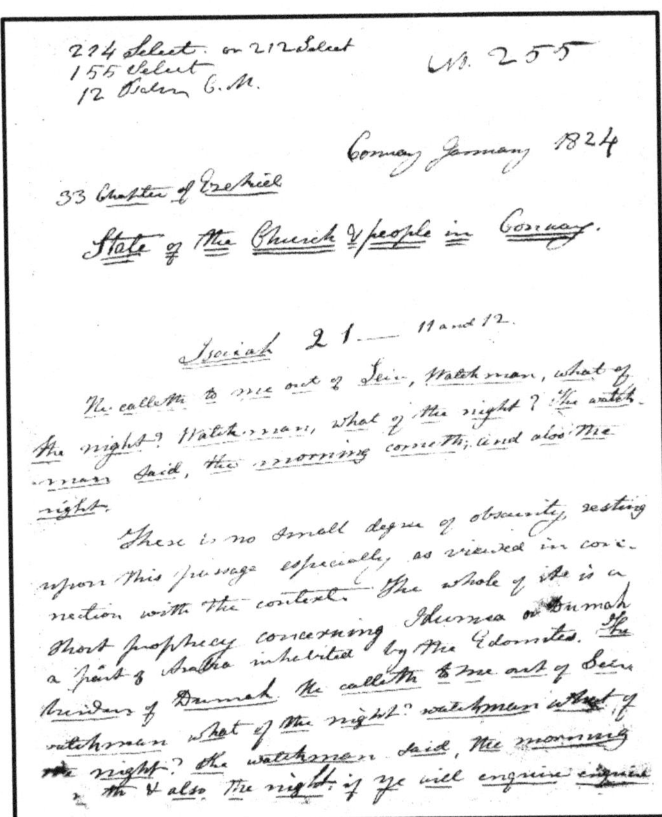

224 Select. or 212 Select
155 Select
12 [illegible] C.M.

No. 255

Conway January 1824

33 Chapter of Ezekiel

State of the Church & people in Conway.

Isaiah 21.— 11 and 12.

He calleth to me out of Seir, Watchman, what of the night? Watchman, what of the night? The watchman said, the morning cometh, and also the night.

There is no small degree of obscurity resting upon this passage especially, as viewed in connection with the context. The whole of it is a short prophecy concerning Idumea or Dumah a part of Arabia inhabited by the Edomites. The burden of Dumah. He calleth to me out of Seir watchman what of the night? watchman what of the night? the watchman said, the morning cometh & also the night: if ye will enquire enquire

Figure 21. "State of the Church and People in Conway," a sermon delivered by Edward Hitchcock in January 1824

By 1824, the tide of spiritual fervor in the parish of Reverend Hitchcock seemed to have ebbed. In a sermon delivered in January 1824, entitled "State of the Church and People in Conway," he used for his text Isaiah 21:11-12: "He calleth to me out of Seir, Watchman, what of the night? Watchman, what of the night? The watchman said, The morning cometh, and also the night." Like the watchman of the Old Testament, he was watching over his own people, and felt obliged to warn them of the night:

> I notice first the declension of religion in the church... Who does not see that a fatal apathy is come over some of our souls? Who does not see that the love of the world has gained over others a dangerous ascendancy and frozen up the warm blood of piety?...Out of a population of 1700 souls but little more than 200 of whom have ever professed religion out of this great number rarely a single instance of conviction or conversion in a whole year!…I have been…cut to the heart to witness the rapid decay of a general sense of religion among us the past year. It has seemed like the melting away of the snow by the rains and the winds of the spring.

He particularly bemoaned the decline in attendance at weekly prayer meetings and other events beyond the Sabbath services.

> …[B]rethren I am free to confess that rarely if ever did I find the prayer meeting and the conference so poorly attended as with us. In other places it is customary for the youth whether pious or not to be constant at such meetings. But here with a few honorable exceptions they seem to avoid the place where prayer is wont to be made.

Here he was quite willing to point the finger of blame inwards:

> But on the subject of weekday religious meetings a very solemn enquiry suggests itself to my mind. Are not these meetings so this thinly attended because they are so poorly conducted? Does not the whole difficulty lie in my incompetence or unfaithfulness? I am willing to believe that this may be the fact…. let not my unfaithfulness in this respect be the means of the loss of your souls. On this account forsake not the assembling of yourselves together. Lay the blame holy upon me if you will—I deserve to bear it—tell me plainly of my deficiency—send me away from the vineyard of the Lord as an unfaithful steward—do anything to me if you will not sacrifice your souls.

Perhaps in those words Hitchcock reveals a certain prescience, for soon he would indeed depart from "the vineyard of the Lord."

Burial Hill

9 The Sovereignty of God

"The heart must bleed for a season."

Conway, March 21, 1824

On a dreary Sabbath in late winter, the congregation rose to sing the second selection of the morning service, number 97 from the Hartford Hymnal. With only the reedy tones of the small organ to accompany them and led by the few choir members who could carry a tune, they sang together a traditional hymn, "As thy days, so shall thy strength be." By the fifth and sixth verses many a strong voice was fading, even as the words of the hymn echoed off the sanctuary walls. Their power may have been lost on many in the Conway church that morning, but not on all:

When call'd to bear the weighty cross,
Of sore affliction, pain, or loss,

Or deep distress, or poverty,
Still as thy days, thy strength shall be.

When ghastly death appears in view,
Christ's presence shall thy fears subdue ;
He comes to set thy spirit free,
And as thy days, thy strength shall be.

The hymn now finished, the pastor rose slowly from his seat and stepped up to the lectern to begin his morning discourse. He fumbled for an unusually long time with his notes, then with his spectacles, then cleared his throat repeatedly. Parishioners well acquainted with his habits and mannerisms in the pulpit must surely have been concerned. And where, they might well have asked, is Mrs. Hitchcock this morning? She normally sat at the far end of the first pew with their child. But today, on this particular morning, she was seated at the rear, alone, her face veiled. She had always been the least ostentatious pastor's wife, yet it seemed this morning she wished to disappear entirely... "Still as thy days, thy strength shall be."

Reverend Hitchcock seldom interjected personal matters into his sermons. Perhaps he avoided such subjects out of a sense of privacy. Or perhaps it simply was not customary in those times for a preacher to share personal anecdotes in his preaching. His congregation surely must have been stunned on that Sabbath in March 1824, when, midway through a sermon entitled "Sovereignty of God," it took a very personal turn: "Thus far I had proceeded my hearers in the composition of this discourse when I was called away to witness in the prostrated agonies and final removal of an only child, a painful exhibition of the sovereign dominion of Jehovah."

Barely two months short of his second birthday, little Edward Hitchcock had succumbed, as did so many young children in those times, probably to pneumonia, influenza, or consumption, in his mother's arms. Like all grieving parents, they were struck with a profound sense of loss combined with regret and guilt. Imagine the effect on his parishioners as Reverend Hitchcock describes the emotional impact of their loss:

> We do not ask you to pity us because we who but yesterday were parents are childless today—nor because we meet when we go to our desolate habitation instead of the cheering salutation of infant affection nothing but a thousand mementos all leading our thoughts to yonder graveyard...[we] ask only with sincere earnestness for your fervent and effectual prayers.

He seems then to be seeking for some mitigation for their loss:

> That children should be called out of the world before they are capable of knowing good and evil might in itself considered be regarded as a mere expression of mercy in God who thus saved them from the dangers of a wicked world and early transplanted them into his Paradise above.

But the painful reality intrudes again:

> …[W]hen we see that death preceded by an agonizing struggle between disease and nature it casts a mystery over the subject and leaves the mind at once to resolve it all into the holy sovereignty of God. We see something of darkness in it—something that our actual researches cannot fathom…It forcibly impresses us with the sentiment that God has a right to do as he pleases with us without explaining to us the reasons of his conduct.

At that point a sentiment is revealed that Reverend Hitchcock would have his congregation believe sheds some light into that darkness:

> But if God does exercise his sovereignty in sending afflictions he does not therefore act without reason although that reason may be hid from us. In the removal of our child we believe he has an object perhaps many objects to accomplish. We have no doubt that one of these objects was the punishment of our sins: and if there is one feeling within us stronger than the rest it is a sense that we deserve that punishment: and it lends smarting poignancy to the wound to know that the arrow which has pierced us passed first through the heart of our child.

As deep as is a parent's pain at the loss of a child, the agony of Edward and Orra Hitchcock seems to have been aggravated and compounded by the belief that their own sins—whatever they might have been—were somehow the reason for their young child's suffering and death. From that day forward, some might recall in later years, their hearts were indeed pierced. And the pastorate of Reverend Hitchcock would never be the same.

Hitchcock shared his grief with Benjamin Silliman in a letter dated only two days following the death of his son.

> Dear Sir, It becomes painfully necessary for me to begin this letter by informing you that it has pleased the Most High after a very distressing sickness of fourteen days to remove from us our dear & only son. We yesterday committed his remains to their cold bed where they must sleep till the resurrection and although we hope that we bow submissively to the kind hand that has connected us yet as you well know from repeated experience the heart must bleed for a season…

Figure 22. *Carex hitchcockiana,* drawing by Orra White Hitchcock, 1826

Sadly, Professor Silliman and his wife were well positioned to share their friends' grief, for they had suffered such a loss only a few years earlier, as is clear from Silliman's reply:

> My dear sir, I most cordially and feelingly condole with you on the late afflicted bereavement in your family. I know indeed, from early experience every pang you have suffered, & hope you may sooner recover from the shock than I did from my first loss of this kind—that of my eldest son. You will present my respectful condolence to Mrs. Hitchcock, whose suffering will of course, embrace all that belongs to yours with the addition of what a mother only can know.

Professor Silliman then addresses a point of faith that must surely have weighed on the hearts of Edward and Orra, the doctrine of original sin. Many Calvinists believed that even an infant was subject to eternal punishment, not for the child's own sins but for those of its first parents, Adam and Eve: "…I consider the declarations of our Saviour, as deciding the point that his sacrifice will cancel their original taint, and neither scripture nor reason will justify us in believing that there will hereafter be a penal retribution awarded to any thing but actual transgression."

What effect did the death of their first child have on mother and father? Orra no doubt found ample time to wrestle with her private grief even as she prepared for the birth of a second child. As to Edward, one hint as to his suffering may be found in an abrupt change in his preaching style. Just a month after his son's death, he adopted a new and radically different mode of discourse. The usual format of his sermons was to select a few lines of scripture on which he would expand at length. But this Sunday, he announced to his hearers, would be different. "This is what is called expository preaching," he explained, "and has been earnestly recommended and successfully practiced by many of the ablest and most pious dispensers of the truth."

He chose for that discourse chapter one of Paul's Epistle to the Ephesians.

> Where is the Christian that has not noticed the unusually elevated style in which this is written, and who has not felt his heart burn within him while this great apostle not in words which man's wisdom teacheth but in the words which the

> Holy Ghost teacheth illustrates the glorious truths and enforces the holy duties of the Gospel?

He proceeded to read the entire chapter, a verse at a time, with commentary on each. The sermon is only about two-thirds the length of his usual discourse, although he no doubt added a good deal of commentary *ex tempore*.

This was the first of twenty discourses he would deliver in the "expository" style over the coming months. Perhaps they were easier for him to compose when his mind and heart were otherwise engaged. Furthermore, they addressed some of the thorniest questions of orthodox dogma such as election, predestination, and original sin. Hitchcock may have preferred to present these difficult subjects in this way, allowing his hearers to consider what the scriptures had to say without adding his own commentary. These were matters with which he himself had once struggled. Perhaps he still found them troubling. He delivered these expository sermons over the last eighteen months of his pastorate exclusively to his own parish, never in other churches. The frequency of his visiting preacher duties also dropped sharply in that period.

The grief that consumed Edward and Orra Hitchcock with the loss of their first child must have been relieved to some degree by the arrival, four months later, of a daughter, Mary. On the other hand, the death of a child was not an uncommon event in those times. Parents were well aware of the probability of such a tragedy. When the worst happened, they grieved, but they moved on. A lost child could be replaced. And, of course, there was solace in the belief that the family would be united again one day in heaven.

During his years in Conway, Hitchcock got his physical exercise in what he referred to as the "geological gymnasium." In a letter to Professor Silliman in August 1821, he wrote,

> …I have reserved five weeks to myself in the year…to devote to geology as I know of nothing better fitted to merit my vigor...if you could without inconvenience occasionally send me by mail one of these Journals it would much gratify me as I am shut out mostly from the scientific world, yet I want a loop hole through which I can look sometimes & see what they are about.

Considering his spiritual duties and labors, his scientific productivity in those years is most impressive. He published at least a dozen papers in the *American Journal of Science and Arts* during those four years including five in geology, three in the physical sciences and astronomy, and two in botany. His reviews of two new and important European works in geology show that he was well abreast of the latest developments in the field. In 1823 he wrote two reviews of *Reliquiae* by British theologian and geologist William Buckland, one for the *AJS*, one for the *Christian Spectator.* In the same year he wrote a review of *Outlines of the Geology of England and Wales* by British geologists Reverend William D. Conybeare and William Phillips that also appeared in *AJS.* These lengthy critiques give strong evidence that this minister from an out-of-the-way New England parish was able to peer through the "loop hole" into the wider scientific discourse of his time. All were published anonymously, a common practice by reviewers in that period, although it seems likely that the identity of the author would have been apparent within the small geological community that existed at the time. They also clearly demonstrate the willingness of Edward Hitchcock, despite all his limitations, to take on some of the most respected scientists of his day and to tackle the contentious issue of science versus the words of revelation.

For all his scientific endeavors in this period, Reverend Hitchcock did not slight religious writing, authoring a treatise entitled *A General Survey of the Works of God* for the *Christian Spectator* as well as a tract on the evils of Unitarianism in *The Evangelist.* Nevertheless, from the earliest days of his pastorate, Hitchcock felt torn as to his duties and affections. In December 1822, he reveals all to his colleague, Benjamin Silliman:

> As I write this Sabbath evening, I take the liberty to propose to you a case of conscience. I have frequently found that my botanical and geological pursuits when zealously attended to, although generally conducive to health, still to have the effect of...deadening religious sensibilities to render me less solicitous to fulfil the duties of my ministry...the thought has occurred to me that you might have had the same trials to go through & therefore might be able to counsel me. Pray tell me if you have the remedy in such a case. Must these pursuits be altogether abandoned? Or is there such a thing as pursuing them with a supreme reference to the glory of God?

On October 6, 1825, Reverend Hitchcock submitted his letter of resignation as pastor of the Conway church. His stated reason: "the feeble state of my health which has continued to decline for a number of years." A resignation for any reason other than health he seemed to believe would have been a violation of his Christian duty. Furthermore, he had received an offer of a faculty position at Amherst College, a position he believed would be more favorable to his health than the ministry.

The pastor had been laying the foundation for this decision for some time. In his letter of resignation he states that he had communicated his doubts about his health to church members "ever since I settled in the ministry in this place."

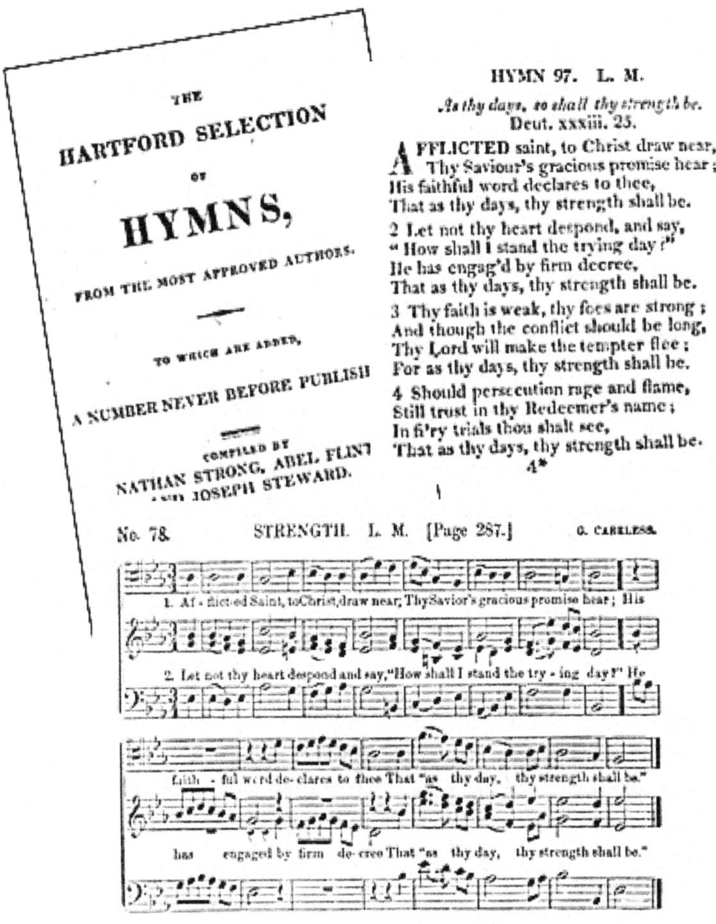

THE
HARTFORD SELECTION
OF
HYMNS,
FROM THE MOST APPROVED AUTHORS.

TO WHICH ARE ADDED,
A NUMBER NEVER BEFORE PUBLISH

COMPILED BY
NATHAN STRONG, ABEL FLINT
AND JOSEPH STEWARD.

HYMN 97. L. M.

As thy days, so shall thy strength be.
Deut. xxxiii. 25.

AFFLICTED saint, to Christ draw near,
Thy Saviour's gracious promise hear;
His faithful word declares to thee,
That as thy days, thy strength shall be.

2 Let not thy heart despond, and say,
" How shall I stand the trying day?"
He has engag'd by firm decree,
That as thy days, thy strength shall be.

3 Thy faith is weak, thy foes are strong;
And though the conflict should be long,
Thy Lord will make the tempter flee;
For as thy days, thy strength shall be.

4 Should persecution rage and flame,
Still trust in thy Redeemer's name;
In fi'ry trials thou shalt see,
That as thy days, thy strength shall be.

4*

No. 78. STRENGTH. L. M. [Page 287.] O. CARELESS.

Figure 23. "As thy days, thy strength shall be," a hymn selected by Reverend Hitchcock to be sung on March 21, 1824, the Sabbath following the death of his infant son.

In "Rights of God," a single paragraph has been inserted perhaps intended to prepare his parishioners:

> God has a right also to do what he will with the pastors of his church to give or withhold them in any part of his vineyard and to continue or remove them as will best accomplish his purposes. And let it never be forgotten that whenever a faithful minister is given or taken way it is God who does it although he employs the instrumentality of man…that he intended the event whether pleasant or painful for the good of his church and the advancement of his glory.

Whatever his true motive for separating from his Conway parish, Hitchcock clearly harbored guilt over this decision. When he returned to Conway in 1845 to speak at the ordination of a new minister, he waxed reflective about his departure two decades earlier:

> Amid the many delightful recollections which the retrospect of my short ministry affords I can confess that a sense of unfaithfulness and deficiency in duty outweighs all other considerations and prevents my ever looking forward to the final reckoning but with solemn trembling. For how overwhelming the thought that I may meet some soul there who will charge his eternal ruin to my unfaithfulness.

In his final sermon in Conway, he places his ministry in an eternal context:

> I know not, indeed, what Providence may yet have in store for me in this world; but the impression is strong within me, that my work on earth is nearly ended—that the toils and sufferings of this life, at least, are almost over...How solemn then the consideration, that the account of my ministry in this place is now sealed up to the judgment of the great day. There I shall soon meet you all; and that account will be opened...to the everlasting joy of some...to the everlasting grief of others.

In truth his life was far from over, yet he would carry with him guilt and remorse about abandoning his ministry for the rest of his life. Nevertheless he must have been well remembered by his Conway congregation. He was invited to preach there again no fewer than twenty-eight times over the next thirty-five years including delivering the sermon at the funeral service for Reverend Emerson in 1826.

Figure 24.
The grave of little Edward
(1822-1824), Conway

A Chemical Laboratory, 1854

10 Silliman's Apprentice

"Never attempt an experiment in public which you have not within a few hours performed in private."

Late October 1825

A one-horse shay with a black leather canopy carried Edward and Orra Hitchcock and infant Mary along the rutted way that followed the Mill River in its descent from Conway to the Connecticut River. Close behind them rumbled a wagon loaded with all their earthly goods and driven by neighbor Henry Billings. On the bench next to Henry sat Emilia Hitchcock, sister of Edward, clinging to the plank seat for dear life as the wagon bounced harshly over boulders and through muddy ruts.

Orra was cradling her daughter and singing softly to her to distract her from the bumpy ride. When the child was finally asleep Orra looked up at her husband. He was grim faced, fiercely grasping the reins. She reached over and touched his hand.

"Edward, she's asleep."

He turned and looked at the little girl, then at his wife, smiling faintly. "We can thank the Lord for little blessings."

"Yes, we can, indeed. With little Edward he punished us—but now he is blessing us. It is one of the mysteries of life," she observed.

"Perhaps he is rewarding us for remaining steadfast through our trials," said Edward.

Just then they approached another stream crossing and the horse slowed, placing each hoof carefully into the bed of the stream. When they were safely on the dry roadbed once again they halted and Edward turned to watch the wagon, concerned that its weight might mire it in the streambed. But Henry had a steady hand on the reins and spoke to his horse reassuringly as they moved though the water and up onto the dry roadway.

"'Tis very good of Mr. Billings to offer a neighborly hand today. He has been very attentive to our needs of late—a true Christian."

"Yes, indeed, he has been, Edward." She could see Henry and Emilia laughing as the wagon began to lurch forward again. "But Edward—I believe Henry's recent attentiveness may have to do more with your sister."

"With Emilia? How so?"

Orra smiled and sighed, tucking the blanket around Mary's shoulders. "Have you not noticed a certain—attachment?"

Edward appeared bewildered. "Attachment?"

"Dearest Edward, how is it that one so schooled in the literary and scientific arts, so worldly and well-read in religion, can be so poorly informed as to matters of the heart? Your sister and Mr. Billings, surely you can see."

"You mean..." answered Edward with surprise.

"Yes, Edward. If a woman's instincts tell her anything, I predict that soon—very soon—you will have a third brother."

The exodus of Edward and Orra Hitchcock from Conway was surely bittersweet. They were leaving behind little Edward whose remains had been interred in "yonder graveyard" only a year and a half before, and still harbored a deep sense of loss. No doubt the couple had forged many friendships in that town. But almost from the start of his pastorate, Reverend Hitchcock felt "out of the way," as he might have expressed it, in the town. The pressures of writing and delivering at least two sermons a week, visiting with parishioners, performing weddings, baptisms, and funerals had taken their toll on his constitution. It is true he had warned the church from the very beginning that his health might not hold up long. And when he finally submitted his resignation it was on the grounds of poor health, although that plea, Edward would admit years later, was somewhat disingenuous. A sense of guilt over his resignation would follow him for the rest of his days.

His new position was the kind of challenge he relished—he would throw himself into the work with all his strength, knowing that he lacked adequate preparation, particularly for teaching chemistry. In a curious way his worries and fears about the frailty of his health were powerful motivators now and throughout his life. In a most revealing letter to his eldest son, Edward, Jr., nearly a quarter century later, he would admit to frequent bouts with what he called nervous despondency, but added that they had "...enabled me to do what little I have done as a literary man."

As to Orra Hitchcock, she was the serene and steady anchor of the family—she would go wherever her beloved husband's ambition led them. She too may have been glad to put the pains and sorrows of Conway behind her; surely the prospect of moving to Amherst must have buoyed her spirits. It was, after all, her hometown. No doubt the presence of a baby girl thrilled her, as did the knowledge that yet another addition to the family was well along.

For the next two months, the couple settled in New Haven, Connecticut, thanks to the kindness and encouragement of Professor Benjamin Silliman of Yale. Hitchcock and Silliman by now had developed a strong relationship, mainly through the exchange of personal letters. In fact it may well have been Silliman who first informed Edward about a vacancy on the faculty at Amherst College and about rumors that the college was interested in him. Six months later, after he had been offered the position, Hitchcock wrote Silliman with some of the details. He was to teach chemistry, geology, mineralogy, and religion, explained Hitchcock. Silliman took the opportunity to offer his younger colleague a warning, based no doubt on his own experience at Yale:

> A Chemical course while it is going on is a complete engrossment of all your time & all your powers & I would never undertake again to teach anything collaterally with it...

Silliman's approach to teaching chemistry was experimental, and that, he warned, presented still additional challenges:

> As to undertaking a course of chemical demonstrations without a previous apprenticeship in the practical part, I must say that I think you would meet with much embarrassment & lose much time & expense which must be saved by going through with an experienced person...Should you conclude on any such arrangement you need not be afraid that I should do every thing in my power to aid you...

And aid him Benjamin Silliman most certainly did, welcoming Hitchcock into his laboratory for a brief but intense apprenticeship in practical chemistry.

Hitchcock's notes from that period, totaling nearly 500 pages, are divided into three sections. The first encompasses some of the fundamental concepts of physical science under headings such as "Heat and Caloric," "Chemical Attraction or Affinity," and "Atomic Theory." Much of this material appears to have been copied directly from Silliman's own notes, possibly from an early draft of a manuscript that Silliman published as a textbook in 1831.

The notion of atoms as the fundamental particles of matter was already well developed at that time. Interestingly, however, Silliman reserved the term *molecule* for crystals. But it is clear that he regarded molecules as tiny crystals, that is, precise geometric arrangements of atoms. And while the system of symbols for the elements (H for hydrogen, O for oxygen, etc.) existed at that time, neither Silliman nor his understudy utilized it, nor did they employ the shorthand of chemical notation, but rather described a reaction in words. Thus for the reaction symbolized as $H_2SO_4 + MgCO_3 \rightarrow MgSO_4 + H_2O + CO_2$ Hitchcock writes, "Pour sulphuric acid upon carbonate of magnesia of the shops and sulphate of magnesia will be formed with effervescence and remain in solution."

Hitchcock's notes then turn to the chemical elements familiar to science in the early nineteenth century—nitrogen, hydrogen, potassium, sodium, lithium, barium, magnesium, silicium (silicon), aluminium, zircon, glucine (beryllium), and others—some twenty-three in all. He describes each element and discusses its properties as well as its economic or practical importance. Under the properties of oxygen, for instance, his notes include the following:

> 1. It is not absorbed by water
> 2. Heavier than common air
> 3. Refracts the rays of light less than any other gas
> 4. Luminous by compression
> 5. Eminent supporter of combustion…
> 6. Oxygen is an eminent supporter of animal life
> 7. It has an effect on the colour of the blood—oxygen unites with all the simplest bodies except nine.

The third and longest section of Hitchcock's chemistry notes includes descriptions of experiments—strictly speaking they were demonstrations—that illustrate key physical principles and the properties of elements and compounds. For these he refers repeatedly to some of the world's leading authorities on "practical chemistry" of his day—William Brande, James Cutbush, Sir Humphry Davy, John Gorham, William Henry, Robert Hunt, Samuel Parkes, Abraham Rees, and Thomas Thompson—all of whose works were no doubt in Silliman's personal library.

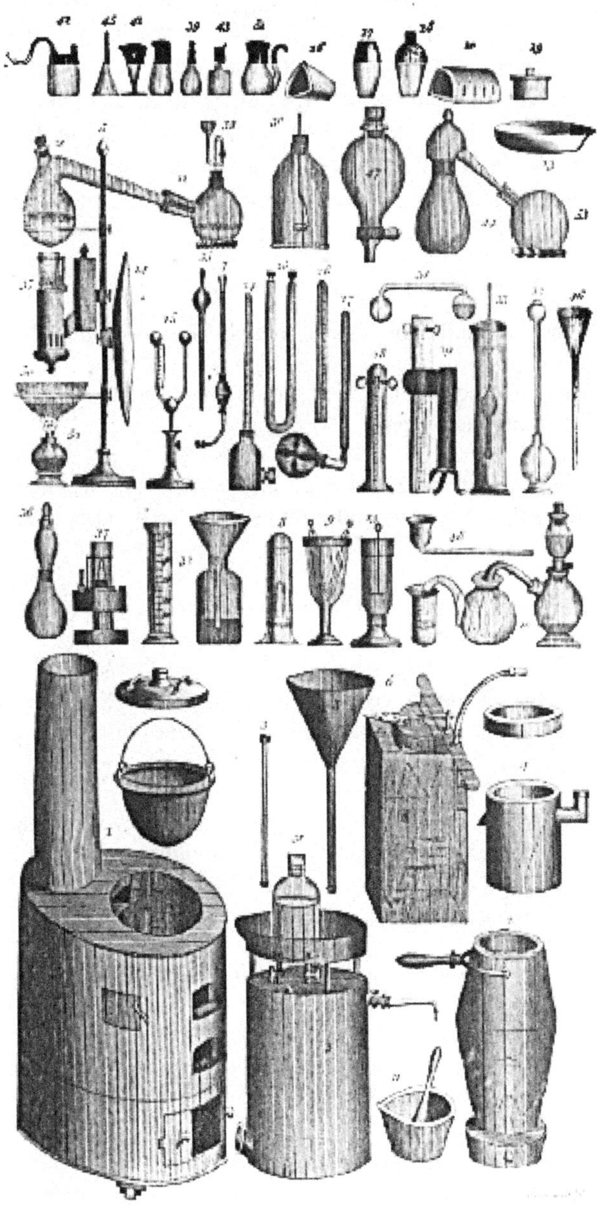

Figure 25. Small apparatus for the chemical laboratory, 1834

One fascinating aspect of Hitchcock's chemistry notes is the array of vessels, devices, and other pieces of apparatus he describes and utilizes, including the blow pipe, colorimeter, cryophore, deflagrator, endiometer, galvanic pile, gasometer, iron furnace, manometer, mercurial cistern, Nooth's apparatus, Papin's digester, pneumatic cistern, reverberatory furnace, tribulated receiver, universal furnace, and Wedgewood pyrometer. We may assume that most if not all of these were available in Silliman's lab, for Hitchcock describes each along with its uses in considerable detail, sometimes with dates of his experiments, often with notes on the results, good and bad. For oxygen he lists eight such experiments:

> Experiment 1. Lower a candle into a jar of the gas. [It burns intensely.]
>
> Experiment 2. Blow out the candle leaving some fire upon the wick and relight it [by re-inserting it into the oxygen].
>
> Experiment 3. Coil a small wire, put it through a cork, and to its lower end attach the end of a sulphur match...and light the match. [It burns intensely but without flame.]
>
> Experiment 4. Repeat the same experiment with a watch spring inserted into a cork and not bent.
>
> Experiment 5. Put a candle under a receiver filled with common air and another under one filled with oxygen—light them at the same time. [The flame in oxygen burns brighter.]
>
> Experiment 6. Attach the compound blow pipe (one arm of it) to gasometer. Light the stream of oxygen issuing from the candle holding a piece of charcoal beneath and on this hold a watch spring or iron wire—A most brilliant combustion will take place.
>
> Experiment 7. Do the same with copper wire. As soon as more than one kind of gas is collected in the laboratory let the jars be labeled to prevent mistakes.
>
> Experiment 8. Put two animals under receivers [beakers] one containing common air the other oxygen. In the latter life will be longest preserved.

The blow pipe Hitchcock refers to was perhaps the most often employed device in chemistry laboratories of the early nineteenth century. The operator blew steadily through a simple blow pipe which was directed at a candle or alcohol burner creating an intensely hot fire. Its successor, the compound blow pipe, a forerunner of modern welding torches, employed streams of hydrogen and oxygen. A sample of a chemical compound or mineral thus could be ignited and heated to its melting point, thereby vaporizing many impurities and yielding a pure substance. Often the color of the resulting flame was characteristic. "Before the compound blow pipe," Hitchcock notes, the mineral barite "burns with a peculiar yellow flame," while strontium "fuses with a red flame." The blow pipe could also be utilized for fusing or bending glass tubes. A gasometer was often utilized for collecting and holding the gases under pressure. Hitchcock refers to its use in conjunction with the compound blow pipe. Black's furnace consisted of an iron outer shell lined with firebrick in which wood or coal could be burned. Flasks of reagents could be heated inside or on the top. The device could also serve as a heat source for the entire laboratory. An ingenious apparatus invented by an Irish chemist, Peter Woulfe, utilized a series of flasks to safely handle noxious gases.

To read Edward's notes from Silliman's laboratory one could almost imagine the somewhat saturnine professor actually having fun, feeling the excitement of mastering an entirely new set of skills different from any he had possessed before. He recorded notes on over 400 experiments or demonstrations. Some appear to have been intended to put on a show:

> Add an alkali such as baking soda to "cabbage liquor" [an extract of cabbage and it turns green, to alkanet [an extract of borage] and it turns bluish purple, to turmeric [an extract of ginger] and it turns brown; add an acid to each and the natural color will be restored.
>
> Hold glass tubes of differing lengths and diameters over the flame from a compound blow pipe and "various musical sounds will be produced."
>
> Suspend several threads in a glass tube filled with alum dissolved in boiling water; as the solution cools "beautiful octahedra" [crystals] will form on the threads.
>
> Dip a quill pen into a silver solution, then write on a card. The writing will be invisible. Dip the card into "liquid sulphuretted hydrogen" [hydrogen sulfide] and the writing will become legible.
>
> Place four fluids, mercury, cabbage liquor, oil, and alcohol tinged with alkanet in a tall flask. Drop different solids into the tube and each will come to rest on a different layer: lead shot on the mercury, oak wood on oil, pine wood on alcohol. "Agitate the whole together they will return to the original position…Used mercury water and oil and succeeded well; put a piece of lead into wood to make it just swim on water and a brass weight on the mercury."
>
> "Attach a common blow pipe to a gasometer filled with common air and put a glass tube about 1/3 inch diameter…into the flame—let the assistant take hold of one end of it and draw it out gradually and it melts and with care a glass wire tube 20 or 30 feet away may be drawn not larger than a knitting needle. Two

> tubes 28 feet long were drawn in this manner December 6th 1825 in Yale laboratory and hung up for exhibition the next day."

In some of his experiments Hitchcock sought to demonstrate practical applications of chemistry, such as these boons for treating an ill family member:

> Fill a matrass with carbonate of ammonia [smelling salts], then insert a cork with glass tube a foot long. Invert a phial [vial] over the tube, then heat the matrass. "Carbonate of ammonia will be volatilized and condensed again in the phial."
>
> Combine a small amount of nitrate of potash [potassium nitrate] and strong sulphuric acid. "The white fumes that rise afford an excellent destroyer of contagious expulsion in the rooms of the sick. It is not injurious to the sick."
>
> Place nitrate of potash [potassium nitrate] into an iron tube; insert a lead tube into a cork and seal the end of the iron tube. Place the iron tube in Black's furnace. Oxygen will be produced from the lead tube which may be collected in a cistern. He adds, "This is the best way to prepare oxygen for cases of sickness," although he advises placing the iron tube at a 45° angle in the oven lest the heat drive out the cork leading to an explosion "loud as a common gun."

Many of Hitchcock's experimental notes reveal in the young professor a certain fascination with what might today be called pyrotechnic displays:

> Mix two parts of atmospheric air and three parts of hydrogen and fill with this mixture an air pistol holding the finger up on the vent. Cork the orifice before it is withdrawn from the water then apply a sulphur match to the touch hole and a violent explosion will take place and the cork be driven across the laboratory.
>
> Do the same with two parts hydrogen and one part oxygen. The explosion will be more violent.

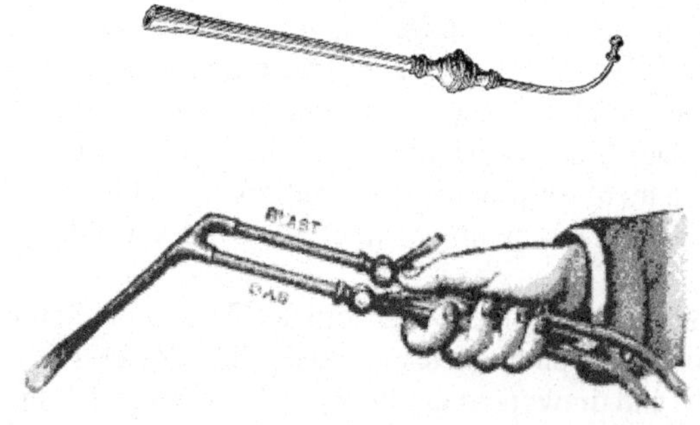

Figure 26. A simple blow pipe and a compound blow pipe

Take two volumes hydrogen one of oxygen mixed together and let it rise in bubbles through the shelf of the pneumatic cistern and as it rises apply a burning paper dipped in spirits of turpentine. Loud and successive explosions will take place.

Mix three parts of oxygen with one of olefiant gas [ethylene] and put the mixture in the tin air pistol and apply a candle and a tremendous explosion will take place.

Take a glass globe open at the two axes (the larger the better). Let the lower end be stopped by a metallic plate and let a small piece of copper plate be raised an inch or two from the bottom to receive the phosphorus. Hold the globe to the tube of the compound blow pipe and let the tube go down to the bottom. Then let in the oxygen and it will expel the common air—it may be known when the vessel is full by holding a candle to the mouth. Put the globe on the table and put into it one or two pieces of phosphorus an inch long and set them on fire. Darken the room and the illumination will be most brilliant and phosphoric acid will be condensed in the flakes on the inside (The globe used at Yale 1825 broke in the midst of the experiment). No danger in these cases from explosion.

Pour (nitric acid) upon powder and charcoal taken fresh from the fire and thrust into a crucible or (which is much more beautiful) into a glass vessel. The charcoal will immediately take fire and burn in a brilliant jet resembling a volcano—the glass always breaks but no danger attend it.

On one page of his notebook Hitchcock recorded these "Canons of the laboratory at Yale":

1. Hot water
2. Dust the stove tables etc.
3. A place for everything and everything in its place
4. Clean towel on or near table
5. Candles and lamps always ready
6. Bottle or pitcher of water on lecturing table
7. Every bottle and vessel clean
8. Nothing put up without a label
9. In cold weather fire in the office—office dusted and clean
10. Saturday—lecture room swept and dusted throughout
11. No dirty hands on walls
12. After each lecture clean and put up everything.

No doubt Hitchcock intended to observe these rules in his own chemistry laboratory at Amherst—that is, were he ever to have such a laboratory at Amherst.

Four decades later in *Reminiscences*, Hitchcock would write of Benjamin Silliman,

> ...by whose kindness and instruction my sojourn there [at Yale] was made most profitable. I there learnt how to perform chemical experiments so that they should rarely fail, and this is the grand secret of success in that department. The two principal rules for securing success were these, and I had them fixed to the wall of the laboratory: 1. Never attempt an experiment in public which you have not within a few hours performed in private. 2. No apology to be ever given or received by any one in the laboratory for a failure, but it is to be set down as detracting so much from the skill of the operator.

In early January 1826, after about eight weeks in New Haven, Edward and Orra returned to Massachusetts. Edward likely would have stayed longer were it purely a matter of adequate preparation for his new teaching assignment, but by now his wife was very much "in a family way." Furthermore, Yale was ridden with an epidemic of influenza from which all the Hitchcocks would likely have wished to distance themselves.

AMHERST 1826-1844

Amherst Town Common

11 A Vast Laboratory

"What is the difference between the laws of nature and the agency of God?"

Amherst, April 1826

Early on a chilly morning a flock of ragged Marino sheep grazed idly on the meager tufts of grass on the town common, steam rising in braided wisps from their newly shorn coats. They looked up and stared vacantly at a gaunt figure making his way up College Hill, clutching his black academic robes about him against the damp spring air. That figure was the new professor, Edward Hitchcock, en route to his first class at Amherst College. As he lumbered along, jaw set with determination, body leaning into an icy wind that made every step an effort, his lips moved ever so slightly, perhaps offering a prayer for strength, fortitude, inspiration—all the blessings of Divine Providence necessary to serve his students in this day and those to come.

In late January 1826 Edward and Orra moved into their new home near the center of Amherst with their eighteen-month-old daughter Mary. It was a modest house of white clapboards about a half mile from the campus. Orra naturally would have felt at home here. She had been taught from an early age in one of the town's schoolhouses. At age twenty she had accepted a position as preceptress at Deerfield Academy, but when that institution closed temporarily in 1819, she returned to Amherst where she served as preceptress at Amherst Academy, within sight of their new home. Her father, Jarib White, had been a prominent figure in the town, a wealthy farmer, successful businessman, justice of the peace, constable, tax collector, not to mention a generous benefactor of Amherst College before his death in 1821. One of her brothers, Jay White, was a grocer in town as well as postmaster and town treasurer until his untimely death in 1825. The White family was well-known and respected in this town.

As for Edward, he too found Amherst to his liking, its rolling landscape, broad fields and pastures reminiscent of his hometown, Deerfield, just a few miles to the north. While in New Haven he had thrown himself full throttle into the task of preparing for his new position, performing experiments under the supervision of Benjamin Silliman during the day, reading and recording those hundreds of pages of notes by a flickering candle at night while Orra and little Mary lay fast asleep nearby. But the more he learned of the necessities of a well-equipped laboratory, the more he must have worried over the conditions awaiting him in his new post.

From the very beginning Professor Hitchcock considered the facilities for teaching chemistry at Amherst College inadequate and did not hesitate to make his feelings known. Exactly how his predecessor, Professor Gamaliel S. Olds, taught chemistry is not recorded, but it seems clear that Hitchcock intended to go his own way pedagogically—very much in the Yale mold. As soon as he returned from New Haven he began to accumulate much of the apparatus and supplies essential to his work, furnaces, gasometers, cryophores, cisterns, receivers, matrasses, and retorts, as well as supplies of dozens of reagents needed for the experiments he had planned. At the same time he lobbied for a laboratory to be a part of the new building already under construction. His plea had been heard by the trustees, and they assured him that a laboratory would be part of the new structure, although they proposed to locate it in the basement as mentioned in a letter to Benjamin Silliman:

> They have commenced digging for the new chapel here. After all the Laboratory is to be put partly under ground. I have warned them as loudly & plainly as I can: but they feel too poor to put up a separate building. I hope however by urging them still more to get it nearly all above the soil.

The winter term at Amherst would normally have begun in February but the start of Hitchcock's chemistry course had been delayed, possibly due to illness or perhaps in order to allow for preparation of a temporary, minimally equipped teaching facility. The faculty record for March 7, 1826, includes this entry:

> Voted: That it is expedient to give the Junior Class information as to the time when the Chemical Lectures will commence, and the cause of their delay: Also, That Prof. Hitchcock be requested to meet the class, and inform them on these points and such others connected with them as he may think best.

A letter to Professor Silliman dated 21 March bore all sorts of news:

> Some of us have been sick almost every moment since we came to this place & this with the hurly burly of moving here made my hands pretty full. Mrs. H. is now confined & has a little daughter four or five days old. She is comfortable as we could expect considering her previous indisposition & she desires to [be] affectionately remembered to your self & Mrs. S. The weeks we spent at N. Haven are recollected by us, I assure you, with a great deal of pleasure. The effect upon my health of returning to the north in the winter was bad as I expected it would be…I have yet done nothing in Chemistry.

Thirty-seven years later in his memoir, Edward would recall those early days at Amherst with uncharacteristic humor. There was as yet no laboratory and he was forced to share a small lecture room with President Humphrey:

> I recollect how my risibles were tried one evening after I had been manipulating with chlorine during the day to hear Dr. Humphrey in his introductory petition, apparently unconscious of the odor that was in the room, which the students were snuffing at, pray that the Lord might smell a sweet savor from our offering.

With considerable effort the professor ascended the stairway to the cramped fourth floor lecture hall on that April morning, mounted the podium, and faced his first group of scholars. Like his parishioners in Conway five years earlier, they were no doubt curious about their new teacher, perhaps somewhat daunted by his reputation as a scientist. Some may even have harbored doubts about the value of a course in chemistry—particularly for those who were preparing for the ministry as were most of them.

Fortunately for us Professor Hitchcock prepared a handwritten script for that first lecture. It was equal in length to two or three of his sermons, and reads much like a homily, but with one noteworthy difference. In his sermons *Reverend* Hitchcock presented an air of complete confidence both in himself and his message. But on this day, *Professor* Hitchcock struck a surprisingly different tone, diffident and self-deprecating. Some of his doubts were stated explicitly, others were veiled in lengthy justifications of both himself and his subject matter. The professor's recent career change was still very much on his mind—perhaps on his conscience as well—as he began:

> ...God, in his righteous Providence, has seen fit to render me through bodily debility incapable of properly performing the duties, and sustaining the cares, of a profession that yields to none in importance and sacredness, and in which, therefore, I could have wished to spend the remnant of life. But though Providence may remove us to another sphere of action, no change of circumstances or relations, can release us from the observance of that most comprehensive rule revelation discloses—whether ye eat or drink or whatsoever ye do, do all to the glory of God.

He then admitted to both a "failing heart and a heavy heart" and to the fear that "instead of exciting within you a deep interest I shall produce in your mind an incurable disrelish for a valuable science." He confessed to insufficient preparation for the task before him, for the inability to measure up to the standard of instruction expected in a modern literary institution. The inadequate facilities for teaching chemistry were also cited. He even suggested that it may have been better never to have undertaken the course at all, or that it might have to be abandoned subsequently.

Finally the professor turned his attention to two questions that he suspected were on the minds of many of his students: What is chemistry? and Why should we study chemistry? Here he referred to English chemist William Henry who defined chemistry as "The science the object of which is to discourse and explain the changes of composition that occur among the integrant and constituent parts of different bodies." Chemistry, wrote Hitchcock, thus has a vast domain, encompassing "an almost endless variety of phenomena" from plants and animals to the air we breathe to rocks and minerals:

> From this view of the nature of this science, it is obvious that it has a most comprehensive range, and embraces an almost endless variety of phenomena... Every man witnesses an abundance of them on every side: and indeed every man is a practical chemist...and the world is a vast laboratory, where immeasurable chemical processes are going forward in ceaseless succession.

He went on to argue that no one, not even a former preacher of the Gospel, should be free of the obligation to strive always for the greater glory of God. To do so within the sphere of chemistry, he continued, should present no difficulty: "I refer here to the constant superintendance of Divine Providence, and to man's dependence upon it for life and its comforts." Then he provided a concrete example of that "superintendance" in the chemical composition of earth's atmosphere:

> Mixed together in proportion of one part of oxygen and three of nitrogen these gases constitute the air we breathe and without which we could not exist. Invert these proportions, that is less than three parts of oxygen and one of nitrogen be united and nitric acid will be formed; a gas exceedingly hostile to life, and a most powerful agent in the destruction of vegetable and animal substances. Vary the proportions yet differently, and the result will be nitrous oxide; a gas most remarkable for its exhilarating and intoxicating qualities, and which therefore would be almost equally unfit for respiration. In still different proportions other suffocating gases would be formed, whose prevalence would be destructive of life.

He then asserted that the skeptic, the atheist, the infidel, will deny the very existence of God and any "superintendance." Instead they posit that the universe is regulated merely by the laws of nature as revealed by science. To this argument Hitchcock countered that the two perspectives are really and truly identical: "What is the difference between the laws of nature and the agency of God? Are they not essentially one and the same thing? Is it not God who acts as much in the one case as the other?" Here we see a remarkable transmogrification taking place—a dour professor to evangelical preacher, a vulgar discipline to inspired revelation; the everyday processes of life to the most sublime works of Almighty God, Creator of Heaven and Earth!

Hitchcock proceeded next to a wide-ranging discussion of the many benefits of this science in their lives, what might be described by a phrase from the twentieth century, "better living through chemistry." He enumerated discoveries of chemists that have benefited medicine, metallurgy, embalming, cooking, agriculture, glassmaking, the manufacture of housewares, of pottery and porcelain, bleaching, mordanting, and dyeing of fabric. He placed special emphasis on agriculture, referring to it as the most important of all arts. His words on that subject seem to presage his lifelong effort to promote agricultural education:

> ...[I]f ever agriculture shall make any important progress, she will be indebted directly or indirectly to chemistry for the clew to her improvement. For the whole process of vegetation is a chemical process; and all that it is wanted for greatly increasing the produce of the soil, is to discover a mode in which the chemical agencies of that soil shall be made to lend their greatest energy in supporting vegetable life.

The following year Hitchcock had printed a twenty-four-page booklet that may have served as a course syllabus, albeit a lengthy one that might have discouraged more than a few students. He set out for himself and his students an ambitious prospectus that must have filled many hours in the preparation and delivery. The course no doubt included lengthy discourses, but interspersed with chemical experiments, some of which involved bright flashes of light and loud explosions that gave his young audience no end of fascination and amusement, but may have had a rather different effect on other faculty or townspeople within earshot.

The weeks passed, spring came and went in Amherst, and finally summer. Early in July his chemistry course finally drew to a close, four weeks or so later than the usual termination of the winter term. In a letter to Silliman dated July 7, 1826, Edward brought his friend up to date.

> I closed my chemical course yesterday…Over the latter part of the subject I hurried rapidly…I worked hard & incessantly but was amply repaid by the almost uniform success of the experiments: and I have reason for thankfulness that I have gone through without receiving scarcely a scratch.

So ended Hitchcock's first term of chemistry at Amherst College, the young professor not much the worse for the wear. He would teach the same course nineteen times from 1826 to 1845, usually in the fall term, three lectures and one recitation per week according to his own recollection.

Amherst was a young town in 1826, at least by comparison with several of its neighbors. Hadley, to its west, had been among the first towns established along the Connecticut River in western Massachusetts, being incorporated in 1661. The northeastern portion of Hadley, known for a time as the Third Precinct, consisted of an area "…ten miles and three Quarters in bredth and Seven miles in length," five miles from the center of the town. By the middle of the eighteenth century the maintenance of roads and of schools in that far-flung corner of the town had convinced the town fathers to authorize its separation. It took the name Amherst after a then much-admired Englishman, and the town of Amherst was born in 1776, although it would not receive the official sanction of the Commonwealth until 1787.

In those times the citizens of Amherst had a reputation for being a cantankerous lot, ready to pick a fight at the slightest provocation. Unlike their neighbors Hadley and Northampton which in that era were known for a particularly unsightly brand of political and religious intolerance, folks in Amherst were more inclined to mind their own affairs and allow their neighbors to do the same. The men of Amherst lived up to their feisty reputation when they responded quickly to the call for assistance in Boston following the battles of Lexington and Concord in 1776. A decade later, when Daniel Shays from nearby Pelham gathered a small ragtag army to confront what they regarded as the many egregious misdeeds of the state of Massachusetts, dozens of Amherst men joined him. According to legend, when the small contingent was chased out of Springfield in January 1787, some took refuge in a rock crevice high on the Holyoke Range known locally as the Horse Caves on the southern border of Amherst. The rebellion ended officially with an agreement that Shays's men sign an oath of allegiance to Massachusetts. Over 100 men of Amherst were among the signatories.

But by the third decade of the new century, the town of Amherst had become a more settled, mature community. Perched on a hill only two miles east of Hadley center, it was a town of farmers, tradesmen, and entrepreneurs of all sorts. One account of that period by an early student of the college describes the town as cloaked in a "forest primeval," but all the artists' views of the town at that period suggest otherwise (see page 145). They show mostly open crop fields alternating with pastures dotted with cows, horses, oxen, and sheep. Trees are shown along the stone walls separating the fields and pastures with an occasional small woodlot here and there.

The town in 1826 consisted of some 1400 souls and a few hundred homes, most located along three major thoroughfares, one running east and west, two running north and south. The town common was long and wide, and surrounded by homes, churches, and businesses. Among the shops were several dry goods stores, groceries, a butcher, and a milliner. Small mills were scattered all over the town center, as well as in the outlying districts to the north, east, and south. One of the industries at the time was a rambling structure on the east side of the common where apple cider was distilled to brandy.

Spiritually, Amherst toed the mark of orthodoxy in that era. It had had its own meetinghouse ever since it achieved independence from Hadley a half century earlier, but in recent years the town's spiritual life had proliferated with no fewer than five churches now to be found. It was no doubt much to the relief of Edward and Orra that these churches were all of orthodox Congregationalist persuasion, the threat of Unitarianism having been recently and successfully repelled to the nearby town of Leverett.

Above all else, Amherst was a community that esteemed education, not just for the sons of the wealthy but for all, even for young female scholars. In 1814 Amherst Academy opened its doors for the first time, occupying a large wooden structure on Amity Street in the heart of town. It was largely the work of Reverend Dr. David Parsons, pastor of the First Church, author and lexicographer Noah Webster, and Samuel Dickinson, whose granddaughter Emily would attend the Academy nearly three decades later. The academy drew students not only from the town but from all over New England. Among its first students had been a young woman, Mary Lyon, who harbored some modern notions about female education. There she would meet and befriend the new preceptress, Miss Orra White, an acquaintance that would continue after Orra and Edward married. Thus it could be argued that Amherst Academy gave rise

Figure 27. A portion of an 1833 map of the town of Amherst with the college shown in the lower center. The house labeled "Prof. Hitchcock" adjacent to the college was purchased by Edward and Orra in 1828.

to two institutions of higher learning, Amherst College and Mount Holyoke Female Seminary, later to be known as Mount Holyoke College.

Just a few months after the arrival of Edward and Orra, the town of Amherst welcomed its first newspaper, the *New England Inquirer,* an enterprise of two local businessmen, Samuel C. Carter and John S. Adams. From the start the editors of the *Inquirer* reported news relating to national and international affairs. Featured in early issues were the complete text of a speech by President John Quincy Adams; news about the political activities of General Andrew Jackson; and a report of a New Hampshire cattle show. As to matters of local interest, wrote Carpenter and Morehouse, "...National politics, foreign intelligence, literature, history, these were the essentials, to which were subordinated and relegated almost into nothingness, the gathering and chronicling of purely local news."

Interestingly, the single item of "local intelligence" appearing in the first issue of the *Inquirer* pertained to Professor Hitchcock. He and a group of students, it was reported, had recently launched a hot air balloon some fifteen feet in diameter from the top of College Hill. Just a few months later he would publish an article on the project in the *American Journal of Science and Arts* in which he described the "two or three expedients for causing (the balloon) to ascend more surely and higher," one of which was the provision of a small sponge soaked in alcohol and set alight to heat the air inside the balloon. With a few adjustments after a first trial, he added, "it rose gently till it had attained the height of nearly 2000 feet; being carried, by a slight breeze, nearly two miles horizontally, before the alcohol was exhausted."

If the journalistic content of the *Inquirer* gives but slight insight into the life and culture of Amherst in those days, the advertisements offer considerably more. "LOOK TO YOUR OXEN" reads one prominent display ad by Ebenezer Eames, blacksmith, urging farmers to pay attention to their beasts of burden and not neglect the care of their hooves. Another reads, "Wanted—Boy of 15 or 16 yrs of age as an apprentice in the shoemaking business." Others offer flour and axes, crockery, glassware, salted codfish, fire insurance, as well as the services of a cabinet maker and a coach and wagon maker.

Amherst provided outlets aplenty for Edward's wide-ranging interests in science, in agriculture, and in religion. He likely found the college community agreeable; three of his six colleagues on the faculty were ordained ministers of similar religious persuasion to his. Furthermore, President Humphrey and the Board of Trustees seemed determined to accommodate his needs.

Amherst was an agricultural center in that time, having within its borders dozens of farms. Corn, wheat, rye, and oats were the major crops–cows, oxen, sheep, and swine the major farm animals. Butter production on the town's farms was the fourth largest in the state in 1840. During his youth Edward had engaged in farm work alongside his brothers in Deerfield, and although he would say later that he was ill-suited to that kind of work, he retained a lifelong interest in agriculture. Thus he found he had much in common with his townsmen who farmed, raised cattle, and grew crops. The Hitchcocks always had horses and cows of their own that they pastured on their neighbors' lands.

Even as Edward's energies were devoted principally to his teaching, he also found time to preach. He delivered sermons on at least a dozen Sundays per year in the college chapel or in churches up and down the Connecticut Valley. Perhaps this work was necessary to supplement his college salary—he was paid about five dollars per Sunday—or perhaps he did it out of a sense of obligation. But it was not an easy addition to his labors. In a letter to Professor Silliman he wrote, "I find that one day's preaching injures me more than a whole week's work in the laboratory."

In addition to teaching and preaching, Hitchcock also submitted at least five manuscripts for publication in 1826. Three appeared in the *AJS* including the brief item about the balloon experiment and two papers on his recent mineral explorations. His review of the text used in his chemistry course was published in *North American Review*. He also authored a long treatise entitled "Influence of Nervous Disorders Upon Religious Experience" that appeared in the *Christian Spectator* published at Yale. Ever since Edward's illness and temporary blindness, we find him reporting on almost constant health complaints. In "Nervous Disorders" he explores the link between body and spirit, arguing that diseases of the mind can affect the body and vice versa:

> How soon is a vigorous frame broken down by the ravings of insanity, or the tumult of excited passions! And how often is the giant mind shorn of its strength, and reduced to the feebleness of infancy, through the influence of its disordered and enfeebled tenement.

He seems to identify with those who suffer with such conditions, not only with their battle with pain and mental anguish, but with the ridicule of friends, family, and medical professionals:

> Those who enjoy firm health, are led to impute all to imagination; and to say it is spleen, or hypochondriasis, or hysterics, or vapours...[I]n order to cure such complaints, these persons think it necessary only to divert the attention of the patient from himself, and convince him that he has no disorder upon him, and that he will be well enough, if he leaves off attention to diet and regimen, and eats, and drinks, and lives, like other folks.

Edward Hitchcock would soon become a fixture at Amherst College, quickly earning a reputation as an innovative teacher with a flair for showmanship, an indefatigable researcher, and an inspired preacher. To such a list of accolades the professor might well have made one addition of his own: an old man enfeebled in both body and mind who must be ready at any moment to be called home to his Maker.

Hitchcock Home in Amherst

12 The Balance of the Universe

"...You have not yet seen nature but mineralogy has furnished you with eyes for her examination."

Amherst, July 13, 1828

Several dozen parishioners sat in the front pews of the college chapel on a Sunday morning, the sun's rays bathing the chancel in a soft glow. The structure was newly completed as the smell of fresh wood and paint testified, and this occasion had special significance—it would be the first christening performed there.

Edward Hitchcock stood stern faced before the pulpit. At his side stood his wife, Orra, holding their infant son, gazing on the child much like the Madonna gazing on Jesus in a painting of Raphael. The baby was dressed in a white, hand tatted gown. Next to her stood their two daughters, Mary and Catherine, looking wide-eyed at the large space and the audience before them.

Reverend Humphrey read several passages of scripture on baptism. He reminded the parents of their duties in the Christian upbringing of a child. He spoke to the congregation of their duty to support the family, to love the child as their own. He then performed the rite of baptism.

"Edward, I baptize thee in the name of the Father, the Son, and the Holy Ghost."

Edward Hitchcock, Senior, then offered a prayer, one he had written on the day of the boy's birth just six weeks earlier: "I do now most solemnly and unreservedly and so far as I know my heart sincerely consecrate this child to God in body and soul for time and eternity. O God accept the consecration and employ this child as an instrument of doing thy will. Whether it will promote thy glory most to call him early out of life or to make him a minister of thy gospel or missionary of the cross O God thou knowest—but I know not. Do with him therefore as seemeth good in thy sight."

Following the benediction offered by Reverend Humphrey, the small congregation rose and sang a hymn of praise to God.

The child who was anointed on that day would live all but about eight years of his life on the campus of Amherst College, even longer than his father or mother. He would attend thousands of services in that very chapel, the last of which would be his funeral service, February 18, 1911.

By 1828, the year in which Edward Hitchcock, Jr., was baptized in the new Johnson Chapel, Amherst College must have seemed to many of its faculty, students, and friends, as an old, well established institution. In truth it was very young and still struggling to establish itself. It had been born less than a decade earlier in a most unlikely time.

The Panic of 1819, as it came to be known, was a recession, probably a depression by present-day standards, and one that was felt by every citizen. Jobs became scarce, inflation spiked, banks failed, bankruptcies were commonplace. At Deerfield Academy enrollment fell and the school was shuttered. Yet just ten miles away in Amherst, a group of citizens was contemplating what would have been considered a bold move in the best of times. The founders of Amherst Academy, with a few new faces, were about to launch a literary institution, as yet unnamed, also to be located in Amherst, and dedicated to the education of "young men of hopeful piety" for the Christian ministry.

At about the same time the trustees of Williams College, located about forty miles from Amherst in the far-flung northwest corner of the Commonwealth, were petitioning the state legislature for permission to relocate the campus, perhaps to Northampton, perhaps to Amherst. Edward Hitchcock was at that time an unofficial student at Yale. He weighed in on the debate in a letter published in the *Franklin Herald* of December 8, 1818, that he entitled "A Dream Respecting the Removal of Williams College." In this dream, he describes the many favorable qualities of Deerfield Academy, and offers a proposal:

> I then dreamed that the Academy on which I sat (Deerfield), contained near thirty rooms, twenty of which were study rooms, two for recitation, one dining hall capable of accommodating 80 persons, and the rest for the accommodation of a steward...I also dreamed that the...Trustees of said institution had offered to give all this property, amounting to 21,000 dollars, to the Board of Williams College, provided they would locate that College in Deerfield: and to this sum I dreamed the inhabitants of the place had added a few thousand dollars. My dream was proceeding and I doubt not would have completely removed and located Williams College, had not my wife, at that moment, in endeavouring to revive the fire, thrown down a pair of tongs, which awakened me.

The Amherst group expressed an interest in having Williams relocate to Amherst, but it was not to be. The petition to the state legislature was denied—Williams College would remain in Williamstown. Two years later, its president, Zephaniah Swift Moore, who had favored the move to a more populous location, accepted the position of first President of the new literary institution in Amherst. To add insult to injury, Moore took with him fifteen Williams students, thus ensuring his status as *persona non grata* with his former institution in perpetuity.

Despite this initial setback, the Amherst group proceeded with plans to establish its own literary institution in Amherst. Funds were raised, mostly from local subscribers, for the construction of a single building on a large parcel of land donated by Elijah Dickinson close to the center of town. On September 19, 1821, the college opened officially and admitted forty-seven students. The original building was put up rather hastily. Although early views of the campus suggest a handsome building in a bucolic setting, the true state of affairs was considerably less grand. South College, as it would later be known, was square and austere. It contained some thirty-two student rooms, had no lighting fixtures, no central heating, and no plumbing. The bedroom and study of two seniors in the first class also served as a recitation room during the day. The college library totaled 700 volumes and was contained in a single bookshelf in the building's foyer. The college grounds, according to King, were maintained in "a natural state," i.e., no paths, no landscaping, no plantings. Edward Hitchcock, Jr., who grew up on the campus in the 1830s and later

Figure 28.
Reverend Zephaniah Swift Moore (1770-1823), first president of Amherst College

attended the college, remembered the early campus as an unsightly gravel pit with few walkways and mud everywhere.

The second commencement at Amherst College took place on Wednesday, August 23, 1826. The following day, prospective entering freshmen took qualifying examinations to determine their readiness for college studies. A week later, the new academic year began.

Professor Hitchcock's teaching schedule for this and the next five or six academic years included chemistry in the first or fall term, chemistry and mineralogy in the second or winter term, botany and geology in the third or summer term. His classes normally consisted entirely of juniors, although other students were permitted to sit in as space permitted. In most years he could expect between forty and fifty students in each class.

For Professor Hitchcock the new term began much as had the previous one, he and his students jammed together in the crowded fourth floor room of North College. But there were hopeful signs that his chemistry laboratory would soon be completed. As indicated in a letter to Silliman dated October 4, 1826, the preparations were considerable: "I hope, by the leave of Providence, to commence lecturing in chemistry in a week or two in the new laboratory, which is approaching to completion. I find there is no end to the labour of fitting up the rooms."

That his new home would be in the basement of the just completed chapel was a source of worry and annoyance, but still it had to be a great relief to at last be better situated for his teaching. He may also have been heartened by the support of the college administration which, despite the financial constraints of the young institution, would soon commit to both manpower and wherewithal for the laboratory. For the first two terms he recruited Orra's brother, George White (AC 1825), as his assistant in chemistry. By the next academic year Lucius F. Clarke (AC 1827) had been hired. The trustees also allocated $110 per academic year for supplies for the laboratory beginning in 1828.

Even at the end of his second term of chemistry, Professor Hitchcock must have felt the need for further improvement of his chemistry skills. Once again he trundled off to New Haven, this time in spite of winter's assaults on his frail constitution. In one of his letters from Yale he tells Orra that he has been ill and confined to bed for two days with rheumatism, indigestion, and a pain in his side induced by cutting too much wood for his host. That letter also reveals that he was sharing a room with two Amherst acquaintances, Sylvester Hovey and Joseph Ware, but was thankful that they were away presently as there was only one bed in the room.

Back in Amherst, he began his first class in mineralogy in February 1827. This was a discipline in which he must surely have felt more at home than chemistry. He had been a collector of rocks and minerals since boyhood and had accumulated a large personal collection. He read extensively in the field. And he had published six papers in the *American Journal of Science and Arts* on geology and mineralogy. His lecture notes begin with a tribute to the Maker for the incredible beauty of the mineral kingdom:

> Gentlemen, So confusedly blended are the inorganic materials of our globe to the eye of common observation and so defaced are the surfaces of rocks and minerals by the hand of time that it would seem improbable such a science as mineralogy could ever exist. Yet when careful observation turns its keen eye upon this department of nature and reveals the internal structure of the mineral masses of our globe, a scene of beauty and order is laid open little expected exhibiting the same evidence of Divine wisdom as is found in the animal and vegetable world.

He proceeds to define mineralogy as "…the science that has for its object a knowledge of all those bodies destitute of organization which exist within the earth or on its surface," the phrase "destitute of organization" meant to distinguish minerals from living things. Here he limits the term "mineral" to homogenous bodies while rocks, the objects of the science of geology, consist of an agglomeration of multiple minerals.

As the text for his course that year Hitchcock selected a new work, *An Elementary Treatise of Mineralogy and Geology,* by the Harvard trained geologist Parker Cleaveland. In his notes he quotes Cleaveland often, including his typology of minerals based on geometry: cube, regular tetrahedron, dodecahedron with rhombic faces, octahedron with triangular faces, rhomb, four-sided prism, and regular hexahedral prism. He appends to that list another eight forms based on the British crystallographer Henry James Brooke. His lecture notes include frequent reminders to himself to use visual aids such as, "Exhibit the models that illustrate this subject." He then launches into an extended discussion of crystals, at the end of which he digresses for several pages to a biography of the eminent French crystallographer, Rene Just Haüy, often referred to as Abbé Haüy.

Finally, Hitchcock enumerates the characteristics, both external and internal, that distinguish minerals. He begins with color, although he says of color in minerals that it is, "…one of the most striking but least valuable characteristics." He proceeds to name nearly one hundred mineral colors. Of white alone he lists eight variations: snow white, reddish white, yellowish white, silver white, greyish white, greenish white, milk white, and tin white. Other external characteristics of minerals include luster, transparency, refraction, geometrical forms, surface, touch, coldness, odor, taste, adhesion to the tongue, soil or stain, streak and powder, concretions, flexibility, elasticity, sound, cohesion, hardness, structure, fracture, tenacity, magnetism, electricity, phosphorescence, specific gravity, fusiblity, reaction to acids and other tests, chemical composition, and optical properties.

Geology followed Mineralogy in most years. In fact, Professor Hitchcock treated them as parts of a single course. Again we are fortunate to have his lecture notes for the first geology class in which he offers some introductory remarks on the subject.

> Gentlemen, We are now to direct our attention to those vast mineral masses that constitute the mountains the crust and indeed in so far as they have been penetrated the internal parts of our globe. By attending to mineralogy you have acquired a knowledge of those simple or homogeneous minerals that either singly or united to one another compose those extensive and solid deposits around us denominated rocks. To apply a lively remark of the Abbé Haüy you have not yet seen nature but mineralogy has furnished you with eyes for her examination.

While mineralogy focuses largely on minute objects, he observes, geology has a much wider scope, including all the inanimate matter of the earth. But it is a discipline with a number of difficulties associated with it. For one, rocks are so highly variable in their characteristics that: "He (the geologist) finds rocks so gradually passing into one another that in many cases the extremes meet and he cannot tell to which side a given specimen belongs."

Still further complicating the field are the many changes that rocks have undergone over time, changes due to "air, water, and fire." And there is the vast area of the earth to be understood:

> It is not enough that a man examine his own district. He must know what are the appearances in other regions and in every quarter of the world that has been examined. Multitudes mistaking their own narrow sphere of observation for the world have gravely made inferences and framed hypotheses which served only to show their ignorance of other regions and to bring their labours into neglect and contempt.

Much of the material of interest to the geologist, he adds, is buried, sometimes under just a few inches of soil, but sometimes under hundreds of feet: "The only point which can unravel the apparent chaos of a complex region of country may be covered up by the loose soil too deeply to be investigated or that point may be buried in the oceans unfathomable depths."

Finally, he adds that a difficulty for many in acquiring a knowledge of geology is what we might call "preconceived notions." In Hitchcock's own words, "…no small difficulty exists in the influence of theory over the judgment of the geologist causing him to see facts in false colouring."

To what theories does he refer? The professor alludes to "two conflicting hypotheses," those of a German geologist, Abraham Gottlob Werner, and a

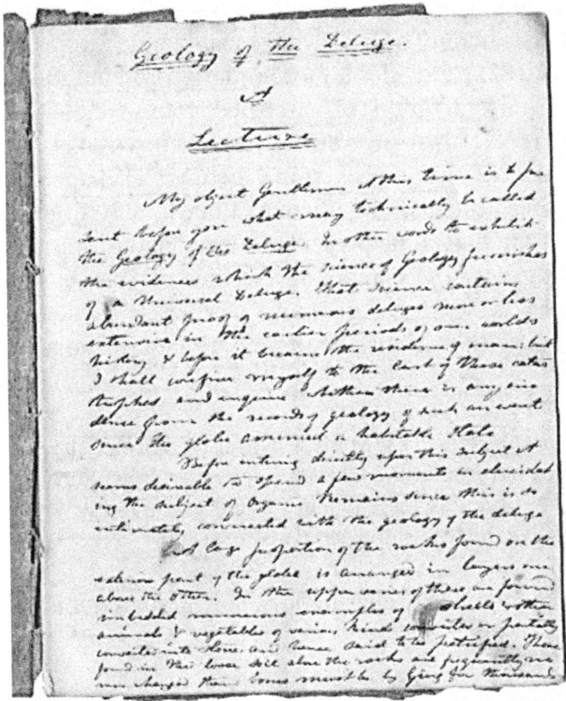
Geology of the Deluge.
A
Lecture.

Figure 29. The first page of Edward Hitchcock's lecture, "Geology of the Deluge," ca 1828

Scottish geologist, James Hutton. Werner postulated that earth's rocks were formed by crystallization from the waters of a great ocean, a theory later dubbed Neptunism. He argued that the structure of the earth was like that of an onion, with similar layers of rock deposited in the same sequence worldwide. Hutton argued that those rocks were products of magmatic activity, then laid down on the ocean bottom. His theory became known as Plutonism. Hutton is best known for the principle of uniformitarianism, the idea that the processes that created the earth in the past were the same as those going on at the present time.

Many geology texts of his day began with an explanation of these major systems of thought in the field, but not Professor Hitchcock. In fact, he explains, he will reverse that order, beginning with accounts of rocks and rock formations themselves, and only toward the end of the course introducing those competing theories. Why? He offers this analogy: "Let any man witness the conflict between two pugilists whom he never saw and it will be impossible for him not to acquire a prepossession in favor of one of them and a desire that he should be the conqueror…" Not wishing to prejudice his students, he proceeds to lay out the facts of geology as he perceived them. Of course, the professor suffered from one weakness in geology, his own limited horizons. He had traveled extensively in western Massachusetts by this age, but had seen little of the larger world, although he had read extensively on the subject.

The remainder of that notebook includes a lengthy outline of the rest of his geology course, although it consists mainly of lists of rocks and land features. A later notebook (likely from after 1835) includes a more orderly presentation of the course, beginning with a consideration of stratified rocks, including sedimentary and metamorphic rocks, then unstratified or igneous rocks. He discusses the mineral composition of rocks, rock strata, geological maps and sections. He then discusses ores, metals, ornamental stones, and organic remains. Finally, as promised at the outset, he presents an extended discussion of the history of geology, ending with the competing theories of Werner and Hutton as well as some new ideas of the French geologist Cordier.

His introductory lecture ends with a discussion of the intimate relationship between geology and religion:

> Still greater attention has been attracted to the subject in consequence of the bearing many of its discoveries have upon the Christian revelation. Geology has long been regarded by the infidel as his vantage ground and not a few defenders of the Bible have, to say the least, ably contested the field.

To his audience, many of them young men preparing for the Christian ministry, he adds:

> This relation of geology to Revelation renders it very desirable that every man who wishes to be thoroughly acquainted with the evidences of Christianity should be conversant with this science. For I hesitate not to say that the Christian ignorant of the subject cannot defend the Mosaic history against the attacks of the infidel geologist.

With the benefit of several centuries of hindsight, historians of science might today be inclined to regard "Christian revelation" as one of those theories or systems of thought that had a detrimental effect on the investigations of many geologists. The scriptures tell of a Great Flood, and for centuries scientists sought for evidence of such a flood. Soon, very soon, geologists would have to admit that the evidence was abundant that a Great Flood, if there ever was such an event, was not the most important influence in shaping the earth, that life had existed on the planet not just for a few thousand years as indicated in the scriptures, but for millions, even billions, of years. And that humankind, far from being a special and separate entity, was a product of that selfsame process.

Professor Hitchcock applied the same attention to his teaching methodology as he did to his scientific and religious pursuits. In chemistry he utilized demonstrations of chemical reactions, often with dramatic effects. In mineralogy he employed models of molecules and crystals to help his students visualize them. In geology he turned to his wife for assistance in illustrating rock formations, cross sections, and maps with murals that could be displayed across the recitation room walls for all to see. They were rendered in pen and

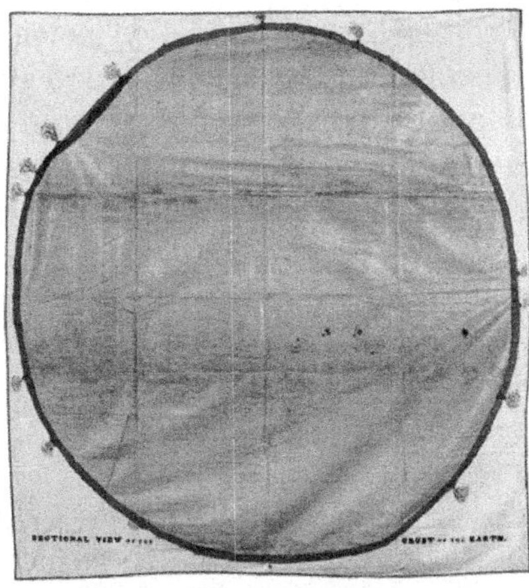

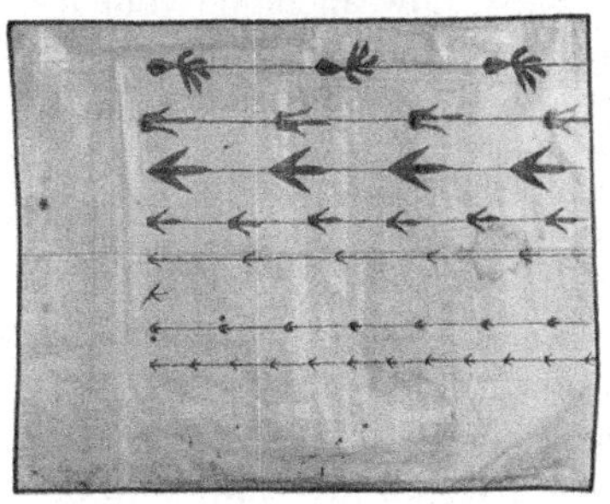

Figure 30. Posters by Orra White Hitchcock for use in Edward Hitchcock's classes at Amherst College. Above, sectional view of the earth, 72¼" x 73¼"; below, *Ornithichnites* tracks, 27" x 65½"

ink on linen, often brightly colored, labeled in bold lettering, with features emphasized which Edward would be commenting on. Many of these were very large; her cross section of the earth is six feet in diameter, her chart of the mollusks when fully extended, nearly sixteen feet long.

Geology was the one course that Professor Hitchcock continued to teach throughout his presidency and during his retirement. On November 8, 1862, just a year and three months before his death, he recorded this entry in his notes:

> I finished my course of instruction with the Class of 1863 in Geology which makes my 37th or 38th class since 1825. It has been a hard struggle this year but has not perhaps injured me. Towards the close I have not been able to walk up College Hill but my horse has carried me up.

Despite Professor Hitchcock's demanding teaching schedule, he continued to do research and publish papers and reviews in scholarly journals. From 1827 to

1830 he published three articles on mineralogy in the *American Journal of Science and Arts.* Two other publications in this period involved his students. In 1828 he set them to the task of translating a paper of the French geologist M. Louis Cordier, *Essay on the Temperature of the Interior of the Earth,* then penned a lengthy review of that paper and another on volcanoes by English geologist George Julius Poulett Scrope that appeared in the *North American Review* the following year. In the same year his students took the initiative in seeking publication of their professor's *Catalogue of Plants Growing Without Cultivation in the Vicinity of Amherst College* to which they added this introductory note addressed to Professor Hitchcock:

> Respected Sir,—Understanding that you have prepared in manuscript a catalogue of the plants, which are found in the vicinity of this place, the members of the Junior class, now attending your lectures on the subject of botany, in the belief that their knowledge of the science, and the interest of their botanical tours, may be increased by the possession of such a work, request your consent to the favour of its publication.

All this exertion on behalf of science apparently did not diminish in the least the professor's interest in matters spiritual. During the same period he published two articles on religion in Christian journals: "Importance of an Early Consecration to Missionary Work," and "Why Do You Not Exchange with Unitarians?" Another paper, "Essay on Temperance Addressed Particularly to Students and the Young Men of America," won an award from the American Tract Society which published it in 1830.

One of Hitchcock's published articles during that period may well have set the course of his research interests for the next decade. In 1828 *AJS* published his review of *Report on the Geology of North Carolina* completed several years previously by Denison Olmsted. A Connecticut native and Yale graduate, Olmsted undertook a geological survey for the state of North Carolina beginning in 1824 at a time when there were rumors of gold in that state. Besides the geological content of the report that Hitchcock found of interest, he was at pains to point out that here, for the first time in the history of the nation, a state legislature had authorized and underwritten a geological survey. Hitchcock hailed Olmsted's project as "a good example to hold up before other legislatures, to induce them to adopt a similar course," a pronouncement that would be fulfilled in large measure by Hitchcock himself just two years later.

In summer 1828, just a few weeks before the birth of Edward, Jr., the Hitchcocks moved from their modest lodgings in the village center to a rambling farmhouse adjacent to the Amherst College campus. From its front porch could be seen nearly all the buildings of Amherst College. Now with three children, Edward, Mary, and Catherine, life would never be the same for Edward and

Orra. Their new home would quickly become a beehive of activity as the lives of the entire family intertwined with the life of the college.

For Professor Hitchcock the third or summer term beginning in 1827 was given over to botany. Again we have the benefit of the professor's detailed script for the first class as well as a small notebook in which the entire course is outlined. In early June of 1827, he once again mounted the podium in North College:

> The science in whose investigation I invite you this morning to engage embraces one of the grand divisions of natural history, and in extent and variety it far exceeds the two other departments. While not more than 30,000 species of animals have been described, and only a few hundred minerals, 50,000 plants have been already registered in the calendar of the botanist.

Consistent with other botanists of his time, he includes fungi and algae in the plant kingdom. Plants are living organized beings springing from seeds and deriving their nourishment from inorganic substances. He further limits the discipline when he adds,

> It belongs to chemistry to ascertain the simple principles that enter into their composition and medicine develops their salutary efficacy upon the animal system. But botany distinguishes their external forms—arranges them into distinct groups or families—exhibits their internal structures—their histories, their habits, their geography and natural affinities.

He reminds his audience that botany is supremely suited to the attentions of Christians: "The noble and ingenious mind, which is fired with whatever is grand and beautiful does not need a logical array of arguments to induce it to the study of the works of God."

With these introductory remarks concluded, he proceeds to outline the discipline of botany. It includes plant nomenclature, taxonomy, phytography, anatomy, phytochemy, and phytonomy ("the manner in which plants originate, grow from their parts, and propagate themselves"). He proceeds to a detailed survey of the anatomy of plants, from roots and stems to leaves, flowers, and fruits. Along the way, he identifies a number of the chemical compounds known then to occur in plants—resins, gums, sugars, acids, tannins, waxes, pigments, and silex (silica). He also describes the absorption into a plant of essential minerals from the soil.

It is interesting how little mention he makes of what we know today to be the most fundamental feature of a plant's physiology, photosynthesis. Of course, the term had not yet been invented and would not be for some decades to come. But he seems to attribute little importance to the process by which a plant manufactures its own organic molecules. Nevertheless, he does make this interesting comment toward the end of the course based on the work of the English scientist and theologian Joseph Priestley:

> …[T]he leaves of vegetables during the day absorb from the atmosphere carbonic acid and give off oxygen and a small quantity of nitrogen. In the night… this process was in part reversed and that carbonic acid is given off into the atmosphere and oxygen absorbed... that animals both by respiration and perspiration generate large quantities of carbonic acid by the former process take from the atmosphere a portion of its oxygen…How natural then to suppose this to be one of those examples of compensation by which the Creator maintains the balance of the universe! No wonder philosophers have adopted such a beautiful hypothesis even if it had the slightest evidence in its favour!

He goes on at some length on the possible relationships between plants, animals, and the atmosphere—what we know today as the carbon cycle. He seems to harbor doubts about the idea, and at the end of his discussion reminds himself to add a warning to his young listeners "on the dangers of putting large flowerpots in small rooms and sleeping there," presumably for fear that the plants will exhaust the oxygen in the room and thus asphyxiate the sleeper.

Again the professor employs visual aids in his teaching, with frequent reminders in his lecture notes to display various plant artifacts such as bark samples, stem sections, tree rings, and pith. He makes notes of dozens of Orra's drawings and paintings to display in the lecture room including illustrations of xylem and phloem, plant cells, flower stalks, inflorescences, and floral structures such as pistils, stamens, and corollas. At one point his musings take an unexpected turn. Botanical studies, he asserts, are beneficial for health:

> I would recommend the study of botany because it affords an opportunity and an inducement to that kind and degree of bodily exercise which is indispensable to the health and success of the student…Now botany not merely furnishes an inducement to give exercise to the body, but it gives also that diversion of mind which is wanted. It exercises the student's faculties in his rambles just enough to turn them off from severe studies but not enough to fatigue.

And he has a warning for his young audience: "Depend upon it that if you once suffer those hundred headed diseases to get firmly seated in your constitution which are now making such dreadful ravages in the learned world—if you get once firmly locked in their grasp they will never let you go." That cause, good health through temperance—in food, in drink, in all things—soon would become Professor Hitchcock's new passion, for himself and his students.

Amherst from Mount Pleasant, 1835

13 The Blessings of Temperance

"This trait in my character has enabled me to do what little I have done as a literary man."

Deerfield, October 1833

Dr. Stephen West Williams had been chopping firewood outside his home when he saw the lank figure of his cousin approaching. "Professor Hitchcock, my good sir," he said exuberantly, burying the ax in the chopping block and turning to extend his hand.

Hitchcock doffed his hat, then shook hands. "Dr. Williams. You look in good health."

"Well, sir, I suppose I am," he replied. "My bride keeps me well provisioned," he added with a smile, at the same time patting his belly, as if still savoring his last meal. "And you, sir, are well?"

Hitchcock grimaced. There was a pause. "Are you managing to keep the good people of this town free of disease?" he replied, clearly avoiding the question.

"I wish I could say as much, Cousin, but there is a good deal going around this season. And I fear for the long winter to come. What brings you to the town of your birth?"

"Mrs. Hitchcock and I have been visiting with my brothers and their families—and Mother. Henry and Charles have promised me a wagon load of hay which we need dearly. And of course the ladies love to dote on the children." Another pause. "I see your name often in the intelligence from Boston. You have been widely spoken of by the learned men of that city."

Dr. Williams smiled sheepishly. "Well, they sometimes go on a little too much, I fear, of flattery. But I have been studying the diseases of Deerfield and Franklin County—croup, dysentery, scarlet fever, typhus, consumption—accumulating numbers that might reveal the distribution and possible causes of disease."

Hitchcock was interested. "Yes, I read one of your papers—on scarlatina. Most informative. That you apply the laws of physics and mathematics to disease is a refreshingly different and modern approach."

"Well, thank you, sir. I take that as high praise from a man of letters such as yourself. I am hopeful that it will lead in time to new measures to fortify our citizens against these plagues and pestilences." Then he posed the question again. "And your health, is it satisfactory?" Hitchcock's glum demeanor gave the doctor the answer he was seeking. "Is it the dyspepsy? I recall you made mention of it when we last met at the Agricultural Fair last summer."

Hitchcock nodded. "Never have I felt so acutely the effects of that illness, Doctor. It will be my undoing, I have no doubt. Do your researches offer any insights for sufferers like myself?"

"I confess that I have not studied it in depth. Not to say that it is not common amongst us, but it seems so often to be confounded with other conditions—overindulgence, ardent spirits, nervous disorders. And it seldom in my experience leads to mortality." Hitchcock nodded. "But there is a physician in London who has been carrying out some interesting investigations, especially with regard to nervous conditions in women," offered Williams. "A Dr. Thomas if I recall. I'll try to find one of his papers and post it to you."

"I would much appreciate it, Cousin," replied Hitchcock. "I confess that I have little in the way of scientific evidence to support my beliefs, although I do have a body and a spirit that are stark evidence. I have actually written a volume on the subject myself."

"A book. My goodness, that is a great undertaking. With all your other duties, how do you manage to find time for such an endeavor?"

An ironic smile broke across the professor's face as he looked into the eyes of his longtime friend. "Writing a book about dyspepsia has taught me one thing of which I have no doubt: should one wish to avoid dyspepsia, the last thing one should do is attempt to write a book about it."

"There is no probability that I shall live until my children (if God spares their lives) have known me from their personal observations of the character, opinions, and feelings of their father," wrote Edward Hitchcock in 1828 in the first entry in his notes. "It has occurred to me that some short remarks of mine relating to my history, feelings, and opinions might be no unprofitable or unacceptable legacy to leave them." Providence, as it turned out, would be generous far beyond his expectations. He would live another thirty-five years—and his "short remarks" would run to nearly 500 pages. While his notes offer many details of his spiritual and professional life, they also speak volumes of the fragile condition of his physical and mental health over that period.

In that first entry Hitchcock recounted his past struggles with illness and debility. First, there was his encounter in his teens with "a slight epidemic disease." The illness passed, but the long-term effect was devastating:

> From that day to the present I have never spent an hour in reading without suffering severely from pain in my eyes: and for a year or more such was their weakness that I was compelled to abandon almost entirely my classical studies. All my plans for life—my high hopes of distinction among men of science were thus blasted in a moment.

He also reported having suffered from digestive maladies since the age of eighteen, a condition he referred to as dyspepsia. "In early life," he recalled, "I had been troubled with what seemed to be a scrofulous diathesis to which was added a dyspeptic habit, before the age of twenty…" It was a condition he believed he had inherited from his mother's side of the family.

Hitchcock's notes over the succeeding decades reveal a man consumed by worry about his health. Believing dyspepsia to be the most common malady afflicting modern man, he felt it was a subject that would be of the greatest interest to the students of Amherst College. He was troubled by the dietary habits he observed in them such as eating between meals, particularly apples, nuts, raisins, and other fruits.

> Indeed, some cannot cease their champing, during the short hour of lecture or recitation; and they make it a rule, just as some animals do, to strew every room where they are admitted, with the husks, the shells, and the cores.

He was convinced that the mental exertions of the scholar put demands on his body that required modifications in diet and regimen.

In 1830 he delivered a series of lectures on dyspepsia to the students of Amherst College. Later that year he published, at his own expense, a book based on those lectures entitled *Dyspepsy Forestalled and Resisted: Diet, Regimen, & Employment; Delivered to the Students of Amherst College; Spring Term, 1830.*

Dyspepsy, he begins, refers to difficulty in digestion characterized by a sense of fullness and uneasiness after eating, of heartburn, nausea, chilliness, lassitude, drowsiness, disturbed sleep, vivid dreams, headache, nervousness, disordered bowels, and a variety of associated symptoms. It is a nervous disorder, he asserts, but this should not be understood to mean that the condition has no physical basis or that it is a mere product of a nervous personality. In its advanced stages dyspepsy governs all the functions of the body including mental and spiritual. Dyspeptics often suffer from despondency, melancholy, hopelessness, self-doubt, and paranoia:

> The mere throbbing of the temples, or a shooting pain, which the healthy man would scarcely feel, will sometimes produce such an anxiety in the mind of the invalid, as to make him fear that his last sickness has come and then his imagination will paint before him, all the terrors of the final struggle; the agonizing parting of friends; the failure of sensation; the ravings of delirium; the shroud, the funeral, and the dark grave. And still worse, his hopeless prospects in futurity, will be arrayed in all their blackness before him, awakening intolerable forebodings, and realizing to him all the horrors of a hardened sinner's dying hour.

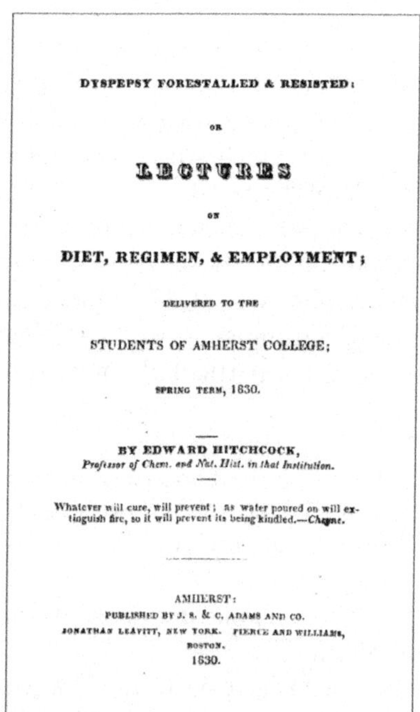

DYSPEPSY FORESTALLED & RESISTED:

OR

LECTURES

ON

DIET, REGIMEN, & EMPLOYMENT;

DELIVERED TO THE

STUDENTS OF AMHERST COLLEGE;

SPRING TERM, 1830.

BY EDWARD HITCHCOCK,

Professor of Chem. and Nat. Hist. in that Institution.

Whatever will cure, will prevent; as water poured on will extinguish fire, so it will prevent its being kindled.—*Cheyne.*

AMHERST:

PUBLISHED BY J. S. & C. ADAMS AND CO.

JONATHAN LEAVITT, NEW YORK. PIERCE AND WILLIAMS, BOSTON.

1830.

Figure 31. Title page of *Dyspepsy Forestalled and Resisted*, 1831

In the first lecture Hitchcock marshals a good deal of evidence for his theories about the causes and remedies of dyspepsia, much of it from the works of contemporary physicians. He enumerates at great length examples of individuals, many of them famous, who overcame digestive disorders by limiting the quantity and types of food and drink in their diets. One limited himself to milk, water, and vegetables, another to bread and water, another to half a pint of gruel twice a day. Some followed general guidelines, but others observed strict limits—for example, no more than twelve ounces of solid food and fifteen ounces of water per day. He discusses regimen, including under that heading "Exercise, Air, Clothing, Cleanliness, Evacuations, Sleep, Manners, and the Influence of the Imagination and Passions upon health." Here again he cites the testimony of illustrious men, one who walked 2000 miles and rode 3000 miles per year to great benefit.

Some digestive maladies, he argues, are the result of all manner of activities that may contribute to a "disordered imagination" and hence to dyspepsia. He then cites a long list of common causes of dyspepsia compiled by an unnamed English physician, a list he admits is somewhat amusing: theatres, hackney coaches, places of worship, indulgence in wine, spirits, or smoking, indolence, sudden changes in the atmosphere, prevalence of the North or East winds, force of imagination, gluttony, quack medicines, love, grief, gambling, contagion, study, and reading novels.

The remedies for dyspepsy, Hitchcock goes on to argue, are moderation in eating and drinking, plenty of physical exercise, and rest. He devotes the bulk of his lectures to a series of proscriptions: "Eat vastly less in quantity than you do—eat of one dish only at a meal—eat little or no animal food—drink much less—drink water—walk ten miles where you now go one—retire early to rest, and rise early." In short, be regular and temperate in all things. He places particular stress on the benefits of bread and milk, arguing that these were placed around the world by God for man's benefit and were therefore healthful. He warns sternly against the dangers of consuming "ardent spirits."

Regarding regimen, he recommends that literary men should devote several hours per day to outdoor exercise, preferably preceding meals, and when possible combined with "…some interesting object of pursuit or harmless diversion" such as natural history or gardening. He also commends the benefits of fresh air, of loose, comfortable clothing, and of frequent bathing. As to "evacuations" he has this advice for his students:

> The grand object is, to secure a movement of the bowels, in most cases, once a day—in some cases, it does not seem necessary more than once in two days. Let there be, however, a stated time, and immediately after breakfast is the best time, for attending to this business. Even if no desire for the exoneration of the bowels be felt, let the proper place be regularly visited at the stated time, and habit will help nature.

In his litany of proscriptions and advice, Hitchcock does not hesitate to take on one uniquely American institution:

> But what shall I say of that chef d'oeuvre of licensed gluttony, a New England Thanksgiving? I would not be thought to condemn an institution, so hallowed by religious, patriotic, and domestic associations; and really so happy in its influence upon the community. But I condemn its monstrous abuses by stuffing and gormandizing, and even sanctioning gluttony by religious acts.

We can well imagine the reaction of his students to such a compendium of proscriptions. Late in life he would admit that the reception was not entirely favorable:

> In no way, perhaps, have I made myself more widely, and perhaps I may say unfavorably known than by my lectures in the College…on Diet and Regimen. I did indeed give some severe, and perhaps uncharitable blows, against some of the dietetic habits of the community.

The response of the students of Amherst College was much more enthusiastic toward another related cause. In the same year that he delivered his lectures on dyspepsia, Hitchcock and his friend, John Tappan, founded the Antivenenean Society at Amherst College. Members were required to sign a pledge promising not to indulge in "Ardent Spirit, Wine, Opium and Tobacco," except for medicinal purposes and for celebrating the Lord's Supper. According to his own careful records, nearly 1500 Amherst students signed the pledge over the following thirty-two years, close to three quarters of the student population in that period. This was a matter of considerable pride for Edward Hitchcock, as he noted in *Reminiscences* late in life: "I have succeeded, by the help of my colleagues, in keeping the temperance flag flying for more than thirty years. Let those who come after me see to it that it be not torn down and trampled in the dust."

Several years after his lectures and the publication of *Dyspepsy Forestalled and Resisted,* Hitchcock took up the subject again, this time in a series of three articles—they were called sermons—published in 1834 in *The American National Preacher*: "Nature of Intemperance in Eating," "Consequences of Intemperance in Eating," and "Blessings of Temperance in Food." A handwritten manuscript entitled "Pleas for Intemperance in Eating Considered," possibly intended as the fourth in the series, was never published.

Despite his claim to understand dyspepsia and the means of avoiding it, Hitchcock suffered from gastrointestinal disorders throughout his adult life. "I thought I had known before nearly everything that could be known of the horrors of dyspepsy," he wrote in his notes, "but I had scarcely entered the vestibule of this inquisitor's torturing house." Dyspepsy, he would observe late in life, took hold of him at an early age "and has never since let go its hold."

By 1834 Edward's cousin, Dr. Stephen West Williams, had made a name for himself both as a physician in Deerfield and as a scientist. Around the age of twenty, Williams had decided to follow in his father's footsteps and pursue a career in medicine. He apprenticed with his father, then studied medicine at Columbia College in New York City from 1812 to 1813 before returning to

Deerfield to start his practice. In Dr. Williams's time, contagious diseases such as dysentery, cholera, scarlet fever, and tuberculosis took an enormous toll in New England. Like any physician of that era, he saw patients suffering with these illnesses daily. In addition to his work as a physician, Williams also distinguished himself as a pioneer in the field of epidemiology, gathering statistics on incidence and mortality. He published over seventy papers in a number of medical and scientific journals in his lifetime including some seventy in the *Boston Medical and Surgical Journal,* predecessor of the *New England Journal of Medicine.*

Mineralogy.

THE Subscribers are endeavouring to collect specimens of the minerals and compound rocks in this vicinity, and they respectfully request gentlemen in this County who are disposed to favour such an undertaking, to send them any rare stones, earths or ores, they may find. They would state that their chief object in making such collection is to obtain a knowledge of the minerals in this section of the country, and that they do not intend to retain them as their private property, but to deposit in Deerfield Academy, hoping thereby to make a beginning that may hereafter be extended by others to the benefit of posterity.

EDWARD HITCHCOCK.
STEPHEN W. WILLIAMS.
Deerfield. Sept. 15 1817.

Figure 32. Advertisement in the *Franklin Herald*, 1817

Growing up together in Deerfield, Williams and Hitchcock shared many interests. In those days they often went on natural history forays together, seeking out interesting minerals and plants to add to their collections. Whether Edward ever consulted his cousin about his own medical conditions or about the etiology of a condition such as dyspepsia as suggested in the vignette is not known. His writings on the subject appear to be little more than expressions of pet theories and remedies regarding his own health, relying largely on anecdotal evidence. They stand in sharp contrast to the scientific productions of his cousin, and to his own carefully reasoned analyses in geology and paleontology.

Ill health and fears of his imminent demise dominated Hitchcock's adult life. He made about eighty entries in his notes over thirty-five years. Nearly every entry contains a reference to his health; in two-thirds he expresses certainty that death is close at hand:

> …[M]y health has suddenly failed me and I am rapidly wasting away so that if his Providence does not save me I shall soon be in my grave [1833]…Blessed be God for giving me strength for all of this. Instead of it I expected a year ago to be in my grave ere this: and perhaps my present state of health is only a short respite from the grave [1834]…Oh that the little remnant of time and strength

> left me might be devoted directly to address my own soul in holiness and promote the glory of God! [1841]...My personal prospects are becoming more and more dark...the College will rise and flourish but I must die soon [1847]...I cannot but feel that the probability is faint of my seeing another year and I long to be prepared to go [1859].

One motive he had in recording his troubles and fears was that his children be forewarned and forearmed:

> I do now earnestly entreat my children...to adopt the grand principles of that system of hygiene which they will find works...If inclined to neglect the system through the example of companions or acquaintances I beg them to remember that the testimony of their departed father ought to weigh more than that of all the world beside and that they cannot disregard his advice and be happy.

Hitchcock did not limit his ruminations on the state of his health to his notes. In nearly one-third of his letters to Benjamin Silliman and close to one half his letters to John Torrey, he mentions poor health. We might expect him to confide about such matters in letters to his wife while traveling, but it is surprising to find that he did not hesitate to reveal his fears even to his young children. Once after a fall, he advised his twelve-year-old son, Edward, Jr., that he would soon perish (see page 177). In a letter to his seventeen-year-old daughter Mary, then attending Mount Holyoke Female Seminary, he pleaded for her to accept Christ: "We feel as if we could not leave this world until that change has taken place: and yet our growing infirmities admonish us that the time cannot be distant when we must leave it whether you are prepared or unprepared for eternity." Perhaps he thought it good for children to contemplate their own death or the death of a parent, that it would strengthen their faith.

Hitchcock's notes show that his colleagues and close friends were aware of his difficulties. Some apparently took him to task, suggesting he himself was responsible. In a February 1834 entry in his notes, he wrote of the reactions to his complaints from friends, placing them in three classes. One class believed he brought the problems on himself: "...[A]ll my present troubles," they say, "result from the preparation of my Geological Report and that it is just what I deserve for my inordinate ambition in writing that book." A second class accused him of following too closely his own dietary restrictions: "You have starved yourself say they—and you must eat more and of more stimulating richer and generous food..." A third class took the very opposite position, that he had not been sufficiently abstemious: "They feel as if an imperious obligation lay upon me to let the world see that my system of diet will save me and restore me, otherwise that system will be regarded with contempt."

At times he seemed to feel that he had been abandoned by those closest to him: "All with whom I am familiar have heard me complain so long of feeble health and have seen me yet live and work hard that they suppose it will continue to be thus." As to medical advice, often it was received with some skepticism. "The physicians will not allow that as yet there is any actual disease in the substance of the lungs yet I know how liable they are to be deceived and how flattering such complaints are. My hope is not in their skill, kind and able as they are…"

For all his fears about his health and imminent death, Hitchcock pressed on—with his teaching, with his research, with new projects. Far from depressing him or diverting his energies, his maladies drove him forward. He acknowledged this in his writing on several occasions. In a letter to his elder son, written while in Europe in 1850, he reflected on this:

> …I wish all the children to know that probably this trait in my character has enabled me to do what little I have done as a literary man. It always had a strong hold in my system and it was mainly that which roused me to effort and urged me forward…If there be any poetic inspiration in any of my writings it too sprang from this trait in my constitution. So that though now in advanced life its freedom in cases has become painful let me not forget it has been a powerful spring in all my intellectual efforts.

Was Edward Hitchcock a hypochondriac? If the term is understood to mean possessed of irrational fears about one's health, it seems clear that he was. But those fears were not entirely groundless. His own testimony and that of his colleagues and family members makes it clear that he suffered a good deal from a variety of very real ailments and conditions. That he was able to accomplish what he did, to achieve far, far beyond what most teachers, scientists, and administrators of his day achieved, is unequivocal evidence of a determined will and faith in his own abilities.

In 1830 Edward Hitchcock went through a particularly trying period of ill health. He was by that time convinced that vigorous physical exercise was his greatest defense against disease. He concluded that what he needed was a new pursuit to reinvigorate his body and spirit. He wrote in his notes of 1832,

> More than two years ago on a journey to Pennsylvania being satisfied that some thorough and systematic course of exercise was very important to give more vigor to my constitution and to save me from sinking, I addressed Governor Lincoln of Massachusetts suggesting to him the expediency of appointing someone to make a geological survey of the state.

His proposal met with a favorable response in Boston, and the new pursuit did seem to reinvigorate his health, at least for a time. More importantly, it secured for him a prominent place in the history of geology in a young America.

Figure 33. Rocking stone in Fall River,
woodcut by Orra White Hitchcock, 1841

A view of Cape Ann

14 The Diluvial Current

"I never saw such direct evidence of a diluvial current and powerful one too from the North in early times."

Troy, Massachusetts, August 6, 1830

"They are remarkable, Professor, truly remarkable. I have never witnessed such a thing in all God's creation." Story Hebard was kneeling on a granite ledge in southeastern Massachusetts, running his fingers across the rock face that was scored with deep grooves. "Dozens and dozens of them across the face of this rock," he continued, almost as if he were describing it to his disbelieving self, "all straight as arrows, all oriented the same, just west of north—almost parallel."

Edward Hitchcock stood over his young assistant smiling. "Indeed, Mr. Hebard."

"I wish I could bring all those skeptics and atheists to this spot, Professor, to see the work of Almighty God displayed in its most unambiguous form. They would I believe be converted on the spot, would they not?"

The professor nodded.

"Right here, written boldly in stone, is the entire book of Genesis: the fall of Adam, the wrath of the Almighty, the anointment of Noah and his sons, the Ark... the Deluge. What could be more unequivocal, Professor?"

"It is most astonishing, Mr. Hebard, I quite agree."

"Surely this place is unique, like no other."

"Actually I have already seen dozens of similar examples, in the valley of the Connecticut, in the hills of Berkshire, and on the island of Martha's Vineyard a few years since. All similar in shape and orientation. And additionally boulders, Mr. Hebard, huge boulders like that one."

He pointed to a large block of a coarse conglomerate not far from them, resting on the bedrock. "That boulder is puddingstone, and yet it sits on a bed of granite."

The young man's brow furrowed as he considered the implications. "You mean it was carried here, from farther north, by the same waters that scoured these grooves?"

"Precisely, Mr. Hebard."

Hitchcock was enjoying watching and listening to the young man swooning over a revelation both geological and spiritual.

"But, Mr. Hebard, I frankly have some doubts."

"Doubts, Professor? What kind of doubts, sir?"

"For one thing, consider the amount of force needed to make just one of those grooves in granite. Then consider that force applied over wide areas of the earth's surface, and all in precisely the same direction and with equal force." Hebard, now standing, was trying to grasp the implications. "Further, imagine the force needed to pick up yon boulder—50 or 100 tons I would guess—and transport it, in the same direction, many miles."

"That must have been a diluvial force of unimaginable power, sir, must it not?"

"Unimaginable...precisely, Mr. Hebard...beyond the ability of the human imagination to comprehend."

A horse-drawn wagon rumbled down a dusty country road in western Massachusetts on the morning of July 29, 1830. It carried two men, Professor Hitchcock and a young assistant, Story Hebard, along with a jumble of equipment and supplies: hammers, trowels, tape measures, compass, clinometer, an assortment of vials and tins, linen bags, wrapping paper, valises, rucksacks, and a supply of oats and hay for the horse. However rustic and humble this assemblage of man, beast, and materials may have appeared, its mission was important: to carry out the first comprehensive survey of a state's mineral resources.

Just five months earlier, the Massachusetts state legislature, at the urging of Governor Levi Lincoln, had authorized a trigonometric survey for the purpose of producing a precise map of the Bay State, its boundaries and major features. Hitchcock was in Hartford, Connecticut, when he read a newspaper account of the proposed legislation. Immediately he wrote a letter to the governor proposing an adjunct to that project, a geological survey. Lincoln must have found the idea to his liking, for just a few days later he sent a message to the legislature recommending such a geological survey. The main purpose of the survey, he added, would be economic:

> Much knowledge of the natural history of the country would thus be gained, and especially the presence of valuable ores, with the localities and extent of quarries, and of coal and lime formations, objects of inquiry so essential to internal improvements, and the advancement of domestic prosperity, would be discovered...

The governor it seems had little difficulty persuading the legislature of the benefits of such a survey. On June 5, 1830, they passed a resolution authorizing him to appoint "some suitable person to make a geological examination of the Commonwealth" and appropriating one thousand dollars for that purpose. Barely three weeks later, Edward Hitchcock received a commission as the first State Geologist of Massachusetts with the responsibility for carrying out the survey he had only recently proposed.

The Massachusetts survey was from the outset a most ambitious, comprehensive undertaking, and its scope expanded even after the work had commenced. In February 1831, the legislature passed a resolution adding a third element to Hitchcock's portfolio, the compilation of a list of all plants, animals, and minerals occurring in the Commonwealth–amending his duties, but not his compensation. Hitchcock himself seems to have further expanded the project by the addition of a summary of the scenic features of the state which he entitled "Topographical Geology." The project thus came to embrace four categories as stated in his report: "Economical Geology," "Topographical Geology," "Scientific Geology," and "Catalogues of Animals and Plants."

Hitchcock began his survey in July 1830 and concluded it in September 1833 (see Figure 34). He spent some 135 days in the field over four summers, traveling an average of twenty-five miles per day, logging more than 3000 miles, almost all in that rude horse-drawn wagon. He visited 266 cities and towns, about ninety percent of the state's municipalities at that time. His travels were carefully planned and systematic, crisscrossing the state, first easterly from Amherst, then westerly. Additionally he made forays into the neighboring states of New Hampshire, Vermont, New York, Connecticut, and Rhode Island. He paid particular attention to Rhode Island, making at least four trips there

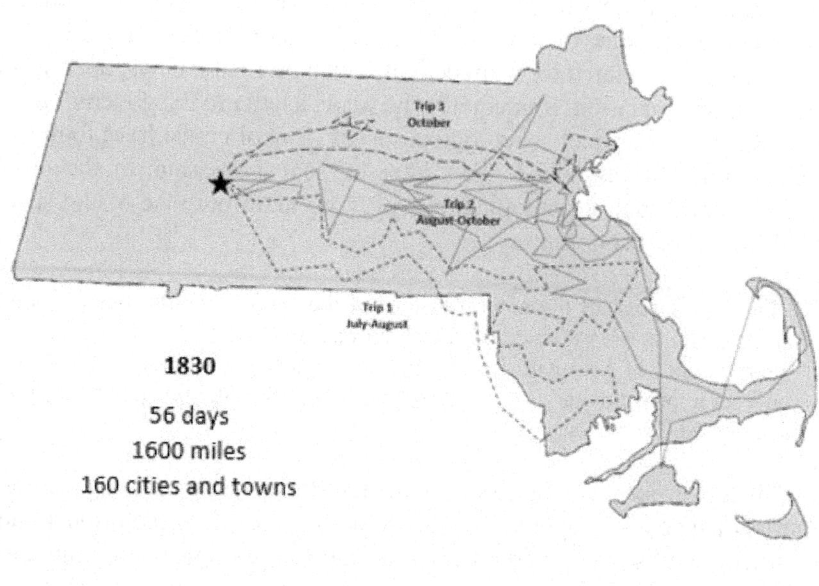

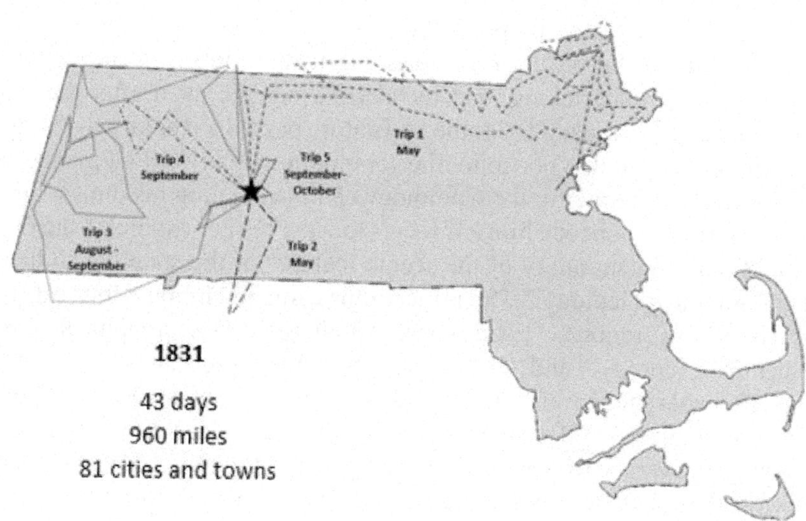

Figure 34. Edward Hitchcock's travels for the Massachusetts Geological Survey, 1830-1833

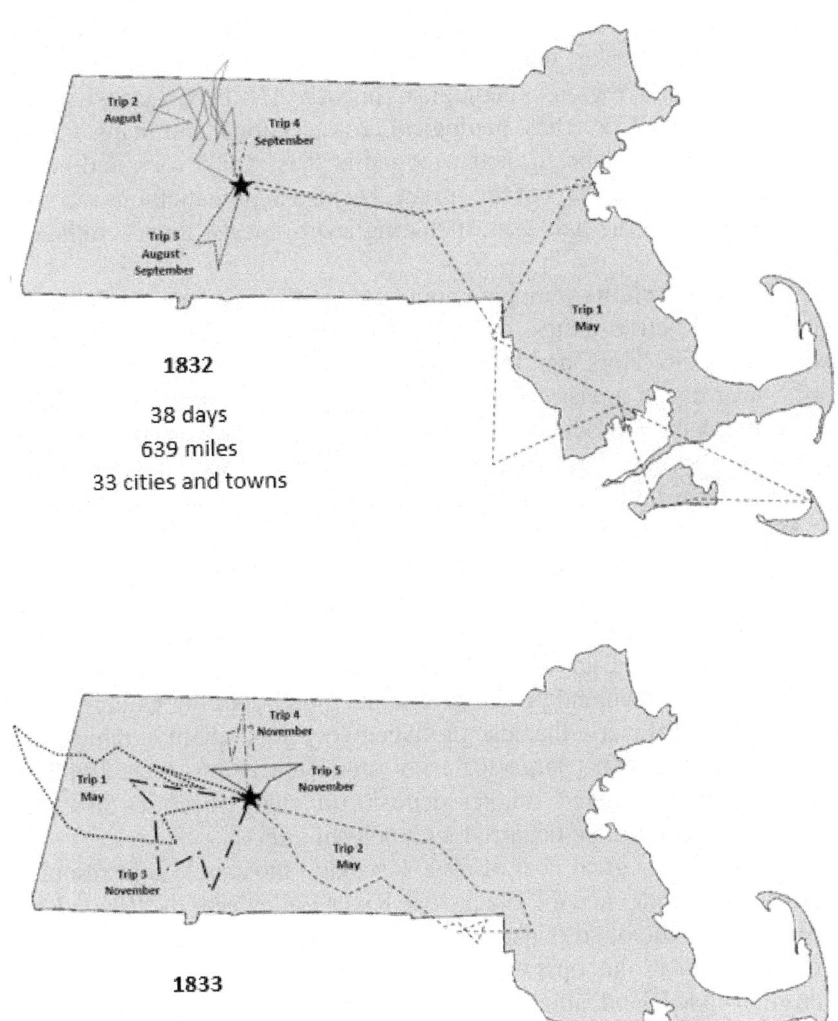
Trip 2
August
Trip 4
September
Trip 3
August -
September
Trip 1
May
1832
38 days
639 miles
33 cities and towns
Trip 4
November
Trip 5
November
Trip 1
May
Trip 2
May
Trip 3
November
1833
14 days
435 miles
37 cities and towns

over the course of his first survey, convinced that it had valuable coal resources to be exploited, some of which extended into Massachusetts.

In each town he visited, Hitchcock recorded his observations of surface geology, rock type, strike and dip of strata, as well as reflections on his understanding of the region's geological history. He kept extensive notes including rough pencil sketches, geological cross sections, and maps drawn in the field. He collected, labeled, and wrapped at least 5,000 rock and mineral specimens over the three years of the survey. He also kept meticulous records of expenditures down to the half cent, including room, meals, ferries, tolls, even "horse dinner."

As economic benefits were paramount among the priorities for the survey, Hitchcock toured active mines, quarries, and manufactories, conferring with owners, workers, investors, and local officials. He visited the Tantiusques lead mines of Sturbridge, a gneiss quarry in Uxbridge, a lime quarry in Smithfield, Rhode Island, a factory producing a pewter-like metal known as Britannia and a textile mill producing calico fabric, both in Taunton, a soapstone mine in New Salem, an iron mine and bloomery forge in Somerset, Vermont, a marble quarry in New Ashford, and an iron mine in Richmond.

The two most valuable mineral resources in Massachusetts at that time were granite and limestone. Hitchcock visited granite quarries in Quincy and Randolph, then spent nearly a week in Essex County where he reported on two quarrying operations on Cape Ann, one at Squam, known today as Annisquam, that employed thirty men and produced granite "much like the Quincy though harder," a second at Beverly that also produced very good quality granite. As to limestone, he observed that large-scale limestone formations were limited to Berkshire County, but noted smaller deposits in many localities in eastern Massachusetts where it often occurred with beds of gneiss.

Hitchcock spent a great deal of time surveying the state's coal resources, particularly in Worcester and the Blackstone River Valley near the Rhode Island state line. A coal mine of sorts had recently been opened in Worcester, and he was anxious to visit the operation. He also observed active coal mining operations in Rhode Island, notably at Cumberland on the Massachusetts border. In his report of 1833, he admitted that the coal of Rhode Island and Massachusetts was inferior to Pennsylvania coal; it ignited with difficulty and once lit produced less heat. Yet he refused to be discouraged, assuring his readers that, "the anthracite of Rhode Island, and even that of Worcester, will be considered by posterity, if not by the present generation, as a treasure of great value."

Another fossil fuel that interested Hitchcock was peat. He reported on many localities of peat in eastern Massachusetts. In some towns he saw peat being dug, although he intimated in his report that it was less often used as fuel than as fertilizer. On the islands off the southeast coast, he saw peat much in use. Referring to its use both as a fuel and in agriculture, he wrote, "I cannot but regard the existence of so large quantities of peat, on Cape Cod and Nantucket, as a great blessing to the inhabitants."

Then as now, iron was a product of great economic importance. Since colonial days, a major source of iron in Massachusetts had been bog ore, a low-grade source of iron leached from bedrock and deposited in low-lying wetlands. Some Massachusetts bog iron operations such as at Saugus had been successful, but by Hitchcock's time most bog iron sources had already been depleted or proven uneconomical. Hitchcock observed bog iron operations in Warwick and Royalston and iron furnaces in Freetown and Cumberland, Rhode Island, on the state line.

During the second year of his survey Hitchcock spent several days in southern Vermont including a visit to an iron mine in Somerset where he made a tantalizing discovery. "The gold in the rocks at Somerset is globular," he wrote in his notes. "One of these nodules which Mr. Wilder gave me…he valued at $1.15. . . I myself picked out several small bits of gold from the soil before it was washed." Back in Amherst at the end of his tour he reported that, "The gold which we got from 6 quarts of dirt in Somerset weighs 7 grains and the large pieces from the brook 29 grains." Their value today would be about seventy dollars. He concluded that the gold of Somerset was associated with the iron and suggested that iron deposits in nearby Massachusetts might hold similar promise: "How far south the gold may be found remains to be shown. May we not expect to find it near the Hawley [Massachusetts] mine of iron since this is in talcose slate." In his report he wrote of gold,

> It may perhaps excite a smile, to see gold occupying a place in a description of the minerals of Massachusetts. It has not indeed been found in this state; but I am able in this place, to announce the existence of a deposit of this metal, in the southern part of Vermont; and I feel no small degree of confidence, that it will be found in Massachusetts.

He concluded with a cautionary digression on the "wild and ill-directed efforts" made by men in search of precious metals, obtaining nothing for their labors but pain, misery, and death.

Edward Hitchcock was a meticulous observer of the world around him, gathering evidence cautiously and objectively. But he also had a sentimental, almost romantic side, and this inspired the second part of his survey entitled "Topographical Geology," the section he himself had added to the project. "In the following sketch of the scenery of Massachusetts," he wrote in the introduction to this section of his report, "my principal object will be to direct

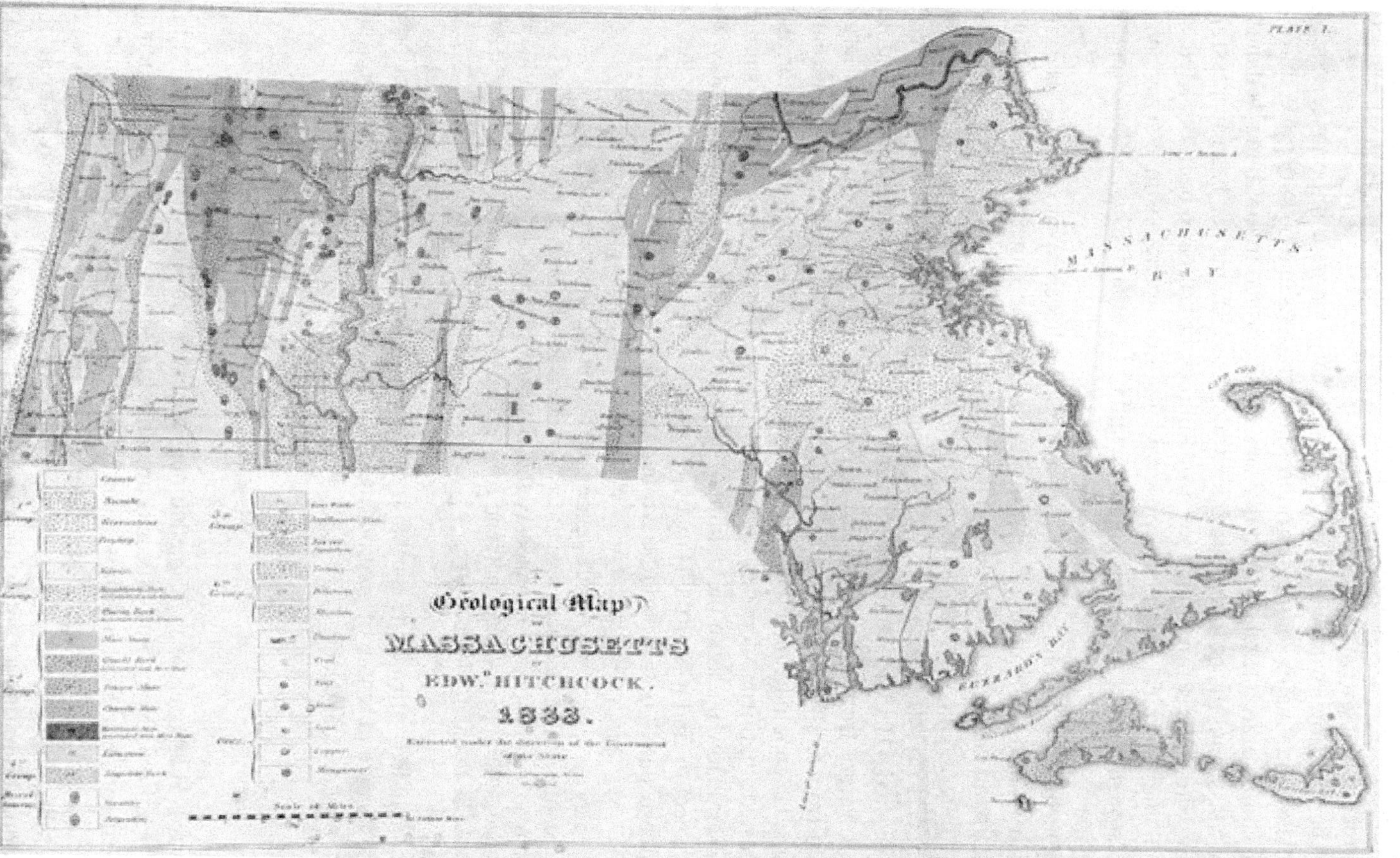

Figure 35. Hitchcock's first geological map of Massachusetts, 1833.

the attention of the man of taste to those places in the State, where he will find natural objects particularly calculated to gratify his love of novelty, beauty and sublimity." He proceeded to enumerate and describe the state's tallest mountains, the major river valleys, the coastline from Cape Ann to Cape Cod and the islands, as well as many of the state's waterfalls, gorges, cascades, fissures, caverns, and purgatories. At a purgatory in Sutton, he had an interesting encounter that he recorded with uncharacteristic humor: "I met with a rattlesnake among these rocks but as he kindly warned me that I was invading his dominions I suffered him to retire into his den and he suffered me to leave his precincts in peace—mutually willing to be rid of one another's company." He concluded the section with comments on each of nine elaborate lithographed landscapes included at the end of the report, adding the following acknowledgment:

> It has been in my power to obtain sketches of some of the most striking scenery which has been described in this part of my Report. . .I am indebted for them to Mrs. Hitchcock; as I am for nearly all the drawings and maps accompanying every part of this Report. The landscapes are chiefly confined to the Connecticut Valley; it not having been convenient for her to accompany me to distant parts of the state.

In his September 1823 address to the members of the Lyceum of Natural History in Pittsfield, Massachusetts, Hitchcock had warned his audience of the dangers of conjecture uninformed by facts, and praised certain European geologists who he said were ". . . men whose grand object is the collection of facts, and who are extremely cautious of hypothesis; adopting none, except such as seem absolutely necessary to explain appearances." Such was the role Hitchcock saw for himself as a scientist, not to weave elaborate and fanciful schemes, but simply to collect facts. And his geological survey afforded him an opportunity to do just that on a grand scale. Everywhere in Massachusetts that he traveled over those three years, he recorded his observations of rock type, soils, landforms, and geological curiosities. And those facts, over time, led him to some startling conclusions.

A principal object of his work was the creation of a detailed geological map of Massachusetts. To do this he employed a scheme of rock classification based on that of his mentor Amos Eaton, including twenty rock types in two groups, stratified rocks and unstratified rocks, the stratified rocks roughly equivalent to sedimentary and metamorphic rocks in modern terminology, the unstratified to igneous rocks. At each stop he recorded the rock type as well as the strike and dip of the strata, and collected, labeled, and bagged samples.

The completed map was large, unfolding to approximately 20" x 30", drawn at a scale of about six miles to the inch. It showed the nearly 300

Massachusetts cities and towns that existed at the time plus those on the border in neighboring states as well as the major rivers, bays, and offshore islands. The twenty rock types were grouped into six categories indicated by colors, "so strongly marked, that they can readily be distinguished by candlelight." Each rock type was indicated by a number and symbol on the map keyed to the legend in the lower left corner of the sheet. Additionally, specific locations of deposits of nine other important minerals or ores—steatite, serpentine, plumbago, coal, peat, iron, lead, copper, and manganese—were indicated by special symbols. It was a map of surficial geology only; no stratigraphic data were included, although more than a dozen cross sections were provided elsewhere in the report. Although the classification scheme employed was soon superseded, this was the first large scale geological map ever published for an entire state, and many of the details of that map, the rock types and their extents, compare favorably with twentieth-century geological maps.

Sketched in Hitchcock's field notebooks are many cross sections of stratigraphic sequences inferred from his observations and measurements. For example in August 1832 he recorded in his notes the strata adjoining the Connecticut River near Turners Falls; along the margin he drew a cross section based on these observations which his wife redrew for his report (see Figure 36).

Another stratigraphic sequence drawn by Hitchcock and discussed in his report is of particular interest for American geology. It crosses the Taconic Mountains along the Massachusetts-New York State line. Here he observed what appeared to be an inversion of the strata, with the oldest rocks lying on top of the younger.

> We are driven then to the alternative of supposing, either that there must be a deception in the apparent outcrop of the newer rocks from beneath the older, or that the whole series of strata has been actually thrown over, so as to bring the newest rocks at the bottom. The latter supposition is so improbable that I cannot at present admit it.

His doubts about such a possibility were shared by many other geologists and contributed to the "Taconic Controversy" that occupied American geology for decades. The very idea that entire rock formations hundreds of feet thick may have been overturned due to ancient paroxysms in the Earth's crust forced geologists to reconsider long held assumptions about geological history.

How the Connecticut River could have deposited sediments as much as 100 feet above its present level was a subject of great interest to Hitchcock. In his 1818 paper he addressed this question, suggesting that the "alluvial region" identified on his map was "formerly the bed of a lake." The river, he argued, may have been obstructed by the sandstone and basalt of the Holyoke Range, but eventually wore through those obstacles. As the lake waters were drained away, the lake bottom sediments were exposed. The terraces along the

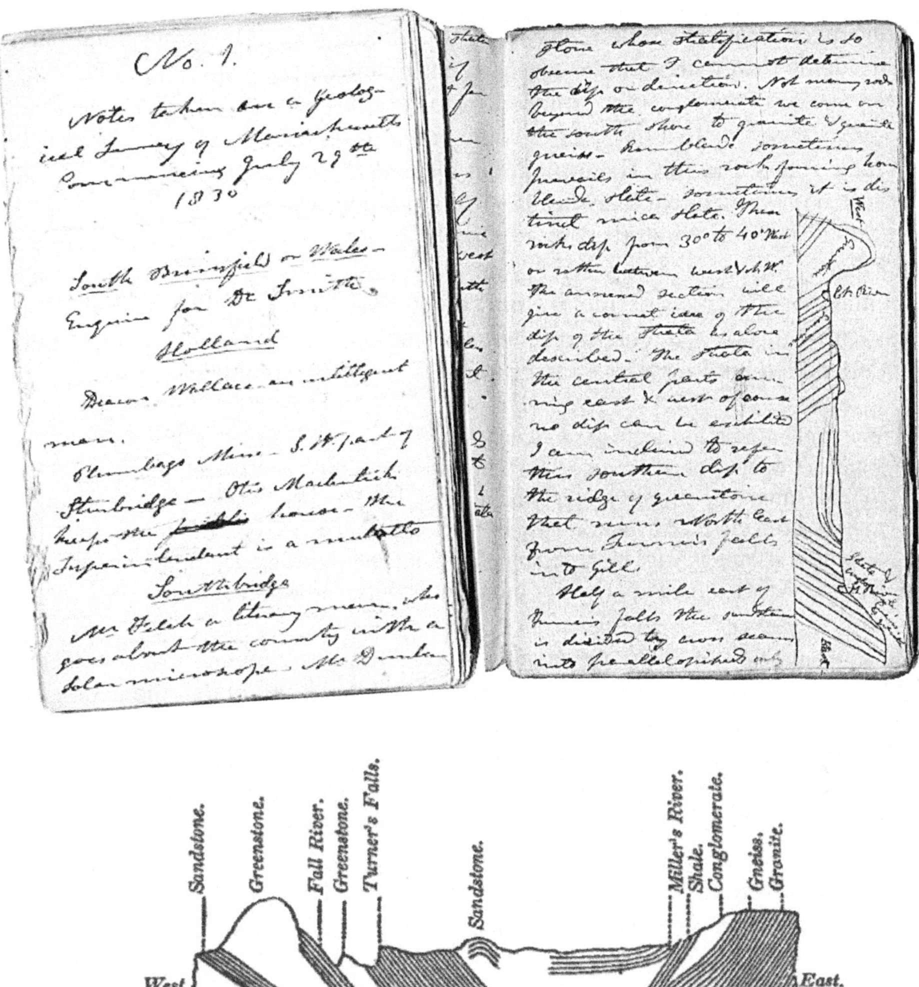

Figure 36. Top, left, a page from Hitchcock's 1830 geological survey notes; top, right, a page from Hitchcock's 1832 notes including a cross section through the Connecticut River; below, the same cross section redrawn by Orra White Hitchcock as it appeared in his *Report on the Geology of Massachusetts.*

Connecticut and Deerfield Rivers, he proposed in his 1833 report, were left as the rivers cut through the bottom sediments of that lake. It was an important early step toward reconstructing the events of the late Pleistocene in the Connecticut Valley. Over a century later, Dartmouth geologist Richard J. Lougee named that body Lake Hitchcock.

One stratigraphic sequence that Hitchcock worked out that had important implications for understanding the region's geological history was that of the

Connecticut Valley from Deerfield to Sunderland. By combining his stratigraphic data with precise measurements made by the state's trigonometric survey, he confirmed that the strata on opposite sides of the river were identical, strongly suggesting that the river or some previous body of water had eroded the riverbed at this location. He argued that the rest of the valley of that river was excavated or formed by other means. "I am in doubt whether there is more than one valley in Massachusetts that is, strictly speaking, a valley of denudation. And that is the passage between Mount Toby, in Sunderland, and Sugar Loaf Mountain, on the opposite side of Connecticut river." On that subject Hitchcock was clearly mistaken, but his careful reconstruction of the strata at Deerfield and Sunderland led him to make an assertion with profound implications:

> The immense period requisite to wear away such a mass of rock as this theory supposes to have once occupied the whole valley of the Connecticut, will seem to most minds the strongest objection against its adoption: I mean supposing it to have been effected by such causes as are operating at present. But this is not a solitary example, in which geological phenomena indicate the operation of existing causes through periods of duration inconceivably long.

"Periods of duration inconceivably long"—this was a remarkable statement for Edward Hitchcock to make at this time because it implied that the geologic history of the region encompassed not merely a few thousand years as suggested in the Holy Scriptures, but tens of thousands of years, perhaps hundreds of thousands of years or more. That he made no suggestion of an absolute age is not surprising. Few geologists of his day were willing to venture such an assertion for reasons both scientific and religious. The fact that Edward Hitchcock, an ordained minister of the most orthodox stripe, was willing to contemplate such a possibility no doubt gave other scientists license to do the same.

Another enigma of New England geology began to reveal itself as Hitchcock traveled through Rhode Island and southeastern Massachusetts: boulders, sometimes massive, and of a different rock type than the underlying bedrock or, as he often referred to it, "the rock in place." He made this prescient observation in Cumberland: "The north end of Rhode Island is a good place to teach the geologist not to rely on bowlders for the character of the formations since there the bowlders are chiefly sienitic granite whereas the rock in place is the shale associated with coal." He made a similar observation a few weeks later south of Boston, noting, "We uniformly found also bowlders south of the beds but rarely even a few rods north."

The following summer he was astounded to see similar evidence high in the Berkshires. As in eastern Massachusetts, he observed many huge boulders that appeared to have been plucked from bedrock and transported, in some instances dozens of miles, from their parent rock. High in the Hoosac Mountains, better known today as the Berkshire Highlands, he observed large boulders that appeared to have been moved uphill many miles from their source by diluvial action:

> Large and very numerous bowlders of the peculiar granite with blue quartz so common in rolled masses in this region and also of granular quartz are found lining the steep escarpment of the Hoosak on the west even almost to the top. Some of them six or eight feet in diameter. The same appears commonly on top of the mountain and even several miles east of it. These facts indicate pretty clearly a diluvial current from the northwest.

Like many American geologists of that time, Edward Hitchcock held firmly to the creation story of Genesis. So when he observed evidence of ancient geological debacles, he saw them through the lens of Holy Scripture. The "diluvial current" to which he referred was a great flood—the Great Flood—the flood of the book of Genesis, of Noah and the Ark. According to the Bible, that event was the single greatest event since the Creation, and by all accounts a global catastrophe of enormous destructive power. And yet there was something about the facts observed by Hitchcock that did not seem to fit the biblical narrative. In his report he hinted at these doubts:

> For bowlders of several tons weight, are found lodged at various elevations, on the steep western escarpment of Hoosac mountain; and as already remarked, these bowlders, in large numbers, have been actually carried over the top of the mountain, and driven south easterly from 10 to 20 miles. . .To suppose that these quartz bowlders were forced by a current of water up the steep side of this mountain, from 1000 to 1500 feet, if that current was at right angles to the direction of the mountain, is absurd. . .Making every allowance for the reduction of the gravity of these bowlders when in water, I confess I cannot conceive how such a work could have been effected by this agency.

Figure 37. Confluence of Deerfield and Connecticut Rivers, woodcut by Orra White Hitchcock, 1841

His doubts regarding those "bowlders" were further reinforced by another geological curiosity. In August 1830 he made this entry in his notebook after a visit to Troy, known today as Fall River:

> 100 rods east of Troy Center I observe the surfaces of the granite exhibiting grooves in a direction nearly North and South—evidently produced by the abrasion of hard substances dragged over them by determined action. Some of these puddingstone bowlders would weigh from 50 to an hundred tons. I never saw such direct evidence of a diluvial current and powerful one too from the North in early times.

A few weeks later he observed furrows in granite in several towns south of Boston, noting, "We uniformly found also bowlders south of the beds but rarely even a few rods north."

Yet another geological quandary confronted Hitchcock in September of 1830 when he and two assistants were traveling on Cape Cod, his first visit to those fragile coastal outposts. He was intrigued by the many large boulders, most of them granite, scattered about the otherwise sandy peninsula. Despite his own admonition of a few weeks earlier in Rhode Island that geologists should not rely on boulders for the character of formations, here he seems to have done just that:

> September 13. From Falmouth to Plymouth 36 miles diluvium all the way. But in the west part of Falmouth and Sandwich the bowlders are so large and thick and so numerous and the hills so high that there can be no doubt that granite and gneiss are in place a little below the surface.

In his report, Hitchcock reiterated his belief that the boulders of Cape Cod were evidence of bedrock, and his geological map for that report indicated as much. Nevertheless, he seemed to leave the subject open to further discussion:

> The map will show...that I have extended a strip of granite from Plymouth into Barnstable county as far east as Brewster, and carried another branch into Falmouth...Others must judge, whether the evidence of the existence of granite in place in the region under consideration, is probable enough to justify me in the course I have taken.

But in his 1841 revision of that map, the granite bedrock of Cape Cod had been removed. In his explanation he hedged a bit on the question: "...as the entire surface is diluvium, I thought it better to color it as such; thus representing what I know exists there, instead of something about which I am not certain."

Hitchcock may be forgiven his equivocation on this point. Not until the mid-twentieth century would the matter be resolved once and for all when a team of geophysicists performed seismic tests, bouncing sound waves off the buried bedrock. The depth of the bedrock beneath the region was found to range from 25 meters at the Cape Cod Canal to over 500 meters at Nantucket. Most of Cape Cod was in the range from 25 to 200 meters. A map from that study shows the highest elevation of the bedrock extending from Bourne eastward to Barnstable and southward to Falmouth, comparing very favorably with Hitchcock's map of more than a century earlier.

Trains of transported boulders, furrows and grooves engraved in bedrock, all with similar orientations, these were evidences that impressed Hitchcock strongly. Even the most violent flood could not account for such effects, a conclusion which he finally came to confirm in a most public forum eight years later.

Early in the third year of his survey, Hitchcock spent more than a week on the islands of Nantucket and Martha's Vineyard. There he learned of another curiosity about the island's past from the captain of the vessel that transported them:

> Lieutenant Prescott informs me that he found portions of cedar maple oak and beech trees some of them in an erect position 1/3 of a mile from the shore in Nantucket Harbour and 4 feet below the surface of the sand and about 8 feet below low water mark. He obtained peat also in the same place.

A few days later he moved on to Holmes Hole on Martha's Vineyard, known today as Vineyard Haven, where he also encountered reports of tree stumps in shallow waters.

Hitchcock heard similar anecdotes about cedar stumps observed at low tide in Cape Cod Bay at Yarmouth, three miles from shore. "Geologists are not a little perplexed satisfactorily to account for submarine forests," he explained in his report. ". . .[I]n general it has been supposed that these forests have subsided in consequence of earthquakes, or other internal movements of the earth." That those boulders, furrows, and grooves as well as rising sea level might be evidence of continental glaciation in the recent past was an insight still unknown to American geology. And yet Professor Charles H. Hitchcock of Dartmouth, in a memorial to his father a half century later, made this interesting revelation: "He once remarked upon the possibility that these hillocks [of Cape Cod and the islands] might have been the terminal moraines of this imagined ice-sheet, which is the earliest allusion to such a view that can be found anywhere in the annals of American geology." Charles Hitchcock was an eminent geologist in his own right and is credited with being the first geologist to recognize Long Island as a moraine of the last Pleistocene glacier.

Hitchcock submitted his report to Governor Lincoln in September 1833. Although he promised "to avoid all unnecessary prolixity," the document ran to more than 700 pages and a quarter million words. But it was a true *tour de force*, weaving thousands of observations in the field into a coherent narrative on the state's natural resources and integrating what he had observed with the geological and religious thinking of his day. He employed Orra's artistic abilities to great advantage, including nearly 100 of her illustrations for the text, the map and cross sections, as well as sixteen lithographs of her drawings illustrating the scenery of the state. The last section consisted of a series of catalogs compiled by experts in their fields, listing all species of mammals, birds, reptiles, fishes, shelled animals, crustaceans, spiders, insects, radiata, and plants known to occur in the state. An appendix included a complete listing of the mineral specimens to be deposited in the state's archives along with a brief description and location for each.

The report was well received in the halls of government, in the scientific community, and among the public. The state authorized printing of 1200 copies of the first edition in 1833 and 500 additional copies of a revised 1835 edition. Governor Lincoln, in his message to incoming Governor John Davis after losing his bid for re-election in 1833, lavished praise on both Hitchcocks:

> It was the good fortune of the State, that an individual was to be found within her own Halls of Science, of gifted intellect, enthusiastic in his devotion to Geological studies, and peculiarly qualified by habits of patient and persevering industry to thorough investigation of the nature and properties of the objects of his research; and it must forever redound to the honor of Massachusetts, that under her exclusive patronage, the first systematic work of this description ever undertaken in the new world, has been happily accomplished.

The governor then offered a well-deserved acknowledgment of Orra Hitchcock's contribution:

> I cannot deny myself the gratification of adding to this tribute of respect for the talents and labors of Professor Hitchcock, the interesting fact, that the beautiful sketches of scenery and other drawings, exhibited in the Atlas, which accompanies and enriches the volume of the Report, are gratuitous contributions of the taste of his accomplished Lady to the value of the work. Surely, so acceptable an offering demands grateful notice, if it shall receive no more substantial acknowledgment.

The state legislature must have been pleased with Hitchcock's work as well; he was reappointed to carry out additional surveys in 1837, 1841, and 1852. Orra continued to contribute her artwork to his reports, although there is no record that she ever received any compensation from the state for her labors.

Prominent geologists of that period were quick to praise the report. An anonymous reviewer, likely Massachusetts geologist Charles T. Jackson, writing in the *American Monthly Review*, said of a preliminary edition of the report, "...when we consider the short space of time in which Mr. Hitchcock has gone over the ground, we are lost in admiration at his industry and perseverance." A much longer commentary, probably also written by Jackson, was published in the same journal in 1836. Praise came from abroad as well including some of Britain's most eminent scientists, Dr. Gideon Mantell, Robert Bakewell, and Henry de la Beche. In a letter to Hitchcock dated November 6, 1845, a young English scientist praised the revised and updated 1841 edition of his report as "a magnificent work." The writer of those words of praise was Charles Darwin.

Although the primary objective of the survey had been economic, it is doubtful whether any significant economic benefit accrued from Hitchcock's work. By far the most important mineral resource in Massachusetts at that time was granite, and nearly all the state's largest granite quarries were already being worked prior to his survey. The same may be said of the limestone and marble quarries of the Berkshires, although, as Hitchcock predicted, they would benefit a great deal from the extension of railroad lines in that part of the state, the first of which opened just three years after his report.

Some untapped mineral resources that Hitchcock thought held promise failed to live up to his expectations, including bog ore, peat, gold, and, most notably, coal. It is safe to say that no one ever made a dollar's profit mining coal in the Bay State. A short-lived "coal rush" did take place in Mansfield, Massachusetts, in 1835. Whether it was prompted by his report is unknown, but it yielded little if any marketable coal. As to Rhode Island coal, it was mined in limited quantities, but the quality of the coal was poor and it was difficult to ignite. An oft quoted witticism of the late nineteenth century alluded to this when it suggested that the wicked should seek refuge in Rhode Island on the Judgment Day because it would be the last place to burn.

If the economic benefits of Hitchcock's survey were slight, what then were the fruits of his work? Among the scientific insights Hitchcock gained from the survey, those regarding the boulder trains and furrowed bedrock were perhaps the most important. To him and to most other American geologists of that period, glaciers were phenomena of the world's great mountain ranges. Yes, they were known to be powerful in their effects, but only in a limited region on and surrounding those mountains. Nowhere in his 1833 report does Hitchcock even mention glaciation. Again and again on his excursions he recorded evidence—boulders, bedrock furrows, great thicknesses of sediment—that he argued were effects of "diluvial action," even as he harbored doubts that they could have been caused by the most violent floods imaginable. But when a young Swiss geologist, Louis Agassiz, and a German-Swiss geologist, Jean de Charpentier, proposed the notion of continental glaciation in 1837, Hitchcock was a ready and willing advocate for the concept.

In his address to the Association of American Geologists in 1841, Hitchcock confessed that he had harbored doubts about the diluvial action hypothesis for some time: "Yet so many difficulties attend any theory of mere currents [of water], that many geologists have become sceptical. . .in regard to every particular theory that has been proposed. I confess myself to have been long of that number." He went on to describe the theory of the glacial origin of those effects with evangelical fervor. Of Agassiz's *Études sur les Glaciers*, published in 1840, he said,

> While reading this work and the abstracts of some papers by Agassiz, Buckland and Lyell, on the evidence of ancient glaciers in Scotland and England, I seemed to be acquiring a new geological sense; and I look upon our smoothed and striated rocks, our accumulations of gravel, and the tout ensemble of diluvial phenomena, with new eyes. The fact is, that the history of glaciers is the history of diluvial agency in miniature. The object of Agassiz is, first to describe the miniature, and then to enlarge the picture till it reaches around the globe.

Almost as soon as he spoke those words, he began back-pedaling. That summer, he and Orra went on an expedition to the top of New Hampshire's Mount Washington. What he saw there was evidence he believed contradicted Agassiz's theory. After a visit to Mount Monadnock in southern New Hampshire, he had a similar reaction:

> The facts stated above relative to the occurrence of striae on the north and south slopes of Monadnoc, might lead to the conclusion that they were the result of glaciers sliding down each way from the summit. But the fact that the roches moutonnees are rounded only upon their northwestern side, shows that the force which has produced these effects had a southeasterly direction. Indeed, I see no way to avoid the conclusion that the ice, which probably was the agent, must have been forced upward over the top of this mountain.

The evidence, he concluded, argued against glacial action alone, for glaciers in his experience always originated at the summit of a mountain, descending in all directions.

While Hitchcock's doubts about the glacial theory may have been strongly influenced by his firsthand observations, they were likely reinforced by Sir Charles Lyell. Lyell had recently developed his own drift hypothesis based on the action of icebergs, not glaciers. He visited Amherst that summer and Hitchcock showed him around the Connecticut Valley. Lyell believed that what he saw on that tour confirmed his iceberg hypothesis. His opinions had great weight, not only with Edward Hitchcock, but with most American and European scientists.

In his *Final Report* and in the second edition of his textbook, *Elementary Geology*, both published in late 1841, Hitchcock developed his "glacio-aqueous" theory. It combined the effects of glaciers, icebergs, meltwater, and sea level fluctuations to explain the drift deposits, striae, furrows, and boulder trains he had been observing around New England.

Figure 38. Louis Agassiz (1807-1873)

> To conclude: the theory of glacial action has imparted a fresh and a lively interest to the diluvial phenomena of this country. It certainly explains most of those phenomena in a satisfactory manner. It seems to me, however, that the term Glacio-aqueous action more accurately express this agency than the term glacial action: for the effects referrible to water are scarcely less than those produced by ice.

One problem with Agassiz's theory had to do with the change in global climate that would have been necessary to allow such vast expansion of glaciers, icebergs, and sea level fluctuations. What might have caused such a rapid change in climate, he wondered. At this point he floated the idea of a sudden change in earth's orbit. But Hitchcock the empiricist could allow himself only a brief wade in such speculative waters, ending the section with this warning to himself: "But I forbear: for enough of dreamy hypotheses on this subject have already had an ephemeral existence, and passed onward into the caves of oblivion."

Edward Hitchcock's geological survey of Massachusetts provided evidence of a wide range of geological phenomena, from the erosive effects of rivers and glaciers, to rising sea level, to inversions, to metamorphism, to those "periods of duration inconceivably long." These were all pieces of a complex puzzle to Hitchcock and other geologists of his day, a puzzle that would not be fully assembled until long after his death. In the early twentieth century George Perkins Merrill, geologist and curator of geology of the National Museum of Natural History in Washington, D.C., known today as the Smithsonian, wrote that Hitchcock's report ". . .marks an epoch in American geological work. . ."

One legacy of his geological survey that Hitchcock himself often asserted with considerable pride was that the survey and report soon became models for many other states. And so they did, with some fifteen states appointing state geologists and launching their own surveys within six years.

The proliferation of state sponsored geological surveys had another beneficial effect on the profession. The scientists contracted to carry out those state surveys were the very same men who gathered in Philadelphia in 1840 to form the Association of American Geologists. Hitchcock was a central figure in that organization, serving as chair of their first meeting, and delivering his famous keynote address at the second meeting. That organization is still alive and strong today, although renamed the American Association for the Advancement of Science. The roots of the nation's oldest, largest scientific organization can thus be traced back through the Association of American Geologists to the state surveys spawned by Edward Hitchcock.

Edward Hitchcock was a scientist of enormous energy and ambition, a keen observer and gatherer of data, an incisive analyst, and a tireless writer, speaker, and champion of the scientific enterprise. But for all his intellectual gifts, the success of his survey was also a credit to the character of the man:

> In many ways Hitchcock was the ideal state geologist. Well-trained in the field, he had a social and intellectual standing that was respected by the legislature, a sense of responsibility to the public, and a smooth, politic manner that readily won him friends and enabled him to influence people.

Some of history's most eminent figures have had greatness thrust upon them unbidden, while others have through their own devices shaped events to their own ends, determined to some degree their own fate. Edward Hitchcock surely belongs to the latter group. He conceived the Massachusetts geological survey, he advocated for it, and he nominated himself for the post of State Geologist. In the commission of his charge he went far beyond the call of duty to the Commonwealth. Nearly two centuries later, we can only speculate whether, as his horse-drawn wagon rattled off down that dusty road in Amherst in summer 1830, he already had a sense that he was embarking on an enterprise of great weight and consequence both for himself and for American geology.

In 1830 Hitchcock wrote in his notes that "some thorough and systematic course of exercise was very important to give more vigor to my constitution and to save me from sinking," and this prompted him to pursue his appointment to the geological survey in Massachusetts. Three and a half years later, with the work complete, he gave thanks for his good health throughout the enterprise. On the last page of his report, he wrote,

> Finally, and above all, I would not close without acknowledging my supreme obligations to Him whose providential care and kindness have followed me in all my wanderings, not permitting even a hair of my head to be injured; and who has enabled me to bring at length to a conclusion, one of the most laborious enterprises of my days. To Him I desire to consecrate the fruits of this labor and of all the subsequent labors of life.

Barely three weeks later he fell ill, convinced that the project he so recently credited with his good health would now be responsible for his final undoing:

> While I have occasion to praise God for sustaining me through it I have also reason to humble myself in view of his judgments. For though he guarded me in all my wanderings from accident and injury yet now my health has suddenly failed me and I am rapidly wasting away so that if his Providence does not save me I shall soon be in my grave. I impute this failure almost entirely to excessive labour.

Here then is the contradiction that held Edward Hitchcock in its thrall for most of his adult life. Hard work was his greatest ally, necessary for his health and vigor, mental and physical, and his fiercest foe. He was also able to take a project of massive scale that accomplished a great deal, and turn it against himself:

> It is a work of great labour. But if I do not mistake my feelings I hope I may be able to glorify God in the enterprise—and do some service to the cause of learning. God grant that I may be kept from unhallowed ambition—from the desire of worldly distinction by this labour!

Figure 39. Gay Head, woodcut by
Orra White Hitchcock, 1841

"The Return" by Orra White Hitchcock, 1839

15 A Wreath for the Tomb

"...a home which material comforts and intellectual tastes conspired to render truly delightful."

Springfield, June 1838

"Walk on," ordered Edward Hitchcock to his horse as he gave the reins a shake. Seated beside him on the wooden bench was ten-year-old Edward, Jr., as the wagon creaked and groaned along the road from Springfield to Chicopee. Father and son had traveled the nearly fifteen miles from Amherst that morning to deliver some specimens to the Springfield railroad station. It was slow going and the wooden crates were heavy burdens to lift off the wagon to the ground, then up onto the loading platform.

When they had finished the unloading, Professor Hitchcock disappeared into the freight office to complete the necessary forms and make the payment. Edward, Jr., walked the horse to a water trough on the street corner and stood by the horse as it drank.

Finally his father emerged from the office onto the platform. As he descended the stone steps toward the street, he lost his footing, his feet went out from under him, and he fell back hard against the steps, his head striking the rock sharply.

"Father!" called the boy. He left the horse and wagon and ran toward his father who now lay motionless on the gravel surface, then knelt by him. "Are you hurt, Father?" There was no reply. The man lay motionless on his side, his eyes staring expressionless. The freight clerk came running and crouched next to him.

"Mr. Hitchcock—Professor—sir—can you hear me?" At first there was no reply. "Go get your father some water, son," he instructed the boy, pointing to a metal cup perched on the edge of the watering trough.

By the time the boy returned with the cup of water his father was sitting up. He accepted the water, took a sip, then spoke softly. "Thank you, Son." He started to get to his feet but fell back to the ground.

"Professor," said the clerk. "Why don't you stay put? I'll get the doc. Won't take but a minute to run up to the..."

Hitchcock shook his head. "No, thank you, Mr. White. That is not necessary. We will be on our way." With some effort the professor clambered up onto the wagon and grasped the reins as his son climbed up beside him. But all was not right and he sat, breathing heavily. He stroked the back of his head and examined his hand.

"Are you bleeding, Father?"

"No, Son." He shook the reins, and the wagon pulled away.

After several minutes of riding in silence Hitchcock finally spoke. "Son, I must tell you, though it gives me great pain, I am gravely injured, I fear." The boy stared at him, fear written in his eyes. "If I cannot drive us all the way home, you must be prepared to take the reins. Can you do that, child?"

"Yes, Father, I can. Does your head hurt terribly? Mama can make you feel better, I am certain."

But his father shook his head. "I am afraid, my child, that I will not survive this happenstance. If I am fortunate enough to make it back home, I doubt I will live the night. My time has come, I am certain of it."

The boy did not reply. The pair sat in silence as the wagon rumbled along. Soon they entered into Chicopee. At the entrance to the quarry just south of the center of town, Hitchcock halted the wagon.

"What is it Father? Shall I take the reins, sir?"

He handed the reins to his son. "Wait here, boy, I'll only be a few minutes. There are some specimens in the quarry I have meant to retrieve."

He soon returned with a bag full of specimens, loaded them into the wagon, then climbed into the seat next to his son. They made their way back to Amherst without another word about Edward's fall or his grievous injury.

By 1835 the Hitchcocks were well settled—in their home, at Amherst College, and in the town of Amherst. After losing a newborn child in 1832, they had been blessed a year later with the birth of a third girl whom they named Jane Elizabeth. With four children ages two to eleven, the household now bristled with activity.

During the years of his geological survey, Edward's attentions had been divided between his college duties and his field work. It is hard to imagine how he could have devoted much time to his family during that period. But those extended absences were now, at least for a time, at an end; the father had returned to his fold. Orra captured the moment of his homecoming in a drawing entitled "The Return" (see page 177). Based on an oil painting by Robert Peckham, it shows her and all six children in front of their house greeting Edward as he stepped from a horse-drawn coach with Orra's mother looking on from a window.

In the years since the Hitchcocks arrived in Amherst, the town had been remarkably transformed. What was once almost exclusively a farming community was fast becoming an industrial center with dozens of small shops and factories, from paper mills, cotton mills, and woolen mills, to shops manufacturing hats, planes, carriages, harnesses, cooking stoves, cutlery, and pistols. One of the fastest growing enterprises in the town was L. M. Hills, manufacturer of palm leaf hats; by 1845 it would employ seventy workers, mostly women, and produce nearly a third of a million palm leaf hats annually.

Much of what we know of the Hitchcock family life in this period comes from the couple's account book. That document, begun on the day they moved into the new house in 1828 and maintained for the rest of their lives, offers many insights into the lives of Edward, Orra, their children, and other household members.

Professor Hitchcock, we learn, was paid $700 per year, four or five times a year, often by "order" (i.e., check), sometimes in cash, from John Leland, the college treasurer. Periodically, he was also paid for his preaching services to the college and reimbursed for expenses incurred for the chemistry laboratory. Also recorded were many cash expenditures for goods and services, from seeds, hay, butter, and molasses, to the repair of a shovel, pasturing of livestock, and killing of a hog. The account book also shows that Caroline White, widow of Orra's brother Jay, and her daughter Amelia lived with the Hitchcocks for a time in 1828 and 1829. Orra's mother, Ruth White, was also accommodated; her name appears in several entries until her death in 1839.

Another interesting revelation from the account book is that the Hitchcocks had many domestic workers in their home over the years to assist with cleaning, laundering, cooking, and attending to the children when their mother was otherwise engaged. Many were women under twenty-five years of age, especially in the early years, but older women were often employed later on. One, Selestia Montgomery, was African-American; several who worked

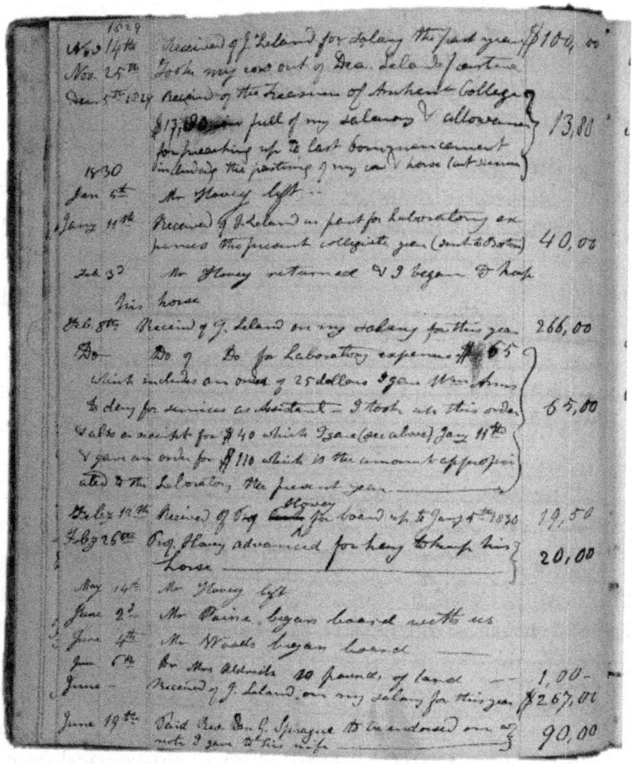

Figure 40. A page from the account book of Edward and Orra White Hitchcock, November 1829 to June 1830

for the family after 1845 were recent immigrants from Ireland, including Bridget McMann, Anna Carry, Hannah Collins, and Ellen Murphy. All were paid in cash, although the account book indicates that purchases were sometimes made for them by the Hitchcocks. In 1837, for example, they purchased a book, *Barnes' Notes on Acts*, for Mary Abercrombie, to encourage her religious studies.

It is surprising to learn how brief was the tenure of most of the family's domestic workers. The account book documents forty-four individuals, nearly all women, who were employed by the family between 1828 and 1864. Most stayed less than a year. Bridget McMann was one exception—she worked for the family for six years between 1846 and 1854. Why the frequent turnover in domestic help? Some of the younger workers may have gone on to better jobs, to school, or to marriage. Perhaps the work was difficult. Mrs. Hitchcock by all accounts was sweetly disposed, but the Professor may have had good days and bad days. He likely also insisted on daily devotions for the household staff, a requirement that may have been more acceptable to some than to others. Some of those domestic workers clearly became close to the family. In a letter to Edward, Jr., in 1852, Orra signed off with, "All send love—Bridget in particular."

A neighbor, Moses Cooley, performed work for the Hitchcocks for nearly thirty years including cutting wood, haying, and gardening. Often he was paid in cash, but just as often he accepted other forms of payment including "6 pounds of lard," "26½ lbs of pork," and "two bushels of rye." John Deignan, another recent arrival from Ireland, did similar work for the family from 1855 to 1864.

To add further to the level of activity in the household, the couple often boarded students and tutors from the college. According to the account book, they put up only two boarders in 1829, four in 1830. By 1831 that number had swelled to ten including one professor, two tutors, and seven students or recent alumni, at least four of whom worked as assistants in the chemistry laboratory. Among those boarding with the Hitchcocks in subsequent years were interesting and influential people such as abolitionist Henry Ward Beecher and educational pioneer Mary Lyon. William S. Tyler, who boarded with the Hitchcocks for several terms while a tutor for the college, wrote that the Hitchcock domicile was "…a home which material comforts and intellectual tastes conspired to render truly delightful." Nearly fifty years later, Edward, Jr., recollected of his family life during the 1830s and 1840s:

> As to the entertaining of relatives, friends of the family, and specially those interested in the church and College work, there was no end, and the amount of [it] now seems to me a marvel. It was continual, for nobody ever was allowed to go to the hotel. From a man from Deerfield with a load of grain, the men in the hay field, up to Mary Lyon and every stray minister, there was always a place at table and a bed for them. We children had to squeeze and be turned out of table and bed, but we always got round somehow.

What was the Hitchcock house like? According to one source, the rooms were large, the walls papered in dark colors with bold antique designs. "The kitchen, with hospitable air, seemed to invite the visitor to sit before the blazing fire upon its immense hearthstone and await the dainties sure to be produced from the great brick oven." The dining room was furnished with mahogany tables and chairs. The downstairs was well heated with fireplaces in every room, but the upstairs bedrooms were cold and furnished with feather beds on high bedsteads.

Just a few steps from the kitchen door was a garden where the family grew potatoes, corn, and beans for their own consumption or for barter with neighbors. They also had apple and peach trees. There was a small menagerie of farm animals as well, including one or two cows, a horse, pigs, and chickens. In winter the animals resided in the barn; the family purchased several tons of hay from a neighbor each year. In late spring some of the livestock were moved to the pastures of neighbors John Leland or George Baker where they remained through the summer. In his memoir Edward, Jr., recalls the sights and sounds of farm life:

> …[E]ven now I can hear the flails of one two or three men threshing rye & wheat. And then the farming mill as it blew the chaff out of the door. And I can see George & Enos Baker pumping water in the barn yard for the cattle to drink.

The family purchased meat, mainly pork and veal, from neighbors or from Mr. Howe, the local butcher. They obtained fish, flour, sugar, salt, lemon, and molasses from the markets of E. W. Storrs and Luke Sweetser, fabric such as cotton, muslin, and calico, shoes, gloves, and bonnets from the store of Messrs. Kellogg and Whitcomb. Orra's cooking skills, as Edward, Jr., described them, were remarkable. Among his favorite foods as a child were his mother's fried salt pork, hominy scrap, cider apple sauce, freshly churned ice cream, and homemade cheese.

When not in school, the children participated in the family economy as well. In his memoirs Edward, Jr., recalled taking the horses and cows to pasture daily, not always willingly. But he did enjoy the several times each summer when he was called upon to drive the team and wagon to Deerfield for a load of hay or corn. It was an all-day excursion highlighted by a visit on his return to a favorite shop in Sunderland for a piece of mince pie. The girls learned needlework from their mother, perhaps also from some of their domestic helpers, and sewed much of their own clothing.

The Hitchcock children naturally benefitted a great deal from the early instruction provided by their mother. Beginning as early as age five, each child attended a small school just a few doors away run by the Misses Emily and Julia Nelson, daughters of the Baptist minister. When Mary Lyon came to live with the family in 1834, the children took an immediate liking to her. She tutored Mary, Catherine, and Edward, Jr., for a time until her departure in 1836.

In winter Edward, Jr., brought his sled to school and would sometimes give a ride to a neighborhood friend, Rebecca Snell. "…[W]e once agreed on a good sledding day that we would be married and go to Jerusalem together," he recalled. "But she got to the New Jerusalem at least 65 years before I shall." Rebecca died in 1841 at age twelve.

With a large home and growing family to oversee, not to mention the constant flow of boarders, guests, and friends, Orra Hitchcock might be forgiven for finding little time for her art. And yet she was fully as productive artistically during this time as she had been earlier in her married life. Not the least of her undertakings was the creation of murals, maps, cross sections, and diagrams for Edward's lectures. By Edward's own estimation, the drawings his wife created for use in his lectures totaled more than 1800 square feet. His botany lecture notes contain references to over one hundred paintings by his wife.

For Edward's 1833 *Report on the Geology of Massachusetts* alone Orra drew over 100 illustrations including fifteen lithographed plates for the "Topographical Geology" section. Some years later Edward would recall Orra's artistic contributions to his work, even as she tended to her family's needs:

> Finally I could not forget that for nearly nine tenths of the drawings attached to my works I have been indebted to the pencil of my wife. It has cost her many a painful sacrifice in the midst of the cares of a numerous family thus to assist me: but she has done it cheerfully…Truly if I have done anything for science it is because Providence gave me such a wife.

As to Edward Hitchcock's writing during this period, the previous five years had been devoted almost entirely to the Massachusetts geological survey. He published a preliminary report of the survey in 1832 and a complete report in 1833. In 1835 he published a revised report as well as several shorter articles on geology. At that point he turned his attentions to a subject especially dear to his heart, the relationship between science and religion, particularly in regard to the book of Genesis.

That science and religion were intimately connected was by now a guiding principle for Edward Hitchcock. He had first heard this formulated by Professor Eleazar Fitch at Yale, but for Hitchcock it was much more than a theological construct, it was a reflection of the man himself. Love of God and love of science mingled inextricably in him. He could no sooner remove one or the other than he could sacrifice one half of his heart, one half of his mind, or one half of his soul.

He had begun to articulate his own thinking on the subject with *Utility of Natural History* and his reviews of Buckland's *Reliquiae Diluvianae* a decade earlier. In 1835 and 1836 he published a series of three articles on the subject in the journal *Biblical Repository*. To Hitchcock the supposed conflict between geology and the words of revelation amounted to little more than a question of chronology. There was no real conflict, he asserted, not when one carefully examined the geological evidence. God did create heaven and earth in six days, but "days" not in the strict sense of twenty-four-hour periods, but in the Hebrew meaning of the word, that is, periods of indefinite length. God did populate the earth with organic beings, plants, animals, etc., although not all at once but in several episodes of creation; some of those creatures

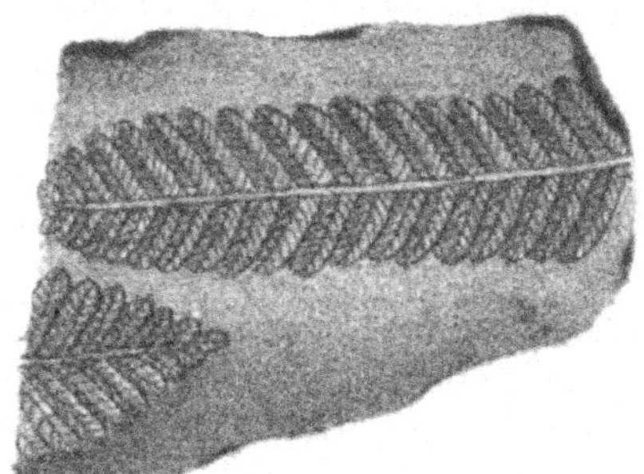

Figure 41. Fossilized fern by Orra White Hitchcock, 1833

Figure 42. Bashapish Falls in Mount Washington, Mass., woodcut by Orra White Hitchcock, 1841

thrived, while others had long since become extinct. And God did create man—as it is writ in Genesis—after all other creatures. Yes, he insisted, the fossil record had proved it again and again: God saved the best for last.

In a subsequent issue of the same journal, Reverend Moses Stuart, Professor of Sacred Literature at Andover Theological Seminary, offered a lengthy response to Hitchcock's trilogy. Stuart had no argument with geology. It mattered not to religion what geologists found, he believed, because the Bible was never intended to be understood as a scientific document. It taught religious truths, not scientific truths. To Reverend Stuart science and religion were independent, while Hitchcock saw them as intimately linked.

Edward Hitchcock responded to Stuart's critique with a rejoinder in the next issue of the *Biblical Repository*, pointing out what he regarded as contradictions in Stuart's thinking. But his challenge accomplished little except to reinforce the fundamental difference between the two men: Hitchcock sought to unite science and religion, Stuart wanted to keep them apart. Hitchcock published a similar response to Stuart's critique in the *American Journal of Science and Arts* just a few months later.

In 1837 and 1838 he authored another trilogy for the *Biblical Repository,* this time regarding Noah's flood, once again arguing that science and religion were in unison. In the first of the three articles, Hitchcock also took issue with Sir Charles Lyell and the theory of uniformitarianism. Like many geologists of his day, Hitchcock was at the time a strict catastrophist, one who believed that earth's early history had been marked by great catastrophes–floods, earthquakes, volcanic eruptions, etc.–all of which he attributed to the hand of God. While catastrophism prevailed among many early nineteenth century geologists, an alternative view of earth's history was beginning to gain ground, a view known as uniformitarianism or gradualism. James Hutton, the Scottish geologist, was among the early advocates of this view, asserting that the slow, gradual forces influencing the earth today such as erosion, deposition, sea level fluctuations, and temperature changes were the same forces that had been at work in the past. In the early 1830s Charles Lyell took this argument a step further in his *Principles of Geology*, arguing that most of the features of earth's surface were formed by slow, gradual processes, not cataclysms. Furthermore, Lyell suggested that no divine agency was necessary, that these gradual forces were simply the work of natural laws. Hitchcock challenged Lyell's insinuation in the strongest terms, suggesting that Lyell was an atheist or, at least, a promoter of atheism through such ideas.

In these eight articles, Hitchcock's tone was decidedly defensive. And those defenses seemed to be raised against enemies on both sides, men of faith who dabbled ineptly in science, and men of science who were not well versed in theology. He pleaded for mutual respect and understanding between those two constituencies. If that was his intention, he must have felt frustrated at the response. His 1836 paper in *AJS* would be the last on the subject to appear in that journal or in any other major scientific publication in America. The scientific community, it seems, had lost interest in the matter. If anything they may have adopted Stuart's position, that science and religion should be allowed to go their separate ways.

To Edward Hitchcock death was an ever-present reality. Nearly every entry in his notes from 1828 until his death bears a reference to impending doom. He shared these premonitions often with colleagues, his wife, even with his children. According to Edward, Jr., those solemn words spoken to the ten-year-old after his fall in Springfield, for example, were not unusual, they were typical, and Orra and their children seemed to accept them as part of his desponding nature.

We might today be tempted to brand this as a morbid obsession, an unhealthy preoccupation, one that could only lead to a life of sadness and depression. But Hitchcock's interest in death was not that unusual for his time. Average life expectancy in mid-nineteenth-century America was half what it is today, due in large measure to the high rate of infant and childhood death. As Hitchcock reminded his young parishioners in that 1823 sermon (see page 87), barely half the children in his congregation would live to the age of twelve. Furthermore, concern with death, its terrors as well as its promises, was fundamental to Christianity.

In 1839 Hitchcock published a book on the subject of death entitled *A Wreath for the Tomb*. Much of the volume is devoted to essays by prominent theologians and writers of his day and earlier—Charles Drelincourt, John Williamson Nevin, Thomas Chalmers, and Hannah More. It also includes a sermon entitled "Lessons Taught by Sickness" that he delivered at Amherst College in 1839.

The book begins with a long essay that reveals a great deal about Edward Hitchcock's attitudes toward death. "The uncertainty of life and the nearness of eternity," he writes, "have one advantage when presented as religious motives, possessed by no other. The most latitudinarian scepticism never doubts their truth." Every human being knows that "the body must ere long, and may soon yield to the King of terrors." And yet men have ever succeeded in deceiving themselves about their mortality, at least for a time.

He proceeds to enumerate some of the ways in which men of all ages and walks of life delude themselves about death. In youth, in middle age, and even in old age, they allow the world and its labors and attractions to distract them from their mortality. Men of all occupations—merchants, farmers, physicians, ministers, poets, philosophers, teachers—find the means to avoid the simple truth that they know too well, that one day they will die. All try to avoid the subject, to avert their eyes from the sight of it, to separate themselves from it in any way possible.

But why separate ourselves from death, asks Hitchcock. An awareness of the nearness of one's death can be beneficial. First, it has a restraining influence on that person. It promotes humility, temperance, and purity, and it helps discourage sensual indulgence. "When he daily feeds upon the manna of heaven, how feeble will be the attractions of the dainties of the table; and how ready to abandon at once every indulgence that impedes or interrupts his communion." Furthermore, an awareness of one's mortality will discourage one from becoming a slave to the "riches, honors, and pleasures" of this world, but rather it will help fix one's attentions on the distant prize of eternity:

> Pride of intellect is the besetting sin of literary men. And nothing but the influence that emanates from a constant realization of eternity, can curb this most indomitable of all sins. But in a near view of the throne…With the glories of heaven full in view, how little will he feel the reproaches of earth; and how can he but pity those, who manifest a spirit that must exclude them from that happy world.

Some men, he admits, are discouraged and depressed by the prospect of their own demise.

> …[I]n a few cases of real piety, where bodily disease has thrown a settled melancholy over the soul, the apprehension of death may unnerve the

> Christian's resolution and energies. While in this morbid state, a dark cloud has come over his prospects for eternity; and until that can be dissipated, he has no heart for labor…

For such men the imminence of death may sap both their bodily and mental capacities and lead to spiritual paralysis. But an awareness of one's mortality, Hitchcock argues, far from being a dispiriting influence, can be a powerful engine both for the reform of one's moral life and for the exercise of one's intellect:

> "Is the time so short," he will say, "and the work I have to do so momentous and great, and shall I suffer one precious hour to be lost? Oh, it needs the whole of the short period left me to prepare my own heart for heaven: it needs the whole to study and understand anything of the works and character of God: it needs the whole to accomplish any thing for my fellow-men. God help me so to select the objects of my pursuit, that none of my time shall be spent in laboriously doing nothing. God help me so judiciously and skillfully to engage in every labor, that the greatest amount shall be accomplished in the shortest period."

It is clear from his notes that this was the role of death in the mind and soul of Edward Hitchcock. It was a kind of motivational device that propelled him again and again to complete unfinished projects or undertake great new endeavors. The prospect of death for Edward Hitchcock was not a bottomless pit of hopelessness, it was a driving force of productivity.

Near the end of the essay, Hitchcock notes that the nearness of death, far from dragging a man down to the depths, can motivate him to take on new projects, to open new horizons: "[H]e who knows the history of religious men, cannot but have often noticed how a transformation of heart has brought out new energies of intellect and of action…new fields of investigation."

In March 1835, just such a "new field of investigation" was opened up to Edward Hitchcock. A curious letter from Greenfield would redirect his attentions to an entirely new domain of geology—new to him, new even to science. It had to do with footmarks in stone, an enduring legacy of earth's past. Just as those indelible marks in stone have survived, so too have Edward Hitchcock's efforts on their behalf survived and outlived him by centuries.

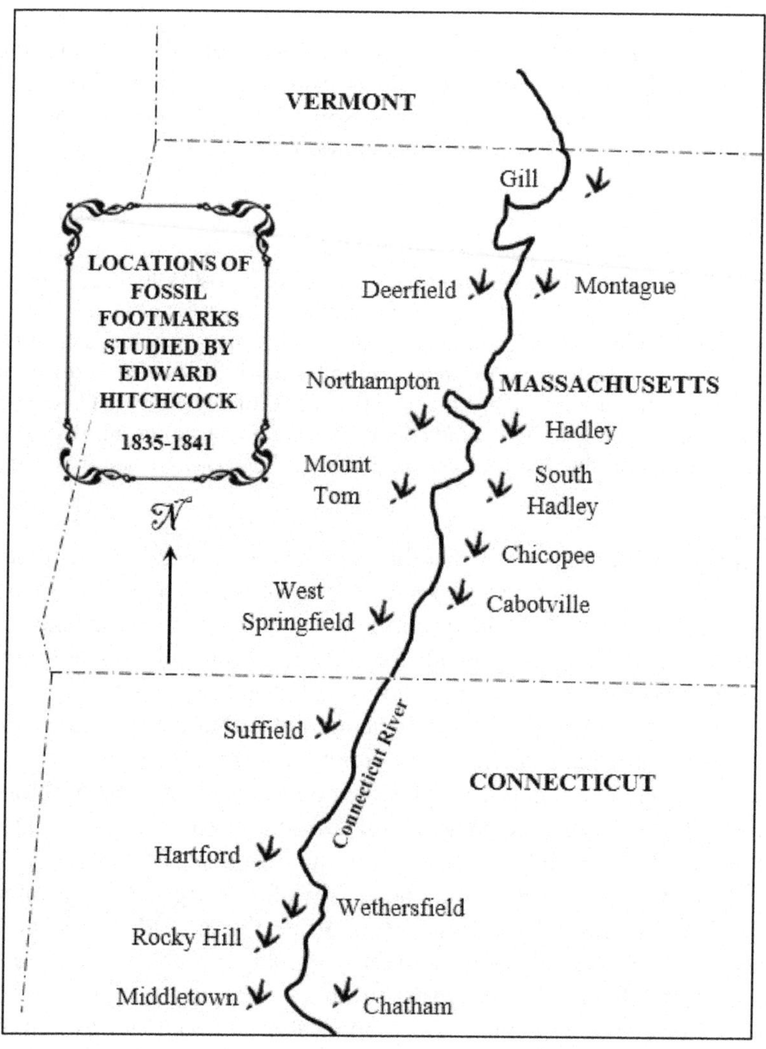

Figure 43. Locations of fossil footmarks mentioned in Edward Hitchcock's *Final Report on the Geology of Massachusetts* in 1841. Specimens listed for Deerfield, Northampton, and Hadley were found in sidewalk paving stones but were likely excavated nearby.

A view of the Moody Footmark Quarry

16 Footmarks in Stone

"The evidence entirely favors the views of Professor Hitchcock"

Greenfield, early April 1835

The tall roan strained as he climbed the last hill, a short but steep pitch, leading from the banks of the Green River to the center of Greenfield. The driver leaned forward in his seat, straining to keep his balance as the buggy lurched through muddy ruts. At last the street levelled out and the driver halted at the wooden sidewalk. He tied his horse, then paused and looked up at the sign hanging above him. "JAMES DEANE, M.D.—Physician—Surgeon."

He entered the office and handed his card to a young woman seated behind a desk. "Professor Edward Hitchcock, Miss, to see Dr. Deane." At that moment a door into an adjoining office opened. A middle-aged woman emerged looking pale and distraught followed by the doctor.

"Apply that tincture daily, then, Mrs. Allen. You should see a rapid improvement," he said smiling pleasantly. The woman nodded, then departed.

The doctor pivoted toward his new visitor, his expression turning more serious as he greeted the figure before him. "Professor Hitchcock, sir. How very good to see you."

"How do you do, Dr. Deane," replied Hitchcock as they shook hands.

"Your trip from Amherst was I pray without incident?"

"Quite so, Doctor, quite so. But the highway through Deerfield was frightfully wet and rutted. I had all I could do to keep my buggy aright. And the bridge at Cheapside is in a sorry state as well."

"Yes, well, the county roads are a travesty these days, I will admit to that. Everyone uses them, yet no one it seems wishes to incur the expense of proper upkeep." He paused. "Well, do come in, Professor."

Hitchcock entered the doctor's office and was seated in a hard wooden chair intended for patients. The odor of ammonia salts wafted through the air.

"Pardon the dishabille, Professor. All in a day's work for a physician, you know. And thank you, sir, for making the trip. I do hope it will not prove a waste of your time. I know how very taxed you must be at the college at this time."

Hitchcock smiled briefly. "I have perused the red sandstone up and down the valley, Doctor, yet I have never seen anything remotely resembling the tracks of beasts as you described in your letter. I feel certain they will prove to be derived from some other cause, although what cause I cannot guess."

"Yes, I daresay that is probably so. And I naturally lack the trained eye that you possess. Which is of course why I wrote you." The doctor paused. "Well, then, shall we?" He rose and directed the professor through a side door to a low shed at the rear of the building. In the first stall stood a horse, a gray mare, chewing idly on some hay. The adjacent stall was empty, except for what Hitchcock immediately recognized as a slab of red sandstone, actually two slabs nestled together, resting against the wall.

"There it is, Professor."

Hitchcock stooped before the stones. They appeared to be etched with four arrow shaped marks. He ran his fingers over each, then shifted his position and looked at the marks from a lower angle. He drew a loupe from his vest pocket and examined the marks more closely. With the doctor's assistance he inverted the stones and looked carefully at the undersides and the edges, then righted them. He stood and looked down on the stones, frowning.

"I fear I have brought you out of your way for nothing, Professor Hitchcock," said Dr. Deane glumly. "I am very sorry for the—"

The professor interrupted. "Quite extraordinary."

"Sir?" Deane seemed shocked at the professor's response. "You mean, sir—"

"Doctor Deane, I believe what we have here are, as you suspected, avian footmarks in stone. Everything about them argues for it—these are fossilized bird tracks."

Figure 44.
Dr. James Deane
(1801-1858)

No one by 1835 was as well acquainted with the geology of Massachusetts as Edward Hitchcock. He had explored the Connecticut Valley since a boy, accumulating a large collection of rocks and minerals. He had published more than two dozen papers on the state's geology and mineralogy since 1815. He had served as State Geologist for five years under two Massachusetts governors, crisscrossing the state again and again, recording data, collecting samples, speaking with miners, manufacturers, and landowners about the local mineral resources. The report on his geological survey, now in its second edition, had been widely publicized, praised, and adopted as a model for other states to follow.

As to organic remains, Hitchcock had discovered, observed, sketched, and recorded hundreds of fossils, plant and animal, from the sandstone of the Connecticut River valley. Fishes, insects, ferns, crustaceans, marine organisms—he had seen them all. But never before had he seen anything resembling the fossilized tracks of animals, least of all of birds.

We can well imagine his reaction, then, on receiving from Dr. Deane the first letter and sketch of the impressions in that sandstone slab from Turners Falls, Massachusetts. He was likely possessed of two instincts, one to dismiss it as an artifact, a random disfigurement of the stone having no bearing to living things. In reply he wrote, "I am not without strong suspicion that the case you mention may be a very peculiar structure of certain spots in the sandstone which I have often seen in a red variety of that rock." At the same time, however, Hitchcock had learned not to treat such a report cavalierly, especially one from a man of education and discernment. "I should be quite glad to see these…specimens," he wrote in closing. "If you can prevent their being defaced for a month or two until I shall visit Greenfield I shall be much obliged to you." Barely three weeks later he fulfilled that promise.

From the first moment that Professor Hitchcock laid eyes on those sandstone slabs, the inference was clear and compelling: these were not random disfigurements of the rock due to chemical or erosive action. They were traces of life, ancient life, ancient avian life. It went against every notion of paleontology he had ever read or contemplated, that creatures as advanced as birds should have lived in the distant past represented by the new red sandstone. This, he knew, would be a hard sell in the scientific arena, and he, Professor Edward Hitchcock of Amherst College, State Geologist of Massachusetts, was fully prepared to meet that challenge.

As invigorating as the prospect must have been to the professor, we might guess that there was another dimension to his reaction to Dr. Deane's discovery. How, he may well have asked himself, how during all my years of geological exploration in this very valley, could I have failed to notice such extraordinary artifacts? And he may also have been struck by one particular irony, that the very specimen he gazed on that day in Greenfield had been unearthed barely three miles from the village of Deerfield, the place of his birth and childhood. Was it possible, could it be, that beneath that surface of cool detachment and objectivity the professor presented to the world lurked rich lodes of emotion, hidden strata of humiliation, perhaps even a vein of jealousy?

In typical fashion, Hitchcock immediately flew into a frenzy of activity, traveling up and down the Connecticut Valley in a rickety wagon, covering more than 500 miles in barely six months. In Massachusetts he visited quarries from Gill southward to Greenfield, Turners Falls, Deerfield, Sunderland, Northampton, Easthampton, and South Hadley. He made several forays into Connecticut as well, visiting sites at West Enfield and Hartford. He talked to quarrymen, rockhounds, landowners, anyone who had any experience with such curious rock samples. To his amazement he also observed slabs of rock with similar marks on the steps of the Hampshire County Courthouse in Northampton and on the sidewalks of Greenfield and Deerfield. Is it possible, he must surely have asked himself, that I, as a young lad of Deerfield, stepped upon that very stone without observing it, without wondering about it, without recognizing it for what it truly was?

Between geological forays, he wrote Benjamin Silliman about the possibility of publishing a paper on the discovery in an upcoming issue of his journal. Silliman was agreeable but urged haste as others, including Deane himself, had similar intentions to publish. Silliman knew that the matter would be controversial and feared that if a nonscientist like Deane were to report such a proposal in his journal, it would place the publication in a bad light. It would require someone of the highest respectability and credibility in the scientific community both in America and abroad to make a strong case, and there was no doubt in Silliman's mind who that someone should be.

Hitchcock submitted the first draft of his paper to Silliman in October 1835. "Ornithichnology—Description of the Foot marks of Birds, (Ornithichnites) on new Red Sandstone in Massachusetts," would appear in the January 1836 issue of the *American Journal of Science and Arts.* Despite the feverish pace of preparation, the paper was a masterpiece of what Hitchcock did best—observe, describe, illustrate, and cautiously, ever so cautiously, draw conclusions. He began with a description of the specimens themselves:

> They consist of two slabs, about forty inches square, originally united face to face; but on separation, presenting four most distinct depressions on one of

> them, with four correspondent projections on the other; precisely resembling the impressions of the feet of a large bird in mud.

He gave similar descriptions for samples he had observed in four other localities, three in Northampton, one in South Hadley.

The footmarks, as he termed them, were nearly all ternate, the three toes pointing in the same direction and joined in some at the heel, although in many the imprint of the heel was absent, as if the creature's weight were projected forward. In some a smaller fourth appendage could also be discerned, usually pointing in the opposite direction and covered with bristles or fine hairs.

Invariably the footmarks occurred in pairs, with distinct left and right feet. But the creature must have been bipedal, "for we search in vain to find any corresponding or parallel row of impressions" such as would be created by a four-footed creature. Furthermore, the footmarks could often be found "in succession," that is, in a line across the surface. "The interval, also, between the different steps, varies; sometimes several inches in the smaller impressions, and even a foot or two in the larger: just about as much, indeed, as we should expect in an animal moving at different paces."

Not until he had presented six pages of description did Hitchcock draw a conclusion as to the most likely explanation of the tracks: "I trust I have proceeded far enough in these details, to justify me in coming to the conclusion, that these impressions are the tracks of birds, made while the incipient sandstone and shale were in a plastic state." He based this statement, one that would raise the eyebrows of nearly all geologists and paleontologists of his time, on three observations:

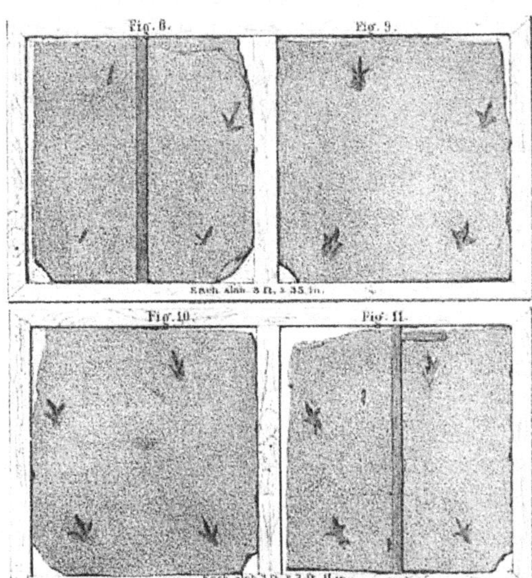

Figure 45. Red sandstone slabs with tracks described by Dr. James Deane in a letter to Edward Hitchcock, March 5, 1835

> 1. These impressions are evidently the tracks of a biped animal. For I have not been able to find an instance, where more than a single row of impressions exists.
>
> 2. They could not have been made by any other known biped, except birds. On this point, I am happy to have the opinion of more than one distinguished zoologist.
>
> 3. They correspond very well with the tracks of [modern] birds.

But how had these tracks been formed and preserved? It seemed clear, he argued, that they were formed in a soft material, mud or clay, that subsequently hardened without disturbance. The birds must have been foraging in shallow water at the time the tracks were formed, much as modern wading birds do. And while the waters lapping on those stones today are fresh, based on the many fossil marine organisms found up and down the valley, he concluded that those waters in ancient times were saline—the birds were wading in a shallow bay of an ancient sea. And although the rock strata where the footmarks occurred are today tilted, some as much as 30°, there appeared to Hitchcock no evidence that the birds were walking on a slanted surface. Thus the inevitable conclusion, "…that these tracks were made before the rock was elevated to its present situation; that is, while it was horizontal or nearly so…."

One difference between these ancient birds and modern-day avians, however, could not be overlooked—their enormous size. The largest track was some eighteen inches long; he would name the creature responsible for that track *Ornithichnites giganteus*. Considering, he pointed out, that the largest living bird species known to humankind, the ostrich, has a foot about ten inches long, *O. giganteus* must have been much larger. "May we not infer, that some of these ancient birds, whose feet are sixteen or seventeen inches long, must have been almost twice as heavy and high as the ostrich?"

It might be assumed that those footmarks in stone provided little data on which to base a taxonomic analysis. In fact his paper utilized at least a dozen traits including toe width, number of toes, length of foot, length of claws, length of step, and others. As was the convention, each distinct type was assigned a two-part name in Latin consisting of the genus

ORNITHICHNITES.

1. *Pachydactyli.*

O—— giganteus.
O—— tuberosus.
α dubius.

2. *Leptodactyli.*

O—— ingens.
α minor.
O—— diversus.
α clarus.
β platydactylus.
O—— tetradactylus.
O—— palmatus.
O—— minimus.

Figure 46. Hitchcock's first effort at a taxonomy of the fossil footmarks and species. Since he was the first to ever attempt such a task, he was free to create new names. He assigned all seven creatures in that first paper to a single genus, *Ornithichnites,* from the Greek meaning birds in stone. He listed these in two subgroups, Pachydactyli (wide-toed) and Leptodactyli (narrow-toed). Several of these he further divided into what might today be called varieties or subspecies.

The Latin species names are in every case descriptive: *Ornithichnites giganteus,* the largest track by far; *O. tuberosus,* having "tuberous swellings on the underside of the toes"; *O. ingens,* large though not quite as large as *O. giganteus; O. diversus,* a highly variable species; *O. tetradactylus,* a four-toed creature; *O. palmatus*, having four toes all pointing forward, not unlike a human hand; and *O. minimus,* the smallest track, ranging from half an inch to one and one half inches. This was only the beginning of Hitchcock's efforts to describe and classify creatures that neither he nor anyone had ever seen. All he had on which to base his system were those enigmatic marks in stone. In response to some of the doubts raised about his attribution of these creatures as birds, he altered the genus name in 1837 to *Ornithoidichnites,* the Greek term *Ornithoid* meaning "bird-like."

Edward Hitchcock was far from a revolutionary. If anything he was a conservative at heart, clinging steadfastly to established notions in matters both scientific and spiritual. Yet in this one paper he had created a new discipline (Ichnology) and a subdiscipline (Ornithichnology). He had proposed a taxonomy of creatures entirely new to science, never even hinted at by paleontological researchers on several continents. Furthermore, were his findings correct and the tracks made by birds, his work pushed back the time of the earliest evidences of avian life. And although he would not say as much at this point in his career, others in the field would conclude that the difference amounted to several geological eras and millions of years.

As might be expected, "Ornithichnology" was received with considerable interest by scientists on both sides of the Atlantic. Within two years reports had appeared in a number of American and European publications. The journal *Annales des Sciences* in Geneva published a French translation of the entire paper that broadened its audience on the Continent.

The first mention of Hitchcock's paper in America appeared in the April 1836, issue of the *North American Review*. It amounted to just a few sentences in a lengthy review of his recently released *Report on the Geology of Massachusetts.* The review was published anonymously, although several comments by the author suggest it may have been the work of Massachusetts geologist Charles T. Jackson. He expressed enthusiasm regarding both the

Report and "Ornithichnology," referring to the latter as "an able and very interesting memoir" that included "some remarkable discoveries."

A different tone was set by a lengthy, more detailed review just two months later. It came from an unlikely source—a small, relatively new literary magazine called *The Knickerbocker*—and from an equally unlikely critic, an Episcopal minister from Glastonbury, Connecticut. The Reverend Alonzo Bowen Chapin began by professing to be an admirer of Hitchcock, at having "read many of his works with unmingled pleasure." But he went on to suggest that the public had been for some time too quick to Hitchcock's defense, too willing to accept something less than excellence in his writing, citing the paper in the *North American Review* as an example. "We fear," wrote Chapin, "that he gives himself more credit for accuracy than he actually deserves."

Chapin had some geological credentials and expertise to bring to the subject, but his criticisms of the paper's scientific merits were weak and ill-informed. He dismissed the marks as "septaria and stria," suggesting they resulted from erosion or chemical action rather than the footmarks of ancient creatures and arguing that Hitchcock's illustrations generalized and misrepresented the specimens. Near the end of his review, he took issue with Hitchcock's knowledge of Greek, such as his use of the medial sigma (σ) instead of the final sigma (ς) at the end of *ορνισ,* the Greek word for bird. Such comments do nothing to support his critique but seem petty, as though the author was more interested in showing off his knowledge of classical Greek than of advancing science. Hitchcock's reply was published a few months later in the same journal, followed by a rejoinder from Chapin.

The response among European critics, on the other hand, was generally favorable. Most writers accepted that the tracks were of bipedal animals, although several doubted that they could be birds. One reviewer wrote in the *Bibliothéque Universelle de Genéve* that it seemed impossible that these could be the footprints of birds, though he admitted that "the resemblance of these fossil footprints with those of the present birds is striking." He went on to add another reservation: "It is only peculiar that animals of an organization as complicated as that of birds may have existed at such a remote period, especially without any trace of the bones which they ought to have left in the fossil state." Wrote a German reviewer, "Much of a stir was rightly made by the bird tracks discovered by Hitchcock on the shores of the Connecticut in Massachusetts…There is no doubt that this is really to do with bird footprints." Similarly, an anonymous reviewer in the *British Critic* stated,

> This class [Aves], however, is now shown to have existed at a much earlier geological period than those above mentioned, for tracks, obviously imprinted by the feet of birds, have been observed in laminated flagstones of the new red sandstone formation, and described by Professor Hitchcock.

Two eminent European geologists weighed in early on the discussion of "Ornithichnology." William Buckland in the 1837 English edition of the *Bridgewater Treatises* wrote of the footmarks, "…[they] are of the highest interest to the Palaeontologist, as they establish the new fact of the existence of Birds at the early epoch of the New Red Sandstone formation…" Charles Daubeny, having visited the Connecticut Valley for a personal tour of the footmarks, wrote in 1838 that the marks "…could have been produced in no other way, than by the treading of birds of various sizes upon a soft and plastic material." Charles Lyell, perhaps the most influential geologist of that era, was slower to lend his support to Hitchcock's work. But in an address delivered before the Geological Society of London in 1842, Lyell stated that based on his recent visit to those sites, he had no doubts that the marks were the footprints of "some creature walking on mud or sand." Furthermore, the arrangement of those tracks in single, uniform lines convinced him that, "the animal was a biped, and the trifid marks resemble those which a bird leaves…"

While influential European geologists such as Buckland, Daubeny, and Lyell were convinced, a good deal of skepticism seems to have prevailed among American geologists, although none appeared in print. In April 1840, a small group of American geologists including representatives from seven states assembled in Philadelphia. Edward Hitchcock was appointed chair of the group. Their first order of business was the establishment of a new society to be known as the Association of American Geologists. After several days devoted to organizational matters, they proceeded to topics of scientific interest, one of which was Hitchcock's paper: "Specimens were next presented of the sandstones of Massachusetts, exhibiting the fossil footmarks, so called, and observations made in regard to them. This subject was of so much interest as to induce the Association to appoint a committee to visit the localities, and to report their conclusions at the next meeting."

That the fossil footmarks were "of so much interest" may have been a considerable understatement. The truth is that there were several members of that small group who were clearly skeptical. The committee appointed included five eminent American geologists, Henry D. Rogers, Lardner Vanuxem, Richard C. Taylor, Ebenezer Emmons, and T. A. Conrad. They deliberated for a year; Vanuxem and Emmons visited Amherst to observe the specimens firsthand. The committee's conclusion, presented at the Association's second meeting in April 1841, must surely have warmed the heart of the professor from Amherst: "From a comparative examination of the facts on both sides, your committee unanimously believe, that the evidence entirely favors the views of Prof. Hitchcock." At that same meeting, he would be named vice chair of the Association and would make his landmark address on the emerging glacial theory. Clearly he stood now at the very center of current thinking on a range of subjects in American geology.

And yet in looking back on that period late in life, Edward Hitchcock recalled it quite differently: "I remember well the discouragement and heart sickness that often came over me during those six years when I had to maintain the conflict alone," he wrote in 1858. He was a proud man, particularly regarding his scientific endeavors, and all the encomiums in the world it seems could not assuage lingering emotions about a few criticisms. "I shall be happy to be corrected wherever I am erroneous, even if it be in my fundamental conclusions," he wrote at the end of "Ornithichnology." But happiness about criticisms of his work was an emotion he seldom experienced in life.

No doubt Hitchcock's memories of that period were also colored by a bitter personal challenge from a most unexpected quarter. In 1843 Dr. James Deane published the first of a series of scholarly articles on the footmarks of the Connecticut Valley in which he claimed to be the original discoverer of the tracks, questioned some of Hitchcock's interpretations of those impressions, made light of the professor's taxonomic efforts, and, worst of all, suggested that he, Dr. Deane, not the professor from Amherst, deserved credit for priority in the field of ichnology. For the next decade and a half, that conflict took on a life of its own, often overshadowing the more important scientific questions raised by the footmarks (see Chapter 24).

The years 1840 and 1841 stand out as a pinnacle in the career of Edward Hitchcock, geologist. In 1840 the first edition of *Elementary Geology* came into print. By then he had been teaching geology for fifteen years. While his lectures were based largely on his research, he did recommend for his students recent works in the field, notably Lyell's *Principles of Geology*, de la Beche's *Researches in Theoretical Geology*, and Bakewell's *Introduction to Geology*. All were by European authors reflecting a European point of view. Hitchcock was determined to publish a truly American text, one that reflected his own experiences, his own perspective on geology.

Elementary Geology was written with his Amherst audience in mind, young men with limited exposure to the sciences. He started with the fundamentals—the types of rocks and rock formations, basic rock structures such as dikes, stratification, lamina, etc. He proposed his own terms and classification system while recognizing those of other authorities. The format of the book was formal, almost stilted, with major concepts set off by headings such as "Proposition," "Principle," "Proofs," etc. A large portion of the book was devoted to organic remains including of course his now well-known work on fossil footmarks. He also devoted considerable space to the subject of glaciers, although not until the second edition of 1841 did he take up the "glacial theory" of Agassiz and others. Near the end, in a chapter entitled "Connection between Geology and Natural and Revealed Religion," he presented his views regarding religion and science, developing his idea that there was little conflict between the two. Also included was an illustration entitled "Palaeontological Chart" that revealed a great deal about Hitchcock's evolving concept of the relationships among living things (see Chapter 29).

Elementary Geology was a success from the start. A review in the October 1840 issue of the *American Journal of Science and Arts*, probably written by Benjamin Silliman, extolled the author: "[Hitchcock's] transatlantic reputation is such, that no American name is considered of better authority in geology, or more highly esteemed." He was no less enthusiastic about the book:

> ...[Hitchcock] has attempted to prepare a work which shall fill a vacancy long felt by the instructors of geology in this country, a work which, while it gives a good view of the progress of the science in other countries, draws its illustrations mainly from American facts. From the rapid glance which we have been able to bestow on this performance, we should think that Prof. Hitchcock had succeeded in imparting this feature to his book.

The review did include one point of criticism: "The style of execution in the work is not equal to its value, particularly some of the wood cuts."

A few months later in the *North American Review* an anonymous reviewer, possibly Lowell chemist Samuel L. Dana, heaped praise on the author: "Professor Hitchcock has been too long and favorably known to scientific men, both of the new world and of the old, to make it necessary for us to say, with what ample qualifications he undertakes the task before him." The reviewer then went on to recommend the book: "His work...bears the impress of acute and original observation..." He was particularly impressed with Hitchcock's treatment of the topic of organic remains: "We walk with our author in the Zoological Garden founded ages before the creation of man. He points out the gigantic plants of other days, in cages the great beasts, and 'draws out with a hook the great leviathans.' We almost hear their deep expirations, and witness the flapping of tails and fins in the 'death flurry' of huge Saurians." This reviewer, too, found fault with the illustrations and the typography: "in too many places the typography, is equaled only by some bad impressions of the penny press." Perhaps the standards of reviewers of those times were very high—in perusing century-and-a-half old copies of a dozen or more editions of the book, I could find little fault with their quality.

Hitchcock's text was widely used in American colleges over the next two decades, running to thirty-one editions. As to production quality, that never changed, perhaps because of Hitchcock's concern that the volume should be affordable for all. If that was his aim, he was apparently successful: the first edition sold for one dollar; the price of the twenty-eighth edition was $1.25.

In 1841 Hitchcock published a revised and expanded edition of his 1835 *Report on the Geology of Massachusetts*. It included some forty pages on the soil survey completed in 1837, as well as sixty pages and twenty-two plates on the fossil animal tracks. By now he had expanded his list of species to thirty, all but one of which were discovered and named by him.

But Hitchcock's research on the fossil footmarks was far from complete. He added thousands of specimens to his collection over the next two decades, constantly revising his taxonomy as new evidence emerged. The rules of nomenclature were only beginning to be formalized when he began this work, and the field of naming and classifying animal tracks was almost entirely his own, so he felt free to manipulate his "ichnotaxa" as he saw fit. For example, one track he identified in his first paper in 1836 as *Ornithichnites ingens* he renamed four times, *Ornithoidichnites ingens* in 1841, *Steropoides ingens* in 1845, *Steropezoum ingens* in 1848, and *Tridentipes ingens* in 1858.

In an 1845 paper Hitchcock announced an important change in his taxonomy. "…[H]itherto names have been given to the footmarks and not the animals. But since all geologists now admit that these impressions are real tracks, this paper attempts to name the animals that made them, and to classify and describe them, so far as it can be done from the data hitherto obtained." At the suggestion of Yale paleontologist James D. Dana, he renamed all the previously identified species and added new ones, placing them in five families, two of which were accepted names of existing animal families, the Struthionidae or flightless birds and Pteropodidae or bats. "I have no great confidence in the arrangement into groups, except in a few instances," he admitted. By 1858 he had abandoned those family names, reverting to the much more general "groups" including pachydactylous and leptodactylous birds, ornithoid lizards, lizards, batrachians (frogs or toads), and chelonians (turtles).

In several papers Hitchcock asserted that his species designations were probably conservative, that the number might well be considerably greater than he had estimated: "What I call species…among the footmarks, would probably only be genera in natural history." But the actual number of species represented by his collections would ultimately prove to be fewer than he reckoned, not more. Hitchcock's nomenclature and classification schemes have not fared well in the test of time. Paul E. Olsen and Emma C. Rainforth, modern day paleontologists who have devoted years to a reexamination of his taxonomy, describe it as a "nomenclatural morass."

Identifying an ancient organism solely from its tracks is somewhat akin to painting a portrait from the subject's shadow. While Hitchcock's taxonomy was flawed, science would ultimately come around to many of his conclusions regarding the fossil footmarks and the creatures that made them. In the end the professor from Amherst would be proven far more right than wrong about those denizens of a salt bay in the Triassic.

Amherst College, 1821

17 A Terrible Incubus

"My mind shrinks from this cross with the strongest aversion..."

Amherst, December 16, 1844

Wet snowflakes splattered against the windowpane as Orra Hitchcock, her brow knit with worry, stood in her parlor looking out toward the college. A few hours earlier, Lucius Boltwood, secretary of the trustees of the college, had come to the door: Professor Hitchcock's presence was requested at a meeting at the President's House.

Her husband had tried to calm her as to the nature of the call. Perhaps the trustees merely wished to confer on a matter regarding completion of the mineralogical cabinet. Despite his reassurances, Orra watched with apprehension as he made his way haltingly up the gravel pathway to the campus, his black winter cloak drawn around him against the wind and snow.

But that was nearly four hours ago, and still he had not returned. He had been in a particularly dark mood of late. It was the perilous condition of the college that was troubling him, she believed, though he shared few details with her. He had confessed to her his discomfort on another matter of a more personal nature, the most recent round of accusations and recriminations passing between himself and Dr. Deane of Greenfield. Deane's actions felt to him like a personal affront, an attempt to rob him of nearly a decade of labor with the cryptic fossil footmarks.

"My dear, I am going up to the President's House to fetch your father," Orra said to her nineteen-year-old daughter who was home from the Mount Holyoke Female Seminary at South Hadley for a few days.

But Catherine was not about to allow that: "Mother, you are not yet recovered from your illness." She was referring to the several months of frail health her mother had suffered over the summer. "I shall go for Father."

Despite her mother's protests, Catherine soon was bundled against the elements as she climbed the hill toward the residence of President Humphrey. As she approached the front door, a figure emerged. It was Lucius Boltwood. The meeting at the President's House had concluded nearly an hour earlier, he reported. Surely her father would be home by now. Catherine was worried. She turned and looked across the campus toward Johnson Chapel. At that very moment the chapel door opened and her father appeared. She thanked Mr. Boltwood, then turned and walked swiftly toward her father.

"Thank goodness you are all right," she said as she approached him. "Mother and I were terribly worried about you." But when she drew close enough to examine his face, she was alarmed at what she saw. "Oh, Father, you look unwell. Why did you not come home straightaway after the trustees' meeting?"

Never had she seen him so pallid, so diminished. She took his arm and guided him along the snow-covered path homeward, the glow of the fireplace in their parlor visible even from this distance.

"What kept you so long, Father?"

"I am very sorry, child, but I could not come home until I spent some time before the Throne of Grace. I have been with Him, begging His forgiveness and praying for His help, though I feel certain He will not be so inclined."

"His help? With what, Father? What help do you need?"

He stopped, turned to his daughter, and tried to speak, but could not.

"Father, what is it?"

He breathed heavily, paused, then looked away as he spoke, shaking his head. "My dear, they have asked me to accept the Presidency of the College." This was news to Catherine, although not entirely a surprise. But she could see that her father was deeply emotional at this turn of events—a single tear was coursing down each cheek.

"That...that is surely a great honor, Father, is it not? Why are you distraught?"

He shook his head slowly, then turned and faced his daughter, his voice barely a whisper, his words fraught with despair. "Because I shall fail, Catherine—I shall fail you, your brothers and sisters, your mother, the college..." He paused for a long moment: "And I shall fail Him."

From its very beginnings Amherst College was a child of adversity. Its parent organization was founded and the first subscription drive launched in the midst of the Panic of 1819, the young nation's first economic recession. So limited were resources in those times that the college's first buildings had to be constructed mostly with donated materials and volunteer labor. And despite the public support the young institution enjoyed in its early years, the Massachusetts legislature twice rejected applications for a charter before approving it in April 1825, after more than two years of effort.

The college's first president, Zephaniah Swift Moore (see page 135), was by all accounts a popular figure among both faculty and students. Unfortunately, his tenure at Amherst was to be brief—he died in June 1823, less than two years after assuming the presidency. Moore's replacement, Reverend Heman Humphrey, a highly regarded preacher from Pittsfield, Massachusetts, would serve in the office over twenty-one years.

The young college thrived for a decade and a half under Presidents Moore and Humphrey. Enrollment, which totaled fifty-nine when it opened in 1821, had swelled to 259 by 1836 and its faculty had doubled, making it the second largest college in New England. Religious revivals were common on the campus in those days, and the college became the largest source of new preachers in New England. Of the 469 men graduated from Amherst College up until 1836, about half went into the ministry, filling pulpits around New England and across the nation, while at least twenty-five more accepted posts abroad as missionaries, proudly carrying forth the Gospel to the heathen world.

The year 1836 witnessed an abrupt reversal of the fortunes of Amherst College, a downward spiral Professor William S. Tyler referred to as a "period of reaction and decline." The college's eclipse was triggered to some degree by another national economic downturn that led to a deep recession and declines both in enrollment and donations. The rising cost of an Amherst College education had its effect as well; in the three-year period from 1834 to 1837, Tyler reported, student expenses increased from $96 per year to $150 per year, cheaper than Harvard and Yale but more expensive than other New England colleges.

Figure 47. Reverend Heman Humphrey (1779-1861), second president of Amherst College

But a good share of the college's wounds were self-inflicted. It was inevitable, argued Tyler, that the rate of growth enjoyed by Amherst College in

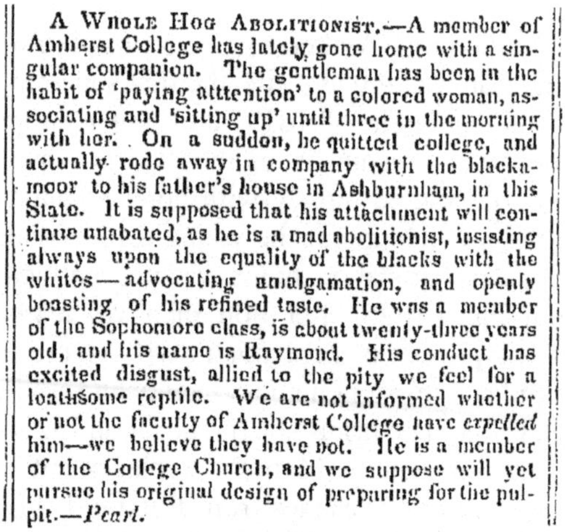

A Whole Hog Abolitionist.—A member of Amherst College has lately gone home with a singular companion. The gentleman has been in the habit of 'paying atttention' to a colored woman, associating and 'sitting up' until three in the morning with her. On a sudden, he quitted college, and actually rode away in company with the blackamoor to his father's house in Ashburnham, in this State. It is supposed that his attachment will continue unabated, as he is a mad abolitionist, insisting always upon the equality of the blacks with the whites—advocating amalgamation, and openly boasting of his refined taste. He was a member of the Sophomore class, is about twenty-three years old, and his name is Raymond. His conduct has excited disgust, allied to the pity we feel for a loathsome reptile. We are not informed whether or not the faculty of Amherst College have *expelled* him—we believe they have not. He is a member of the College Church, and we suppose will yet pursue his original design of preparing for the pulpit.—*Pearl.*

Figure 48. "A Whole Hog Abolitionist," published in the *Boston Investigator*, July 22, 1836

its first fifteen years could not have been sustained indefinitely. For one, religious revivals were fewer than in those early days, "...zeal for orthodoxy and evangelical piety was no longer at a white heat." Even relations with the town suffered. "The people of the village were still friendly to the college," asserted Tyler, "but they had ceased to regard it as their own offspring or foster-child."

Perhaps an even more important influence on the school's decline had to do with student-faculty relations. During the first decade of its existence, the college community was like a close-knit family. But that changed dramatically in the 1830s. In part due to sheer numbers, faculty dealings with students became less personal. "There are evils, difficulties, and dangers inevitably connected with a large college," wrote Tyler, "...which almost preclude the possibility of its realizing the ideal of a college, or doing in the best way its whole and proper work."

One flashpoint in the college's internal relations that was particularly emotional and wrenching had to do with the antislavery movement that had gained momentum throughout New England by 1830. Many northerners advocated the outright abolition of slavery, while others favored colonization, allowing slaves to be granted their freedom and returned to Africa. Two student organizations were formed by Amherst College students in 1833, the Anti-Slavery Society and the Colonization Society, both affiliated with national organizations. The Anti-Slavery Association grew rapidly; by November 1834, one-third of the student population had joined. During the summer of 1834, the Board of Trustees decreed that both societies should disband. The Colonization Society complied, but the Anti-Slavery Society refused. In a petition to the faculty the students argued eloquently for their cause:

> ...[W]e look again over two millions of our Countrymen—we hear the clanking of their chains. We listen to their moving pleas for deliverance—their deep-toned wailings are borne to us on every breeze;—we remember that we are the disciples of the Compassionate Saviour, who commands that "all things that we would that men should do to us, we should do others"—and our hearts are ready to burst within us. We would gladly comply with your request if we could do it consistently with the dictates of conscience, and the wants and woes of perishing millions.

The faculty replied with a letter that seemed to offer the Anti-Slavery Society a compromise, setting up a number of conditions under which it might continue. But President Humphrey took a decidedly harder line. In a carefully worded letter dated February 19, 1835, he expressed sympathy for the group's motivations, but argued that it would not be proper for the college to support such a movement:

> ...in the present agitated state of the public mind, it is inexpedient to keep up any organization, under the name of Anti-Slavery, Colonization, or the like, in our literary and theological institutions....we are not aware, that such a society as yours now exists in any respectable College but our own in the land.

The president's position was endorsed by the faculty. The vote was reportedly unanimous, although several faculty members including Professor Hitchcock were known to support the student group. The decision was widely reported in the press; abolitionist publications such as *The Emancipator* and *The Liberator* upbraided the college in the harshest terms. Barely a year later the trustees reversed themselves on the matter of the Anti-Slavery Society, allowing it to reorganize. But the damage had been done.

Just six months later, tensions reached a crescendo when a racial controversy erupted at Amherst College. A student, William Raymond, had been observed in Amherst in the company of a young African American woman. *The Boston Investigator* got wind of the matter and on July 22, 1836, published a brief but inflammatory item entitled "A Whole Hog Abolitionist" (see Fig. 48).

The William Raymond story received even wider publicity than the college's antislavery decision—in twenty-first century argot we might say it "went viral." Within days it had appeared in more than a dozen newspapers from Maine to Georgia. At a meeting a few weeks later the faculty took up the matter. Raymond pleaded that he had been merely tutoring the woman and several other African Americans living in Amherst at the time. According to the minutes of that meeting, the faculty believed Raymond's misdeeds were not too extreme, but felt that the publicity had done injury to the college:

> Raymond examined in relation to his "connexion with a coloured girl"... Whereas reports highly derogatory to the character of William

> Raymond...have been extensively circulated, the Faculty have felt bound to examine them; and whereas they find evidence against him, though not of such guilt, as to require his expulsion, yet of such a glaring and disgraceful impropriety as cannot be passed over. Therefore resolved that the said Raymond be and he is hereby dismissed [for a year] from Amherst College.

Almost from the day of Raymond's dismissal, the social fabric of the college seemed to unravel. At the same time tensions developed around a range of other issues such as the selection of recipients of honorary distinctions, the system of student monitors, and conflicts among the various student societies.

A large-scale student rebellion took place at the annual Exhibition exercises the following year. A number of students refused their awards and declined to make their presentations for reasons of conscience related not to the antislavery decision or the expulsion of William Raymond, but to the way that the faculty selected recipients for such honors. Instead of delivering his oration, one student gave a harsh indictment of the college faculty. A few days later he was dismissed and a number of others were reprimanded.

As with the Raymond decision, this action by the faculty attracted widespread attention in the press. A brief item appeared in the *Greenfield Gazette and Mercury* in July 1837, entitled "Troubles in college." It described the rebellion that had occurred at Exhibition and reported that one of the students "couched his declinature in disrespectful language," that he was later expelled, and that a number of other students had been suspended. Within days the item was copied in dozens of other newspapers across the country.

The social amity that once typified student-faculty relations at Amherst College was no more. The college's internal strife was spread not only by the press but even by the institution's own alumni:

> Year after year too many of the graduates went forth, not to invite and attract students, but to turn them away by reporting that the government was arbitrary, the president stern, severe, unsympathizing, unprogressive, and even in his dotage.

Inevitably the college's internal strife became public knowledge:

> The causes of the decline of the college were discussed in newspapers and pamphlets, and writers who were confessedly graduates and professedly friends of the institution, published to the world that the alumni were dissatisfied with the management of the college, and it never would prosper with out a thorough reform, not to say a complete revolution.

The internal strife of Amherst College did further damage to the institution's already weak financial condition. Enrollments declined and the resulting loss of revenue in turn led to the deterioration of the campus and buildings. Edward Hitchcock, Jr., never one to mince words, put it bluntly:

> The buildings in the 40s were shabby. Even in carpenters repairs there was sad neglect, & as for paper (on the walls) it was very rarely seen, & generally if a dormitory room was painted it was done by the student himself. The entries were awfully bare and neglected, save that a pretty liberal supply of whitewash was administered all inside the buildings in summer vacation. The rooms of the students were simply the walls, a fire place, a lock and key to the door. The windows were very loose and let in any amount of cold air & the entry doors were left to swing all day and all night. How the students were comfortable… I cannot now understand.

Despite deep cuts in expenditures in 1840 and 1841, income fell short of what was needed for the operation of the college. To make up the difference funds were borrowed from the Charity Fund and other funds designated for scholarships and endowment. Interest payments on these loans became greater each year. That debt, recalled Hitchcock, "…hung like a terrible incubus upon the Trustees, the Treasurer, and the whole College, and came near proving its ruin."

With financial troubles mounting, the trustees in 1841 hired one of their own, Reverend Joseph Vaill of Monson, Massachusetts, as a full-time "agent" charged with launching a new subscription drive to raise $100,000. Vaill was tireless in his pursuit of donors, raising nearly $25,000 in about three years. A series of letters to the editors of the *Boston Recorder* relayed the promising news but called still more attention to the school's "financial embarrassments."

The timing of this fundraising effort was unfortunate, coming amidst another national recession. In his 1843 report to the trustees, Vaill noted that "we could not have fallen upon a period so unpromising for making this effort as the years 1842 and 43." By 1844 donations had dropped off still further, even among the college's wealthiest patrons. The shoe industry was the Bay State's economic powerhouse in those days, but with uncharacteristic humor Vaill reported that even "…in the boot and shoe districts I found everything down at the heels." He further admitted that the college might be doing itself more harm than good by continued appeals for assistance.

By spring 1844, President Humphrey was ready to retire, and the trustees seemed anxious to see him go. At a trustees' meeting held at Worcester in June probably anticipating his dismissal, Humphrey tendered his resignation, but agreed to stay on until his successor could be named. At the same meeting the trustees offered the post to Professor Edwards A. Park of Andover Theological Seminary—Park declined. Eight weeks later the position was offered to

Professor George Shepard of Bangor Theological Seminary in Maine—he too declined. A third offer was made to the Reverend Albert Barnes of Philadelphia and declined. No one, it seemed, was interested in taking the helm of a sinking ship.

As the new academic year began, the college's prospects were grim, and the members of the faculty were all too aware of the gravity of the situation. A year earlier they had been asked to take a salary reduction of $200; now they were asked to accept an additional $200 reduction. It must have been clear to them that only extreme financial strictures could save the college from shuttering its doors.

Reverend Vaill played a critical role in formulating a plan to save the institution. Vaill had been one of the earliest supporters of the college, serving on the Board of Trustees since it was formed in 1823. The solution he and the Prudential Committee believed was to ask the faculty to take yet another salary reduction, but with one important difference: this time they would be asked to accept a salary limited to the funds received in student term bills after necessary expenditures had been paid each year, not just for the coming year, but indefinitely.

In November 1844, Reverend Vaill brought this proposal to the faculty. It may be a measure of his negotiating and mediating skills that the professors were willing even to consider the plan. A few days later, Vaill returned to the Prudential Committee with the faculty's response. It contained three additional conditions that may well have come as a shock to the committee. First, the faculty would agree to the new salary arrangement only if they were given complete independence in the operation of the college including making only those expenditures they felt were essential. Secondly, they would insist on an indefinite suspension of all public solicitations which they believed served only to further aggravate the school's shaky public standing.

Finally, the faculty insisted that they be granted the authority to select the next president of the college. It would have to be someone from within their own ranks who was knowledgeable of and sympathetic toward the college—someone who already enjoyed the respect of the students, the alumni, friends, and potential donors—someone of the highest moral standing who could restore the reputation of Amherst College in the halls of government—someone with a reputation for honesty and courage in the face of adversity. In short, it would have to be Professor Edward Hitchcock.

Perhaps the strongest argument in favor of Edward Hitchcock was simply that he was a known quantity to Amherst College, a man whose loyalty to the institution was unquestionable. He had served the college for nearly two decades, longer than all but three of the trustees. He enjoyed the personal friendship of several trustees: Reverend Theophilus Packard had chaired the ecclesiastical council that oversaw his ordination and installation at Conway in 1821; John Tappan had accompanied him on one of his earliest geological

Figure 49. Samuel Williston (1795-1874), founder of Williston Seminary and Amherst College trustee

surveys; Samuel Williston delivered letters from Edward, Jr., on his frequent visits in Amherst. He was admired and respected by all, students and faculty alike, as a teacher, as a scientist, and as a man of faith. And he had managed to establish himself in the halls of power in Boston, serving as State Geologist under four governors from three parties, connections that might aid in the continued effort to obtain state aid.

At the same time, the trustees must surely have been aware that Professor Hitchcock suffered from a variety of health conditions and tended to despondency and pessimism. Despite these weaknesses, he had a way of instilling confidence, by virtue of both his scientific acumen and his character: when he gave an opinion on a matter, it was always well informed; when he took on a task, he could be relied on to give it his all.

On Monday, December 16, the trustees approved the plan. Whether or not they liked it or believed it would succeed, it must have been clear to them that there simply was no alternative. All that remained was to convince Professor Hitchcock to accept this highest of academic honors, the Presidency of Amherst College, an institution that they feared might well be in its death throes.

Hitchcock's appointment was publicized within days in the *Greenfield Gazette* and many other newspapers. The only record of his response is a letter dated nearly a month later in which he subscribed to the salary reduction plan but made no mention of his appointment or his acceptance.

Why the delay? Clearly, the professor had doubts—deep-seated, heartfelt doubts—about whether to accept the position. Two decades later in *Reminiscences*, he enumerated his reasons. First, he felt he lacked the ambition and talent necessary for the job, particularly for soliciting donations. Furthermore, he feared it was inappropriate for someone to be the head of such an institution who had never completed a college education himself. Additionally, he felt that as president he would be unable to continue his scientific research and publishing. And lastly, he was certain that his health was too fragile to sustain him.

In March 1845, just a few weeks before his inauguration, Hitchcock wrote, "This is certainly a post which I have never sought out here or elsewhere. Nay I have done all in my power when I saw that affairs were tending to my election to prevent it." Furthermore, he was certain that he would fail in his new post:

> ...Amherst College is at present in the state of great depression and those who expect that I shall bring it up will be assuredly disappointed. Indeed according to my best judgment little else is before me but anxiety perplexity trial and defeat if I shall ever actually enter the office as I have agreed to do if life be spared. Often my mind shrinks from this cross with the strongest aversion and it is only agonizing prayer that prevents me even now from cutting loose from my engagements.

It seems his apprehensions were shared by Orra:

> My wife too sympathizes with me in this aversion: and while the world supposes us exulting in our new honours and elevations as they are called we actually dread them as likely to prove sore evils. We feel as if it were too late in life and as if we were too much invalids to engage in new enterprises especially in those which are full of unpleasant duties and bring little else but care.

On the other hand, Edward and Orra were given much encouragement:

> Nevertheless if we could only believe that we should promote the welfare of the College we can cheerfully engage in the work trusting in God for wisdom and strength. And we yield our judgment to that of our friends who seem almost unanimously to urge the place upon us. If a short period shall prove that we are right and they wrong in judgment let not posterity charge it to inordinate ambition on our part that we assume these duties.

In the end, and despite all his misgivings, Edward Hitchcock accepted the nomination. It seemed to him that he had no choice: "The truth is that the new plan for bringing the expenses within the income of the College could not be adopted unless I took the place: and this I deemed indispensable to the existence of the College."

PRESIDENT HITCHCOCK 1845-1854

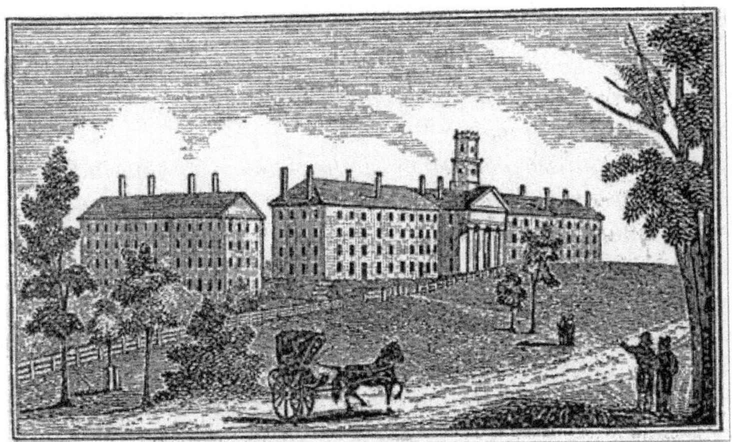

North-western view of Amherst College, 1839

18 The Highest Use of Learning

"They forgot themselves in their efforts to aid others."

Easthampton, March 1845

Samuel Williston sat in his study at a large, ornate desk of the darkest, richest walnut, polished to a mirror-like shine, leaning over a thick, leather bound ledger. A tap sounded lightly on the door.

"Uh-huh, what is it?" he muttered absently.

A maid opened the door but stood without. "Sir?"

"Well? Speak up, girl."

"Sir, 'tis a student, sir...to see you. He says you are expecting him."

At that a thin, fair-haired young man appeared behind the maid, smiling broadly.

"Ah, Master Hitchcock, do come in, young man." As Edward Hitchcock, Jr., entered, Williston closed the ledger and gestured toward a chair. "Have a seat, then." Edward seated himself while the stout, florid faced man leaned back

in his chair. His gruff demeanor softened as he stared intensely at the boy. "Well, then, you are doing well in your studies, I trust?"

Edward, Jr., nodded. "Yes, sir, I hope so, sir, I..."

"Let me see, you are reading Latin with Mr. Alden, hmm? Top notch fellow, him." Edward nodded. "And rhetoric with Mr. Russell Wright?"

"Mr. Monroe Wright, sir. He..."

"Ahah, yes, of course, Monroe. Hired him myself in New Haven last year. Knew at first glance he was the man for the post. In business and in education, you gain a certain sense about such things...an intuition as to who has what it takes. Do you know what I mean?"

"Oh, yes, sir. You are admired by all the students for your judgment in such matters, sir. That's what makes this institution so...so exceptional."

A broad smile crept across the gentleman's face. "Quite so, quite so. And your lodgings this term are acceptable, then?"

Again Edward smiled and nodded enthusiastically. "Oh, yes, sir, I am back in my old room on the third floor, sir. Most suitable, sir. Mr. Wright saw to it, sir."

"And how is your father doing? He must be very busy, I trust, what with such a great responsibility about to be laid upon his shoulders? The fifteenth, if I recall aright, is the day of his inauguration."

"Yes, Mr. Williston, I believe so."

"A man of great intellect and character, your father."

"Thank you, sir, yes, sir, he certainly is, sir."

Williston smiled. "My intuition tells me he will do well, very well, indeed."

"Father has the highest admiration for you, sir—your courage and foresight both in business and in founding the Seminary. He speaks of you ever so often, sir."

"Does he, then? Well, I am heartened to know that I have at least one admirer, at least one."

"Oh, you have many, many admirers, sir. Everyone says so, sir."

Mr. Williston sat back in his chair, smiling, gazing at the ceiling. "And what again is the day of his ascension?"

"April the fifteenth, sir."

The inauguration of the third president of Amherst College took place on Tuesday, April 15, 1845. It was by every measure an auspicious occasion, for the new president, for his wife and family, for Amherst College, for the community. The proceedings began at ten o'clock in Johnson Chapel with the installation of Edward Hitchcock as pastor. The minutes of the Ecclesiastical Council were read, dissolving the pastoral relationship between the church and Reverend Humphrey, with words of praise and thanks for his more than two decades of service to the church, then an introductory prayer, an installation prayer, the charge and right hand of fellowship extended to the new pastor, a concluding prayer, and a benediction by Reverend Hitchcock.

The actual inauguration ceremony followed, not in the college chapel, but in the village meetinghouse a short distance away, attended by students, faculty, trustees, family members, as well as many townsfolk. After an introductory prayer, President Humphrey delivered his farewell address, a brief history of the college that was, according to one newspaper account, "exceedingly interesting." The retiring president, speaking on behalf of the trustees, then declared Edward Hitchcock the duly elected president of the college, ushered him to his seat in the presidential chair, and presented him the keys of the college.

At that point President Hitchcock delivered his Inaugural Address, "The Highest Use of Learning." Some may have expected the newly inaugurated president to confine himself to a few timeworn platitudes about education, some effusive words of praise for the institution, and an optimistic message about its bright and glorious future. But that was not at all what President Hitchcock had in mind.

"The cause of education…is almost universally popular," he began. "Yet were we to pass around the enquiry among the different classes of society, why they regard it so important, we should probably receive very different answers." Some would contend that education's chief value lay in enhancing one's reputation as a learned man, or in acquiring wealth, or increasing the "comforts and luxuries of life." Others would argue for the benefits of education to the larger society, "…elevating the lower classes above the condition of mere drudges and animals…giving to men just views of their rights, relations, and destinies." Finally, he concluded, still others would see in education a greater spiritual dimension, believing that "…the religious applications of learning are by far its most important use."

President Hitchcock next acknowledged the many secular advantages to be derived from education.

> When we compare the present condition of the world, and our own condition, with what they were in our early days,—we cannot but be deeply impressed with the rapid progress of society, and the multiplication of secular advantages, and the means of comfort and happiness, growing out of the advancement of learning.

He spoke at length of the applications of learning to the "useful arts," offering as an example the use of steam power in Great Britain at that time, where "steam performs a work that would require the unaided labor of more than four hundred millions of men…"

And yet for all the secular benefits derived from education, argued President Hitchcock, the religious benefits are still greater, and to that thesis he now turned. "Accompany me now, my friends, as we rapidly pass around the circle of literature and science, in order that we may see what are the relations between religion and the different branches of human learning." What followed was a lengthy review of the contributions of these fields of knowledge to religion, accompanied by occasional but forceful disparagements of those skeptics, heretics, and atheists who would find conflict between the two realms.

The ancient classics, Hitchcock noted, while filled with atheistic notions, offer many benefits to the study of religion: "The very absurdity of the mythology and philosophy of the classics, brings out by contrast, in bolder relief the beauties and glories of Christian doctrines and Christian philosophy." Furthermore, an understanding of the Greek language is an essential tool for a full understanding of the scriptures: "…how unfit to give a correct interpretation of Scripture is he, who is unacquainted with the languages in which it was originally written."

As to literature, Hitchcock conceded that "not a little of the influence of modern polite literature has been very disastrous to religion," having been written by men who were "intemperate, or licentious, and secretly or openly hostile to Christianity…and their writings…deeply imbued with immorality, or infidelity, or atheism." But for all the "sophistries and cavils" of the likes of Voltaire, Gibbon, and Hume, the great mass of literature is favorable to religion, including such eminent authors as Ramsay, Muller, and Goldsmith.

Poetry, Hitchcock argued, is the "natural handmaid of pure religion…Hence it was chosen by the Holy Ghost as the appropriate language of prophets and other inspired men." And while he conceded that many poets were infidels, he named some—Milton, Cowper, Watts, and Wordsworth, for example—whom he deemed "Christian lights."

The president next turned his attention to mathematics. No more powerful evidence of the existence and benevolence of the Deity can be found than in the study of mathematics, he argued, a discipline which "furnishes us with the noblest examples of abstract truth in the universe…." For example, "…the contemplation of an endless series in mathematics, gives us the nearest approach to an idea of the infinite, which we can attain." If one is troubled by the notion of the Trinity, he noted, how three can be as one, let him study mathematics, and "…after you have demonstrated to him the properties of the hyperbola and its asymptote, the apparent absurdity disappears." Furthermore, the laws of mathematics regulate "with infallible precision" the movements of the stars and planets. "Mathematics then forms the very framework of nature's harmonies, and is essential to the argument for a God. Instead of having no connection with religion, it lies at the foundation of all theism."

Chemistry had been the first discipline to which Professor Hitchcock had directed himself at Amherst College, so it is not surprising that he would recognize the virtues of chemistry for promoting religion. "What admirable skill and benevolence does the doctrine of definite proportions and atomic constitution in chemical compounds present!" He saw the hand of God as well in the "isomeric constitution" of organic molecules, in the remarkable properties of water, and in the immutable laws of thermodynamics.

As to anatomy and physiology, Hitchcock argued, "No sciences have furnished so many and so appropriate facts, illustrative of natural theology, as anatomy and physiology." So precise are the structures of living things, for example, that modern anatomists can with a single fragment of bone reconstruct the entire anatomy of an animal, a striking testament to the skill of the Creator. But for modesty, he might here have added the even more remarkable fact that one could infer a great deal about ancient creatures—strange, enormous creatures never seen by human eye—by examining footmarks preserved in rock!

Hitchcock concluded with a nod to "...the wide dominions of natural history, embracing zoology, botany, and mineralogy," arguing that they have been found to be "crowded with demonstrations of the Divine Existence and of God's Providential care and government." At this point he paid special tribute to "inductive science" and its champions for promoting religion, men such as Newton, Kepler, Galileo, Linnaeus, and Owen:

> The very same argumentation that leads such original discoverers to derive the principles of science from facts in nature, carries them irresistibly backward to a First Cause: and, indeed, the inductive principle, as developed by Bacon, forms the true basis on which to build the whole fabric of natural religion...

That the sciences had from time to time promoted attitudes contrary to religion was also admitted: "Scarcely any important discovery has been made in these branches, that has not been regarded for a time, either by the timid and jealous friends of religion, or by its superficial enemies, to be opposed at least to revelation, if not to theism." One such notion that he addressed at some length was that of spontaneous generation. Scientists such as Lamarck and Étienne Geoffroy Saint-Hilaire argued that life could generate itself without benefit of a Creator. They suggested that primitive life forms "...[B]y an inherent tendency to improvement and the force of external circumstances become animals of higher and higher organization; until at last the orang-outang abandoned his quadrupedal condition, and stood erect as man, with all his lofty powers of intellect." But with the aid of modern optical instruments such as the microscope, argued Hitchcock, "the origin of nearly every animal visible to the naked eye, has been found to be by ordinary generation...not a single example of the spontaneous production of living beings can be adduced." Furthermore, he contended, "physiology demonstrates that species are permanent and can never be transmuted."

Finally, Hitchcock turned his attention to geology, asserting that the more geologists learn of the history of the earth, the more the biblical principles are strengthened. Modern geology, he argued, shows us that there was a time in earth's past when there was no life; hence, there had to have been a creation event. Second, the record of organic remains demonstrates that since the Creation there have been a number of "extinctions and renewals of organic life, each of which demands the agency of such a Being." And finally, that man has only recently been created, as is stated in the Bible.

At last Hitchcock reached his conclusion regarding learning and faith:

> We have now taken a glance at the entire and vast circle of human learning. And is not every mind forced irresistibly to the conclusion, that every branch was originally linked by a golden chain to the throne of God: and that the noblest use to which they can be consecrated, and for which they were destined, is to illustrate his perfections and to display his glory. If so, let me conclude my too protracted remarks, by a few inferences.

Some in his audience may have felt a measure of relief that the end was in sight, but they were to be disappointed. For now the President turned to the matter at hand, Amherst College. On this subject he was forthright, some might say brutally honest, in stating the facts that confronted him as President. These included what in modern-day parlance might be termed the "elephant in the room," the college's financial straits:

> It is well known, that an impression prevails abroad extensively, that the College is in a state of severe depression, and struggling for existence. And to some extent this impression is correct. But to omit minor causes, the grand source of our embarrassments is not well understood. It is a deficiency of pecuniary means.

No one, Hitchcock observed, has reason to doubt the value of the work of the institution. "There is no complaint that we send forth men of corrupt principles, to contaminate the community; nor that they are deficient in scholarship, in comparison with graduates from other Colleges."

One reason for the college's difficulties, he argued, was simply the desire in its early years to meet the demand of the growing student population for more instruction and better facilities. "The unusual prosperity of the College in its earlier days, compelled the Trustees to provide more ample means than were subsequently needed; and thus they incurred debt." Then he turned to the other factor that loomed large in the college's current financial situation: "But the grand reason is, that the College has never received any pecuniary aid from the State Government." No other New England college, with the possible exception of Brown University, was ever so deprived of its state's support. His criticism of the state was softened by one note of praise:

> For one thing at least we sincerely thank the Government. Without an exception, the gentlemen whom they have designated as Trustees, have entered

> cordially and efficiently into the work of building up this Institution, and of relieving it of its embarrassments; and we could not have done without them.

A third reason for the college's pecuniary straits could truly be marked as an admirable quality. For Amherst was founded to provide an education for indigent students, and that is where most of its funds had been directed.

> The truly devoted men, who commenced the Institution... directed all their efforts to obtain a fund for that purpose: and they succeeded nobly: for that fund now amounts to $50,000. But it can be used only for such students....they raised no funds for the general purposes of the Institution...they forgot themselves in their efforts to aid others; or rather, to advance the cause of religion.

The college's present-day financial difficulties were proof of the steadfastness of the founders to their cause.

He then turned to a consideration of some of the "bright spots" in the condition of the college. The foundation of the college is the cause of pure religion, he argued; it is blessed with a large Charity Fund; and it has enjoyed some sizable gifts from wealthy men interested in the college. He also alluded to the plan agreed to between faculty and trustees to keep the college's debt in check and praised the faculty for their devotion to the institution even in a time of great difficulty. He praised the college's facilities and extolled the attractive setting of the college. And he praised the college's alumni, including the 400 now ministers, and thirty foreign missionaries.

Finally, he confessed to all those doubts he had been harboring since that snowy day in December.

> Here it is right to confess... that I am unadapted to meet the present exigency...But I yield to the judgment of the Trustees and friends of the College, so far as I know it to have been expressed, and cheerfully attempt the experiment in reliance upon able coadjutors, upon the liberality of the friends of the College, and above all, upon help from on High...

Lest his audience should read into his words a lack of resolve, he added,

> ...[T]hough I enter upon these duties with a deep sense of incompetency, think not that I, or my colleagues, take hold of our work with a faint and irresolute heart. Having made up our minds that this is the post of duty, we mean to stand firm by it, so long as God shall add his blessing, and the public shall patronize our labors.

Figure 50. Edward Hitchcock and Orra White Hitchcock, ca 1863

He then returned to his original thesis: "We boldly avow it as our leading object, to make science and literature subservient to the cause of religion: and we will not believe, till a fair trial has been made, that a religious public, or the noble minded youth who come hither for instruction, will wish us to adopt a lower standard."

At this point the President's discourse had run to well over two hours and he acknowledged that it was time to "...relieve this exhausted audience." When at last it was over and the crowd poured out of the meetinghouse into the April sun, it must have felt to all as though a new era had begun for Amherst College. Despite the daunting challenges faced by their new president—the college's financial condition, tensions between faculty and students, the public perception that the college was teetering on dissolution—despite all that, a new era of optimism had begun, shared by the trustees, the faculty, students, the larger community, if not by the new president.

Buttons—what could be more common, more mundane? And yet buttons were critical to the revival of Amherst College, for Samuel Williston was a "button baron." A native of Easthampton, he married Emily Graves in 1822. They owned a shop where, as the story is told, Emily admired the buttons on a houseguest's coat. She secretly removed one and examined it. Realizing that it was European-made and unlike anything available in America, she shared her findings with Samuel. Within months the couple had begun a new business, manufacturing fabric covered buttons—a business that would soon make them Easthampton's wealthiest citizens. The couple endowed a new academy, Williston Seminary, that opened its doors in 1841. In the same year Williston was appointed by the legislature to the Amherst College Board of Trustees.

Williston's appointment came just as the depth of the financial woes of Amherst College was becoming apparent. By 1844 he was convinced that extreme measures would be necessary to reverse the college's downward spiral. He was a member of the committee appointed on December 16, 1844, to undertake the final negotiations with the faculty on a plan to save the college, including recommending Edward Hitchcock as president.

By this time Samuel Williston was a friend and admirer of Edward Hitchcock and supported his appointment as president. At a meeting of the Board of Trustees on the evening of April 14, 1845, barely twelve hours before the inauguration, Williston made an astounding gesture of support for Hitchcock and for Amherst College, a pledge of $20,000 toward a Professorship of Rhetoric and Oratory. It was the largest single gift the college had ever received, and although the funds were to be transferred in installments over the next three years, it was a source of enormous relief and satisfaction to the college and, in particular, to its new president.

View from Mount Holyoke, 1839

19 A New Millennium

"A splendid mountain like this deserves a splendid name."

Hadley, July 4, 1845

Three young men, earnest determination writ on their brows, climbed a steep mountainside in the morning sunlight, shouldering axes and saws. At their hands every oak, chestnut, and pine fell with a thud, then was hauled aside. Not far up the incline another crew was employed similarly, though with less earnestness and more laughter and horseplay.

After several hours of labor the trio paused and turned to admire the prospect opening up before them. On the slopes below dozens of their classmates labored, shirtless and glistening in the morning sun, carving their way up the mountainside. Through the gap created in the foliage, the sinuous course of the mighty Connecticut could now be seen, its banks bordered by broad fields bristling with corn. Far beyond rose the Berkshire Hills, their highest summits still cloaked in morning clouds.

One of the trio sank onto a tree stump, wiped his brow, then looked up at his companions, breathless.

"I've had it, boys. I need a rest."

"Come on, Brewster, get a move on. We're only a few rods from the top." He pointed upwards toward a rocky prominence not too far distant.

"Tell me again, brother James, why are we doing this?" demanded Brewster. "Why when we could be rusticating in the shade on College Hill, or bathing in the cool waters below?"

"You, Brewster, you of all people should understand," replied Burns. "We are climbing Mount Zion, young man, just as it is writ."

"Oh? And to what end?"

"Have you learned nothing from your Bible studies, silly boy? Beulah Land—New Jerusalem—the Promised Land."

Brewster shook his head. "I wonder if it is worth the effort. I truly do."

"Well, how about luncheon, then—the chance to share a small feast with Miss Lyon's young ladies? Now there's a reward you surely would not malign."

"Well, that does alter the picture some, I'll admit. But dainties, sweets, and lemonade are not exactly my kind of fare."

Burns smiled. "What if we were to improve the opportunity?"

"Improve it? In what way?"

Burns reached into his rucksack lying on the ground at his feet and drew out a small, shining flask. "Add a splash of this elixir to lemonade and see if that doesn't bring a smile back to those lips. And it is guaranteed to relieve your aching muscles at the same time."

Brewster looked up and grinned, then rose slowly to his feet. "Well, considered in that light, I can already begin to feel my resolve restored." He paused, a look of mirthful curiosity in his eyes. "But I fear old President Humphrey must be rolling in his grave to see all this."

"Humphrey's not dead, Brewster, he's merely retired. But you are right. A new day has dawned for Amherst College. And when we sup with those fair maidens from South Hadley, let us raise a glass and offer a toast to the new college, the new president, and the new millennium!"

There were cheers all around. Then the three resumed their labors.

As important as the inauguration of a new president was for Amherst College, it was no less so for Edward, Orra, and their family. First, there was the matter of where they would live. The official residence of the President of the College was situated on the campus just a short distance from the Hitchcock home of the past seventeen years. It had been constructed in 1834, replacing one that had been built rather hurriedly for the accommodation of the college's first president. An imposing three story brick structure in the Georgian style with six tall brick chimneys rising above a slate roof, it had been designed to do honor to the college's president.

But the new president had no relish for the prospect of moving into that particular house. He had no qualms about the structure itself, finding it "large, commodious, and in good architectural proportions," but in *Reminiscences* he admitted to several reservations. One was its location: "It is too near the College, and overlooks it too much, and is too much overlooked by the College. For a President should not be obliged to see every small impropriety of students, because he must notice them all." Furthermore, he believed that its construction had nearly bankrupted the college. "If I were again to take the Presidency, I should prefer, all things considered, to live in the old one," he wrote. Apparently Orra shared her husband's distaste for the place as reported by Edward, Jr.: "My Mother said more than once in my hearing that there were two things she never would do, to live in the Presidents house, ...and to go to Europe. But she did both of them."

Despite their reservations, the Hitchcocks moved into the President's House. It was not an easy adjustment. The house was considerably larger than their former home, and furnishing the additional rooms proved to be a financial burden. Furthermore, there was a backlog of cleaning to be done. As Edward, Jr., recalled: "... my mother, Mary [his older sister], and the hired girl had an immense deal of back-breaking scrubbing to do...And my back and knees can ache now when I think how I put down and took up those big parlor carpets." In addition the place was badly in need of painting and wallpapering, all of which the family had to do at their own expense.

As to day-to-day life in their new home, the family found the place less than commodious, as described by Edward, Jr., with typical candor:

> And the coldness of that house. For though we had 20 cords of wood, the house was never warmed, there was no means of doing it...the parlors had nothing but open fireplaces, which wouldn't both draw at the same time...The whole third story, when we lived in this house, was one great garret, with no light or ventilation save two windows in the west end.

For all the hardships it presented, settling into their new home ushered in a new era for the Hitchcocks and the larger community, as the full operation of that house within the social life of the college soon became a family affair. And the evidence suggests that it was a life that all in time came to enjoy.

Edward Hitchcock was a man of many talents, but entertaining was certainly not one of them, either by nature or nurture. Not that his childhood was cheerless; his father after all was a singing leader in Deerfield, as was his brother Charles. But the pleasures of social intercourse were not a large part of Edward's youth. Furthermore, his disdain for large meals and rich foods was expressed most explicitly in his lectures and publications on dyspepsia.

Orra, on the other hand, seemed to be possessed of both domestic skills and a personal inclination for entertaining. Ever since the Hitchcocks moved into their house near the college in 1828, their home had been an unofficial gathering place for a constant stream of distinguished visitors as well as student and faculty boarders. From Inauguration Day forward, their new home became the official social epicenter of the campus, and Orra White Hitchcock became the first lady of the college, a role she had prepared for well in the preceding years and now seemed to savor.

The Hitchcock children were swept up in the social affairs of the college as well. Mary, now nearly twenty-one and having completed two years at Mount Holyoke Female Seminary and a year at Troy Female Seminary in Troy, New York, had returned to Amherst. Catherine, nineteen, was in her second year at the Mount Holyoke Female Seminary just a few miles away. Edward, Jr., a month shy of seventeen, would soon complete his studies at Williston Seminary, then in September enter Amherst College while living at home. The three younger children, twelve-year-old Jane, eight-year-old Charles, and six-year-old Emily, were still in grade school, although soon enough they too would be conscripted.

We can learn little about the family life of the Hitchcocks from the writings of Edward, Sr. Fortunately, we are compensated amply by his eldest son whose memoirs abound with fascinating details, warmth, and humor. He paints a vivid picture of life for the family of the new president. He attests that the rest of the family took well to this work as well: "My mother was never rattled, impatient, or fretful at any of these calls, or apologised because she hadn't anything better, but always had enough of something on the table and did not sit up nights to make delicacies...We children were all the waiters..."

The Hitchcocks initiated two annual social events at their home known as levees, one for new students in autumn, and another for seniors shortly before Commencement each summer. Recalled Edward, Jr.,

> When my father was President he had what we would call receptions. One, a Freshman party at which a large part of the town, all the Faculty & the Freshmen, were invited in the early fall, and another the Senior Week in July when the Seniors were invited with the same other people. And oh don't my sister Mary & I remember those parties, for we with my mother and one hired girl—after my father was President—and all this extra work to do. I always froze all the ice cream, & took it out at the party.

Commencement, which in those times took place in midsummer, was a particularly difficult period for President Hitchcock. "During my Presidency I found Commencement week to demand almost constant confinement in the meetings of Trustees, Prudential Committee and Faculty, and on the closing day a session of five or six hours in the church." That Commencement week was hard on his constitution is clear, yet he adapted:

> I used to get very nervous, and my head seemed as if bound by a hoop, till I learned to practice great abstemiousness. By taking a little horseback exercise in the morning, and a bowl of arrowroot, the lightest of all kinds of food, for breakfast, I could go through these protracted sessions without the slightest inconvenience or subsequent injury.

The Hitchcock children were very much members of the college community from an early age until adulthood. Both Edward, Jr., and Charles attended Amherst College. As to the daughters, Catherine, Jane, and Emily would eventually marry Amherst graduates.

For all the reasons Edward Hitchcock had mustered against accepting the presidency, one factor that he believed weighed in his favor was an understanding of and empathy for his students, as he recorded in *Reminiscences*:

> ...[T]he experience of my early life fitted me to sympathize strongly with that class of young men the founders of Amherst College intended to educate...I had originated from the same humble class in society, and been obliged to contend with the same difficulties and discouragements. I could, therefore, counsel and encourage those who were struggling along the same rugged path.

It appears that he was correct in that assessment; he managed to forge a close bond with his students while a teacher, a bond that was strengthened throughout his presidency.

One innovation introduced by President Hitchcock that proved highly successful at bond building, one that soon became a college tradition, was mountain excursions. He may well have been inspired by his friend, Mary Lyon, who instituted a "mountain day" at Mount Holyoke Female Seminary shortly after its founding in 1837.

The first mountain excursion at Amherst College took place on Mount Holyoke, a 900-foot summit overlooking the Connecticut River in Hadley, a few miles west of Amherst. On July 4, 1845, he led a large contingent of Amherst men to the foot of the mountain. Armed with axes, shovels, and crowbars, the students carved the first trail to the summit of that eminence. The task was daunting, yet it was achieved most impressively by midday according to

Hitchcock's own account. What motivated the men of Amherst? Besides the inherent reward of a job well done, they may also have regarded favorably a promise of a celebratory dinner prepared by Miss Lyon and some of her students:

> Never did I see a body of men go into any enterprise with such a will and with better success. Before eleven o'clock the road was so far opened that a gentleman rode horseback over it, and by twelve o'clock the young men had the work finished and had made their toilet as well as they could with nothing but rocks for a mirror, and were ready to descend and meet the Holyoke ladies with their dinner ready by the welcome spring.

A year later another excursion was organized to the highest summit in the Holyoke Range and the one closest to the college campus, known then as Hilliard's Knob. Besides clearing a trail to the summit, they announced their intention to officially rename the mountain. The outing attracted both young men of Amherst and young women of Mount Holyoke Female Seminary, 500 in all if a report in the *Springfield Republican* can be believed. When all were assembled at the top, a student read a proclamation:

> ...On this fourth day of July when our fathers asserted claims bolder and more momentous than this mountain's to its rightful appellation, in the name and by the authority of the Senior Class of 1846, in Amherst College, I now denominate this commanding summit Mount Norwottuck.

The rocky podium was then turned over to President Hitchcock who delivered a lengthy geological discourse, ending with a declaration that no doubt earned the heartfelt accord and cheers of all present: "Mount Norwottuck—Hitherto it has been a wall of separation between two literary Institutions. To-day it is a point of union. Let it ever be an object of deep interest by them both!" The new president clearly had a knack for motivating his young scholars, for rallying them to a popular cause. According to written accounts the libations carried to these summits were limited to lemonade, although one wonders if some more invigorating ingredients may also have found their way into the beverages consumed by some of the celebrants when the president and other distinguished guests were distracted.

A third mountaintop celebration in June 1849 took an unanticipated turn to controversy, albeit a lighthearted one. This time the excursion was to Mount Toby in Sunderland where a path was cleared to the summit and a celebratory gathering held. Edward Hitchcock, Jr., by now a senior, addressed the assemblage, offering a justification for the name change that was heartfelt though perhaps a bit too self-congratulatory for some tastes. "A splendid mountain like this," he began, "deserves a splendid name; a classical and euphonical name, not a common or vulgar one; a name that will look well and sound well in poetry, books of travel and history." Furthermore, he argued, the

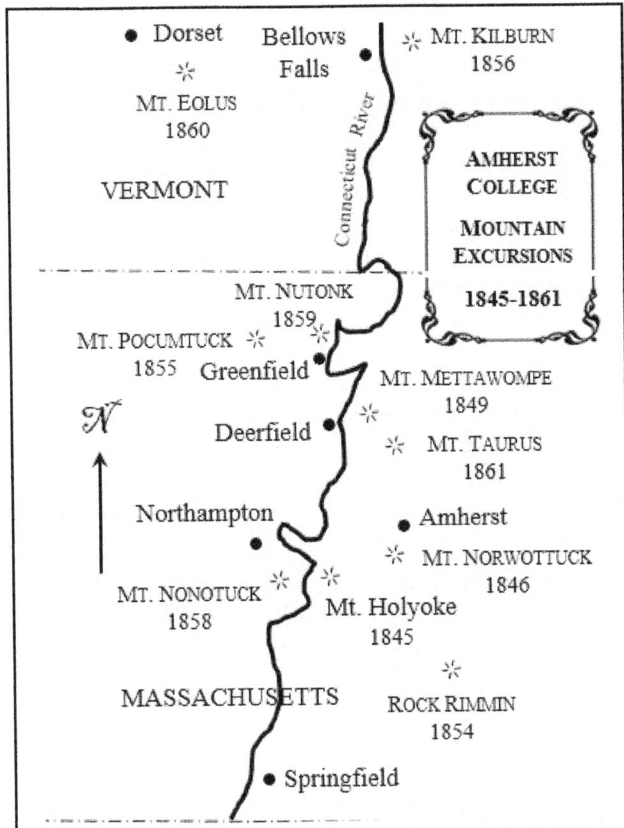

Figure 51. Mountain excursions at Amherst College, 1845-1861

students had earned the right to do so based on their "conquest" of the mountain. "To give a new name, we think a quite moderate exercise of the rights which such battles and such victories confer upon the conqueror." Thirdly, he asserted, there were literary considerations: "…no poet would dare to write a poem, if he must introduce into it the name of Toby. It would kill the finest epic in the world." And finally, said the young Hitchcock, it was high time that the original residents of the region got their due.

> We wish to change the name in order to do justice to the original owners of this mountain…And this act of justice, though tardy, is what we propose to do to-day. His name, although of the purest Indian, is easily spelt and pronounced, and euphonious in either prose or poetry. It is Mettawompe, and by the Senior Class of 1849, in Amherst College, the name Mettawompe is hereby affixed to this mountain.

We can imagine the burst of cheers and applause that this declaration must have evoked that day on the summit of Mount Toby, now, by decree, renamed *Mettawompe*. Some townspeople in attendance that day were apparently less enthusiastic. Five months later, at the Sunderland Town Meeting, a resolution was voted on and approved, reportedly by a vote of six to one:

> Whereas, in the month of June last, the Senior Class of Amherst College saw fit to change the name of the mountain heretofore called Toby, to that of Mettawompe, therefore Resolved, That as the citizens of the town of Sunderland, we consider the associations connected with the history of the past too sacred, and the reasons assigned for the change too trivial, to justify us in assenting to the change.

The resolution, appearing in the *Hampshire and Franklin Express*, provoked a tongue-in-cheek rejoinder a few weeks later under the title, "Mesmeric Meeting of the Senior Class of 1849 in Amherst College." The anonymous writer—it was President Hitchcock himself—seemed to suggest that the senior class had been duly reprimanded:

> We receive with all humility the rebuke of the town of Sunderland as Seniors should receive a rebuke from their Seniors in age and wisdom; and in token of our submission we will stand up with folded arms and lowered crests while it is read to us by the Secretary from the "Amherst Express," with the affecting history of Captain Toby….we duly appreciate the high degree of reverence felt by "six to one"' of the inhabitants of Sunderland for Captain Toby.

But the letter went on at some length to reassert the right of the students to make such changes. The "controversy" no doubt raged for some time in both Sunderland and Amherst. History, however, seems to have cast the final vote in favor of the citizenry of Sunderland: to the present day the town's highest summit is known as Mount Toby. The rebuff apparently did not discourage President Hitchcock or his students—mountain excursions and renaming celebrations continued throughout his presidency and beyond.

These mountain excursions as well as the newly established student receptions give clear evidence that Edward Hitchcock's style of leadership contrasted sharply from that of his predecessor. The spiritual credentials of Heman Humphrey were impeccable, but in personal appeal he was somewhat deficient. Edward Hitchcock, Jr., in his memoirs, made this frank assessment:

> President Humphrey was an austere man. Old style Puritan in his life. He was righteous & solid but not complaisant or approachable…It is said of him that very often when a student was ushered in to his study, that if he was not entirely at leisure, he would instantly the man opened the door, say "what do you want" without the civility of inviting him to a chair. And while he was thoroughly respected as an official he was not what we should call a popular President.

Perhaps President Hitchcock was correct in claiming as one of his few strengths in his new job an understanding and sympathy for his students. Events such as the mountain excursions seem to have solidified his status as a sympathetic, good humored, and popular leader, one to whom the phrase "Hail fellow well met" might apply. Whether he went too far in that direction is an interesting question, one which John M. Tyler, son of William S. Tyler, addressed many years later: "Possibly he [Pres. Humphrey] used the curb a little too hard, while President Hitchcock was afterward criticized for guiding with too loose a rein."

A month before his inauguration Hitchcock wrote in anticipation of his new position, "There is one circumstance connected with this change which I confess I look upon with pleasure. I am to become again the pastor of a church and must engage more than I have done of late in preaching the gospel. The idea certainly seems pleasant to me…" His pastoral duties would include preaching, teaching, and watching over the spiritual life of his flock.

Nearly all the homilies President Hitchcock delivered in the college chapel during his presidency had been written and first delivered more than a quarter century earlier but were now extensively revised and updated for the times and for this new audience. Some addressed the basic tenets of orthodox Christianity, resurrection, atonement, salvation, eternal damnation. Some called on his hearers to examine their souls, to turn away from sin, to avoid backsliding.

Only three of the surviving sermons from those years were new, written specifically for the college community and the times. In May 1846, he took up the subject of war, explaining that "a sense of duty growing out of the present condition of the country constrains me to make the effort." He was referring to the war with Mexico, and he chose as his scriptural text a powerful passage from the fourth chapter of James: "From whence come wars and fighting among you? Come they not hence, even of your lusts that war in your members?"

Hitchcock seldom introduced politics into his sermons, but this misadventure, he argued, called for strong words of condemnation. He proceeded to enumerate in typical Hitchcock fashion the toll of wars in ancient and modern times: five million in northern Africa, fifteen million in the wars of Justinian, six million at the hand of Napoleon, twelve million American Indians at the hands of the Spanish, fifteen million in the Grecian wars, thirty million in the War of the Twelve Caesars, thirty million during the Reformation. "Indeed," he concluded, "Edmund Burke estimates that about one quarter of the human race have perished by the sword that is 35,000,000,000."

In that same sermon he spoke with emotion about the war between the United States and Mexico that had begun only a month earlier:

> The circumstances under which I address you my hearers are indeed most disheartening and throw gloom and despondency over the prospect. While I yet

> speak the toxin of war is sounding all over our land and the requisition comes to our very doors for the young and the middle aged to arm themselves for foreign conquest whenever the constituted authority shall give the command.

A note of frustration can be heard as he added, "…what can my feeble testimony avail at such a time and who will hear my voice in the uproar and fierce excitement of war?"

While Hitchcock generally waded cautiously into matters political in his sermons, he no doubt sensed there was widespread disaffection with the jingoism of President James K. Polk in both the college and the wider community. His outrage over the war with Mexico is clear enough. He even addressed the sensitive question of a Christian's duty to serve in a war that he finds objectionable:

> Now I admit this blind submission to orders and the severe punishments that follow disobedience and this total disregard of a man's conscientious scruples may be indispensable to any efficient military system. But I cannot believe that when intelligent Christian men see it in its true light they will long endure it. … who has a right to come in between me and God and attempt to release me from my obligation to obey him and submit my conscience to the direction of a fellow man?

One of Hitchcock's sermons delivered in the college chapel in May 1847 survives as perhaps his most eloquent statement of God's love for the least of men, and an implicit condemnation of the institution of slavery. This was his most frequently delivered—and presumably most requested—sermon; it was subsequently published by the American Tract Society in 1848 under the title "Blind Slave in the Mines."

The sermon recounts an event that occurred while Hitchcock was touring a Virginia coal mine just a few weeks earlier. Deep below the earth's surface in a dark passage, he heard a voice singing a familiar hymn. "I shall be in heaven in the morning," the voice sang out with deep emotion. Soon Hitchcock's party came upon the subterranean soloist, an old blind man, a slave, who had lost his sight in a mine accident many years previously. Deep in the bowels of the earth that man labored while he sang a hymn of faith and hope, each stanza ending with the line, "I shall be in heaven in the morning." Hitchcock was deeply moved:

> Never before did I witness so grand an exhibition of moral sublimity. Oh how comparatively insignificant did earth's mightiest warriors and statesmen her princes and her emperors and even her philosophers without piety appear. How powerless would all their pomp and pageantry and wisdom be, to sustain them if called to change places with the poor slave! He had a principle within him

> superior to them all: and when the morning which he longs for shall come, how infinitely better than theirs will his lot appear to an admiring universe.

This account reveals as clearly as any other Hitchcock's humanity; his deep and abiding Christian faith; and his conviction that God's humblest children will one day be exalted. In the words of Matthew, "Blessed are the meek: for they shall inherit the earth."

Hitchcock's preaching had a particular impact on one student, Martin Nelson Root. In a diary of his two years at Amherst, Root made frequent references to the president's sermons. He even recorded a lengthy excerpt from the sermon about the blind slave, probably copied from the version published by the American Tract Society. That sermon must have enjoyed a special resonance among the college community; Hitchcock delivered it at least three times in the chapel while president and once during his retirement.

During his presidency Hitchcock also accepted invitations to preach in other churches. These were usually in Amherst or nearby, although on at least three occasions he delivered sermons in Boston including one in January 1850 at the State House before Governor George Briggs and the Legislature at the opening of a new session of that body.

For all his love of science and of learning, nothing was more dear to Edward Hitchcock, closer to the very heart and soul of the man, than saving souls, and he worked at that one student at a time, counting each success as an offering to Almighty God, and each failure as a personal mark against his own soul. One entirely voluntary part of his new pastoral duties that gave him particular satisfaction was hosting a weekly gathering for students devoted to "prayer and religious conference." These meetings took place in his private study on Monday evenings, and they proved enormously rewarding to the new president:

> Not a word was ever said in public about this meeting, yet it never lacked attendants. I told them I should generally call on them for prayers, and that I would then make familiar remarks upon some practical question, proposed at the preceding meeting, and would be glad, also, to hear their remarks. I sat at my study table, and the room was usually so closely packed that we could not even kneel in prayer. It seemed like a great family at morning or evening prayers, conversing upon experimental religion, and I do not doubt that the home feeling this produced had much to do with the interest which the meetings seemed to excite.

So well attended were the meetings that at one point he considered moving them to a large college room.

> I rejoice that I did not: for in subsequent years, by letters from graduates, I found that probably no other religious effort which I ever made was so blessed of God as this. Sometimes thrilling incidents occurred in the

> meetings…sometimes the prayers made by my young brethren had an unction, an eloquence and a power, which I have never heard elsewhere, and whose impression remains upon my memory to this day.

In evaluating the state of the college, Hitchcock counted as the most important of all measures of success the conversion of souls. And so it was that he spoke and wrote often of revivals of religion at Amherst. In *Reminiscences*, he devoted nearly thirty pages to the subject of revivals, and he published regular reports on these revivals in local and regional newspapers. In April 1846, he wrote a lengthy article on the subject that appeared in a local newspaper: "During the term just closed, it has pleased the Lord to bless Amherst College for the eighth time since its establishment in 1821, by awakening a deep interest in the subject of personal religion…" He included in that article excerpts of letters of testimony received from parents regarding the dramatic changes they observed in their sons. As often happened in those times, that story was quickly copied in full or in part in other newspapers from New England to New York and beyond. A Philadelphia newspaper reported of the college, "God has done great things for that institution, and great things for His church by its influence." The *Southern Patriot* in Charleston, South Carolina, reported, "In a recent account of the revival in Amherst College, it is stated, that of the 119 students, 71 are now professors of religion." At last the public narrative about Amherst College had shifted from warnings of "troubles" and "financial embarrassments" to pronouncements of a revival, financial as well as spiritual.

President Hitchcock may well have been surprised at how much of the job of president he found agreeable, the interaction with students, the levees, the mountain excursions, as well as the more serious matters of teaching, preaching, and pastoring. But as he had anticipated, there were some duties that proved to be sources of displeasure, stress, even despair.

First there were the meetings, and of these there seemed to be no end. Trustees' meetings were the least of his concern; they generally took place but once a year. The Prudential Committee, on the other hand, met monthly, sometimes more frequently as needed. But Faculty Meetings were held weekly, and these, it seems, were the bane of his existence. "They often wore very much upon me," he wrote years later, "especially when followed, as they sometimes were, by the admonition, dismissal, or expulsion of delinquents." Edward, Jr., wrote that faculty meetings shortened his father's life and would have killed him sooner had he not resigned when he did.

Another duty that President Hitchcock found "peculiarly onerous" was the great volume of official letters—what he referred to as his "epistolary correspondence"—that he was called on to write, 400 or 500 such letters per

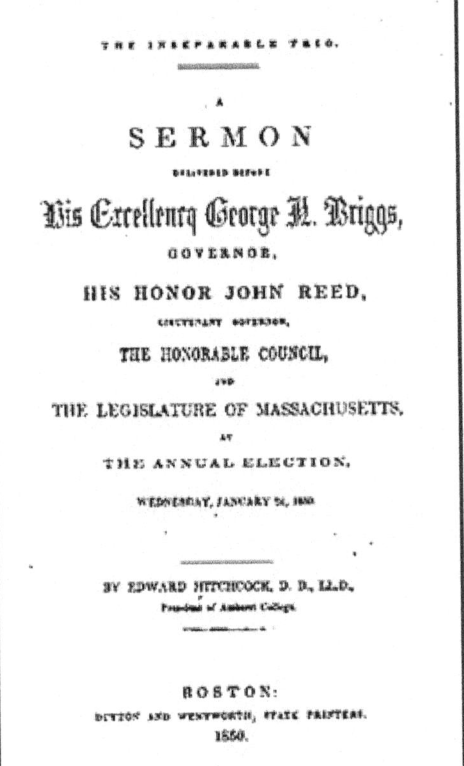

THE INSEPARABLE TRIO.

A

SERMON

DELIVERED BEFORE

His Excellency George N. Briggs,

GOVERNOR,

HIS HONOR JOHN REED,

LIEUTENANT GOVERNOR,

THE HONORABLE COUNCIL,

AND

THE LEGISLATURE OF MASSACHUSETTS,

AT

THE ANNUAL ELECTION,

WEDNESDAY, JANUARY [illegible], [illegible]

BY EDWARD HITCHCOCK, D. D., LL.D.,

President of Amherst College.

BOSTON:

DUTTON AND WENTWORTH, STATE PRINTERS.

1850.

Figure 52. *The Inseparable Trio*, a sermon delivered at the state legislature in Boston, January 1850

year he estimated. Some pertained to his scientific interests which likely were pleasurable and interesting to him, but many were decidedly unpleasant, having to do with students and those "admonitions, dismissals, or expulsions" to which he referred.

> The same mail…might bring inquiries about some point in the theory of temperance—how to employ garnet in making sand-paper—how to reconcile the imputation of Adam's sin with our sense of justice—where to find the best beds of sulphate of baryta…or new views of the relations of geology to Moses—or a new poem—or a new work…During my Presidency, I calculated that I was obliged to answer as many as four hundred or five hundred letters, annually, and to these should be added at least one hundred recommendations to students going out to teach school, and for other purposes, and to graduates.

The business of soliciting donations was one of the duties of a president that Hitchcock did not relish. But he was stunned by the gift from Samuel Williston on the eve of his inauguration, and by a succession of other large contributions that followed it, almost it seemed in spite of his perceived limitations in this area. Soon he would discover a device, a fulcrum he might have called it, for eliciting still more financial support, and one that served his scientific interests perfectly.

At last, it seemed, the era of tense relations between the students and administration of Amherst College was over, enrollments had begun to rise, the financial situation was improving. But optimism was not Edward Hitchcock's stock-in-trade—he was ever able to find an ominous cloud on the sunniest day. In November 1846, he wrote in his notes, "...from all quarters I hear of an impression that the College is gaining ground and rising (Oh how slight a wind will change the current of popular feeling!)."

Nearly a quarter century earlier, in one of his first sermons, he had warned of the dangers of prosperity to the human soul, and now those words seemed relevant, as he wrote in 1847, "Of all things in this world prosperity in temporal affairs is the most dangerous to an individual and why not to a public institution?" Tellingly, he delivered that very sermon, "Prosperity the Ruin of Mankind," in the chapel in October 1847, just as Amherst was once again prospering. With ample cause to rejoice on all sides, with a student body that felt warmly toward him and his style of administration, with a wife and family that took enthusiastically to their new roles in the college—despite all this encouragement, President Hitchcock's soul, it seems, was filled with doom and gloom.

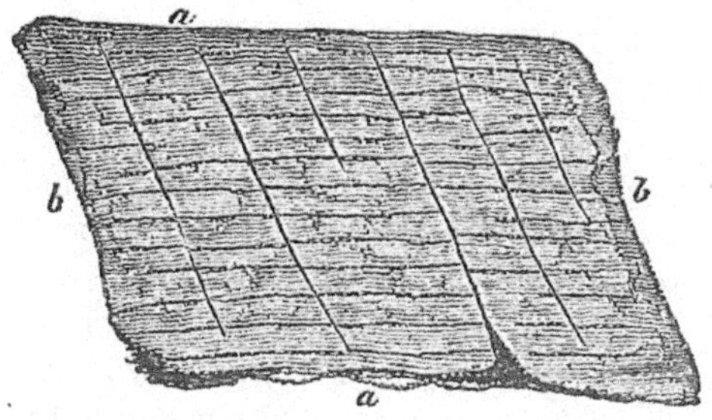

Figure 53. Gneiss with glacial furrows from Billerica, Massachusetts, drawn by Orra White Hitchcock, 1833

Woods Cabinet and Observatory

20 The Cabinets

"The incubus that had so long rested upon us was removed."

Enfield, Massachusetts, Autumn 1845

"Mr. President, you are very welcome, sir, very welcome indeed," began Josiah B. Woods as his guest stepped from his carriage. "How was your journey?" Woods stood before his large, brick home overlooking the little town of Enfield, nestled in the hills of central Massachusetts. It was the most impressive residence in the town, but then Josiah B. Woods was Enfield's wealthiest citizen.

President Hitchcock was returning from several days spent in Boston and Cambridge meeting friends of the college, most for the first time as president. It had been an exhausting trip, in part because he felt ill at ease in asking for contributions for the college. "It has been most taxing on my constitution, I must confess. I do not relish city life, sir. It is all too fast and confusing." He paused, looking around at the sweeping view of the Swift River Valley that lay below, shimmering with autumn color. "One needs a tonic such as this, for the body as well as for the soul."

"I quite agree, Mr. President, indeed." The pair stood in silence for a moment, as if entranced by the view before them, then Mr. Woods broke the spell. "Well, do come in and rest yourself. I very much wish you to meet my dear wife and my daughters...and of course to learn of all the intelligence from Amherst."

A cup of tea and a single wheat biscuit gave President Hitchcock new vigor, and after exchanging pleasantries with Mrs. Francis Woods and several children, he brought Mr. Woods up to date regarding the college. When he had run out of college news, he reached into a small satchel and produced a specimen of glistening yellow crystals.

"This is epidote, sir. I collected it a decade ago not a mile from here—on one of my geological forays." He knew that Josiah Woods, while not a trained scientist, had a particular interest in minerals. On a visit to Amherst a few years earlier, Woods had presented the professor with several pieces of gneiss, the native rock of his hometown, and seemed to delight in the opportunity to discuss their unique attributes. They were, truth be told, rather ordinary, but the professor had a way of making even the most mundane object seem like solid gold.

"Ah, that is marvelous, sir," Woods replied, lifting the specimen toward the window and admiring its shining highlights. "I understand that you have accumulated quite a collection for the college, Mr. President, one that does the institution proud."

This was the moment Hitchcock had been waiting for, the opportunity to bring up a subject close to his heart. "Yes, indeed, no fewer than 14,000 specimens to date, sir, and more arriving every day. But we have some difficulty these days in properly storing and displaying them. I regret to say that most are at present hidden away in boxes or bags like this one where they cannot be seen or appreciated." He paused, hoping that his host would respond.

"A shame, Mr. President, a shame."

President Hitchcock swallowed and breathed heavily, as if trying to steel himself for a feat demanding great strength. "I...I wonder, sir...that is, in consideration of your interest in minerals and ores, whether you might be able to assist the college in the construction of a natural history cabinet." There—he had said it. Exhausted, he fell back in his chair casting his gaze to the floor, as if ashamed at his outburst and preparing for what he was certain would be a rebuff.

"I would, indeed, Mr. President. It would be an honor." President Hitchcock at last looked up, took a deep breath of relief, and smiled weakly at his host. Mr. Woods then added, "But what precisely would this cabinet require?"

"We have a plan, Mr. Woods, for a small but handsome structure—octagonal—wood frame—with an observatory attached." He drew several sheets of parchment from his breast pocket bearing sketches of a preliminary design. "The cost would be approximately five thousand dollars." He winced as he said the number and once again his eyes dropped downward.

There was a long, uncomfortable pause. Mr. Woods rose from his chair, walked to the window, and looked out for a moment. Without turning to his guest, he began: "Mr. President, I would be pleased to...to assist...in this most worthy project."

"Thank you, sir, for your..."

Woods turned and interrupted him. "I will be happy to subscribe, sir, perhaps $200." President Hitchcock smiled at his host, trying his best to hide his disappointment. But Mr. Woods continued. "However, I will make a further proposition, sir. If I may be allowed a few months, I will in my travels for business make further solicitations. I have confidence that I can obtain in cash and subscriptions most if not all of the amount you require. Would that be suitable, sir?"

President Hitchcock's pallor suddenly turned rosy and a broad smile crept across his face. "Yes, sir, that would be suitable, Mr. Woods—most suitable."

Of all the duties incumbent on a college president, the one Edward Hitchcock dreaded most was seeking donations on behalf of the college. Not only was he uncomfortable with solicitations, he was convinced that he was not very adept at it—surely he would fail. But very soon after his inauguration a few of his first efforts at procuring donations brought unexpected success, not so much a result of his skills in solicitation as of the confidence and trust he enjoyed among friends of the college.

One area in which he was favored with some early success was that of endowing the college's first "cabinet." Collections of books, equipment, and artifacts played a vital role in American colleges from the beginning. A good library was essential, naturally, to a literary institution. But equally important were instruments—"philosophical apparatus" as they were known—telescopes, microscopes, globes, astronomical models, and the like, that would permit students to explore the wonders of the universe large and small. Also essential was a collection of natural history artifacts—minerals, bones, skeletons, dried plants—the better to exhibit evidence of God's benevolence in all His creations.

Hitchcock knew well the kinds of facilities a well-equipped literary institution should possess. He had visited Harvard in 1815, in part to examine the college's philosophical apparatus. During his apprenticeship with Benjamin Silliman at Yale, he had learned about fitting out a state-of-the-art chemistry

Figure 54. New telescope in the Lawrence Observatory, 1854

laboratory. No doubt he also learned at that time of Yale's new mineralogical cabinet. But Amherst had the most meager of collections. To compete with the likes of Harvard and Yale, Amherst must build up its collections, and he began advocating for this cause immediately on joining the faculty.

Hitchcock's first priority after arriving at Amherst was equipping the college's first rudimentary chemical laboratory. Through his efforts a proper facility was accommodated in the basement of the new chapel in autumn 1826. In that same year he contributed his own mineralogical collection to the school, and immediately put it to use in his courses. About the same time Orra began work on hundreds of drawings, paintings, posters, and murals that would assist her husband in his teaching as well.

As to the astronomical instruments and related apparatus, the trustees in 1830 passed a resolution authorizing Hitchcock and mathematics professor Sylvester Hovey to raise funds for and acquire equipment. Hovey traveled to Paris that summer, returning with a telescope made by the renowned instrument maker Hippolyte Pixii that would be the college's first astronomical device.

Meanwhile Amherst's mineralogical collection was growing rapidly. Part of Hitchcock's charge as State Geologist of Massachusetts had been to collect samples for the state's three colleges, Harvard, Williams, and Amherst. By 1840 he had acquired at least 1000 specimens for the collections of Amherst College. By his own accounting, several thousand specimens, mostly minerals, also came to the college from its foreign missionaries. And as the years went by faculty members such as Sylvester Hovey, Charles U. Shepard, Charles B. Adams, and Edward Hitchcock donated their personal collections to the college. Clearly a new facility was needed to house these treasures.

In the first year of his presidency, Hitchcock succeeded in influencing Josiah B. Woods, an attorney and industrialist from Enfield, Massachusetts, to make a donation for the erection of a building, called a cabinet, to house all the college's collections. Woods's own donation was modest, but his admiration for Hitchcock led him to undertake a subscription campaign to solicit additional gifts for the project, an effort that eventually garnered $9000. When the new cabinet opened, it held at least 11,000 objects, mainly geological and zoological specimens, including an extraordinary gift from Professor Charles U. Shepard described by Hitchcock as "an almost unequalled collection of meteoric stones, by which the mineralogy and geology of other worlds are brought under our eyes" (see Figure 55). The Woods Cabinet, as it would eventually be named, was the first of a series of new buildings constructed over the next ten years to house the collections of the college including the Lawrence Observatory (1847), the Morgan Library (1853), the Appleton Cabinet for Zoology and Ichnology (1855), and the Nineveh Gallery (1857). These buildings would be the most important physical legacy of Edward Hitchcock at Amherst College.

Despite the sizable donations of Samuel Williston and David Sears and the success of the efforts of Josiah Woods toward the new cabinet, the college's fortunes were not immediately reversed. Total enrollment of 118 in 1845 was the lowest since the school was chartered, and it rose by just two in the following year. Hitchcock was increasingly discouraged about the college's finances and feared that his premonitions of the school's demise were coming true.

But the generosity of Josiah Woods, and, perhaps more importantly, Woods's confidence in Hitchcock, gave the president courage to make a few additional solicitations, however repugnant the task might be. He was inspired by the words of his longtime friend and colleague, Professor Nathan W. Fiske, who had made this prediction at the time of his retirement in 1847: "Amherst College will be relieved; Mr. Williston, I think, will give it fifty thousand dollars, and you will put his name upon it." Wrote Hitchcock in *Reminiscences*, "I felt justified, therefore, in saying to [Samuel Williston] that if his circumstances would allow him to come to our aid in this exigency by founding another professorship, I did not doubt this result was to follow." In other words, Amherst College would be renamed Williston College.

As it turned out, Professor Fiske's prediction was validated in large part. Williston did agree to endow a new professorship and half of a second. Soon thereafter, another benefactor, Samuel Hitchcock (no relation to Edward), made up the difference; within a few weeks two full professorships had been endowed.

Figure 55. The collections of Charles U. Shepard, originally housed in the Woods Cabinet, shown exhibited in Walker Hall, 1868 or later.

President Hitchcock did lobby the trustees for some years after regarding the change of the college's name, but it was never approved. According to Hitchcock, Williston himself seemed unenthusiastic. Perhaps, he had told Hitchcock, they might want to make the change posthumously. But even after Williston's death in 1874, the idea was never seriously pursued.

In winter of 1846, President Hitchcock wrote to the state legislature appealing for aid for the college. He was not optimistic; similar requests had been denied any number of times over the last twenty years; some members of the Board of Trustees had expressed doubts that it was worth the effort. Nevertheless, in April 1847, legislation was finally approved; the college would receive $25,000. In Hitchcock's mind it had required nothing short of a literal act of God to overcome the obstacles. The bill came up on a Saturday and was met with strong opposition. Its supporters gathered that evening to pray to God for the bill's success. All present agreed to make similar entreaties on the Sabbath.

> Monday came; the Bill was read; but to the amazement of these praying men, opposition had almost disappeared, and with a few remarks it was passed…how can we, avoid the conviction that prayer was the grand agency that smoothed the troubled waters and gave the College the victory after so many years of bitter opposition and defeat!

Williams College received a similar endowment from the legislature in 1849. Harvard was unsuccessful, perhaps for political reasons.

At last the college's financial worries were abating. Even the usually pessimistic president had to admit that the tide had turned. "And, oh! what a load did these benefactions take from my mind!" he wrote. Not until their meeting in July 1847 were the trustees informed of the news:

> This was the most delightful trustee meeting I had ever attended. Those venerable men…whom Dr. Humphrey and myself had so often met with a discouraging story of debt and an empty treasury, were now for the first time to be told of God's wonderful goodness in turning our captivity and answering their long-continued and earnest prayers.

With the college's coffers now replenished, steps were taken to settle accounts. The first was in paying off their debt: "The incubus that had so long rested upon us, was removed; the cord that had well-nigh throttled us, was cut asunder, and the depletion of our life-blood was arrested." Second was repaying the faculty the salaries they had foregone for the past two-and-one-half years, a generous and apparently unexpected gesture. Also, Hitchcock was quick to see that necessary repairs were made to the college buildings, including the installation of blinds on the dormitory windows, a change most welcome by the students.

The intelligence quickly spread that the college's financial worries had been relieved. According to Martin Root, word was circulated on campus in July to the effect that John J. Astor had given the college half a million dollars, a rumor President Hitchcock himself was quick to squelch. It is a measure of the wisdom of the president in promoting good relations in the college that when he did go public with the good news, he chose to announce it first to the students, and to do so at an all college event:

> ...I took the opportunity at evening prayers to read the above votes, and I shall never forget the scene that followed. At first they did not seem to comprehend the matter, and they gave no demonstration of their feelings...But as the successive announcements came out, they could not restrain their feelings and began to clap, and by the time the last vote was read, the clapping was tremendous, and when they were dismissed and had reached the outer door of the chapel, they stopped and the cheering was long and loud.

With the support of the state and of many donors large and small, the school's pecuniary situation had been stabilized. Amicable relations between the faculty and students had been restored. Student enrollment was on the rise; it would nearly double by the end of President Hitchcock's term of office. He was acclaimed by many as the reason for the abrupt reversal of fortunes of the institution. Amherst College was once again on solid footing, having risen from the ashes like the phoenix of mythology.

The "New Cabinet and Observatory," later to be named the Woods Cabinet, was dedicated on June 28, 1848. Architecturally it was not a traditional American college building. At Hitchcock's insistence it was octagonal, like his personal cabinet built a decade earlier (shown in "The Return," page 177). While a traditionalist in most other respects, Edward Hitchcock had a particular partiality for such a structure, although he knew that opinion was not shared by all.

> Some of our good friends who have never seen the architecture of Europe, were greatly scandalized because the building had so many angles, and its longer axis or front was not perpendicular to the face of the row of buildings behind, but quite oblique, conforming to the crest of the hill.

He got the idea from an Amherst graduate, O. S. Fowler, who had made a name for himself in the pseudoscientific field of phrenology. Fowler, according to Stanley King, "...became convinced that the octagonal form was desirable in construction, both for reasons of economy and for reasons of health."

Three years into his presidency, a renewed sense of unity and spirit had embraced the college, and Edward Hitchcock was quick to give the credit where he felt it was due:

> Never, it seems to us, was his special Providence more manifest than in this whole business, from its inception to the present hour. If ever I had doubted God's special agency in influencing the hearts of men to deeds of benevolence, the experience of the last two years would have removed my skepticism. Permit us then from a full heart, to praise God for our increased means of honoring Him by promoting the cause of education.

One of Hitchcock's concerns on ascending to the presidency was whether those duties would prevent him from continuing his research and writing. In fact he threw himself vigorously into that work, even as the duties of his new office pressed on him. In the first five years of his presidency, he published three books on religious topics, *The Coronation of Winter, Religious Lectures on Peculiar Phenomena in the Four Seasons,* and *A Chapter in the Book of Providence*. He also published nine scientific papers in that period, three in geology, six related to the fossil footmarks, in the *American Journal of Science and Arts* or in the *Proceedings of the American Association for the Advancement of Science*. While most of these were brief, there was one notable exception, a major revision of his taxonomy of the fossil footmarks, with much new data and many new insights. Published in the *Proceedings*, it ran to 125 pages and nearly 50,000 words with 135 figures.

Another continued source of pleasure for the new president was teaching. One condition of the position had always been that in addition to his administrative duties, he should also teach. President Hitchcock's new title was Professor of Natural Theology and Geology, and so with much pleasure he resumed some of his teaching duties. Most of his courses—chemistry, mineralogy, and botany—were taken over by the newly appointed Professor of Chemistry and Natural History, Charles U. Shepard, an early Amherst College graduate. It remained to Hitchcock to teach geology, and that was by his own account an entirely pleasurable duty, and one he would continue even after his presidency was concluded and he was in retirement.

Despite all the successes of the first four years of his presidency, or perhaps as a result of his efforts, Hitchcock's health had by late 1848 become tenuous. On November 12, 1848, he made this entry in his notes:

> During the present term as the cold weather has come on my cough has become very urgent and last Thursday as the immediate result apparently of the labours of preaching and administering the communion on the Sabbath and of some unpleasant excitement bleeding at the lungs commenced and has continued more or less to this time. Of course I have been obliged to suspend at once all my labours in College and shut myself in the house…

The implication of this state of affairs was undeniable:

> ...I have reason to fear that this is the final termination of those labours and not improbably of all others on earth...I am brought to a solemn pause and am trying to bring myself into perfect acquiescence with the Divine Will.

Despite the progress in easing discord on the campus, tensions still existed. In his diary Martin Root suggested that the state of the President's physical and mental health was well known to students. He mentioned hazing, pranks, secret societies, and "rowing" as bearing on the president's health. Root makes particular reference to this in his diary:

> Mrs. Hitchcock has been of great advantage to the Pres. The Dr. is liable to fits of despondency and gloom. The least obstacle is apt to discourage him and make him give up in despair...she goes into his study, and uses all the art of females to make him forget his troubles, talks in a cheerful manner to him, and in a short time returns his mind to its proper degree of temper. She fills out his sermons, and it is probable he would not have been anything great, if she had not assisted by her drawings of everything appertaining to his study of Geology.

His source for such intimate details of the president's health was no doubt his classmate and friend, Edward Hitchcock, Jr.

Word spread that President Hitchcock's condition was dire. "We understand that the health of President Hitchcock of Amherst College has failed him, and it is feared he will be obliged to resign his office in that Institution," reported the *Springfield Republican* on November 28, 1848, a report that would be repeated in dozens of newspapers around the country in the next two weeks. A Maine newspaper a few days later reported incorrectly, "President Hitchcock of Amherst College has resigned in consequence of ill health."

Figure 56. Cascade in Leverett

By this time his family and some colleagues had come to doubt his repeated complaints of ill health: "All with whom I am familiar have heard me complain so long of feeble health and have seen me yet live and work hard that they suppose it will continue to be thus." Even his doctors had underestimated the gravity of his situation, or so he believed:

> The physicians will not allow that as yet there is any actual disease in the substance of the lungs yet I know how liable they are to be deceived and how flattering such complaints are. My hope is not in their skill kind and able as they are: but if God should speak the word I might be spared. I am trying to leave myself entirely in his hands and to wait quietly to see what is his will.

He then let it be known that he would soon resign.

> I had given the Trustees to understand that just so soon as they could find another man to take my place, I should consider it a great favor to be released…there was a sort of understanding when I took the Presidency, that when the College had passed through its pecuniary exigency I might be allowed to fall back to my former professorship. That exigency was now over; the institution was free from debt, and with funds sufficient to enable it, with economy, to go successfully forward; the question of its permanent existence was now settled; its numbers were increasing, and I did not cease from time to time to remind the Trustees of my wishes.

If Hitchcock believed that resigning was the only hope for his declining health, the trustees had a different solution. They had succeeded in urging him to travel to Richmond, Virginia, in spring 1847, for nearly six weeks, and he had admitted to feeling much improved on his return. If a little travel could yield such benefits, perhaps a longer excursion would be even better for him. Edward resisted. "Instead of heeding [my wishes]… in 1849 they voted, without any suggestion of mine, and even contrary to my wishes, to give me leave of absence for six months, for a tour to Europe."

Orra had long expressed an aversion for such a journey. As to her husband, he was convinced that, should they undertake the voyage, they would end up at the bottom of the Atlantic. He turned, naturally, to the Great Arbiter: "I have prayed long and earnestly over the subject and I trust with an agonizing desire to know my duty…it does seem as if the finger of Providence pointed me towards the rising sun." Nevertheless he seemed to be hoping for a reprieve when he added, "I have decided to endeavor to go earnestly desiring however that if neither God's glory nor my good can be promoted by the trip my way may be hedged up."

The transatlantic steam ship Liverpool

21 Towards the Rising Sun

"So strong is the feeling…as if I were preparing for my own funeral."

Edinburgh, Scotland, August 9, 1850

The Hitchcocks were attending a soirée at the home of Professor Robert Jameson of the University of Edinburgh, an elegant residence situated on the Royal Circus, one of the city's most fashionable neighborhoods. The event was a small affair, with only a few dozen guests, men in evening jackets and kilts, ladies in long dresses, many with fine jewelry and airs to match. It was the kind of event that made both Edward and Orra ill at ease, unfamiliar as they were with the manners of high society in general, and of Scottish high society in particular. And then there was the rich, overly stimulating food, and the ever present ardent spirits.

Orra was engaged in a conversation with Miss Jameson, sister of the host, when Professor Jameson introduced Edward to Lady Randolph, Countess of Moray, a Scottish aristocrat of the first order.

"Professor Hitchcock, I am delighted to meet you, sir," she began. She was looking at him intensely, almost appraisingly.

Unsure whether he should extend his hand to a countess, Edward smiled, then bowed awkwardly. "Lady Randolph, a pleasure."

The countess seemed now to relax. "Are you and Mrs. Hitchcock enjoying your visit in Edinburgh?"

"Indeed we are, my lady. It is a lovely city—without doubt the loveliest we have seen in our travels to date."

Lady Randolph smiled proudly, knowing that the Hitchcocks had already spent time in England and Ireland. "It is indeed." She paused briefly. "I understand, Professor Hitchcock, that you intend to visit schools of agriculture during your stay in Scotland."

"Yes, Lady Randolph, that is my hope. The Governor of Massachusetts has commissioned me to carry out a survey of agricultural schools wherever I travel in Europe."

"How very interesting. And have you visited many such schools yet, Professor?"

"Indeed, madam. One large establishment in England—at Cirencester—very impressive. Another at Hoddesdon in Hertfordshire. And the Irish have a very well-developed program of agricultural education—most thorough. Several are within Queens College, but there are as well what are known as training schools. I was particularly taken with one at Glasnevin—called the Model School and Farm—and another at Larne. Quite elaborate both in facilities and in courses of study, I believe. An excellent means of improving agricultural methods, of keeping up with new scientific findings, and of improving the lot of the farmer."

"Laudable, Professor, and no doubt important in Ireland. But I dare say I doubt such a school has a place in Scotland."

Hitchcock was genuinely confused by this comment. "Oh? Why do you say that, my lady?"

"Professor, we Scots pride ourselves on our refinement, our education, our understanding of our country's history and traditions. But the working class are not like us, you see. Many have no education, no appreciation."

Hitchcock swallowed and nodded as she spoke. "Hmm-uh-huh."

Lady Randolph continued. "To give a crofter an education could be a difficult, even a dangerous practice. It might give him aspirations beyond his status—turn him into a Chartist or a Luddite, do you know what I mean? A farmer, after all, is merely a farmer, and always will be. Surely you would agree, sir?"

Professor Hitchcock bowed. "I understand, Lady Randolph, that you have your traditions and standards. And of those your country, your people, may rightfully be proud. But as an American I see the matter in a somewhat different light. We strive to give the best possible education to all classes, both sexes—to every citizen."

"It sounds to me like a very wasteful system, providing education to the masses."

"In my native town—Deerfield—in Massachusetts, Lady Randolph, every man, woman, and child was encouraged to acquire as much education as possible, regardless of their status in the community."

"Professor, surely you do not mean to say that you received the same education in Deerfield as a farmer's son?"

Hitchcock smiled, bowing slightly again. Then he spoke softly, as if trying very hard not to give offense. "My lady, I am a farmer's son."

Despite serious reservations, Edward and Orra began preparations for their trip to Europe. "I confess that both myself and wife look forward to this voyage with great solicitude and even strong aversion," he wrote in his notes just a few weeks before their scheduled departure.

> My own health is so feeble that I have lost all courage and we both anticipate little else but suffering. Indeed so strong is the feeling upon my mind that I shall never return that I feel as if I were preparing for my own funeral…But when the enquiry comes up what shall I do if I do not go I still persevere in getting ready.

One factor that appears to have made the prospect of the European trip more agreeable was the decision of their friends, John and Hannah Tappan of Boston, to accompany them. The Tappans, both natives of Northampton, were experienced travelers and this no doubt went a long way to allay the fears and anxieties of the Hitchcocks, inexperienced as they were in foreign travel. Knowing well of Edward's frugality, the Tappans also donated $250 toward their passage to Liverpool. All obstacles seemed to have been swept away. There was nothing left to do but prepare to set sail.

And set sail they did from Boston on May 15, 1850, aboard the wooden hulled Cunard steamship *Canada*, bound for Liverpool, England. The trip in those times took ten or twelve days and it was by all accounts a difficult crossing for Edward. "I was reduced a good deal by the voyage," he wrote to Edward, Jr., several weeks later, "and have not yet recovered the tone of my stomach nor my flesh though I hope I am somewhat improving." In a letter to his brothers in Deerfield he described the voyage in a word—"dreadful."

Once in England, however, Edward's health improved as did his spirits. Their first excursion from Liverpool was by rail to the north of Wales where they ascended Mount Snowdon, the highest peak in Wales, on horseback. He had purchased an aneroid barometer in Liverpool which he took along and used to measure the elevations along the way and at the summit. He was naturally fascinated by the geological wonders all around him as he recorded in his notes from the trip: "How interesting to be able to pick out marine petrified shells from the rock, at the summit, now thirty-five hundred feet above the sea level." He also recognized other important evidences not unlike those he had observed on his geological surveys:

> The most interesting phenomena which met me in the mountains of Wales, were the marks of ancient glaciers. Although I had then never seen a glacier, and had forgotten whether English geologists had supposed them once to have existed in Wales, a few days' observation satisfied me that great masses of ice must once have descended from the highest parts of the mountains, through the valleys, wearing down and smoothing their bottoms and sides up to a certain altitude, the whole corresponding to glacier action.

He expressed his view of the role of glacial action in shaping the landscape of Wales to British geologist Sir Andrew Ramsay in a meeting later in the trip. Ten years later, Ramsay adopted the idea in his published geology of Wales; Hitchcock believed Ramsay got it from him. A few days later Hitchcock and John Tappan ascended Cader Idris, the second highest summit in Wales.

The party next traveled by rail to Bristol, Bath, Southampton, and then by boat to the Isle of Wight. Edward was much affected by the unique landscape of that island, particularly "the chalk needles and overhanging cliffs and domes of chalk, and the variegated and upturned strata of Alum Bay." While there they attended a service at Whippingham Church where they were seated only a few feet from Queen Victoria and the royal family who frequently spent weekends at Osborne House nearby. One goal for his trip had been "…to take the privilege of a cat in looking upon a king, a queen, a nobleman, or military chief, should such a one cross my path," and in that chapel he was able to do just that. He was moved to see the queen bow her head in humility when the vicar asked for prayers for Her Majesty.

The Hitchcocks and Tappans then traveled to London where they spent nearly two weeks. Both Edward and Orra had visited New York City, but London in 1850 was five times larger than New York, and the experience was overwhelming. In a letter to his brothers he wrote:

> What shall I say of London except that it is the center of the world and it seems as if all the world were collected there. Some days I have travelled there 4 or 5 miles in one direction through streets with almost a continued line of houses and the same day gone as far in the opposite direction and yet on neither side have I reached the outer limits of the city.

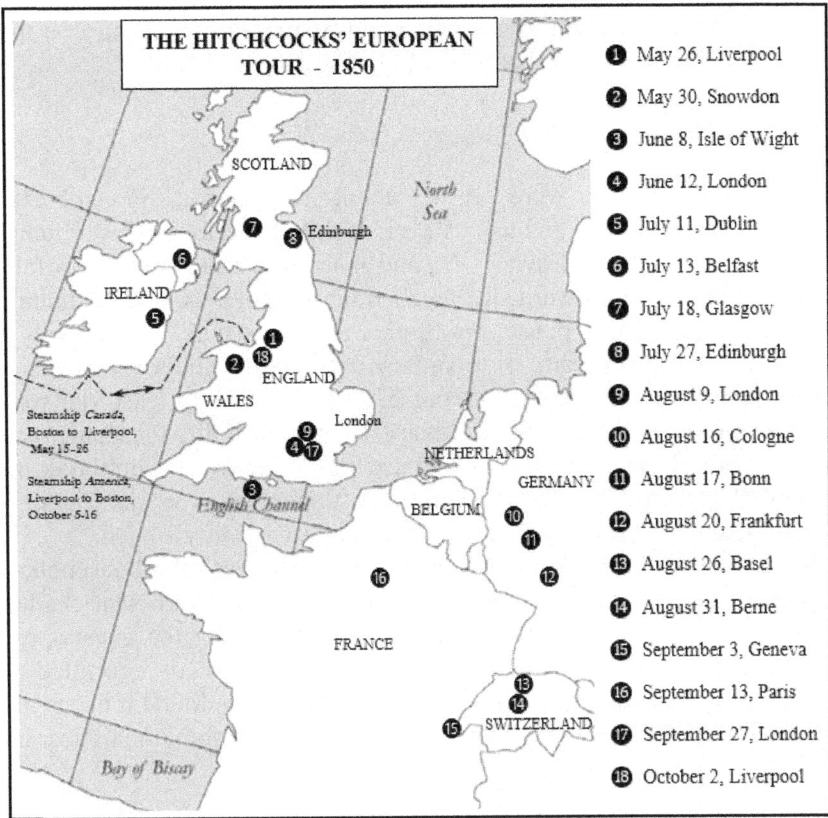

Figure 57. The Hitchcocks' European tour, 1850.

Edward made good use of his time in London, visiting the British Museum, the Museum of Economical Geology, the Botanic Garden at Regent's Park, the collections of the London Geological Society, and the Hunterian Museum. He was particularly impressed by the Hunterian, also known as the Museum of Comparative and Morbid Anatomy. He was wined and dined—without the wine, of course—by England's leading scientists. Dr. Gideon Mantell treated him like a brother, he recalled, and Sir Charles Lyell invited him to dine with the London Geological Society. He enjoyed a "soiree" at the Royal Society of London where he saw a lock of Sir Isaac Newton's hair.

He was particularly pleased at last to meet Dr. John Pye-Smith of Homerton College. A decade earlier Dr. Pye-Smith had favored Hitchcock with an effusive introduction to the second edition of *Elementary Geology*. It would appear in at least thirty subsequent editions. The old man was very frail, and Edward was invited to attend a celebration in honor of his retirement. "I had formed a high opinion of him…from his correspondence," Hitchcock recalled, "and I had an opportunity to state to the company, when they called on me for remarks, my views of Dr. Smith, without the usual embarrassment of speaking in a man's presence; for he was so deaf that he could not hear a word."

While Edward and Orra were touring about Europe, back in Amherst the Hitchcock household was as busy as ever. It fell to the four eldest Hitchcock siblings, Mary, Catherine, Edward, Jr., and Jane, to manage domestic affairs in their parents' absence. Edward, Jr., recalled that summer as devoted mainly to "guarding the President's house, my brother and my sisters." They likely also managed a constant stream of boarders and guests and oversaw several important college social events. Of course, they had help. At least four women were hired for the summer months. Edward had responsibility for seeing that the help were paid; those disbursements appear in the family account book in his hand. By September he had moved to Easthampton to begin teaching at Williston Seminary, after which transactions appear in Mary's hand.

According to the account of Edward, Jr., managing the household was satisfying, even exhilarating. Commencement Week was a particular challenge. They entertained many dignitaries at that time, including the guest speaker, Reverend Frederic D. Huntington of Boston. Edward, Jr., recalled with particularly vivid detail a meal at which he and his sisters found it necessary to disguise the fact that he himself had lugged the ice cream from the freezer in the woodshed:

> In the early morning Mary had made the custard for the ice cream and I had frozen it. Of course it came on as dessert at dinner. But the hired girl had not the ability to get it out of one of those old-fashioned freezers and I was the only one who could. So we put up this ruse. Jane went to the front door—I was at the head of the table—and rung the bell and then came in and said there was some one who wanted to see me. So I excused myself, sneaked around to the woodshed very rapidly, got out the ice cream for the girl, and then got back to the table before the ice cream came in.

Charles, who turned fourteen that summer, had completed his final year at Amherst Academy in July; he would be entering Williston Seminary in September. During the interval, he no doubt had some daily chores to attend such as taking the cows to pasture, a task he was not fond of. But he may well have been assigned more adventurous duties such as driving the wagon to Sunderland for a load of corn and hay as his older brother had done at his age.

Emily, now eleven, was still receiving instruction from the Misses Nelson just a few doors away; she would be starting her first year at Amherst Academy in September. Already she was exhibiting artistic talent well beyond her years. That summer she produced a watercolor of a native orchid, putty root (*Aplectrum hyemale*), that grew in the Notch on the Holyoke Range, just a few miles from her home. It is far from a childish production, demonstrating both skill and a keen eye for detail, attributes no doubt developed under the watchful eye and patient guidance of her mother. We can imagine her excitement at the prospect of presenting that work to her parents on their return.

Letters from Edward and Orra to their family naturally were filled with accounts of their adventures to date, but also with anxious queries, particularly after their two youngest. "We are glad to hear you get along so nicely without us," Orra wrote to her two older daughters, "tell Emily I always try to think of her as a very good girl…Tell Charlie we are glad to hear so good a report..." They were also much concerned about college matters, and in particular with Commencement. Later on their journey Orra wrote a letter that reveals some homesickness, perhaps even a certain longing for the hard work that Commencement week entailed:

> Well, you are all over commencement—and I can well imagine the state of your house today—the groaning of the washtub under the numbers of linen sheets and pillowcases and towels—the desolation of the rooms that have so recently been filled with delightful visitors. These things are so strongly impressed upon me from having them repeated for more than twenty years, that I almost feel the fatigue and loneliness and the relief of having got through commencement week even here in my noisy room.

Just as the Hitchcocks and Tappans were about to depart from London for the Continent, Edward received a letter from the governor of Massachusetts appointing him to a commission to consider the establishment of a state college of agriculture. The governor asked him to visit and report on similar schools in Europe. Hitchcock had been advocating for improvements in agricultural education for some years, including its introduction at Amherst College. Now he would have the opportunity to offer his advice on the subject in the halls of state government. He quickly took up the invitation. Within days the Hitchcocks had altered their itinerary, bid adieu to the Tappans, and departed from London for Ireland.

Educating prospective farmers in America seemed a perfectly natural endeavor to a man who had spent some years farming with his father and brothers. So Edward was surprised to find mixed feelings on the idea abroad, particularly in England, Scotland, and France. In the opinion of one French educator he spoke to,

> …[W]ith few exceptions… the lower classes are not allowed to learn in the schools what they please, and go as far as they can; but only such subjects as

> the higher classes consider appropriate to qualify them for the humble sphere they are expected to occupy.

Nevertheless he found many schools of agriculture in Europe, and visited at least nine institutions over the next two months in England, Ireland, France, Switzerland, and Germany. He met with dozens of school and government officials, gathering information on students, faculty, curriculum, and facilities.

The Hitchcocks spent nearly a week in Ireland and were much impressed with the loveliness of the place as well as the friendliness of the people. Edward visited four agricultural schools while there. In a letter to her daughters Orra wrote of seeing a large steamer setting sail for America, loaded with refugees from the famines that had swept Ireland for nearly five years. But she was struck as well by the living conditions of many of the Irish people:

> The potato crops in Ireland looked beautifully—but the people poorly clad and miserable looking houses—women doing all sorts of outdoor work—many with bare heads and legs—many of the houses deserted the inhabitants gone to America—houses built of stone, thatched roofs, frequently but one small window, the door too short for a man to stand upright, earth floor sunken, no yard or tree or anything that looked like comfort.

Christian sympathy seemed to be in short supply in the hearts of both Edward and Orra in regard to the poor of Ireland, particularly the beggars that crowded around them wherever they went. At the Giant's Causeway in County Antrim Edward observed, "A great annoyance here are the beggars that follow you everywhere with something to sell and if you will not buy them they beg for money to obtain tobacco or rum." Orra was still harsher: "…I was so out of patience that I turned upon them and shamed them hardy looking men as they were able to work & following us along begging." She also contrasted poor Catholics and poor Protestants, writing a few weeks later that in a Protestant region of Switzerland the land looked better, the people cleaner, while in a Catholic region, "The goiter, cretinism & filth & poverty of these people is dreadful." At several points in her diary Orra seemed to remind herself of a Christian's concern for the less fortunate: "I hope I felt some compassion at least for these poor deluded and ignorant people," she wrote after attending a Catholic mass in Martigny, Switzerland. About the Irish forced to flee to America she wrote, "May that day never come that I shall wish to leave the land of my birth for any other land on which the sun shines." Nowhere in Edward's diary did he express any sympathy for the poor of Europe, but in notes scribbled for an address to a college organization after his return to Amherst, he did reflect on one lesson learned from his trip: "I ought to be made more modest and more liberal in my feelings toward all men and more free from narrow prejudice."

In Scotland the Hitchcocks were happily reunited with the Tappans. Edinburgh impressed them as a most beautiful city, although Edward was frank about its shortcomings: "Edinburgh is a magnificent city: yet exhibiting a strange contrast of peculiar elegance and sordid poverty and filth." The Hitchcocks and Tappans shared rooms in a small lodging house, later to be joined by eminent comparative anatomist Professor Richard Owen and his wife. In visiting the natural history museum at the University of Edinburgh, Edward was particularly struck by the style of many of the exhibits:

> I noticed that the stuffed animals are arranged in a very unusual manner. They are placed in various attitudes all over the floor, so that the visitor moves about among bears and hyenas, tigers and lions, with open mouths and life-like aspect. And I should think some persons of sensitive temperament would shrink from the promenade.

For Edward the highlight of their stay in the Scottish capital city was a meeting of the British Association for the Advancement of Science. In two letters to the *New York Observer* he described that meeting in detail. He reported that some 900 attended including several hundred ladies. He bemoaned the cost of admission, five dollars for the general public, ten dollars for members, adding that he feared that in the United States such a high price would exclude many who might like to attend.

Speeches and lectures were delivered by some of the leading lights of British science including Scottish geologist Dr. Roderick Murchison, physicist Sir David Brewster, Irish astronomer Dr. Thomas R. Robinson, and English paleontologist Gideon Mantell. Lectures took place in the halls of the University of Edinburgh, with six or more sessions occurring at any one time, on topics ranging from mathematics and physical science to geology, natural history, and physiology. Of particular interest to Hitchcock was a talk by Professor Mantell on *Dinornis*, the huge extinct bird of New Zealand, which Hitchcock regarded as "the greatest zoological discovery of the present century," one that had been helpful in his effort to convince doubters of his conclusions regarding the fossil footmarks of the Connecticut Valley. Edward himself delivered two lectures at the meeting, "On the Erosions of the Earth's Surface, especially by Rivers," and "On Terraces and Ancient Sea Beaches," although according to Orra's diary he was treated somewhat dismissively by Dr. Murchison who chaired the session.

Both Edward and Orra commented more than once in their diaries on the presence of large numbers of women both at the meeting in Edinburgh and several similar forums in London. While in London, Orra had toured the fossil collection of William Saull, as she wrote, with "two ladies, geologists." Orra was already acquainted with Mary Lyell, wife of Sir Charles Lyell, from a visit to Amherst in 1842. Lady Lyell called on Orra one day in London, and Edward and Orra dined with the Lyells a few days later. Like Orra, Lady Lyell had considerable scientific expertise of her own and was a frequent illustrator of her husband's publications, so the two women no doubt had much in common.

In his letters to the *Observer* Hitchcock devoted a good deal of attention to the social events of the week, including promenades, soirees, dinners, and breakfasts. "I attended as many of these social occasions as time and strength would allow (for I usually half starve at public dinners, because the food is cooked in such modes that I prefer to let alone…)." As to the consumption of spirits he wrote, "Oh what torrents of it were taken down at dinners of two or three hours' continuance…" The Hitchcocks, of course, abstained.

After traveling by rail from Edinburgh back to London, the Hitchcocks and Tappans departed by steamer for the Continent. At Frankfurt, Edward attended the International Peace Congress to which he had been appointed delegate from Massachusetts. Peace was a fragile commodity in Europe at that time with Prussia and Austria vying for control of central Europe, a dispute that would lead to the Austro-Prussian War of 1866.

The two couples spent nearly two weeks in Germany, visiting Frankfurt, Wiesbaden, and Heidelberg, and another week in Switzerland, at Basel, Zurich, Berne, and Geneva. One of Edward's goals for the trip had been to visit some of the great castles, cathedrals, and palaces of Europe. They had seen many in the British Isles, and on the Continent they visited many more, in Ghent, Aix la Chapelle, Cologne, Basel, Berne, and Paris. They were much impressed at what they saw, although these great monuments of religion left Edward with mixed feelings. Besides the architectural wonders to be seen, there were treasures and relics of all manner: a girdle said to have been worn by the Virgin Mary and a lock of her hair; a fragment of the cross on which Christ was crucified and one of the cords that bound him; a bone of St. Simeon; the teeth of St. Thomas, and on and on. Edward wrote, "…having heard that such things were shown we thought best to inquire if it was a reality and to be sure they were exhibited with all sanctity and credulity."

Edward's patience ran thin at times with such outward trappings of faith, especially those of the Church of Rome, which he believed to be a perversion of true religion. In a sermon delivered shortly after returning from their trip he wrote of the matter:

> The architectural magnificence of the arches and aisles and domes of the lofty cathedral would cause you to praise and silently admire: the splendid paintings upon the walls and the ceilings…And then the immense organ would pour its lofty melody upon your ear and near the altar you would see the gold coated priests bowing before the shrine while attendants around were waving their vessels of incense filling the church with grateful odours…: the whole scene

> being in fact as impressive to the senses as human ingenuity and princely treasures could make it.

And yet, he suggested, there was so much that was absent in these glorious houses of God, no personal confessions of faith, no fervent solitary prayers, no moral lessons, hardly any mention of the Gospel:

> …this would be all which you would witness in that cathedral most probably of the worship of God and you would see the multitudes departing after dipping their fingers in the consecrated water at the entrance and making the sign of the cross—and feeling satisfied with such mummery—the remainder of the Sabbath they would pass as a holiday…

In a mountain pass high in the French Alps, Hitchcock described another example of what he believed to be a terrible perversion of the Christian faith, an oratory with a statute of the Virgin Mary and the Infant Jesus. It bore this inscription: "Lord P. J. Rey, Bishop of Arney, grants an indulgence of 40 days to any one who will recite one Pater one Ave Maria and one act of contrition before this Oratory—1836. Vive Jesus! Vive Maria!" Hitchcock was appalled.

> Oh how sickening to me in such a spot with this impious usurpation of Jehovah's prerogative and offering forgiveness not for past sins but for those to be hereafter committed…But the traveller in Continental Europe will meet with such impieties at almost every step and every where find evidence that while the splendid forms of religion remain vitality has been smothered.

The Hitchcocks and Tappans arrived in Paris on the seventeenth of September, their trip fast approaching its end. Edward wrote a long epistle to his son, Edward, Jr., that included a lengthy report on the state of his health. On the whole, he reported, the trip had served to aggravate his existing conditions, although he expressed some surprise that it hadn't been worse. "My system has held out wonderfully. How much longer God wills it to last I cannot say. Though I have enjoyed much the past summer I have also suffered much probably much more than if I had been at home." Then he added, "You will doubtless impute this discouraging statement in part at least to those desponding feelings which with me have such power."

Edward was consumed with apprehension regarding their return voyage. He had just written a lengthy letter to the governor of Massachusetts reporting on the findings of his agricultural school survey. He estimated the project had cost him $574. In the event that the worst happen, he asked his son to "… present this statement to the Government in the confidence that they will be generous in the matter as they always have been to me."

Neither Edward nor Orra had much interest in shopping. Orra wrote in her diary on their first day in Paris that she had resolved not to purchase a thing, but soon enough she changed her mind, purchasing a dress, shawl, buckles, and bracelets. Edward splurged a bit himself, buying a silk gown, shaving apparatus, spy glass, several drawings and portraits. He also purchased a microscope, probably from the shop of the famous Hippolyte Pixii which they visited. It was his single most expensive purchase (80 francs) of the trip.

The Hitchcocks departed from Liverpool on October 5 aboard the steamship *SS America*. Edward's reports of the voyage were similar to those from their earlier crossing, dreadful. His spirits began to lift when the vessel laid over briefly in Halifax, Nova Scotia where. "…I met the pleasant north-west breeze of October which always had exhilarated me in past years…Our run to Boston was a pleasant one." They arrived in Boston on October 22.

Edward summed up the trip in typical fashion: "…having been absent 158 days, and travelled 10,647 miles: 6,000 of which were upon the ocean, 2,444 in Great Britain, and 1,063 on the Continent. This gave as an average for each day of travel, 67 miles."

What of the trip, then? Was it a success? The intention of the trustees had been to give their president a rest, in hopes of improving his health. Whether that goal was achieved is difficult to judge. As was often the case, Edward seemed to be on both sides of the question simultaneously:

> We went, and though I suffered much from wretched health and depressed spirits, yet Providence ordered every thing so mercifully—almost miraculously, sometimes—that we were carried over 10,000 miles of travel without injury to a hair of our heads, and almost without the ordinary discomforts of travel. I did indeed suffer very much on both voyages, not merely from sea-sickness, but from the…aggravation of all my chronic complaints…

He had hoped to meet some of the scientists with whom he had corresponded, and that goal was achieved. Not only did he meet them in person, he got to know them, and they him. His report on agricultural education was well received by the governor and legislature, an important step toward the creation of a state agricultural school for Massachusetts.

The Hitchcocks bid the Tappans adieu in Boston, then embarked by rail for Northampton. For weeks Edward had been worrying about the state of Amherst College on his return. Had his absence injured the institution to which he had devoted himself for a quarter century? Or had the students and faculty gone merrily on their way, quickly forgetting their President, the one who had abandoned them to galivant about in Europe? He would not have to wait long for an answer.

American Railroad 1864

22 The Religion of Geology

"The beast has been wounded...he raves with pain."

Northampton, Friday, October 18, 1850

Under a leaden autumn sky, the train from Boston pulled slowly into the Northampton Depot, brakes squealing, steam engine chugging and hissing. As soon as it shuddered to a halt, passengers began disembarking, pouring down the narrow steps to the platform, clutching valises while looking anxiously about for family or friends. But one couple was still in their seats, marshalling their strength for the last leg of a long, long journey.

"Well, Father," began Orra with a sigh, "we are almost home. Are you excited, dear?" Edward offered no reply. "Won't it be wonderful to see the children?"

Edward looked anxiously through the window at the darkening sky. "I fear we will have a long wait for our ride, Mother. It is a hard drive from Amherst at this time of year, in the dark, especially across that dreadful bridge. The boys may well have forgotten."

Edward rose slowly, then took Orra's hand and helped her down the steps onto the platform. By now the other passengers had disappeared into the gray dusk and the couple stood alone in the gloom.

"Just as I suspected, not a soul knows or cares," grumbled Edward. "I suppose we had best retrieve our valises and wait in the station house. Oh, I just know we will catch our death of cold in that terrible place." The very thought started him coughing.

At that moment a clatter could be heard as a carriage pulled into the station. It was a barouche of particularly elegant design from the livery in Amherst, one used for parades, funerals, and the like, and festooned with a garland of evergreen boughs wrapped with ribbons. It was drawn by a team of handsome Belgian draft horses that looked familiar to Edward. Then he recognized the young fellow at the reins, a student, though he could not recall his name.

"James Balfour at your service," the driver began cheerily, doffing his cap. "President Hitchcock, sir—Mrs. Hitchcock, ma'am—welcome home—your carriage awaits."

Pulling up behind the carriage at that moment was a long hay wagon drawn by another team. In the hay sat a gaggle of young men dressed in trousers and straw hats, laughing and shouting. One of them had a bugle and played several rousing fanfares.

"Three cheers for President Hitchcock," sounded a voice from among them. "Hip-hip-hurrah. Hip-hip-hurrah. Hip-hip-hurrah." Then another voice rang out. "And for Mrs. Hitchcock. Hip-hip-hurrah. Hip-hip-hurrah. Hip-hip-hurrah."

Two fair-haired young men leapt from the wagon. Brushing off the straw, they approached the couple, smiling. It was Edward, Jr., and Charles. "Mother, Father," began Edward, Jr., standing stiffly, ever ready to make a speech. "On behalf of the students of Amherst College, we welcome you home."

Beaming, the young men reached out and shook their father's hand. He greeted his sons with a weak, confused smile. "Thank you, Edward, Charles." Then they turned to Orra. She was at a loss for words, tears streaming down both cheeks, as she hugged her sons.

"Welcome home, Mother. Are you happy to be home?" asked Charles.

Orra looked lovingly into her son's eyes and stroked his hair. "Oh, Charlie, you have no idea." And the tears flowed anew.

Nearly an hour later the small procession made its way up the steep incline of Amity Street toward the center of Amherst. It was nighttime now and only a few dim lights shone through the windows of homes they passed. Edward was slumped down in the carriage, swaddled in a blanket against the cold night air.

As they approached the center of the village, Orra grasped her husband's hand tightly with excitement. "Oh, Father, look," she said, pointing ahead. A crowd had appeared, dozens and dozens, lining both sides of the street. It seemed as though the entire population of the college had turned out to greet the Hitchcocks, joined by many townspeople as well, all cheering and waving. In the village center the throng poured into the street, surrounding the carriage and wagon, and then proceeded to lead them along the Common.

As the noisy entourage ascended College Hill, the Hitchcocks were at first mystified at what they saw. From a distance it looked like a mirage, an incandescent glow, but as they drew nearer the source of the illumination became clear: every window in every room in every college building was lit with a candle. In front of the President's House stood hundreds more well-wishers, students, professors, townspeople, many bearing lanterns or torches, all waiting to greet the President and Mrs. Hitchcock on their return.

"My heavens, it's like a dream," said Orra to her husband as their carriage drew to a halt in front of the President's House. Just then she saw her four daughters, Mary, Catherine, Jane, and Emily, standing together on the front step of the house, waving.

Through her tears, Orra spoke: "Father, we are home at last."

"Yes, Mother, by the grace of Almighty God, we are home—home where we should be," he replied.

Life soon returned to normal for the Hitchcock family. Edward, Jr., was well into his first term as a teacher at Williston Seminary. He had graduated from Amherst College in 1849, then spent a year studying with doctors in Northampton and at Harvard Medical School. After accepting the Williston position, he enrolled at Harvard, although how he was able to do both is something of a mystery. Orra once described Edward, Jr., as much like his father, but his handwritten reminiscences brim with good spirit, optimism, and humor, the very antithesis of his father's. Of his first two years on the faculty at Williston he wrote that his memories of that period were among the sweetest of his life. "I was more of a man than a college student. I was teacher and the boys were scholars; it seemed an enlargement of my life. And all through those two years of my life there was very much that was very delightful." Fourteen-year-old Charles was also now at Williston. From letters we learn that he had suffered from homesickness for a time, but with the help of his older brother he soon seemed to adjust.

As to the Hitchcock daughters, twenty-one-year-old Catherine taught for a time at Monson Academy while seventeen-year-old Jane continued her studies at Ipswich Female Seminary. Emily was still at home and attending Amherst Academy as had all her siblings before her. The whereabouts of twenty-six-year-old Mary following her parents' return is uncertain. Several family letters suggest she had been suffering some health problems; she spent time in 1849 in

New Lebanon, New York, receiving a form of hydrotherapy under the care of a Dr. Bedortha. A few years later she was apparently living with the family of her cousin, Caroline White Sprague, first in West Chester, Connecticut, then in New Jersey. Caroline's husband, Daniel G. Sprague, was a minister and the couple had several children. Perhaps Mary was serving as a governess to the Sprague children.

Orra no doubt was pleased to throw herself back into familiar domestic routines, accommodating a constant flow of boarders and visitors as well as college social events. Her letters reveal her concern for her children who were away, including offers to mend her sons' clothes and inquiries after Mary's health. Thanksgiving had always been a joyous family occasion for the Hitchcocks. In a letter to Edward, Jr., dated a few weeks after their return, we learn that they were planning a large Thanksgiving dinner and had invited Edward's siblings, Charles, Henry, and Emilia, their spouses, and families, just the kind of large social occasion that Orra seemed to relish.

President Hitchcock promptly returned to his college duties. He was of course concerned at what he might find, but to his surprise all was well. The rumors of troubles at the college seem to have been in error or exaggerated. True, enrollment had declined that fall among juniors and seniors, but the loss was more than offset by a large incoming freshman class. His spirits were surprisingly good—the trip had apparently fulfilled its chief purpose, at least as he recalled in *Reminiscences* more than a decade later:

> … [M]y health went on improving for a considerable time. Health was not indeed restored, but simply new power acquired to contend with disease for a longer time. This recuperative influence was not wholly lost upon me for many years, and I doubt not that this European tour has enabled me to perform double the labor since which I could have accomplished without it.

The major project at the college over the next eighteen months was the construction of a new library. For too long a library had been something of an afterthought. The first was a set of a few hundred volumes in a single bookcase. Once Johnson Chapel was completed in 1828, the collection was moved to the third floor of that structure where it remained for nearly a quarter century. But the college's book collection attracted the interest of many donors. When Professor Hovey made his trip to Europe in 1832 to acquire philosophical apparatus, he was also authorized to purchase books with a fund which by that time totaled over $4000.

In the 1840s benefactors David Sears, John Tappan, George Merriam, and others established a fund for the construction of a new library. It was a cause that was championed by one member of the Board of Trustees in particular, Bela B. Edwards, an Amherst graduate. The trustees were quickly convinced of the

Figure 58. Morgan library, 1855

value of the project; they named Edwards to chair the building committee. Fundraising was spearheaded by Professor Tyler. Major contributions by some of the college's most generous supporters including Messrs. Merriam, Sears, and Williston, made up the largest part of the campaign, but many smaller gifts were received as well.

Although the trustees were favorably disposed toward the library project, the details of its design created considerable disagreement and controversy. Bela Edwards was particularly aggrieved with the choice of location, next to the President's House, as well as with some of the design elements. It fell to President Hitchcock to navigate the contentions of the board on the matter, a task that took a toll on his spirits. The library was completed in 1853 at a cost of $15,000. It was built of gneiss, the first campus structure to be constructed of stone rather than brick. Sadly, Professor Edwards died before the completion of the project. In his retirement valedictory a year and a half later he offered this tribute to Bela Edwards:

> It was this earnestness of so judicious a friend that led me, more than my own preferences, to urge strenuously the adoption of his views, though obliged to thwart the wishes of other friends; and it is certainly gratifying to know, now that he is gone, that the results accord so well with his wishes and plans, though their accomplishment cost me more care and anxiety than almost any other college enterprise of the last ten years.

Hitchcock's writing interests seemed to change on resumption of his duties. For the remainder of his presidency he published not a single paper on the fossil footmarks. On other matters geological, however, he was prolific, penning nearly a dozen papers in four years. He delivered three brief papers at a meeting of the American Association for the Advancement of Science in Albany in 1851 that appeared in the association's proceedings of the following year. He published four articles in the *American Journal of Science and Arts* between 1852 and 1854 on geological subjects. Coal seemed to be a topic of special interest to him at this time in his career. Two of his *AJS* papers dealt with coal deposits, one in Vermont, the other in Rhode Island, with particular attention to the fossil remains found in those strata. He also submitted another geological report to the state, most of which was devoted to a discussion of coal in the Blackstone River Valley. He seemed convinced more than ever of the promise of coal mining in Massachusetts.

Another geological writing project in this period was the completion of a small book entitled *Outline of the Geology of the Globe*. Intended as a sequel to his highly successful *Elementary Geology*, it included ninety-six lithographs of pen-and-ink or pencil drawings of fossils and fossil footmarks, some of which were the work of Orra Hitchcock. Two large scale hand-colored geological maps, each 24” x 16”, were included as well. The first was a map of the world based on an outline map from Johnson’s *Physical Atlas* of 1848, with geological information from a number of sources. Naturally it was highly generalized, listing only six rock categories. The second was a geological map of the United States and Canada based on maps of French geologist Ami Boué and Charles Lyell. It too was highly generalized, listing fifteen categories of rock. Massachusetts, for example, is shown to consist largely of one type, hypozoic and metamorphic rocks, with smaller areas designated alluvium and tertiary, red sandstone, and coal.

One writing project Hitchcock undertook during this period had a particularly personal dimension, a biography of Mary Lyon, longtime friend of both Edward and Orra. Orra and Miss Lyon had become acquainted as teachers at Amherst Academy before the Hitchcocks were married. Miss Lyon, who grew up in Buckland just a few miles from Conway, had visited the couple frequently when they lived in that town. She boarded with them in Amherst for some months in 1835 and 1836 before her female seminary became a reality. With the success of that institution she had earned an international reputation as a visionary educator.

Miss Lyon’s sudden and unexpected death in 1849 must have been a severe blow to Edward and Orra. It came at a time when Edward’s health, both physical and mental, was at a low point. In fact, it appears that he was not present at her funeral, though it took place in South Hadley barely ten miles from their home. His predecessor, Reverend Heman Humphrey, came from Pittsfield to preach the sermon and eulogy, but it was a task to which Edward Hitchcock, a friend of the deceased and supporter of the seminary from the start, would surely have been better suited.

Hitchcock’s absence from the funeral of Miss Lyon may explain his determination to write a biography and tribute to his friend. *The Power of Christian Benevolence Illustrated in the Life and Labors of Mary Lyon* was a touching eulogy for a woman who was a devout Christian and a true pioneer in women's education and whose friendship was precious to the entire Hitchcock family. The book sold well, going through twelve editions. It was, he noted, the best-selling of all his books to date, evidence both of his reputation as an author and Miss Lyon's as a pioneer of higher education for women.

A lifelong goal of Edward Hitchcock had been the completion of a major work on the relationship between religion and science. Eight years earlier in his notes he wrote,

> During the last summer I completed the work which has occupied my leisure time for two years viz. ten lectures on the Religion of Geology. It is the result of long study upon the subject: and as I consider the religious applications of science to be its most important use I look upon these lectures as the most valuable of my scientific studies.

At that time he also wrote a dedication to the book that gives touching evidence of his debt to his wife. "TO MY BELOVED WIFE," it begins. "Both gratitude and affection prompt me to dedicate these lectures to you…Early should I have sunk under the pressure of feeble health, nervous despondency, poverty, and blighted hopes, had not your sympathies and cheering counsels sustained me."

But the book's publication was delayed, perhaps due to the fragile condition of the college or to the pressures of the presidency. Finally, in spring 1851, *The Religion of Geology and Its Connected Sciences* went to press. Published in Boston, London, and Glasgow, it was carried by booksellers across the United States and Great Britain. According to one newspaper database, over 300 advertisements appeared in newspapers from Massachusetts to Ohio to Mississippi between 1851 and 1854. It proved to be his best-selling book for the general reader, selling 3400 copies in the first six months after its release. Sales continued to be strong for some years; according to the Boston publisher, 9000 copies were printed in 1854, 12,000 in 1857.

The Religion of Geology is Edward Hitchcock's "grand synthesis," an effort to demonstrate once and for all the central thesis of his life, that science and Christian faith need not be antagonistic, that each supports and enhances the other. The book consists of fourteen lectures that he had delivered to his geology classes since 1826. He makes clear in the preface that these thoughts are not new or hurriedly produced: "If my views are erroneous, as exhibited in these lectures, I cannot plead that they have been hastily adopted. Most of them, indeed, have been the subjects of thought occasionally for thirty years."

In the first lecture, "Revelation Illustrated by Science," he enumerates in typical Hitchcock style the scientific principles he believes have a bearing on religion and must therefore be reconciled with the words of revelation. The list

Figure 59. The 1859 London edition of *Religion of Geology*

runs to eighteen, one of very few places in all of literature where adverbs such as "eleventhly," "sixteenthly," and "seventeenthly" appear. In subsequent lectures he addresses a range of questions relevant to religion and geology including the Creation and age of the earth, Noah's flood, death and the diversity of life, miracles, catastrophes, and God's divine plan.

On the matter of the age of the earth, Hitchcock notes, "For while it has been the usual interpretation of the Mosaic account, that the world was brought into existence nearly at the same time with man and the other existing animals, geology throws back its creation to a period indefinitely but immeasurably remote." The great antiquity of earth is undeniable, he argues; even one unschooled in geology can observe the evidence beneath his feet. We can hear the words of his Yale mentors, Eleazar Fitch and Benjamin Silliman, echo as he invokes the meaning of the Hebrew word, "yom," to demonstrate that the true age of the earth need not be regarded as contradicting the scriptures.

Naturally, Noah's flood is also a matter of importance to Hitchcock. In particular he strives in *Religion of Geology* to reconcile what he has observed in the rocks of New England with what he believes to be true from Genesis: "Though it is now generally agreed that geology cannot detect traces of such a deluge as the Scriptures describe, yet upon some other bearings of that subject it does cast light." That there were great floods in earth's past is unquestioned, but they were not universal, and they do not account for the deposition of fossil remains. He also admits the impossibility that Noah's ark could have sheltered so many animals as suggested in Genesis. Furthermore, he asserts, ice has been the major agent of change in earth's surface, and its effects date back far longer than a few thousand years.

As to death, Hitchcock points out that according to the Bible, death was introduced into the world by God as punishment for the sins of Adam and Eve. Geology, on the other hand, testifies to "…the occurrence of death among animals long before the existence of man." The layers of rock containing evidence of ancient organic remains give clear evidence, he asserts, that life had existed for millennia previous to the first man and first woman. Furthermore, it is clear that many of those early life forms had perished in at least five great extinctions: "…[A]s countless millions of these remains are often found piled together, so as to form almost entire mountains, the periods requisite for their formation must have been immensely long…" It is clear, he asserts, that God had the idea of death long before the depredations of the Garden of Eden required him to impose that sanction on humanity. Following each of these events a new creation occurred whereby earth's diversity was replenished, a process sometimes referred to as "serial creation":

> That history shows us clearly, that the earth, since its creation, has been the seat of several distinct economies of life, each occupying long periods, and successively passing away. During each of these periods, distinct groups of animals and plants have occupied the earth, the air, and the waters. Each successive group has been entirely distinct from that which preceded it, though each group was exactly adapted to the existing state of the climate and the food provided…

That idea, that earth's history consisted of a series of creation events yielding ever more advanced lifeforms, each better suited to the changing conditions on the planet, was not original to Hitchcock. It was advocated by the likes of Louis Agassiz, William Buckland, Hugh Miller, and Gideon Mantell, all of whom attributed it to the wisdom of Almighty God. But a similar script soon would be invoked by others, minus the guiding hand of a Supreme Being.

In "The Hypothesis of Creation by Law" Hitchcock expounds at length on a recent work entitled *Vestiges of the Natural History of Creation.* That work asserted that life developed on earth not according to God's will but according to universal laws. Such a notion was, of course, anathema to Hitchcock, an effort to "exalt law into a Creator, as well as a Controller of the world."

No one was a stronger advocate of the laws of nature than Edward Hitchcock; he had affirmed again and again his belief that the universe is highly ordered and obeys basic principles. The stars in the heavens, the organs of the human body, the rocks and minerals of the earth's surface, all he believed were governed by and displayed those laws. But as to those laws acting independently, he was not having it. "What is a natural law," he asks, "without the presence and energizing power of the lawgiver?" *Vestiges* is not overtly atheistic, argues Hitchcock, but "It does apparently so remove the Deity from all concern in the affairs of the world, and so foists law into his place, that practically there is no God." Hitchcock may well have sensed that the central argument of *Vestiges*, that natural processes alone can account for the development and diversification of life on earth, was fast gaining momentum both among scientists as well as the general public.

The Religion of Geology was reviewed in many of the leading theological publications of Hitchcock's time. Some notices were enthusiastic and highly laudatory. One writer in the *Christian Register*, a Unitarian weekly, gave an "earnest commendation" of the work, writing that,

> President Hitchcock...had made an important contribution...both to the interest of general learning and of Christian faith. Indeed, his volume has certain merits in these respects not belonging to any other treatise with which we are acquainted.

Another writer for the *Daily National Intelligencer,* the largest Washington, D.C., weekly of that period, was equally laudatory, asserting that the book,

> ...[W]ill accomplish much good in removing many prejudices entertained by certain individuals against geology, from its conflict with Holy Writ...The work is a thorough one, and, so far as we are aware, grapples with every difficulty which a caviling ingenuity has suggested.

Two Amherst graduates, both ordained ministers, also offered words of praise for the work of their former professor, but praise tempered with reservations. John Stebbins Lee (AC 1844), writing in the *Universalist Quarterly,* expressed his admiration for his former professor. He agreed with Hitchcock's central thesis: "...the hostility between Science and Revelation, we believe, is only apparent, not real. When rightly interpreted and understood, they will appear in perfect unison." But he then proceeded to enumerate what he regarded as the many errors in the book, errors he believed resulted from Hitchcock's austere brand of Calvinism: "...he must be bold who attempts thus to mingle together what can be no more united than oil and water. Calvinism is at war with nature's teachings; an excrescence on her fair face; and we see not how any man in his senses can begin to reconcile them."

In similar fashion, Rufus Phineas Stebbins (AC 1834), by then a Unitarian minister writing in the *Christian Examiner,* offered praise for Hitchcock combined with misgivings about some of his ideas: "We are impressed with the…vigor of his mind, the originality and freshness and clearness of his views, and the reverential spirit in which he has handled doctrines which, though erroneous, are sacred to very many in the religious community." No doubt Reverend Moses Stuart would have weighed in on this discussion as well, although he died only a few months after the book was published.

Then there were the criticisms from nonbelievers, most notably a series of commentaries that began on September 24, 1851, in the weekly *Boston Investigator*, a newspaper that proclaimed itself for "freethinkers." The author, identified only as "Vindex," wrote thirty-two weekly columns over the ensuing eight months in which he excoriated Hitchcock and his writing fiercely and relentlessly. Of the words of revelation quoted by Hitchcock, he wrote: "All this is humbug, moonshine, gammon [rubbish]." Of Hitchcock's arguments: "Were you ever reduced to a more preposterous chain of argument! Absolute assumption! a begging the question! And then running into the vitiosus circulus [circular reasoning]." Of Hitchcock himself: "You are infinitely absurd."

One might have expected such an onslaught to sting the often thin-skinned professor, yet it seemed to have quite the opposite effect, as he recorded in his notes:

> But the most gratifying notice of it *[Religion of Geology]* is in the Boston Investigator a weekly newspaper of infidel or atheist character. Already some 14 or 15 articles have appeared addressed to me and exhibiting more of venom than perhaps I ever have seen in print. This shows that the beast has been wounded that in fact he raves with pain. Had that paper spoken well of my book I should have been distressed because I should fear that I had taken wrong ground.

Apparently, Hitchcock was not injured, not even by the vicious, vituperative Vindex!

Less than two years after the publication of *The Religion of Geology* and nearly fifteen years after his articles on creation and Noah's deluge appeared in *Biblical Repository*, Hitchcock returned to the subject of science and religion once again, this time in that journal's successor, *Bibliotheca Sacra.* The editor was Reverend Edwards Amasa Park of Andover Theological Seminary in Andover, Massachusetts, a former Amherst professor and a longtime friend of Hitchcock. In "The Relations and Consequent Mutual Duties Between the Philosopher and the Theologian" Hitchcock suggested that scientists (he used the term "philosophers"–the word "scientist" was not yet in wide use) and theologians ought to be well informed in both disciplines. He advised theologians against wading in over their heads in the field of geology while issuing a similar warning to men of science against claiming any special knowledge of religion or the scriptures that they did not possess.

As an example of a scientist floundering in unfamiliar waters, he cited Louis Agassiz. Few men of his day had the scientific credentials of Agassiz, but the man also held strong views on race, including the superiority of the white race. In 1850 Agassiz published an article in *The Christian Examiner* entitled "The Diversity of Origin of the Human Races" in which he argued that those who advocated a single origin of humanity based those views on a misinterpretation of a few passages from the Bible: "…To suppose that all men originated from Adam and Eve, is to give to the Mosaic record a meaning that it was never intended to have."

To Edward Hitchcock, those were fighting words on two counts. He could not accept Agassiz's theory of multiple human origins, not from scientific evidence, nor from the words of revelation. But he took particular exception to Agassiz's attempt at biblical interpretation, and he expressed in no uncertain terms his regret that "…an exegesis of Genesis had been thrown out so confidently, which is contrary to the obvious sense and to the almost universal opinion of biblical writers." That exchange proved to be only the first of several points of contention between the two men that would arise on several occasions over the next decade.

Later in the same article, his thinking on science and religion appeared to take an abrupt turn: "The object of philosophy is to explain the phenomena of nature, mental, moral, and material; that of theology is exclusively to defend and enforce the moral relations of the universe. Hence the two subjects are almost entirely distinct in their aim." He seemed to have adopted the position of his old adversary, Moses Stuart. But just a few sentences later he back-pedaled, allowing that those discrepancies were only apparent, not real.

Hitchcock took up another thorny question in the next issue of the same journal. In "Special Divine Interpositions in Nature" he considered whether miracles were exceptions to the ordinary laws of nature that result from "special divine interposition." Hitchcock was at heart a scientist, an empiricist, wedded to the notion that certain physical laws guide all phenomena. He argued that those laws originated in the mind of God. But some nonbelievers of his day—such as the author of *Vestiges*—had concluded that physical laws alone were sufficient to carry forward the processes of the natural world. Hitchcock's formulations appeared to give fuel to the arguments of atheists.

Why did Hitchcock choose to publish those scholarly articles, most of which covered ground already covered in *Religion of Geology?* Perhaps he felt the need to clarify some of his ideas from the earlier work, or perhaps he thought

Lightning Rods!!

OTIS' PATENT INSSULATED LIGHTNING CONDUCTOR—THE ONLY METHOD OF

Absolute Protection against Lightning,

AS DEMONSTRATED BY

Science and Experience.

AMHERST COLLGOE, May 22, 1854.

I have given some attention to Otis' Patent Insu-lated Lightning Conductors, and do not hesitate t give my approval of their construction. The part are well connected together by means of screws, th insulation with regard to the building is ingeniousl effected, and the whole is so constructed and arrange as to ornament the building, rather than disfigure it as is too often done. E. S. SNELL,

Professor of Mathematics and Natural Philosophy

I agree with Professor Suell in the above recom-mendation. EDWARD HITCHCOCK, President.

Figure 60. Three Edward Hitchcock testimonials: left, advertisement for Ayer's Cherry Pectoral cough remedy; top, right, poster for submarine armor; bottom, lightning rod advertisement

articles in *Bibliotheca Sacra* would reach a different audience including clergymen and divinity students who might not have read his book. He would publish three more articles in *Bibliotheca Sacra* in the last decade of his life, all on the relationship between religion and science.

One of the banes of Edward Hitchcock's existence at Amherst College had always been "secret societies." Two literary societies had existed in the college from its earliest days, the Athenian and the Alexandrian. Patterned after similar organizations at Williams, the societies were college sanctioned; each was assigned a meeting room. Membership was originally by random assignment—every student in the college was appointed to one or the other. The societies had constitutions, bylaws, and officers. At weekly meetings the members offered compositions and declamations or engaged in debates. In time each society accumulated a considerable library for the exclusive use of its members.

Without doubt the Athenian and the Alexandrian societies enriched the young institution, but over time they also spawned tensions and animosities. The society libraries became matters of contention in part because of the limited resources of the college's library. By accumulating their own books, each society strove to achieve an advantage over the other, particularly in preparing orations. The first hint of trouble in this connection appeared in the faculty records for October 1826:

> Voted—That the Pres. and Professor Hitchcock be committed to consult on the subject of the pernicious degree of emulation existing between the literary societies of College, particularly in relation to the extravagance practiced in endeavours to increase their libraries.

When the college chapel was completed in 1827, it included space for a library, and it was proposed that the two societies contribute their collections to the new library. The idea was agreeable to most, but a number of students withdrew from the established organizations and formed a new group, the Social Union. It was, according to student George R. Cutting, the college's first "secret society," although like the Athenians and the Alexandrians, it was officially recognized by the college. Exactly what was secret is not entirely clear, except that only members were permitted to attend meetings.

From that time on the rivalries among the three societies grew. Attempts to recruit new members in each entering class became more and more aggressive. The societies became more selective, striving to pick the best possible candidates for their membership. Dues were also levied against the members, creating hardship for students of limited means. The literary societies that had formerly promoted scholarship and polite discourse seemed to have evolved into fractious cliques.

Hitchcock devoted six pages in *Reminiscences* to a discussion of "Secret and Anti-secret Societies" and the problems they created at Amherst and elsewhere. In his notes early in his presidency, he mentioned the problems associated with the secret societies: "...[T]here has been a discontented restless spirit and contentions among the students themselves growing out of secret societies so that so many have left and it does seem as if the College were almost run down."

A solution of sorts was worked out with the urging of the president. It was agreed that all three societies would be dissolved and two new ones created, to be known as Academia and Eclectic. Five years later, a new round of reorganization took place. The result was a reversion to the original names, Athenian and Alexandrian.

By the ninth year of his presidency, Hitchcock was struggling, due in some measure to the societies:

> But what was worse than all this the anti-secret and secret societies having become so numerous that they cannot flourish made an onset upon the Faculty and pressed their unreasonable demands the more because they knew our numbers to be reduced and our health to be wretched hoping in such circumstances to carry points which we should refuse at another time…Such a load of labour and anxiety has been absolutely intolerable…

One of Hitchcock's worries as the prospect of retirement loomed was financial. He would receive a salary of $500. But his notes of December 1854 reveal his concern:

> I have indeed some anxiety about obtaining the means of supporting my family as my salary is to be small…But I must try to eke it out in some way or other and if I have strength I do not fear. I have been trying giving lectures abroad this vacation but though it produces some income it is more than I ought to attempt in the cold weather of winter. I will trust Providence however for the little time that remains.

Another source of income for President Hitchcock was testimonials (see Figure 60). During the latter half of his presidency, he lent his name to at least three commercial enterprises, a cough remedy, a newly patented lightning rod, and an exhibition of "submarine armor." The advertisement for "Ayer's Cherry Pectoral" appeared regularly in newspapers in at least eighteen states from 1849 to 1854. James C. Ayer operated a highly successful pharmaceutical business in Lowell, Massachusetts; according to one source Ayer accumulated a fortune of $20 million. Hitchcock and colleague Ebenezer S. Snell, Professor of Mathematics and Natural Philosophy at Amherst, allowed their names to be used on behalf of "Otis' Patented Insulated Lighting Conductor" in a series of advertisements appearing in the *Franklin Democrat* in 1854. Most curious of all is a poster for an exhibition of "submarine armor," that includes the following:

> Recommendation of Dr. Hitchcock, President of Amherst College, Amherst, October 28, 1854—Messrs. Pratt and Bancroft have exhibited in this Place their Submarine Diving Dress, which they use in descending beneath the ocean…The whole exhibition I consider most interesting…These gentlemen are highly respectable and deserving of patronage, in my opinion.

A careful reading of Hitchcock's notes reveals that tensions related to secret societies as well as disagreements between the President and the Board of Trustees were taking their toll on his mental and physical health. He was increasingly convinced that his life would soon be over and that the time to leave office was at hand.

Just fifteen months after returning from Europe, in February 1852, he wrote, "Never before have I been so conscious that my work on earth has nearly come to a close." He had announced to the trustees at their previous meeting, perhaps in December 1851, his intention to resign. At commencement six months later he had repeated his intention, apparently to deaf ears: "…I presented my resignation to the trustees as I informed them I should last winter. But I found them quite unprepared for it and quite unable to fix upon a successor." Sometime in late 1852 or early 1853, he withdrew his resignation, apparently buoyed by encouraging developments, particularly regarding the cabinets and collections:

> God has put me upon the track of several interesting enterprises for the good of Amherst College and is giving me unexpected success in some of them and I feel bound to follow them up as long as I am possibly able. This makes me hold onto my place still although it is full of trials.

The "interesting enterprises" to which he referred were acquisitions of new artifacts. In April 1853, Dexter Marsh died in Greenfield. Marsh had been a longtime collector of fossils and other wonders of the natural world. His collection had grown so that in January 1850, he opened a small museum attached to his home to display some of those wonders. On Marsh's death, Hitchcock and James Deane had carried out an appraisal of that collection, valuing the items most generously for the sake of Mrs. Marsh and her children.

On September 21, 1853, the collection, Dexter Marsh's life work, was sold off at auction. Hitchcock, of course, was much interested in acquiring some of Marsh's extraordinary collection. Fortunately, Amherst College had recently received several generous donations for that very purpose, and he traveled to Greenfield prepared to spend every dime. On that day he acquired hundreds of ichnological artifacts for his growing collection, spending by his own account $700. It may have seemed an extravagance to some, he observed in *Reminiscences*, then recounted this anecdote:

> After the auction at Greenfield, I employed a wagoner to transport my specimens to the railroad. I happened to be a little out of sight, and heard him describing to a citizen standing by the sums I had paid for them. "The man," said the citizen, "who will waste money like that, should have a guardian placed over him." I could not restrain a loud laugh, which brought us into conversation, when I said, "you will at least acknowledge that my insane prodigality is a good thing for Mrs. Marsh."

The auction and his acquisitions clearly buoyed his spirits for a time. A few months later he wrote in his notes,

Figure 61. Assyrian relief from the Nineveh Gallery.

> I have been greatly favored in respect to the footmarks: but now I want a place to put them as well as the whole zoological cabinet and this is what I am now asking God to help me accomplish. Perhaps he has put me upon the right track: I shall not know for some time.

Another Mr. Marsh, Reverend Dwight W. Marsh, was a source of still further encouragement for the president. He was a missionary in the Middle East and had procured for Williams College some archeological specimens from the ruins of ancient Nineveh, known today as Mosul, Iraq. On hearing of this, Hitchcock contacted Dr. Henry Lobdell, also a missionary and an Amherst graduate. Dr. Lobdell secured another collection that included sculptures, inscribed stones, gems, pottery, and coins, for Amherst College. According to Hitchcock, the specimens were carried by camel 500 miles to the Mediterranean, then by ship 5000 miles to Boston. They arrived in Amherst only weeks after the Dexter Marsh auction. Still there was the problem of where to house these two extraordinary collections.

But the reprieve provided by these "interesting enterprises" was brief. By the following spring, the decision had been made—President Hitchcock would resign. Samuel Williston, long one of his closest friends and allies on the Board of Trustees, was the first to be informed. In a letter to Williston dated May 4, 1854, Hitchcock wrote,

> You may recollect that when a year ago last Commencement I consented to withdraw my resignation, I did so with the understanding that if I found it impossible to go on, I would give the Trustees private notice…That time has now come.

He cited as the reason his failing health, but hinted at internal college affairs that hastened his decision, namely, "the resignation of my officer, the sickness of a second, the absence of a third, and from several other causes…" He asked Williston if the decision could be kept private until his successor was named.

In a reply dated just a few days later, Williston pleaded with the president to reconsider, but added a touching personal note:

> I feel extremely sorry for my own sake, as well as for the College to have you retire. I doubt whether I should ever have done much for Amherst College but for my acquaintance with you, and for the sentiments of affection and esteem which I have long cherished for you.

At last, it seems, the deed was to be done. At a special meeting held in Boston on July 11, 1854, the Board of Trustees accepted with reluctance the resignation of President Hitchcock. By the first of September the post had been offered and accepted by Reverend Dr. William Augustus Stearns, a graduate of Harvard and Andover Theological Seminary and pastor of the Prospect Street Congregational Church in Cambridge. The news of the appointment of Dr. Stearns was "gratifying intelligence" to Hitchcock, as he wrote to Williston. His only reservation was a proposal from the trustees to offer the new president $300 a year more than the incumbent. His feelings on the matter may seem like petty jealousy or resentment, but he went on at some length in that letter to remind Williston of the financial straits the college found itself in. He also reminded him that if the president were to be allowed such an increase, it would be necessary to supplement the salaries of the other officers of the college. That Hitchcock was motivated not by jealousy but by frugality seems clear. Five years later when the faculty, administration, and students of the college presented him with an engraved silver tea set, he thanked them, but then scolded them for their extravagance.

On Wednesday, November 22, 1854, a solemn ceremony took place in the village church adjacent to the campus. President Edward Hitchcock stood erect and proud as he addressed the large crowd of faculty, students, dignitaries, and villagers. As his predecessor had done on the day of his inaugural, the retiring president recounted the history of Amherst College. He went on at some length regarding the achievements of his administration. Lest anyone should think he was merely blowing his own horn, he gave tribute where it was due, to the Divine Administrator on high. Prominent in his oration was the matter of the college's collections, among the largest and finest in any college at his time. He then confessed his disappointment on the matter:

> Yet this fine collection is spread into three apartments and is imminently exposed to fire. To secure a new building to receive it, with the still more exposed collection of fossil foot-marks, has long been with me an object of strong desire and effort; and it is among the deepest of my regrets, on leaving the presidency, that it remains unaccomplished.

Then, like a shaft of sunlight breaking through the storm clouds, came this:

> Thus had I written, only a few days ago, and thus had I expected to leave this subject to-day. But a kind Providence has ordered otherwise. Last evening a letter was received, announcing the gratifying intelligence that the trustees under the will of the late Hon. Samuel Appleton of Boston had appropriated, only ten days ago, ten thousand dollars of the sum left by him for scientific and benevolent purposes to the erection of another cabinet—the Appleton Zoological Cabinet—by the side of the Woods cabinet on yonder hill.

Once again at the eleventh hour, a kind Providence had intervened, albeit through the agency of a wealthy benefactor, to bless his efforts and bless Amherst College. Wrote Tyler, "the close of his administration was marked, like its beginning, by donations that surprised himself scarcely less than they delighted the friends of the institution." Before concluding his valedictory address, Hitchcock reminded his audience of his declining health.

> I have seen too much of God's providential kindness in times past, to doubt its continuance to the end, if I do my duty. It would, indeed, be folly in me to expect to accomplish much more, either for others or myself; or to anticipate a serene and quiet old age…But one, who, like myself, has sustained a forty years' contest with disordered nerves, and who, as he looks back, can see lopt-off fragments of himself, strewed over the wide battle-field, such a one ought to know that these complaints usually gain a complete mastery in advanced life, and make existence a burden. No, no, though God may be better to me than my fears anticipate, yet, at the age of threescore and two, and with such a constitution, it is not for me to calculate upon much more of enjoyment in this world.

What then was the legacy of Edward Hitchcock's presidency? Judged by numbers alone, the record is unambiguous. Enrollment had doubled in those nine years from 118 to 237 as had the number of faculty. The college's debt was entirely disposed of just three years into his term. By the end of his presidency the school's assets had soared, thanks to many major gifts, endowments, and professorships; according to his own estimate in 1858 his efforts had added $115,000. As to the campus, it had grown as well with the addition of the Woods Cabinet and Lawrence Observatory, the new library, and the Appleton Cabinet. Just as importantly, the college's reputation had been restored in the public mind. Newspapers that once ran story after story of troubles at the college now carried reports of new gifts, higher enrollments, and a generally contented campus.

Some of the changes that the college experienced during Hitchcock's presidency may be credited directly to him, particularly in winning back the support and trust of the students with social events and excursions. But the reversal of the school's financial misfortunes is probably attributable not so much to the president himself, but to the confidence he instilled in students, alumni, and donors alike that the college would survive, thrive, and once again be worthy of financial support. "The value of Dr. Hitchcock's presidency to the Institution," wrote Williams S. Tyler, "cannot be overestimated. His weight of character and his wise policy saved the college." In the words of Carpenter and Morehouse,

> The administration of President Hitchcock marked something more than an era in the history of Amherst College; it witnessed a new birth of the institution. When he assumed the presidency, the college was struggling amongst the quick sands of debt, apparently on the verge of dissolution; within the ten years of his term of office it was...placed on the high grounds of financial prosperity... Nor was the success of his administration to be measured by college finances alone. It was the age of growth and expansion in cabinets, collections and materials for the illustration of the physical sciences. It witnessed the erection of a library building and a great increase in the number of books upon the library shelves. It was marked by two great religious revivals, in 1846 and 1850.

Following his oration, Hitchcock presented the keys of the college to William Augustus Stearns, who then delivered his inaugural address.

When at last the proceedings ended, Edward and Orra walked down the aisle, through the wooden church doors into the midday sun. Perhaps they paused for a moment to admire the view from the campus, across the fields, and up the steep shoulders of Mount Norwottuck, before heading homeward. Edward likely offered a prayer of thanks to God to be relieved of his burden at last. As to his wife, Orra no doubt offered a prayer of thanks as well, first, that her husband was now relieved of the onerous responsibilities of the presidency, and, very likely, that they both were at last free to return to their own home to share the warmth of that familiar fireplace with their children and first grandchild.

Appleton Cabinet 1858

RETIREMENT 1854-1864

Interior of the Ichnological Cabinet.

23 Sabbath of Life

"I have never found my hands fuller or my time more occupied than for several months past."

Amherst, November 23, 1854

Edward was hunched in a chair in the front entryway of his home, struggling to pull on his galoshes. Just then Orra emerged from the kitchen.

"Father, what are you doing? Not going abroad, I trust. It is bitterly cold and there is snow in the air."

"Yes, Mother, I know. But I must go to college."

"Have you forgotten, dear, that you are retired now? It is all in Reverend Stearns's hands now, is it not?"

"Yes, of course—of course it is. But I have an engagement. Mr. Sykes, the architect for the new cabinet."

"Surely it can be delayed a few days."

"No, I am afraid it must be today. He advised me yesterday at the inauguration that he already had some ideas for the structure and wished to discuss them. I insisted he come today to look at the site."

"How long, Edward, will you be engaged?"

"Not long, Mother, I promise." He drew his heaviest coat around himself. Then Orra wrapped a woolen scarf around his neck and tucked it snuggly beneath his coat lapels. As he departed she watched anxiously at the front door, then at the parlor window. For the remainder of the morning, every time she passed that window she paused, pulled aside the drapes, and looked out, hoping to see her husband making his way down the hill.

By midafternoon Edward was still in his office with Mr. Sykes, poring over a number of sketches the architect had hastily drawn. The light was poor and he was tired, but he was nevertheless determined to nudge the project forward a little further if possible. Then there came a rap on his office door. "Uh-huh," responded Edward absently, intent on a hurried sketch the architect was making of an alternative placement of the structure. The door opened and a familiar face appeared. It was his eldest son, Edward, Jr., smiling warmly.

His father immediately rose from his chair. "Ah, Edward—well, this is a surprise," he said, shaking his son's hand. "How are you, Son? Everything all right in Easthampton, I trust?"

"Perfectly, Father, perfectly all right. I was so sorry to be unable to be present yesterday for the inauguration ceremonies and of course your address, that I felt I must visit today and wish you well in your retirement."

"Well that is very kind of you, Son." He introduced him to Mr. Sykes who looked up briefly, nodded, then returned to his sketches. "But I really am busy right now and shall be for a while. Mr. Sykes and I are working on some ideas for the new cabinet. I think you will find it to your liking. We want it to be..."

The young man placed his hand gently on his father's arm and spoke softly but insistently. "Father..."

The elder Hitchcock paused mid-sentence. "Can it not wait?"

Edward, Jr., took his father's elbow. "It won't take but a moment, Father, I promise. You have a special visitor." He drew his father toward the office door, then out into the hallway. There stood his wife, Mary Judson Hitchcock. In her arms was a mass of swaddling clothes which she carefully drew back.

"Grandfather Hitchcock," she said with a beguiling smile and a twinkle in her eyes, "someone would like to say hello."

The senior Hitchcock gazed into the shining eyes of two-month old Edward Hitchcock the third, sighed and spoke softly to the infant, "Well, hello there little one, how are you?" The baby gave out a little gurgle. Edward's eyes glistened as he looked up into the smiling faces of his son and daughter-in-law.

"Mother asked us to come after you, Father," explained Edward, Jr., but the old man was too entranced by the smiling face of his first grandchild to respond at first. He continued, "She hoped we could all have dinner together."

Finally Edward seemed to hear. He looked at his son, his daughter-in-law, and then his grandson. "O, well, of course. Just a moment." He returned to his office and bid adieu to Mr. Sykes, assuring him that he would visit him in his

Springfield office in a few days to continue their conversation. With his daughter-in-law's assistance he donned his heavy coat and scarf, and the four of them made their way homeward.

Edward Hitchcock must have been enjoying a rare period of contentment when, just a month after stepping down from the presidency, he wrote: "The change in my condition which I have long been desirous of has at length been accomplished and the circumstances have been as merciful as I could have hoped for." Lest we imagine those merciful circumstances to include hours lounging by the fire, napping, or enjoying the company of his wife, children, and grandchild, we need only look at the agreement worked out with the trustees for his retirement. First, as to teaching, he retained the title Professor of Geology and Natural Theology and agreed to a busy teaching schedule that included both lectures and recitations in geology, anatomy, physiology, and theology, well over one hundred classes per year. That might seem like a heavy load for a man of his age and condition, but he took it on with pleasure provided he would be released from any administrative obligations and—blessed Providence—from the burden of attending faculty meetings. Wrote Tyler of this new phase in his friend's life,

> Professor Hitchcock returned with the freshness of a first love to his lectures and recitations, to geological excursions, explorations, and naming of mountains, to the collection and classification of specimens and the development and perfection especially of his favorite branches, ichnology and natural theology.

In addition to his teaching duties, he immediately threw himself body and soul into a number of new projects—"obligations," as he termed them. Foremost of those was the construction of the newly endowed Appleton Cabinet. Since it would house artifacts accrued by Hitchcock on behalf of the college over the past thirty years, the trustees saw fit to give him nearly complete control over the design and construction of the new building. The structure he had in mind would be 110 feet long by 45 feet wide—nearly twice the size of the original Woods Cabinet. It would be two stories tall and designed specifically to house the college's growing collections, the ichnological artifacts and the Nineveh Gallery. And it would include a lecture room on the eastern end.

Selecting a location for the new edifice proved to be somewhat of a sticking point, as it had been for the new library several years earlier. Hitchcock wanted the Appleton Cabinet located next to the Woods Cabinet, arguing that the classroom would thus be close to both buildings for instructional purposes. But trustee Luke Sweetser, businessman and longtime supporter and benefactor of the college, was of a different mind, and the two old friends struck a deal. The new cabinet would be placed on the south edge of the campus, and Sweetser would provide $1000 for the addition to the Woods Cabinet of a classroom specifically for geology. The projects went forward simultaneously, with Hitchcock very much involved in both. The depth of his involvement is revealed in a letter to Edward, Jr., the following May in which he asked his son to talk to the builder about some modifications to the plans for the Woods Cabinet addition:

> Something must be done to decrease the expense or I fear we shall not be able to build as Mr. Shoals estimate overruns our means considerably. I had rather have it smaller than not to have it built at all." When at last the two projects were complete, he wrote: "I have never perhaps found my hands fuller or my time more occupied than for several months past."

As if all of this were not enough for the "retired" professor, Edward was determined to seek other means of augmenting his salary, including lecturing and what would today be termed consulting. In February 1855, Edward and son Charles traveled by rail to a remote region of western Virginia to carry out a survey of coal resources for the Great Kanawha Company. Just as their work commenced, the weather turned on them. Heavy rains and river ice conspired to make travel impossible and they were marooned in Red House, a small town on the Kanawha River. In a letter to Orra he expressed his regrets about the situation they found themselves in:

> You well know how earnestly I looked forward to some degree of rest on leaving the Presidency of the College. But thus far instead of rest I have been as it were on the top of the billows or deep between them. How freely should I feel the force of the sentiment in one of my sermons that "to him who does his duty there is no satisfying rest this side of heaven."

Nevertheless, Edward and Charles carried out their charge and eventually returned to Amherst. Edward submitted a report to the chairman of the Great Kanawha Company, written while still in Red Hat, that gave a generally optimistic account of the coal resources they had investigated. But the last paragraph revealed his state of mind:

> I will add only, that I have not been led to form too favorable an opinion of this region…For we are here in midwinter, with the ground more or less covered with snow, the temperature very low, the roads frozen and excessively rough, navigation closed, health feeble, and my spirits quite as low as the thermometer. Indeed, I have never been engaged in a geological exploration so unpleasant and trying. Respectfully submitted, EDWARD HITCHCOCK

Back in Amherst two months after Edward's return from Virginia, he and Orra were strolling through the village, perhaps shopping or simply enjoying a spring day, when she fell, striking her head on the brick pavement. She bled profusely and lost consciousness. For a few moments Edward thought his beloved Orra had perished. She soon revived, however, but remained in a bad state for several weeks. He was convinced that her only hope would be divine intervention. At one point she was suffering terribly from "difficulty in deglutition [swallowing] and spasmodic pains in the chest." Her doctors, according to Edward, could make no sense of her symptoms, but he concluded that her difficulties were due to the obstruction of her esophagus by a dental plate. That night the plate at last was dislodged and passed into her stomach. Her pain and suffering were immediately relieved.

Such a sudden and unexpected turn of events was to Edward's mind nothing short of a miracle: "How wonderfully had God interposed!" he recorded in his notes. But he then became worried at the ultimate fate of the plate, "lest such a ragged indigestible body might occasion trouble in some of the more lower viscera." Again he prayed for divine intervention, and at length his orison was answered: "I had scarcely left my closet before it was announced to me that unceremoniously and without injury the teeth had escaped." He then added,

> Such a statement on account of the nature of the subject if made public would exert only a smile or a jeer. But as a matter of private history I leave it on record for those personal friends who may read this journal and I hope that they may join me in ascriptions of praise to Him who so splendidly interposed to rescue my beloved wife in times of extreme peril.

By autumn Orra had recovered from her accident, Edward had returned to his teaching, and the couple had resumed their busy lives. On November 8, 1855, he traveled by rail to New York City. Over the course of the next few weeks he gave lectures in that city as well as in Newark, Elizabeth, and Bloomfield, New Jersey. One letter to his daughter Mary hints that he may have visited with her at the home of Daniel and Caroline Sprague in Orange, New Jersey.

Immediately on his return to Amherst, he and Orra prepared for a longer trip. He admitted in his notes that he might be taking on too much:

> I have made several engagements to lecture abroad the coming winter chiefly on the bearings of geology upon religion…[M]y engagements look formidable when I think of them and the winter. I find my system this autumn to be running quite low and nothing but God's power can carry me through my engagements. I pray for strength to do whatever he wishes me to accomplish and to prepare me for whatever is before me.

Orra had her misgivings about the trip as well, writing to Edward, Jr., "We expect to start in the morning. But not without many apprehensions of suffering from cold etc. I do think after all a quiet home is the best place for enjoyment that this world affords and I believe the best to prepare for a future home of rest too."

On December 12, 1855, they departed for a nearly two-month long lecture tour of the Midwest, with Edward scheduled to speak in dozens of YMCAs, athenaeums, lyceums, and auditoriums. At some point the couple parted and Orra continued alone to Cincinnati where she visited with daughter Catherine and her husband, Reverend Henry M. Storrs. Edward traveled first to Buffalo where he delivered a series of five lectures over the course of nearly three weeks, then moved on to Indianapolis, Cincinnati, Chicago, Milwaukee, Cleveland, and finally Columbus, Ohio. In each city he delivered one or more lectures; in Milwaukee, for example, he gave three lectures within a week. Most were on the topic "Geology and its Bearings Upon Religion," several on "Fossil Footmarks."

In late January Edward joined Orra at the Storrs' home in Cincinnati where they spent some time visiting. During their stay, Edward reported on his travels in a letter that appeared in a Boston weekly, *The Congregationalist.* Under the pseudonym "Geologus," he offered his observations on the cities they had visited, the people they met, the condition of the railroads, and the geology of the Midwest, along with some complaints about the weather. He was particularly impressed with his daughter's new hometown: "But who could have looked at the beautiful valley in which Cincinnati stands, while yet uninhabited…without inferring at once that Providence must have intended that spot for a city."

In early February the Hitchcocks began their journey homeward. It proved to be a harrowing trip in the midst of a blizzard—their train was delayed for long intervals in Buffalo and in Albany. Safely home in Amherst a few days later, Orra wrote to a niece, "Some of the drifts about here are tremendous. In our front yard they are a wall on either side. The cold has not been so intense here as in many places—only 11° below here while at Cincinnati it was 18 and Milwaukee 30." Meanwhile Edward began preparations for yet another ambitious project that would take him away from his family once again.

For someone as consumed with his own mortality as Edward Hitchcock, the decision to take on the geological survey of Vermont, especially at age 63, seems surprising. The survey, which had been authorized by the state legislature in 1844, had been taken up by three different geologists in succession, in 1845, 1853, and 1856. All three had died, the third only months after his appointment. "I could not but confess to a sort of superstitious fear," wrote Hitchcock, "that if I took the post I should be the fourth before the completion of such a work." In spite of his worries, he took on the job in November 1856, on condition that he be allowed to hire his two sons as assistants.

In early May 1857, the three Hitchcock men, assisted by geologist Albert D. Hager, a Vermont native, set out to undertake the survey of a state almost as large in area as Massachusetts and with far more rugged terrain. It did not go well for the senior investigator. Within weeks he had to give up the field work and return to Amherst, leaving his sons and Mr. Hager to carry on without him. "I have got completely upset by my jaunt last week," he wrote Edward, Jr., on May 23. "I never had so hard a time of it—and am still quite unwell. The worst symptom is an irregular action of the heart. I rode two days all day in rain and snow."

On May 27, 1857 he made this entry in his notes that reveals his state of mind:

> This is my sixty fourth birthday. And though every thing around me is bursting into life at this delightful vernal season yet it becomes me to turn my thoughts forward to death and eternity especially as the present state of my health reads to me an impressive lecture on my frailty and liability to be suddenly removed. In consequence of an extremely hard journey in Vermont and exposure to storms I have developed anew a difficulty in my heart of which I have formerly spoken in this journal.

Frugal as ever, Hitchcock spent only a fraction of the funds appropriated for the project, and yet the Vermont State Legislature withheld reimbursement for several years. In the same entry he expressed his regrets on the matter: "I meet too with great difficulties and perplexities in the Vermont survey—so as to make me regret that I ever undertook it. Though I have laboured in it for two years more or less I have never received a cent for my services and doubt whether I ever shall." Eventually funds were provided and the final report was published in 1861, running to two volumes and nearly 1000 pages. A Canadian geologist writing in *American Journal of Science and Arts* described the work as "…one of the best that has been published on this continent."

The Vermont geological survey no doubt had much to do with the career path of Charles H. Hitchcock. For a time he had been contemplating going into the ministry, but after completing the Vermont survey and report, he was hired to carry out similar surveys in New Hampshire and Maine. His vocational choice had been made.

During the 1840s Edward Hitchcock published nearly two dozen papers on his fossil footmark research. But in the last half of his presidency he published nothing on the subject. Then, in 1855, his attention returned to the footmarks as strongly as ever. In a single paragraph from his notes of November 1855, he admitted that his enthusiasm for the footmarks had declined for a time, but went on to cite some reasons for his renewed interest in the subject:

> ...[A]n unusual number of new facts in science have opened unexpectedly upon me and awakened my former enthusiasm as a remarkable fossil (jaw of a fish) from Indiana—fossil bones from Springfield—a fossil shell and fern from Mt. Tom and especially new fossil footmarks.

The remarkable fish jaw he alluded to had been discovered in Indiana and sent to him earlier in 1855. He concluded that it was the jaw of a shark, but one that was unusual for the single rank of teeth. He brought the specimen with him to the August 1855, meeting of the AAAS in Providence, Rhode Island, and presented it before a large audience. Among those present was Professor Louis Agassiz, a distinguished authority on the subject. Agassiz immediately proposed that the fish was actually a swordfish, but an entirely new species possessing not one jawbone with teeth above and below, but two bones fused together, each with teeth only on the outer surface.

The bones from Springfield were of still greater interest to Hitchcock because of their direct bearing on his research. During construction at the site of the United States Armory in that city in spring 1855, fossilized bones were unearthed in sandstone. William Smith, superintendent of the operation, notified Professor Hitchcock who received them with great interest. After examining them, he referred them to Harvard anatomist Jeffries Wyman. Professor Wyman eventually confirmed them to be reptilian, but unusual in that they were hollow, much like the bones of birds—that was surely music to Edward Hitchcock's ears.

By 1855, geology and ichnology had truly become a family affair for the Hitchcocks. The shell and fern to which Edward referred were discoveries related to the fossil footmarks made by his elder son. In two papers published in the *American Journal of Science and Arts*, Edward, Jr., reported on fossils he and his Williston students had unearthed in sandstone on nearby Mt. Tom. In one paper he described impressions of a fern, *Clathropteris rectiusculus*, a

Figure 62. Fossil fern and shell discovered by Edward Hitchcock, Jr., 1856

species that had been found elsewhere in the Connecticut Valley and in Europe. He suggested that the presence of the fern might aid in working out the age of the local sandstone and its possible relationship to similar formations elsewhere:

> If we can rely with confidence upon this geological zone, it will form a convenient starting place for tracing out other older and newer formations....[and it] makes the opinion also probable—long since advanced by my father that the Trias [Triassic] also exists here.

That opinion was further reinforced by a subsequent discovery of a mollusk shell nearby.

At about the same time the younger Hitchcock son was also cutting his teeth in the field of ichnology. Three years earlier, at age sixteen, Charles had come across some interesting impressions in recently deposited clay on the banks of the Connecticut River in Hadley. He identified, described, and photographed tracks of a number of animals—humans, dogs, birds, a batrachian (possibly a salamander or lizard), snails, and worms—as well as impressions of raindrops, ripple marks, and air vesicles (i.e., bubbles). No doubt with the encouragement and advice of his father, Charles wrote an article on the tracks that was published in *AJS* in 1855. In that paper he suggested that some of those modern-day tracks could offer insights into the formation of the fossil footmarks discovered by his father and others in Triassic sandstone. "From the facts obtained at this locality we derive a very clear idea of the manner in which foot-marks on stone were produced," he wrote. He then described how newly deposited mud dried to form an uneven surface, how subsequent rains filled depressions in that surface, and how animals wading in those depressions made impressions in the mud, particularly where it was nearly dried up. He discussed various features of those tracks such as alternating left and right feet and the presence of distinct imprints of claws and hairs. Most interesting to geologists of his day would have been the young Hitchcock's final comment that pertained directly to his father's work:

> For three years I have not noticed on this clay bed any other trace of the animals besides their tracks. As this seems to be the common feeding-ground for many species, if any of them died there, their remains would probably have been devoured or floated away by the water. Such a spot therefore, is the least likely of any to contain organic remains. As it seems to be a type of the spots where fossil footmarks occur, we may reasonably infer that the paucity of such remains in the Triassic rocks is not strange.

Even if all these new and interesting developments had not been enough to renew the elder Hitchcock's interest, another challenge faced him. With construction of the Appleton Cabinet complete in fall 1855, it fell to Edward, with the assistance of Charles, now an Amherst senior, to begin curating and exhibiting the more than 10,000 ichnological specimens he had accumulated over the last two decades. As always Edward girded himself for the task while simultaneously convinced of his inadequacy:

> …I am trying to get my collection of fossil footmarks into the new Ichnological Cabinet—the first one ever erected. It must be done this fall or the larger ones now out of doors will be ruined. All these objects with a course of instruction in geology severely taxes my time. But I want to work just as hard as possible: though I fear that I have been too much diverted of late from my spiritual concerns and sometimes almost believe that Satan has had something to do in presenting before me so many interesting worldly objects in order to draw me away from God and eternal things.

By 1856 the Appleton Cabinet was fitted out with one of the most unusual collections of artifacts to be found anywhere in the world. The first floor was devoted entirely to Hitchcock's fossil footmarks where, in the words of William S. Tyler, "…the eye of his science and imagination could see the gigantic birds, saurians, and batrachians of the primeval world marching down the geologic ages"; while on the upper floor were displayed "…shells of mollusks, casts of the megatherium, skeletons and skins of the gorilla and other animals, and stuffed or preserved specimens of the animal creation in regular gradation from the lowest to the highest orders." The work had been slow and painstaking, but well worth it. The value of the specimens to the college, Hitchcock argued, had increased tenfold as a result. None of this could have been accomplished without the assistance of Charles, about whom Edward wrote with obvious satisfaction,

> I can now also leave one individual who understands it almost as well as myself and who can carry forward the investigation should he live in this valley—I refer to my son Charles who by aiding me the past year has made more commendable progress in the knowledge of the 119 species of Lithichnozoa which I have described. I think he would be able to recognize them all—where as I know of no other man living who could distinguish ten of them.

Later in that year Edward and Charles completed and published a pamphlet entitled *A Synopsis of the Genera and Species of the Lithichnozoa in the Hitchcock Ichnological Museum of Amherst College*. It listed the specimen numbers and Latin binomials for some 150 species as well as the location of each in the cabinet. It encompassed ten animal groups: marsupialoid mammals; pachydactylous or thick-toed birds; leptodactylous or narrow-toed birds; ornithoid lizards or batrachians; lizards; batrachians; chelonians (turtles and tortoises); fishes; crustaceans, insects, and myriapods; and annelids (flatworms). Even after the pamphlet was printed, the collection continued to grow, eventually numbering more than 20,000 specimens. Based on those additional specimens, Hitchcock presented a paper at the Boston meeting of the American

Association for the Advancement of Science in 1863 describing thirty new species.

With the completion of the Appleton Cabinet and its contents, Hitchcock turned his energies to a related project, a report to the Commonwealth of Massachusetts on the ichnological resources of the state. He had included a lengthy chapter on the fossil footmarks in his report on the geological surveys in 1841. But so much had happened in the intervening years, so many new footmarks had been discovered, so many taxonomic revisions had been published, and so many other workers had now joined the discussion, that he felt the need to bring the governor, state legislature, and the public up to date. And so the semiretired professor began work on *Ichnology of New England: A Report on the Sandstone of the Connecticut Valley Especially Its Fossil Footmarks Made to the Government of the Commonwealth of Massachusetts.* It was an ambitious undertaking, the capstone of two decades of work, the *magnum opus* of his paleontological career. It would have been a mammoth effort for anyone—for a man of his age and constitution it was particularly challenging. But it had to be done, he believed; it was another obligation.

Curiously, *Ichnology of New England* begins where most books end, with a bibliography. It lists sixty-three works pertaining to fossil footmarks arranged in chronological order. Included are books and articles by some of the most influential geologists of the period, American and British—William C. Redfield, Henry D. Rogers, Sir Charles Lyell, Professor Richard Owen—as well as fourteen works of his own, eleven of Dr. James Deane, one of Dexter Marsh. Charles H. Hitchcock's 1855 paper also appears. Inexplicably, the two papers by Edward Hitchcock, Jr., are not listed, even though both are cited prominently later in the report. The placement of the bibliography at the front of the book suggests the author wished to show both the breadth and depth of interest this new science had generated. The works are presented in chronological order, no doubt intended to demonstrate the author's priority in this research.

The bibliography is followed by a history of the field of ichnology, beginning with the author's own pioneering work. Here he cites one reason he felt the publication of the book was necessary. Ever since his first paper in 1836,

> ...[T]he work of discovery has...been going on; and within the last two years the developments have seemed to be more wonderful than ever, so that now I am able to describe no less than one hundred and nineteen species from the Connecticut Valley; and the whole subject seemed never to need revision and new descriptions so much as now."

At this point Hitchcock draws the reader's attention to the newly completed Appleton Cabinet. Up until that time, he explains, most scientists had little more than drawings and descriptions of fossil footmarks to examine. But now, thanks to the generosity of Samuel Appleton and others, the collections in the new cabinet could stand as references to anyone who wished to carry on ichnological research. "A sample of nearly every species that has been disinterred in the Connecticut Valley will be found in this cabinet. It is my intention, in this Report, to give a description of them all…"

The greater part of the introductory section of the report deals with the age of the sandstone in which the tracks were found. Here he marshals a broad range of data to support his conviction that the new red sandstone was deposited during the Triassic or early Jurassic. Some of the strongest evidence, he argues, is based on the nature of the fossils that occur so abundantly in that formation. He cites evidence of fishes, mollusks, ferns, and other groups, the strongest of which is from the work of his elder son:

> Still more decisive as to the jurassic, or rather, perhaps, liassic, character of the upper part of the Connecticut River sandstone, are the discoveries of Edward Hitchcock, Jr., M. D., in the strata of Mount Tom, in Easthampton. He has found there a species of Clathropteris, (C. rectiusculus,) a peculiar fern found in Europe, only in the lower part of the lias and upper part of the trias. It occurs not far from the middle of the sandstone of the valley, measuring its perpendicular thickness. It may safely be concluded, therefore, that the rock above this point corresponds to the lias, or lower part of the jurassic series.

One footnote in this section is of particular significance. It quotes a sentence from a letter written by Dexter Marsh to Benjamin Silliman in 1848:

> You will recollect that the first specimen of fossil footprints of birds ever brought into public notice in this country, was the slab I discovered among the flagging stone, while laying the flagging stone near my house, which Dr. Deane first described to President Hitchcock as the footprints of birds.

Here Hitchcock adds, "From this statement it would seem that Mr. Marsh was the first to notice these impressions," an obvious flag to his readers that this was a matter of some importance to him. He would come back to the subject at considerable length in a postscript added just before the report went to press.

Hitchcock next presents a list of the characters of the footmarks he used in formulating his classification system. They include the obvious—number of feet, number of toes, presence of webs, length of toes, length of step, etc.—as well as many less obvious features—pachydactylous toes vs. leptodactylous toes, divarication of the toes, caudal appendages, integuments—a total of thirty-one characters in all.

The ensuing 130 pages, nearly three quarters of the report, are devoted to a description of each track-forming species, the most thorough such listing ever produced. By this time Hitchcock had reworked his taxonomic system yet again, merging some of his previously identified species while at the same time creating several new species. They now totaled 119 species in ten groups, the same groups enumerated in his *Synopsis*. That work had included species from all over North America, some of which were not known in New England, while this work included only species found in New England.

Near the end of the book is a section entitled "A More Popular Description of the Footmarks." Here the author reaffirms his conclusion that most of the tracks were formed by birds, although he hedges a bit with this footnote: "I speak of those animals as certainly birds, though doubts sometimes cross one's mind on this point: and I am aware that with some distinguished zoologists these doubts are strong. But I follow what seems to me at present the most probable view." Nevertheless, just a few pages below, he describes the bones unearthed at Springfield in 1855 that he had referred to Jeffries Wyman. Wyman concluded that they were the bones of a reptile, but different from any reptile known to Wyman, living or extinct. Here Hitchcock seems to open the door to a new view of his tracks:

> … the bones and the tracks will doubtless cast mutual light upon each other; and it seems already settled from the bones that large reptiles lived in the Connecticut Valley in sandstone days; and this, also, was one of the most common sort of animals, judging from the tracks.

The implication was clear: at least some of the creatures responsible for the fossil footmarks he had been studying for decades likely were reptiles, but reptiles with bird-like features.

Finally, the text is followed by sixty plates containing nearly 400 figures of tracks, many engravings of drawings, but over half ambrotypes, an early form of photograph. Some of the ambrotypes display remarkable detail and a striking three-dimensional quality.

The completed manuscript was delivered to Governor Henry Gardner with a cover letter dated April 1, 1857. The legislature approved its publication about eight weeks later. It is not surprising that the book took another year or more to go to press, probably owing to the many figures that needed to be engraved or photographed. In his notes Hitchcock reflected on the work that would soon be in print.

> I have occasion to speak of the Divine Goodness in another respect. I have been spared to accomplish another great work of my life–a work of science yet one on which I have long laboured. I mean the completion of a Report on the Fossil Footmarks of New England made to the Government of the State…

Here he noted that the work had cost him "more than 20 years of hard toil and study." Then he added this somber afterthought: "Oh how little will the world ever know how much of toil and anxiety all this has cost me especially as I have had to accomplish it in spite of a least one very bitter enemy so situated as to be able to do much to thwart me."

The "bitter enemy" to whom Hitchcock referred was Dr. James Deane of Greenfield, the man who first referred that original slab to him in 1835. Eight years after Hitchcock began his research on the fossil footmarks, Dr. Deane began writing and publishing his own accounts and descriptions of the tracks. At times it seemed as though Dr. Deane was trying to steal the limelight from Edward Hitchcock. The two had often exchanged bitter words in print; they had rarely spoken in person for the ensuing decade.

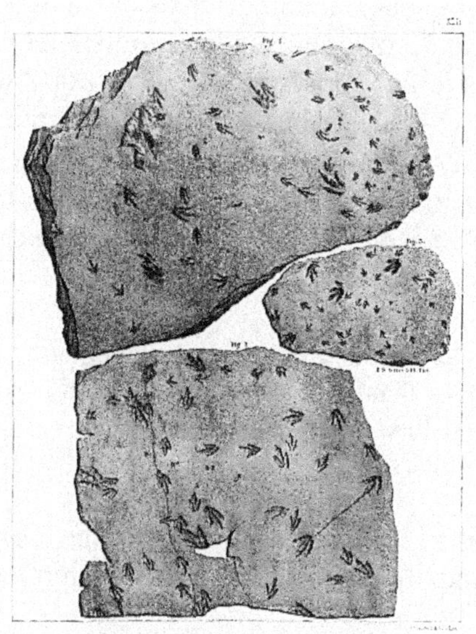

Figure 63. One of 60 plates from *Ichnology of New England*, 1858

On June 8, 1858, barely three months to the day from when Hitchcock wrote those words, Dr. James Deane passed away of typhoid fever in Greenfield at the age of 56. At last Edward Hitchcock's "bitter enemy" was gone, no longer to thwart him…or was he?

Sleigh Ride

24 The Aged Warrior

"How uncertain and unsatisfying a thing then is mere scientific reputation and honor!"

Amherst, December 31, 1858

Mary, Jane, Emily, and Orra Hitchcock stood like statues in the parlor, bundled in woolen cloaks, swaddled with scarves, their heads topped with knitted hats, once their brothers', pulled down and tied under the chin.

"Mother," pleaded her youngest daughter, "must we go out into the cold, the wind, the ice, and the snow?" Mary and Jane no doubt had their own opinions about this ill-advised venture, but chose to let their boisterous younger sister make her plea while they stood in silence.

"Yes, dear, we must—for your father."

" Surely we will all be taken ill, especially Papa."

"Nonsense, child. It will only be a short promenade. And your father has been so low these last days of the year. This, at least, will lift his spirits."

The youngest daughter would not go against her mother's wishes for anything. But she turned her gaze to her older sisters and rolled her eyes in the way she did. Mary and Jane offered her expressions of sympathy, yet stood impassively.

Just then their father burst through the door, he too swaddled against the elements. A gust of wind and a swirl of snow followed him before he had a chance to push the door closed behind him.

"Are we all ready, then?" he asked with a satisfied smile, gazing at his wife and daughters. Orra smiled and nodded; her daughters remained silent and stolid.

With that he led his wife and daughters out into the winter's cold. It was midmorning of the last day of the year. There had been some rain the day before. Overnight the rain had frozen on contact, coating every tree, every limb, every fencepost, every railing.

Edward's spirits had been very low for several weeks, and his bodily complaints multifold. But on rising this last morning of the old year, he looked out the window at the snow and ice covered landscape, and rushed to the kitchen to tell Orra of his plan, his spirits soaring. Her task, he informed her, would be to rally their three daughters to the notion. Then he had been away on foot, off to the livery to hire a sleigh and team. It was an uncharacteristic extravagance for him, the clearest possible sign to Orra that the family should cooperate, if not for their own sakes then for his.

They all clambered into the carriage, Edward at the reins. With a jerk the sleigh was off, first along the road a few rods, then up across George Baker's pasture. A sudden squall had erupted just as they departed, and for a few minutes there was little to see and do but huddle together against the wind, the snow, the cold. But just as suddenly as the squall had begun, it ceased, the clouds parted, and a brilliant sun beamed forth, illuminating the fields, fences, scattered trees and shrubs, as well as the recumbent form of Mt. Norwottuck, white and glistening in the distance.

"Father, it is magnificent," said Orra. Then she turned to her daughters who were huddled together, their faces completely obscured by a woolen blanket. "Girls, look about you, please. You won't want to miss this." One by one the three faces emerged, skin rosy with the cold air, eyes glistening in the wind. Then as they looked about, they all gasped.

"Have you ever seen such dazzling splendor, my dears?" asked Edward with a smile. "The work of the Almighty at its finest, most ethereal, most uplifting."

At the edge of the pasture the sleigh plunged into the forest where an equally resplendent scene was revealed, each twig an icy pendant, each branch a chandelier of crystal, the sunlight highlighting every facet. At times when the angle of the sun was just right, the trees glowed with the soft richness of embossed silver.

Finally the sleigh emerged into an opening in the forest high up on the mountainside. Edward reined the team to a halt where the sun was brightest and the slightest bit of warmth could be detected. Beyond lay the fields they had just crossed, then the road, and their house, and just beyond that College Hill, and then the village, all swathed in glimmering white and silver.

Orra and the girls sighed simultaneously at the sight. "Oh, Papa," began Emily, leaning forward and placing her hand gently on the old man's shoulder. "I have never ever seen anything like it."

He and Orra exchanged smiles. The whole family had witnessed something similar, nearly fifteen years earlier, on a January morning in the first year of his presidency. But Emily was only seven then and could not be expected to remember the occasion.

"I thought you would like it, all of you," replied Edward. For several minutes they remained at that lofty vantage, gazing with wonder at the wintry landscape bedecked in jewels.

Finally with a shake of the reins they were off again, off for home, for the warmth of the kitchen stove and the parlor fireplace, for tea or for cocoa, but with visions of those icy pendants, crystal garlands, and evergreen sprays coated in soft silver dancing in their heads.

Controversy had always been a part of Edward Hitchcock's life. Even at the age of sixteen, he seemed to be spoiling for a fight when he aimed the pointed spears of his "Poetical Sketch" at men of power and influence. Likewise in his adult life he sparred again and again on matters of faith and science with authors, editors, scientists, and ministers alike. That he took a good deal of pride in these skirmishes is clear from his "list of literary and scientific productions" recorded in his notes that included nine controversies. The same list, with a few additions, reappeared fourteen years later in *Reminiscences*:

> With Edmund M. Blunt, of New York, on errors in the Nautical Almanac…
> With the Episcopalians, respecting the time of Easter…
> With Professor Potter, about some points in the Temperance movement…
> With Prof. Amos Eaton, on Geological Nomenclature…
> With Prof. Moses Stuart, on…[the] connection between Geology and the Bible...
> With Dr. James Deane, on the discovery of Fossil Footmarks…
> [With Dr. Bowditch] Defence of my claims [regarding the footmarks]
> [With] Mr. Draper, the first discoverer of the Footmarks…
> With Rev. Mr. Chapin, of Connecticut, on Fossil Footmarks…
> With Rev. Erastus Hopkins, on a Railroad through the Connecticut Valley...
> With…Jonathan Saxton in reply to his attack upon "Exhibition of Unitarianism."
> With one of the editors of the Christian Register…
> With Rev. E. H. Sears and Prof. Haven, especially on Bodily Identity…

Not included in either list was yet another contentious subject for him, the omission from a history of the American Association for the Advancement of Science of his role in the founding of that organization. This clearly vexed him; he devoted five pages to the matter in *Reminiscences*.

Of all the controversies in the professional life of Edward Hitchcock, the most protracted and bitter was with Dr. James Deane. It continued for at least fifteen years in private letters and in published exchanges. And it seemed to bring out the worst in both men: pride, pettiness, even at times untruthfulness.

For nearly eight years following the first letter Hitchcock received from Deane in 1835, the two men seemed to be on amiable and respectful terms. In his first paper on the subject published in 1836, Hitchcock was at pains to acknowledge Deane's role in referring those first specimens to him:

> My attention was first called to the subject by Dr. James Deane of Greenfield; who sent me some casts of impressions, on a red micaceous sandstone, brought from the south part of Montague, for flagging stones. Through the liberality of the same gentleman, I soon after obtained the specimens themselves, from which the casts were taken; and they are now deposited in the cabinet of Amherst College.

In his second paper he named one species, *Ornithichnites Deanii,* in honor of the doctor from Greenfield. He credited Deane twice in his 1841 *Report* and at least a half dozen times in his 1843 paper, "Description of Five New Species." For his part Deane seemed to be content during this period to collect artifacts, deliver them to Hitchcock, and offer his opinions.

That cordial relationship began to unravel in late 1842. Deane had sent some newly discovered tracks to British paleontologist Gideon Mantell, accompanied by a letter with detailed descriptions. According to Deane and others who examined them, the specimens were particularly fine, superior to any previously found. In his narrative the Greenfield doctor recounted his role in the discovery of the footmarks in 1835, suggesting that he had immediately recognized the marks as bird tracks while Hitchcock had been doubtful. Deane was nevertheless generous and fair in his account of what ensued:

> Prof. H. then gave the specimens an inspection which resulted in the unqualified conviction that these foot-prints were genuine vestiges of birds. He subsequently explored the entire valley of the Connecticut River with extraordinary success, the details of which he has given to the scientific world in several treatises of great ability.

Benjamin Silliman published Deane's letter in the *American Journal of Science and Arts* in October 1843, along with communications Silliman had received from Gideon Mantell, Richard Owen, and Sir Roderick Murchison, all of whom had seen the specimens and read the letter. Perhaps sensing that

Hitchcock might feel slighted by the elevation of Deane's role in the affair, Silliman twice reminded his readers of Hitchcock's contributions on the subject, first in his introduction and later in a footnote to Deane's letter.

In his introduction Silliman described Deane as the "original observer" of the tracks, then proceeded to quote the letters he had received, letters that were highly complimentary to Deane. Murchison referred to Deane as the "first observer" of the tracks, Richard Owen called him the "original discoverer." Both men also acknowledged Hitchcock's important role in studying them. Murchison went still further in his address to the Geological Society of London as quoted in the article: "…let us honor the great moral courage exhibited by Prof. Hitchcock, in throwing down his opinions before an incredulous public." Despite the words of praise sounded for him, Hitchcock was alarmed at what he read. It seemed clear to him that Deane was attempting to reclaim priority in the "discovery" of the footmarks. What was worse, Deane apparently had succeeded in convincing the three eminent British scientists of his claim, and Benjamin Silliman as well.

Hitchcock had another beef against his mentor that served to compound his anger. In April 1842, months before Deane's letter, Silliman had delivered an address to the Association of American Geologists in Boston in which he made a few brief comments on the subject of the fossil footmarks:

> It is worthy of remark, that the trifid tracks and impressions on the new red sandstone of the valley of the Connecticut, so zealously explored by Dr. James Dean of Greenfield, and both explored, and figured and described by Prof. Hitchcock, leave no reasonable doubt, that they are, at least in part, due to the feet of birds—some of them of colossal dimensions.

Silliman no doubt believed he was being evenhanded with those words. His friend from Amherst did not see it that way. Hitchcock wrote Silliman about his displeasure. That letter has not survived, but Silliman's response indicates the depth of feelings over the matter:

> I am greatly surprised at the state of your feelings & very much regret that you did not at Boston frankly tell me how you felt & I would at once & before the association have made it all right & I cannot persuade myself that it is now essentially wrong.

A few weeks later, Hitchcock wrote a letter to Sir Charles Lyell in London. Sir Charles and Lady Lyell had visited Edward and Orra in Amherst the previous summer and so Hitchcock considered Lyell a personal friend. He began by acknowledging the compliments he had received from Mantell, Owen, and Murchison in *AJS*. To enlist Lyell's support, he proceeded to review the story of the tracks:

> Dr. Deane did indeed first call my attention to the subject and for this I have given him full credit in all my published reports on the subject. He also said (I quote him from his first letter to me) in describing one of the slabs containing tracks, that "one of them is distinctly marked with the tracks of a turkey (as I believe) in relief." But he did not say this as a geologist for in the same letter he says "I am not a geologist"—nor was it the result of any careful examination of tracks. The opinion that these tracks were those of birds was a common one among the quarrymen who usually called them turkey tracks.

Hitchcock went on to point out that the first tracks had been "discovered" in 1802, long before either he or Deane had seen them. He then suggested that his own study of the tracks made him the true "discoverer." The logic is a bit contorted and leaves the impression that he was determined by whatever means necessary to deny Deane that title. Just a few lines later he stated, "I ought to add that I am now and ever have been on the most friendly terms with Dr. Deane."

A paper by Deane, "On the Fossil Footmarks of Turner's Falls, Massachusetts," appeared in the next issue of *AJS*. The paper painted a striking, almost romantic picture of the vicinity of the falls:

> The narrow compass of the horizon and an air of solitude that pervades the region, is in full contrast with the expanded valley and quiet loveliness that reigns undisturbed above and below the falls, which have been appropriately called the miniature of Niagara.

Deane described the fossil tracks he had observed at the site which he acknowledged had already been documented, stating,

> The readers of this Journal are already aware that their existence during this remote geological epoch is now fully established, and it is to carry on the illustrations, and accumulate the facts that bear upon this very interesting subject, that it is still presented.

He expressed the belief that the tracks he had observed were of the type Hitchcock had previously designated *Ornithichnites Fulicoides*. Aside from the depiction of the site and a few observations on the anatomy of the feet that formed the tracks, Deane's first published paper failed to add much to what Edward Hitchcock had already concluded regarding that species. Why had Silliman accepted a manuscript largely composed of previously documented information? Perhaps he wished to mollify Deane, to defuse the doctor's unhappiness about the failure of Silliman and Hitchcock to give him his due.

Matters came to a head, however, with a second manuscript by Deane entitled "On the Discovery of Fossil Footmarks" submitted to Silliman in 1843. That paper revealed Deane's deep-seated resentment toward Hitchcock for his claims regarding the fossil footmarks. I was the first to discover them, Deane argued. I was the first to recognize their significance, to realize them as the tracks of ancient birds. And yet the professor has repeatedly claimed the footmarks and their investigation entirely as his own. Deane's tone became more and more heated until, near the end of the paper, he obliquely accused Hitchcock of a series of mistakes and distortions in his research:

> If the application of science to this subject, consists in arbitrary classification; in the adoption of terms of non-committal import in essential particulars; in applying to the acknowledged footmarks of birds, terms which belong exclusively to reptiles; in founding species upon distorted and doubtful examples; in throwing doubts around self-evident truths, and in the adoption of erroneous conclusions, and the assumption of theories, then the claim of original discovery rests upon a broad basis.

In addition, Deane pointed to errors in Hitchcock's taxonomy, such as creating one of his early lists of species only to later abandon several of those species. He seemed to be suggesting that taxonomic revision, a fundamental task of science and one that is inevitable as new data are revealed, casts doubt on a scientist's credibility. To add further insult, Deane asserted that Hitchcock was "adequately compensated" by the state of Massachusetts while he was investigating the footmarks.

> Mr. H. lays great stress upon the five years of labor bestowed upon the investigation of footmarks. This is true, but it was a labor that most men would willingly endure when backed by the patronage of Massachusetts. He was adequately compensated from her treasury, and his expensive work was published by her liberality.

Edward Hitchcock was nothing if not frugal, and this criticism no doubt stung as much as the rest, perhaps more. The truth, Hitchcock later pointed out, was that the work was done after his paid work for the state had been completed. In a convoluted addendum to a subsequent article in *AJS*, Deane accepted Hitchcock's account, although he offered no apology for the error.

All three items, the article by Deane, a "rejoinder" by Hitchcock that was even longer than the original article, and a brief "surrejoinder" by Deane appeared together in the fall 1844, issue of *AJS.* At the end of Deane's article Silliman inserted this footnote: "By special agreement between the writers of these discussions, their respective proofs are mutually read, each receiving that of his antagonist, the object being to close the discussion in the present number…" The editor was clearly anxious to put an end to the verbal repartee. No doubt many of his readers shared his hope.

The central issue in the controversy from the start had been who deserved credit for the discovery of the fossil footmarks. The truth was that sandstone slabs imprinted with bird-like tracks had been discovered long before either man was introduced to them—so strictly speaking, neither was the true "discoverer." Furthermore, Deane's claim that he deserved the credit for correctly deducing the essential facts of the footmarks before Hitchcock had little merit. It was Hitchcock, after all, who gathered specimens from dozens of quarries up and down the Connecticut Valley, who described them and analyzed them, who made the claim that they were the tracks of ancient animals, probably of birds, in public forums again and again, and was often in the early years assailed for it. Ultimately it was Hitchcock's careful descriptions and analysis that won over the harshest skeptics. Deane could hardly have read those sixty pages of Hitchcock's 1841 report and honestly concluded that he deserved as much credit as Hitchcock. Edward Hitchcock was a proud man, and it no doubt galled him to witness the rise in prominence of the name Dr. James Deane in the scientific communities both in America and in Europe over the next twelve years.

"Beware the riches, honors, and pleasures of the world," Pastor Hitchcock had warned his parishioners many times. That warning must surely have been ringing in his ears during his battles with Dr. Deane. He admitted as much in a poignant passage of self-criticism from his notes of December 1843: "I place first as the most prominent unfavorable symptom in my case, inordinate worldly ambition or more definitely love of scientific distinction…"

Dr. Deane published twelve papers on the fossil footmarks in the nation's foremost scientific journals between 1843 and 1856. He exchanged letters with influential European scientists on several occasions and was widely praised abroad for his pioneering work with those sandstone tracks. While he did make many valuable contributions, his five papers in *AJS* between 1843 and 1848 were more descriptive than analytical, often expanding on material already introduced by Hitchcock.

After yet another skirmish with Hitchcock in 1847, Deane seemed intent on avoiding further arguments and confined himself to describing and illustrating the tracks he had discovered or examined, relying almost entirely on specimens from his own collection or those of several other Greenfield collectors. "I have no intention of entering fully into the subject," he stated in one paper, "My plan is merely to present some obvious practical views, grounded upon facts, leaving purely speculative conclusions out of the question. I do not even attempt a classification of the footprints." Throughout his writing, he was careful to avoid nomenclatural or taxonomic issues. Indeed, in one paper he dismissed the very idea that an accurate classification system could be derived from such material. "…[T]o embrace the whole, or even the greater part of them, in any system of classification upon principles of true science, is, in my opinion, impossible," he wrote in one paper, an obvious backhanded swipe at his nemesis from Amherst. Many of the illustrations in that publication were exceptionally crisp and detailed, a credit both to the artistic skills of the author and the talents of the lithographer.

In an 1850 paper Deane presented descriptions and lithographs of five new bird species, the tracks of which had been obtained recently from a Turners Falls location. In his last published paper before his death, he followed a similar pattern, describing in some detail a number of impressions, all collected at Turners Falls. It included two lithographed plates from drawings by the author and a pen and ink drawing.

While Deane's scientific expertise was no match for Hitchcock's, his prose was more fluid and readable than Hitchcock's formal scientific style. As to illustrations, Deane's were superior. Art historian Robert L. Herbert writes, "Deane's photographs and his illusionistic lithographs which he drew himself upon the stone, are more remarkable than his rival's illustrations..." Hitchcock's own drawings are flat tracings, adds Herbert, "...their simple forms are a far cry from Deane's subtle renderings."

In the last six of Deane's works on fossil footmarks published between 1845 and 1856, he mentioned Edward Hitchcock's name only once and cited not a single one of Hitchcock's works, although one paragraph, a cursory summary of Hitchcock's "occasional papers," was included in a memoir published several years after his death. During the same period, Hitchcock cited Deane and his works repeatedly, three times in his 1845 paper in the *Proceedings of the Association of American Geologists*, eight times in his 1848 paper in the *Memoirs of the Association for the Advancement of Science,* at least thirty times in *Ichnology of New England* in 1856 (not counting those that were part of his postscript on the controversy). In the bibliography of *Ichnology*, Hitchcock included eleven of Deane's published papers and letters on the subject. While neither man may have been willing to "let bygones be bygones," Hitchcock was

Figure 64. Turner's Falls, Mass., drawing by Orra White Hitchcock, 1833

nevertheless generous in giving credit to Deane for his many contributions to the field of ichnology, a kindness that was not returned by the doctor from Greenfield.

So the controversy stood in 1858 when *Ichnology of New England* was being prepared for publication. Then came the intelligence of Deane's death. Hitchcock immediately added a footnote to the description of *Ornithichnites Deanii* in his manuscript: "This species is dedicated to the late Dr. James Deane, who first called my attention to the subject of footmarks, and who has subsequently investigated it with much success, as its Bibliography, prefixed to this Report, will show."

No doubt the professor was relieved to have the matter behind him at last, but his reprieve would be brief. At a meeting of the Boston Society of Natural History in July 1858, Thomas T. Bouvé, a businessman, amateur naturalist, and friend of Deane's from Boston, offered a tribute that was subsequently published in the Society's proceedings. "Whatever may be said of others who have honorably worked in the same field," wrote Bouvé, "this, I think, may be truly stated of Dr. Deane, that the first scientific observations upon the footprints were made by him." Similar words were spoken by Dr. Henry I. Bowditch, a well-known Boston physician, in a eulogy delivered at a memorial service for Deane in Greenfield on August 4, 1858. His eulogy was subsequently published as a pamphlet.

We can imagine Edward Hitchcock, seated in his study, the pamphlet of Dr. Bowditch in hand, fuming at the errors, distortions, misrepresentations, and lies—as he saw them—in the tribute to Dr. James Deane. No doubt Orra and some of his colleagues urged him not to let it get to him—in modern-day parlance they might have said, "Let it go, Edward, let it go"—and well he might have done. His own words, "Beware the riches, honors, and pleasures of the world," likely rang in his head, and yet he could not resist one more opportunity to right his wronged reputation. He proceeded to draft a nine-page postscript for *Ichnology* entitled "Who first scientifically described the Fossil Footmarks of the Connecticut Valley?" that was inserted just before the book went to press.

Ichnology of New England had a very limited press run; only 1000 copies were printed by the state. Most of those were distributed to cities, towns, and libraries across the Commonwealth—few were available for sale. The only advertisements to appear in Boston newspapers were by Phillips, Sampson, and Company, a firm that had published several of Hitchcock's earlier works. Perhaps because of the limited availability of the book, only two short reviews appeared in American scholarly journals. The one newspaper to carry a story about the book was the *Springfield Republican,* on May 7, 1859. That article ignored the scientific merits of the work, its conclusions, and its implications for the understanding of the history of life on earth. Instead it dealt exclusively with the rivalry between the two men and repeated its claim that Hitchcock had ruthlessly grabbed priority in the work from the doctor from Greenfield.

One in depth review of the book did appear in the *North British Review*, authored by Professor John Duns of the University of Edinburgh. It was a long article discussing the scientific content of *Ichnology* in detail. Near the end of the review, Duns lavished praise on the author and dismissed unequivocally the claims of Deane's eulogists. We can imagine Hitchcock's pleasure as he read that paragraph:

> The controversy is one which admits of an easy settlement; and, after studying it without bias, we have not the least doubt but that, in the pages devoted to it in the present Report, Dr. Hitchcock has settled it. Dr. Deane had accidentally found some specimens of tracks "lying upon the side-ways at Greenfield," and had informed the author, who commissioned the finder to purchase them for him. They fell under the eye of science when Dr. Hitchcock obtained them. Had they been left to Dr. Deane alone, they would have been lying on the "side-ways" still.

He also received letters of support from three eminent European scientists, Adam Sedgwick of Cambridge, Richard Owen of London, and Wilhelm Haidinger of Vienna. In his notes that winter his satisfaction was clear:

> From these sources I learn that my claims as to the footmarks which have been assailed so much in this country are fully admitted by these distinguished savants...and these testimonies have all been unsolicited. Truly it is God who has raised up for me these foreign friends and it ought to fortify me against neglect and abuse at home.

Overseas it would appear that Hitchcock had prevailed in the Deane controversy. But the nearly complete lack of attention to the subject in America, both in the scientific community and in the public media, forces the question, Who other than Edward Hitchcock really cared about it? If his pride had not been so deeply invested in the matter, he might have realized that little benefit could be derived from continuing to do battle with the ghost of James Deane. Furthermore, had the two settled their differences long ago, they might have been able to advance the understanding of the fossil footmarks more effectively together than by expending so much energy composing letters and publishing articles against each other.

"How uncertain and unsatisfying a thing then is mere scientific reputation and honor!" added Hitchcock in the same entry. "Oh if a man has nothing else to rest upon he is poor indeed."

Edward and Orra had much to be thankful for in the last years of the decade. Two daughters, Mary and Jane, were living at home and assisting their parents in domestic affairs. Emily was not far away at Mount Holyoke Female Seminary, and although her health had been a concern for a time, she graduated in July 1859, after which she too lived at home. The three daughters cared for their parents during their frequent bouts with poor health. Meanwhile their fourth daughter Catherine and her husband were fully occupied with their own life in Cincinnati. Their first child, Mary, had died in infancy in 1857, but by 1859 Kate had given birth to a healthy son whom they named Charles Bigelow Storrs.

Charles Henry Hitchcock, who had graduated from Amherst in 1854, served as tutor there for several years before receiving an appointment as Lecturer in Zoology and Curator of Cabinets in 1859, a post he held for five years. For two of those years, 1859 to 1861, he also attended Andover Theological Seminary in Andover, Massachusetts, and it was in Andover that he would meet his future bride, Martha Barrows, daughter of an Andover professor.

Edward Hitchcock, Jr., and his wife, Mary, now lived in Easthampton, just a few miles from Amherst, with their three children. Edward, Jr., had been teaching at Williston Seminary for nearly a decade. His teaching duties were, to use his own word, "legion." They included Latin, chemistry, anatomy, physiology, botany, meteorology, mineralogy, Milton, public speaking, spelling, reading, and bookkeeping. But anatomy and physiology were his first loves, and he lamented the lack of a good textbook on the subject. Sometime in 1857 or 1858, he wrote to Jeffries Wyman, the Harvard anatomist, urging him to fill the gap by authoring a text in anatomy and physiology. Wyman replied that he could not possibly take on the task due to other obligations. Edward, Jr., decided to undertake the project himself, enlisting his father to contribute a brief introduction. Father and son were listed as coauthors when the book came into print in late 1859, published by Ivison, Phinney, and Company of New York.

Elementary Anatomy and Physiology surveys the major systems of the human body—skeleton, viscera, heart, lungs, blood, nerves, sense organs—although the terms employed are those of another era: osteology, myology, splanchnology, ichorology, etc. After describing each system in the human body, the authors compare the system's structure and function in other animals. The text is enhanced by hundreds of anatomical drawings. One feature of the book that sets it apart from others of its day is the numerous drawings of cells and tissues as seen through a microscope (see Figure 65). Notably absent from the more than 400 pages of *Elementary Anatomy and Physiology* is any mention of reproduction or excretion. Edward Hitchcock, Jr., had studied medicine at Harvard Medical School, and was surely well acquainted with these subjects, but perhaps deemed them inappropriate for young students in the Victorian Era.

Elementary Anatomy and Physiology was widely and enthusiastically reviewed in newspapers and journals over the next year. It was particularly well received by journals of education of its day, gleaning such compliments as "Of great merit," "…an excellent work," "the best book for schools on the subject we have seen." One reviewer, however, was not so enthusiastic, the redoubtable Louis Agassiz of Harvard.

Louis Agassiz and Edward Hitchcock, Sr., shared many interests and views regarding geology, paleontology, and anatomy. As to temperament, on the other hand, they could not have been more dissimilar. Agassiz was famously brash, abrasive, sometimes abusive of those who disagreed with him or displeased him. He was an admitted glutton, an imbiber, and an outspoken racist and anti-abolitionist. While he claimed to be a Christian, some would argue that his faith was not apparent in his demeanor, behavior, or opinions.

Agassiz's review of *Elementary Anatomy and Physiology* appeared anonymously in the *Boston Evening Courier* on March 31, 1860. He could not find any merit in the work whatsoever and proceeded to dismember it, chapter by chapter, page by page, pointing out what he regarded as outright errors aplenty: "…in the sections devoted to Comparative Anatomy, amounting to about one hundred and eight pages, there are at least one hundred and thirteen untrue statements, or more than one blunder to a page!" He mocked the authors' style: "…everywhere do we find, even that which is correct, presented in such a raw, dry way…that it will be utterly impossible for any one…to understand what so many, or so few, words mean."

At the time, Edward, Jr., was naturally upset by the review. But in his

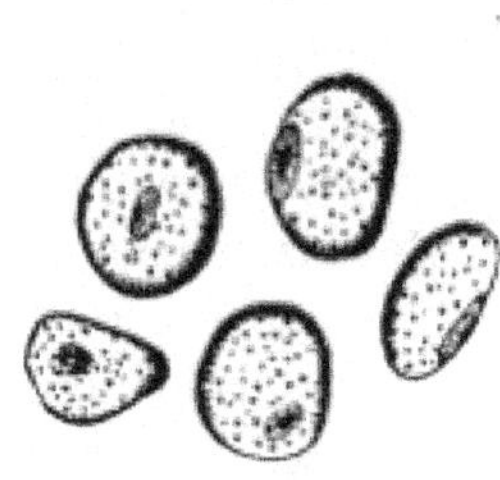

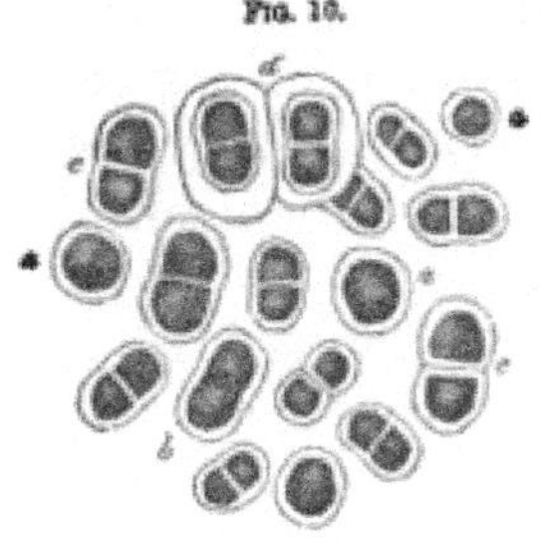

Figure 65. Illustrations from *Elementary Anatomy and Physiology* drawn through the microscope

memoirs written late in life, he seemed to have made his peace on the matter. He suspected that Agassiz's friend and colleague, Jeffries Wyman, was the instigator of the harsh review; that Wyman may have been annoyed to find that the young upstart from Easthampton had published such a volume instead of him, and had then prevailed on his friend, Louis Agassiz, known for his vituperative prose, to exact his pound of flesh. There was at least one silver lining to this gray cloud, reasoned Edward, Jr., that the scathing review had appeared in an "insignificant Boston paper." The harshness of the review might have been a setback to some. Fortunately, the younger Hitchcock was more resilient than his father. "...[I]t was a mighty good experience for me to write the book," recalled the younger Hitchcock late in life, "But it gave me humbling views of my ability at bookmaking."

To read the accounts of that time in the life of Edward Hitchcock—the mountain excursions, winter lecture tours, scientific meetings, battles with enemies living and dead—one might assume that his health had improved on retiring from the presidency. But his notes tell a different story. After his aborted efforts on the Vermont geological survey in May 1857, he wrote, "...the present state of my health reads to me an impressive lecture on my frailty and liability to be suddenly removed." The following winter he was no better, complaining of irregularities in his heart: "I have been strikingly taught of late that my poor physical system has nearly reached the end of its conflict with disease and I must soon give way." Less than a year later he noted, "I cannot but feel that the probability is faint of my seeing another year and I long to be prepared to go."

Winters were always the hardest on his constitution. In January 1859, his health suddenly deteriorated:

> It is the severest sickness I have ever passed through and I supposed it my last. And even now though my friends regard me as getting well my disease appears to have left my lungs and throat in such a state that I regard it as doubtful whether my worn out powers can ever bring me back to anything like health... The type of the disease was essentially that of which my father died and from which I have often suffered and I may add which probably at last will take me out of the world.

His condition was serious enough to be reported briefly in a Boston newspaper: "Ex-President Hitchcock, of Amherst College, is seriously ill with congestion of the lungs, pneumonia, and inflammation of the kidneys." He was confined to bed for six weeks and utterly dependent on his family. And yet toward the end of his confinement he was able to enjoy his favorite winter pastime, a bracing ride on horseback. It was fundamental to Hitchcock's circular reasoning on health that he attributed his illnesses to overactivity while prescribing physical activity as the best antidote.

Hitchcock was not one to let poor health prevent him from working, from meeting his obligations. It was a point of pride for him. Despite successive setbacks, he pressed on with his work. Sickness, fears of decline and death, far from being inhibitors, were actually his strongest motivators:

> I must say that had I neglected to work in past times whenever I felt unable I should not have done half of what I have. Not one in ten of those in vigorous health who have ridiculed my dyspeptic fears and weakness would have stood at their posts as I have done if half my load of infirmities had been laid upon them.

Throughout that and many other crises late in life, Edward's family ministered to his needs. At one point he wrote, "I have been taken care of entirely night and day by my own wife and children and it may be I owe my life to their watchful care." Orra's health must have been reasonably good in those years. She seldom made mention of her own health in her letters to distant family members and seemed to be mostly occupied with caring for those at home. While she was visiting friends in Rockport, Massachusetts, in summer 1856, Edward wrote her of his concerns for her health and his hope that she might gain some benefit from being at the shore. Three years later Edward made brief mention of Orra's health in a letter to Edward, Jr., writing, "Ma is comfortable though I feel anxious about her. It is all a result of that old injury," likely a reference to her fall four years earlier.

By April 1859, Edward had recovered enough of his former vigor that he was able to deliver the sermon in the college chapel—the subject was sickness. He expounded at length on the matter of "fitting up the sick room," including furnishings, lighting, music, paintings, statuary, even perhaps "…the plate of fruit, or other dainty, which some kind neighbors had sent him." At one point in his sermon he brought up the need of a proper infirmary for an institution such as Amherst. Here he addressed the college itself with a bit of uncharacteristic histrionics:

> Oh Amherst, I have somewhat against thee–Thou canst, indeed, show the stranger thy unrivalled scenery, thy convenient dormitories thy fine library rooms—thy superb Laboratory–thy philosophical and natural history Cabinets, loaded with apparatus and specimens; and with just pride do you point out these treasures—the fruit of so much toil and sacrifice. But where among them all can you point to the room provided for the sick and suffering indigent student, whom you have, with Christian liberality, invited hither? Till such an edifice can be shown you ought to blush and be ashamed of all your treasures.

Within a year of that plea, Amherst instituted one of the first college student health programs in the nation.

By spring of that year, however, Hitchcock had recovered some of his vigor, at least to judge by his activities. Much of his energies were devoted to the report on the Vermont geological survey and to revisions of several articles he was preparing. In July he traveled to the White Mountains of New Hampshire. Then, in August he attended the AAAS meeting being held just twenty miles away in Springfield.

In 1859 the second edition of *Religion of Geology* went to press. It was much like the first edition except for two important differences. In the preface to the new edition, dated March 1, 1859, Hitchcock wrote of the previous edition,

> The numerous notices of the "Religion of Geology," which have appeared in the periodicals of different grades, have been, for the most part, commendatory; while its steady sale from year to year, shows that the subjects have a deep hold upon the community. With some writers, however, the work has met with harsher and severer treatment.

That atheists and skeptics like the infamous Vindex showered book and author alike with the strongest, most virulent language came as no surprise to Hitchcock—he never expected to win them over. But he may not have anticipated the adverse reaction from some believers.

One of Hitchcock's harshest critics among Christians was Reverend Henry W. Soltau, an English minister and biblical scholar. In a long, rambling letter, Reverend Soltau had warned him that his writing made him "…an antagonist of God," adding, "I never before read a word which so presumptuously calls His word into question, or treats it with such contempt." Hitchcock seemed to welcome this criticism and used it in the preface of the new edition:

> Now, which of these writers shall I believe? The Infidel raves furiously, because I have endeavored to make Geology sustain and illustrate revelation; but my Christian friend declares my book to be thoroughly infidel. One of the parties must surely be mistaken in its bearing. Till they can settle that question, I think I may rest quietly. Like an acid and an alkali in chemistry, the two attacks neutralize each other, and leave me unharmed.

We might imagine a triangle of opinion regarding *The Religion of Geology,* with each apex occupied by an adversary, while in the middle of that triangle, stands Edward Hitchcock. Reverend Soltau would have Christians reject any science, or scientist, that contradicted Holy Scripture, Reverend Stuart would allow them to coexist peacefully, each in its own realm, Vindex would of course reject all religion as hogwash.

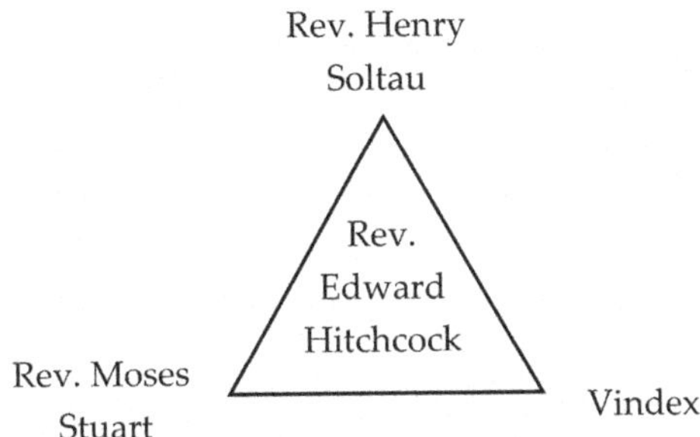

Also new to the second edition was a final chapter entitled "Synoptical View of the Bearings of Geology Upon Religion" which he described as "a brief view of the whole subject as it now lies in my mind." In that lecture he argued that false notions perpetrated largely by Christians suggested that science, particularly geology, was hostile to religion. And those false notions, he observed, "continue more or less to float in the public mind."

But soon the "public mind" would be otherwise engaged. Eight months after the release of the second edition of *Religion of Geology*, another book was published that took all the oxygen out of the discussion, that almost overnight succeeded in capturing the attention of scientists, clergy, and the public. It was a revolutionary treatise on the subject of transmutation entitled *Origin of Species* by Charles Darwin.

Figure 66. Interior of the Appleton Cabinet

By the mid-1850s the American Association for the Advancement of Science had grown a good deal from its modest beginnings in Philadelphia in 1840. It boasted nearly 700 members in 1855, including its first female members. Annual meetings took place for a week each year in various American cities attended by scientists from across the nation and abroad. They included lectures, forums, field trips, and social events.

Edward Hitchcock had been a regular participant at nearly every meeting of the AAAS and its predecessor, the Association of American Geologists, since its founding in 1840, a pattern he continued for several years following his retirement from the presidency. He traveled to Providence for the August 1855 meeting where he delivered six papers; to Albany for the August 1856 meeting where he delivered two papers; to Montreal in August 1857; to Baltimore in spring 1858 where he delivered two papers; and to Springfield, Massachusetts, in August 1859 where he delivered four papers.

The Springfield meeting of the AAAS in 1859 proved to be a most important occasion both for Edward Hitchcock and for Amherst College. The collections of the college—zoological, mineralogical, archeological, botanical, and ichnological—had grown by leaps and bounds in recent years. In *Reminiscences* Hitchcock enumerated those collections most precisely: 14,425 rocks and fossils, 14,188 animals, 20,000 fossil footmarks, 4500 plants, plus nearly 30,000 more in the "Shepard Cabinet," a collection promised to the college by Professor Charles U. Shepard.

It had all begun with the modest collections of Hitchcock himself and the Natural History Society that were donated to the college in the 1820s. Those had been augmented substantially by subsequent donations from Professors Fiske, Hovey, Shepard, Adams, and others, as well as many graduates. Particularly important were contributions that came in from around the world thanks to the generosity of many graduates, later missionaries in all quarters of the globe. Among those was Story Hebard (AC 1828) who assisted with Hitchcock's first geological survey in 1830. A few years later as a missionary in Syria, he had sent many cases of rocks and fossils to Hitchcock. Unfortunately, he passed away shortly thereafter. Naturally, the completion of the Woods Cabinet in 1847 had drawn ever more attention to those collections, and now with the opening of the Appleton Cabinet and the installation of the ichnological, zoological, and Nineveh collections, interest was very high.

Hitchcock was anxious to show off those collections to a wider audience and the August 1859 meeting of the AAAS in Springfield afforded just such an opportunity. On Saturday, August 6, after three days of lectures, the 275 participants were invited to travel by rail to Amherst for the afternoon. According to one newspaper account, some 500 persons including many citizens of Springfield were aboard the seven rail cars as they rolled out of the station for the ninety-minute journey. "Upon reaching Amherst, the party found the students of the college at the depot, who waked the echoes of Pelham across the valley with their cheers of welcome." A long banner was then unfurled, inscribed "Honor to Science." Escorted by the students and entertained by a band from Montague, the party proceeded up the hill to the campus where they visited the cabinets, the observatory, and the library.

Outside the Woods Cabinet stood casts of fossil trees from the Connecticut sandstone. Inside they found thousands of,

> ...specimens of rocks with their characteristic fossils from Europe, from Asia—from Palestine, Syria, Armenia, Persia, India, mainly contributed by the sons of Amherst—missionaries who, though far away in foreign lands, remember their fostering mother with filial regard...

Also to be seen were specimens from across America including 3200 from Massachusetts, every one of which likely had been collected by Hitchcock himself during his first geological survey nearly thirty years earlier. In the Nineveh Gallery they observed magnificent artifacts of ancient Assyria, "the eagle-headed, filleted, and horded divinities, with the sacred tree, arranged just as the deities 4000 years ago in the palace of Sardanapolus." There also were displayed "bricks from Babylon stamped with cuneiform letters, the oldest printing in the world..."

In the lower room of Appleton Cabinet the guests viewed the ichnological exhibit, those extraordinary tracks of beasts on great sandstone slabs. "It is the most wonderful room in the world," wrote the reporter. "More wonderful these than relics relating to human history; those are the records of men; these are God's records. Science stood there reading them—and learning this word alone: Progress!"

In the upper room they saw the zoological collections, thousands of creatures from huge mammals to tiny insects: "...things creeping, crawling, winding, wiggling, hopping, snapping, flying, which had performed their part in life, whatever that may have been, but which now, though dead, are teachers—demonstrators of science." And there were shellfish by the thousands, with their "...limestone houses which crabs, clams, and oysters secreted from the sea, little by little, to build houses upon their own backs...their moveable palaces, more gorgeous than the finest frescoe in St. Mark's in Venice, or St. Peter's at Rome." If the scientists and other visitors that day were only half as moved and impressed as that reporter, Edward Hitchcock must surely have been pleased.

At five o'clock the guests assembled in Williston Hall where they feasted on a "generous collation" provided by the ladies of the college, beneath another banner, *"Interpretes naturae salvete,"* Interpreters of Science, Hail! Princeton professor Stephen Alexander, then President of the Association, gave a few words of thanks, followed by comments by President Stearns and Professor Hitchcock.

Well into evening the train departed from the depot amidst still more fanfare. Shortly after the event Hitchcock recorded his thoughts:

> The meeting of the American Association of Science at Springfield which I was the means of bringing there passed off very successfully: and so did the excursion to Amherst which I also planned and had to take a leading part in accomplishing. We were indebted mainly to a kind Providence in providing a most beautiful day and all seemed so gratified that I cannot doubt the College was essentially promoted. The highest authorities now declare that our collections in natural history are superior to those of any College in the land. How wonderful that providence should have so signally prospered the College early in its history in this respect!

With the AAAS meeting behind him, his health immediately deteriorated. "My efforts however in attending the Scientific Association at Springfield and our Commencement completely broke me down and I have been obliged ever since to remain at home with hoarseness and cough and great emaciation."

By fall he had resumed his normal activities, teaching, preaching, and leading the senior class excursion to Mt. Nutonk in Greenfield. In December he and Orra spent several days in Newburyport. On the last day of the year, his mood seemed to be running the gamut within a single paragraph:

> The hours of another year are almost run out: and yet how wonderful! I am still spared and since the weather became steadily cold I think I have felt even better than for some months past... In looking back upon the year it pains me to see so much evidence in my experience that I have not improved as I ought the severe sickness of last winter.

Orra White Hitchcock, 1860

25 Troublous Times

"She has been teaching you how to live; now she has taught you also how to die."

Newport, Rhode Island, August 2, 1860

Edward Hitchcock and Charles H. Hitchcock were among the 135 members of the American Association for the Advancement of Science attending the fourteenth annual meeting in Newport. Edward was one of the speakers at the first afternoon session. His subject was the fossil footmarks.

Ichnology, he began, is a young science. Only sixty years have passed since the first footmarks were excavated by quarrymen. But thanks to the vigorous investigations of many, we know a great deal about their origin. No one today doubts that these extraordinary markings in stone are anything other than the tracks of ancient animals. But as to the exact nature of those creatures there is a good deal of debate to this day.

At this point he brought up the question of the bird-like nature of many of the tracks. "I acknowledge the position that some eminent naturalists have taken lately that none of the tracks in the Connecticut valley were made by birds. It may be so; and no one familiar with the difficulties of ichnology should by any means be very dogmatic in, or tenacious of, his opinions about foot-marks. Yet no wise man will hastily abandon an opinion which has been sustained by such strong arguments." As he spoke, his son Charles who was seated beside him passed through the audience some of his father's footmark specimens. They were among the most striking artifacts from Edward's collection and they elicited exclamations of amazement from his audience.

The professor spoke for over an hour and eventually his frailty and the lateness of the hour began to show their effects—his voice became softer, his pace slower. Finally he concluded his presentation. "Are there any questions?" he asked.

A rotund gentleman standing at the rear spoke up, smiling as he addressed the speaker. The man was Louis Agassiz. "I have spoken before of my concerns regarding the foot tracks, but I wish to reiterate them at this time. It is not in my view sufficient to draw inferences from modern-day animals. What is needed is to consider other animals known to have existed at the same time as those that formed the tracks. Until that method is applied, Professor, I cannot concur with your conclusions."

Professor Hitchcock nodded and acknowledged Agassiz's comments. At that point Professor William B. Rogers of Boston spoke up. "I heartily agree with Professor Agassiz that it would be more informative to examine the footmarks as they relate to other animals of that era. But therein lies a problem, as there is little agreement as to the age of these tracks. Until we have that information, I believe the insights offered by Professor Hitchcock are the best we have available."

The following morning Charles Hitchcock presented a paper on coal in which he expressed the view that coal deposits across the nation were formed at the same time as evidenced by the fossils they contained. Again Agassiz rose to voice his disagreement. "I would point out to the young man that many coal beds known to be of the same age exhibit quite different fossils. There is in my opinion no necessary correspondence between fossil content and age." Agassiz drew laughter from the audience when he added: "Some of us, young man, may be as old as fossils, but age has its benefits. We have learned to exercise caution in drawing inferences from them."

That afternoon Edward Hitchcock delivered another talk, this one on some of the rocks he and Charles had examined during the Vermont geological survey. Once again Agassiz was on his feet, criticizing some of Professor Hitchcock's assertions as wild and reckless. "Hypotheses in science," he insisted, "...must be formulated with as much precision and pursued with as much care as in mathematics." He then turned to the audience to deliver a stark warning.

"Gentlemen, making such assertions casually and without foundation is dangerous and harmful to our discipline. It leads to wild theories such as those of spontaneous generation, Darwinism, and the like, which now are the disgrace of science."

Again Edward Hitchcock declined to respond.

On the long train ride from Newport to Amherst, Edward and Charles sat in silence, gazing out on the green, rolling landscape that rushed past. Finally Charles spoke:

"I don't like that Professor Agassiz, Father, I don't like him at all."

"He is a brilliant man, Son, a brilliant man. And his views carry a good deal of weight with many."

"Perhaps, but he strikes me as a bit of a grandstander. Do you know what I mean? He takes pleasure in finding fault with others, right or wrong. I can't help but wonder if he has it in for us."

To which his father replied, "Perhaps he does, Charles, perhaps he does."

For Edward Hitchcock the importance of the college's cabinets went well beyond their scientific value. Studying those artifacts, he often pointed out, was the best possible means of showing young men the beauty and majesty of God's creation—they taught piety just as surely as philosophy. But in one of his notes of January 1860, an ominous paragraph appears on the subject of the religious principles of the institution:

> Till within a year or two the thought has scarcely crossed my mind that the funding of Amherst College and its Cabinet would ever be perverted to the support of religious error. But some occurrences within the past year have shown me how easily such an event could be brought about if God should withdraw his guidance and protection and though while the present men continue [as] officers and Trustees of the College such an event would be hardly possible yet others will succeed them perhaps of different views through whose connivance the Institution might pass into the hands of such men as it was founded to counteract and defeat any Unitarians, Universalists and Infidels...Now my feelings recoil from the idea of having the fruits of my labours and donations ever go to the support of such religious or antireligious notions...

Nowhere in Hitchcock's surviving papers or his published works is there any further mention of the source of his fears. But one possibility is William J. Walker. Walker was a Boston physician who had in mid-career redirected his energies to business with great success. Late in life he made large bequests to several Massachusetts institutions including Amherst College. But Walker was an eccentric with a reputation for outlandish behavior—it may or may not be relevant that he was also a friend of Jeffries Wyman and Louis Agassiz. Furthermore, Walker was known to attach "strings" to his philanthropy. When he endowed a professorship in mathematics and astronomy at Amherst in 1861, for example, he proceeded to give advice to the college on what he regarded as the best instructional methods for those subjects.

President Stearns went to great lengths to appease the meteoric philanthropist. Once in 1861 he visited Walker in his Boston office—it proved to be a most unusual meeting, as recounted by Stanley King:

> The doctor received him in his well-furnished study in his Boston home; but the doctor was completely without clothes except for a pair of slippers. The doctor was practicing nudism at home for his health. President Stearns was so taken aback that he almost forgot what he had come to talk with the doctor about. Fortunately, he recovered himself and went on with the conversation without comment on the unconventionality of his rich host. Later in their acquaintance Stearns tried to raise the question of the doctor's religious views, which were reported to be unorthodox, only to be cut off with the statement by the doctor, "I am an Ishmaelite."

We can well imagine Edward Hitchcock's discomfort—to put it mildly—with a man such as Walker and the influence he might have on the future of the college. Whether the "antireligious notions" he referred to were those of William J. Walker may never be known. But whatever their source, they unsettled Hitchcock profoundly. He even considered changing his will.

Another mystery from that same period may be related to Hitchcock's concerns, a fifty-page gap in his notes dating from April 1860, to April 1862. Perhaps those pages were simply lost, perhaps they were removed by Hitchcock himself. "I am almost inclined to erase those pages," he wrote a year earlier after complaining about the officers and students of the college. Whether the fifty missing pages included further comments on the specter of "antireligion" at Amherst College remains a mystery.

One matter weighing heavily on Edward Hitchcock that winter was his textbook, *Elementary Geology,* his most successful published work. Since 1840 it had gone through thirty editions. Most of those "editions" were merely new printings, but the book had undergone two major revisions, one in 1847, another in 1854. In 1860 the publisher, Ivison, Phinney and Company of New York, urged him to undertake yet another major revision. To complicate matters further, they asked him to collaborate on those revisions with another author, possibly David Ames Wells, a former student and friend of Louis Agassiz. Not surprisingly the arrangement did not work out. But a few months later those revisions were accomplished with a far more congenial collaborator, as mentioned in his notes:

> I have to record with gratitude the completion of another literary labour viz. the rewriting of my Elementary Geology for the 31st edition. It has cost me nearly as much labour as its first preparation although I have been very greatly aided by my youngest son for whose sake indeed mainly I have laboured so hard to bring up the book to the present state of the science.

The title page bore the names of both authors, Edward Hitchcock and Charles H. Hitchcock, as well as the subtitle, *Elementary Geology: A New Edition, Remodeled, Mostly Rewritten, with Several New Chapters, and Brought Up to the Present State of the Science, for Use in Schools, Families, and by Individuals.* Edward was particularly pleased with his revisions of the section entitled "Bearings of Geology Upon Religion." In the preface to the new edition, he informed his readers that this would likely be his last edition:

> In this revision I have associated with me my youngest son, who has borne a large share in the work...Should it happen, as most likely it will, that this is the last revision of the work I shall ever make, and he should survive me, I trust he will be found fully competent to keep the work up to the advancing state of the science, should the public call for its continued publication.

Perhaps at the urging of Charles, those formal headings–Proposition, Proofs, Inferences, etc.–had been removed in the new edition. A new chapter devoted to metamorphism had been added. Also omitted was the term "glacio-aqueous action," although it is clear that at least the senior author still clung to that hybrid concept of drift phenomena. But just a few years later, after the death of his father, Charles would be an enthusiastic convert to Agassiz's glacial theory and devote much of his subsequent career at Dartmouth to studying and elucidating the glacial geology of North America.

In August 1860 Edward and Charles H. Hitchcock attended the fourteenth meeting of the American Association for the Advancement of Science in Newport, Rhode Island. Both men read papers on their recent researches, Edward on the newest findings of his ichnological research, Charles on subjects related to the Vermont geological survey. Louis Agassiz was in attendance as well and according to newspaper accounts had a good deal to say, mostly critical, about several presentations including those of both Hitchcocks.

Figure 67. Reverend William A. Stearns (1810-1884), fourth president of Amherst College

On the final day of the meeting, the official announcement was made of the next meeting of the Association, to take place in Nashville, Tennessee, in August 1861. The meeting was never convened. That winter, Tennessee and ten other states seceded from the Union. In April 1861, Confederate troops attacked and seized Fort Sumter, South Carolina. The "War of the Rebellion" had begun.

The AAAS did not meet for the duration of the war. When finally the Association reconvened in Buffalo, New York, in 1866, Edward Hitchcock, one of the founders and most influential members of the organization, was not present. The Newport meeting in 1860 would be his last.

An interesting postscript to the early history of the AAAS may be found in a paper presented at the 1866 Buffalo meeting entitled "Scientific and Religious Character of Edward Hitchcock." It was offered by Almira Hart Lincoln Phelps, noted science educator and author. She wrote that he had spoken on her behalf at the Springfield meeting in 1859, advancing the opinion that "…a woman who had devoted the greater portion of a long life to the study of science…should be honored with an election as a member of this association." Almira Phelps was elected to the AAAS at that meeting, only the third woman to be so honored.

William Augustus Stearns had the good fortune to ascend to the Presidency of Amherst just as the college was entering a period of prosperity. But much to the new president's credit, enrollments continued to rise, donations flowed in, and a collegial atmosphere prevailed among administration, faculty, and students during his tenure.

While President Stearns lacked the aptitude for natural history of his predecessor, he was a willing promoter and participant in several of Hitchcock's mountain excursions during the early years of his presidency. In October 1855, both men embarked with the entire senior class on an excursion by carriage to Colrain, Massachusetts, a few miles west of Greenfield. There they were joined by the senior class of Williams College as well as a large group of local citizens, totaling more than 300 according to a newspaper account. At the summit of Walnut Hill, the highest in the area, a ceremony took place followed by the anointment of that peak as "Pocumtuck," the native name for the Deerfield River that coursed through the valley far below. Charles Hitchcock spoke on the geological history of the region. A melodramatic interlude included a mock confrontation between a "Yankee" and an "Indian sachem." President Stearns and Professor Hitchcock each then spoke, although according to the report the proceedings came to an abrupt halt when a storm arose. That evening at a celebratory gathering at the Shelburne Falls House, President Stearns offered a toast to his predecessor as "…the man who was consulted in the making of Connecticut river and who had left his tracks all along the valley." Similar festivities took place in 1856 on Mt. Kilburn in Bellows Falls, Vermont, in 1858 at the christening of Nonotuck in Holyoke, and in 1859 at the renaming of Nutonk in Greenfield, with Professor Hitchcock present at each.

In October 1860, yet another excursion was planned, this one to the summit of a mountain in Manchester, Vermont. Again the entire senior class participated, led by Charles Hitchcock. The elder Hitchcock traveled with the group most of the way, but for reasons of poor health was prevented from completing the trip. Charles and the students ascended Dorset Mountain, redubbing it "Eolus." In one of very few letters penned by Charles that have survived, he described the event to his brother:

> Our work in Vt naming Mt. Eolus was a complete success. The folks in East Dorset paid all the bills of the students and will use the name henceforth and a history of the town of Dorset is nearly ready to be struck off and Mrs. Fields sent orders to have the work stopped till the mountain had received a new name. He said they had been anxious for a new name for a long time. The students gave two concerts in Ludlow and Rutland much to the gratification of the people.

That may have been the last of the Amherst College mountain excursions for the man who began the tradition fifteen years earlier.

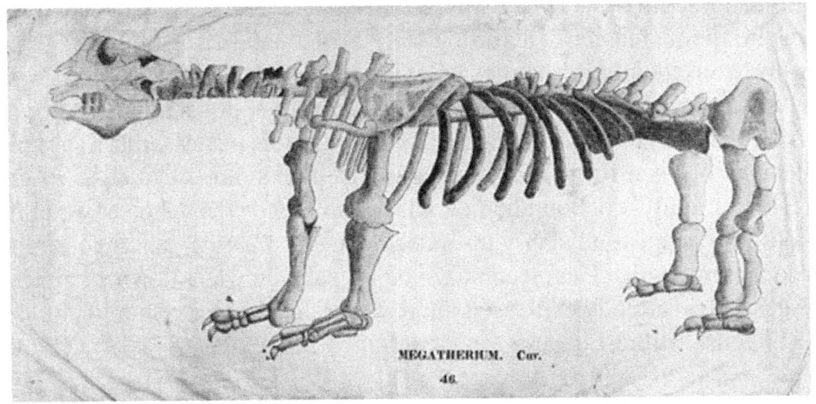

Figure 68. *Megatherium*, poster on canvas by Orra White Hitchcock

Figure 69.
Dr. Edward Hitchcock, Jr.
(1828-1911)

"We had a quiet and lonely Thanksgiving," wrote Orra to Edward, Jr., in London in early December 1860. "...[O]nly us four...Our thoughts were compelled to wander in various parts to gather the scattered members of our household." The four Hitchcocks at home would have included Orra, Edward, Mary, and Jane. As to the "scattered members," daughter Emily was in Cincinnati with the Storrs, probably assisting in the care of their little one; Charles may have been in Andover finishing the report on the Vermont geological survey, studying at the Seminary, or keeping company with Miss Barrows. Edward, Jr., had departed in early September on a European tour where he studied, wined, and dined with the likes of Sir Richard Owen, Sir Roderick Murchison, and Sir Charles and Lady Lyell. During his absence, his wife Mary and their three children stayed in New Haven with her family.

The American political situation was increasingly perilous. "Before this reaches you you will have doubtless learned that a Republican president has been elected," wrote Edward, Sr., to Edward, Jr., in mid-November, a reference to the election of Abraham Lincoln. "We shall now see whether the southern fire eaters will carry their threats of succession into execution." They did. Just six weeks later, a special convention of South Carolina representatives was held in Charleston and voted unanimously for secession, the first state to do so. Over the next two months, six more states would join South Carolina. Troops from both North and South were already on the move. War it appeared was inevitable.

Despite the increasingly alarming state of the nation's affairs that winter, most of the transatlantic exchanges between father and son had to do not with "war or rumors of war," nor with the sights of Europe, but with acquiring new artifacts for the cabinets of Amherst College. The letters of Edward, Jr., are filled with accounts of his efforts to obtain skeletons, tracks, bones, or casts of great creatures of antiquity. At Bonn he met with a mineral dealer who showed him a seven-foot-long sandstone slab with tracks of *Chirotherium*, an ancient reptile similar to the crocodile. The piece might be for sale, he was informed, although Louis Agassiz had already expressed interest in it. In Paris he visited with famed zoologist Henri Milne-Edwards and examined skeletons of a whale and a porpoise. In London he was shown a cast of the skull of *Megatherium*, a sloth the size of an elephant from the Pliocene, that Professor Owen believed could be sold to the college. Also on offer at the British Museum was the cast of a skeleton of *Glyptodon*, similar to the modern-day armadillo, but ten feet long. If all of that was not enough, Edward, Jr., also had information about the pending auction of the complete library of the late naturalist and geographer Alexander von Humboldt who had died just a year earlier in Berlin.

Figure 70.
Charles H. Hitchcock
(1836-1919)

So far as is known the only one of those treasures that Edward, Jr., was able to secure was the skull of *Megatherium*. But later in his stay in London, he was introduced to Ephraim Brown, Esq., who promised to donate to Amherst College the cast of a complete skeleton of *Megatherium* measuring 12' by 5' by 10'. To possess it would be a great accomplishment for Amherst, explained Edward, Jr. "...[I]t would be unique in America," he wrote his father, "for even Agassiz has not got one."

After the attack on Fort Sumter on April 12, 1861, life at Amherst College would never be quite the same. The day following the attack was the Sabbath, and Professor William S. Tyler recalled preaching the sermon in the college chapel on that very day:

> On that dark and portentous Sunday in April 1861...the writer of this history preached in the College Chapel on themes suited to the circumstances, and in a strain intended to inspire courage, heroism, and self-sacrificing devotion. And while the professor was preaching, or at least as soon as he had done, the students were already practising what he preached.

Seventy-eight Amherst College students enlisted, as did two faculty members, two college officers, and 169 graduates. Two of those students died in service to the nation during the "War of the Rebellion." As to the townsmen of Amherst, nearly 300 served in that war as well; fifty-seven died, forty-nine were wounded, nine captured and imprisoned.

On May 25, 1861, Edward, Jr., perhaps stirred by the emotions of the times, wrote an extraordinary letter to his father, one filled with warmth and reflection: "My Dear father, So our birthdays by a kind Providence have once more come around. I have just reached the average limit of human life (33) while you have more than doubled it (68 I believe). I wonder if I ever shall live as long as you have?"

Near the end of his letter, Edward, Jr., noted an important date that was approaching and asked his father if there were any plans for a celebration. The date was May 31, 1861, his parents' fortieth wedding anniversary. Whether the family gathered for the event, or Edward and Orra observed it alone, is not in the record.

Just a few weeks after Edward, Jr., penned that letter to his father, circumstances at Amherst College took a turn in his favor. The newly created position of Professor of Hygiene and Physical Education was again vacant, the trustees had begun a search to fill the vacancy permanently, and Edward Hitchcock, Jr., was a candidate. He had some obvious qualifications, a medical degree, nearly a decade of teaching experience at Williston, and a textbook on anatomy and physiology that had been well received in some, if not all, quarters.

But his letters to his father that summer suggest that Edward, Jr., had doubts about his own abilities. Furthermore, he had been around Amherst College from boyhood and had not always been well-behaved. He worried now that some of those youthful transgressions might weigh heavily on him as a faculty member: "…the thought of being a public man in the same place where I was so long and did all my wicked tricks is not at all pleasant." In spite of his own doubts, at the start of the 1860-1861 academic year, the names of two Hitchcocks could be found in the list of faculty:

> Edward Hitchcock, D.D., LL D., Professor of Natural Theology and of Geology
>
> Edward Hitchcock, Jr., A.M., M.D., Professor of Hygiene and Physical Education

In November 1861, with his health as fragile as ever, Edward, Sr., did what he always did in times of great frailty, he took on an ambitious new project, a history of Amherst College. By the following spring he had made a good deal of progress:

> It is certainly marvelous that during the last six months I have done so much in carrying out the plan suggested in my last entry as to a history of the College. I have actually written the book of some hundred pages in nine Sections although the two last are not completed which I entitled Reminiscences of Amherst College. Excepting College duties I have had little else to occupy my attention and Providence is giving me strength to write as fast as I ever did in my life. I

> would be glad even to print this work before I die. But in these troublous times no publisher can be found who dares run the risk of bringing out such a work and I shall have to leave it for posterity in manuscript.

The work was a big undertaking for the aging Hitchcock, and it occupied nearly all his time for more than a year.

On May 23, 1862, Edward observed a special occasion: "Another birthday has come and gone. Yesterday I was sixty nine years old. How unbelieving I should have been had any prophet thirty years ago or even ten years ago told me that I should enter upon my seventieth year." There were, of course, complaints both physical and spiritual: "…[M]y bodily discomforts and even distress are so great and the cloud over my spirits is so thick that I seem sunk into a state of almost utter hopelessness as to this world." This state of despair seemed to have been aggravated by the loss of his favorite form of leisure: "At this time too I am sadly afflicted by the failure of a favorite horse which I have used almost daily under saddle or in taking my family to ride. I was not aware how dependent I have been upon horseback exercise." He needed something more to motivate him it seems: "But to obtain a new force now is nearly impossible on a variety of accounts and I know not which way to turn."

Despite Edward's discouragement, he and Orra now enjoyed the blessings of a large extended family that included six grandchildren, from Edward Hitchcock III, now eight, down to little Katherine Storrs, barely two months. In that same entry he reported that son Charles had "…again plunged into the wilds of Maine." Charles must not have plunged too deeply into those wilds, for just a few weeks later this marriage announcement appeared in a Boston newspaper: "At Andover, 19th inst., by Prof. E. P. Barrows, of Andover Theological Seminary, assisted by Rev. Edward Hitchcock, D. D. of Amherst College, Mr. Charles H. Hitchcock, Geologist of the State of Maine, to Miss Martha B. Barrows, daughter of the officiating clergyman."

By October 1862, Hitchcock was convinced that the end was near:

> The long and desperate struggle between nature and disease is almost over. My complaints have reached such a constancy and intensity of suffering that they cannot be endured much longer. Nor does anything which I do or my physician can do afford anything more than a slight temporarily relief...My days with the exception of the hours in which sleep produces an oblivion of pain are little else than prolonged distress.

He offered a range of diagnoses in his notes: chronic bronchitis, dyspepsia, inflammation of the entire alimentary canal, the larynx, the trachea, the bronchial tubes. And yet, he admitted, his brain was holding out remarkably well. That term he was occupied with daily lectures and recitations in geology, although he was too weak to get to class on his own and had to rely on his horse to get him up College Hill. He also completed a descriptive catalog of the fossil

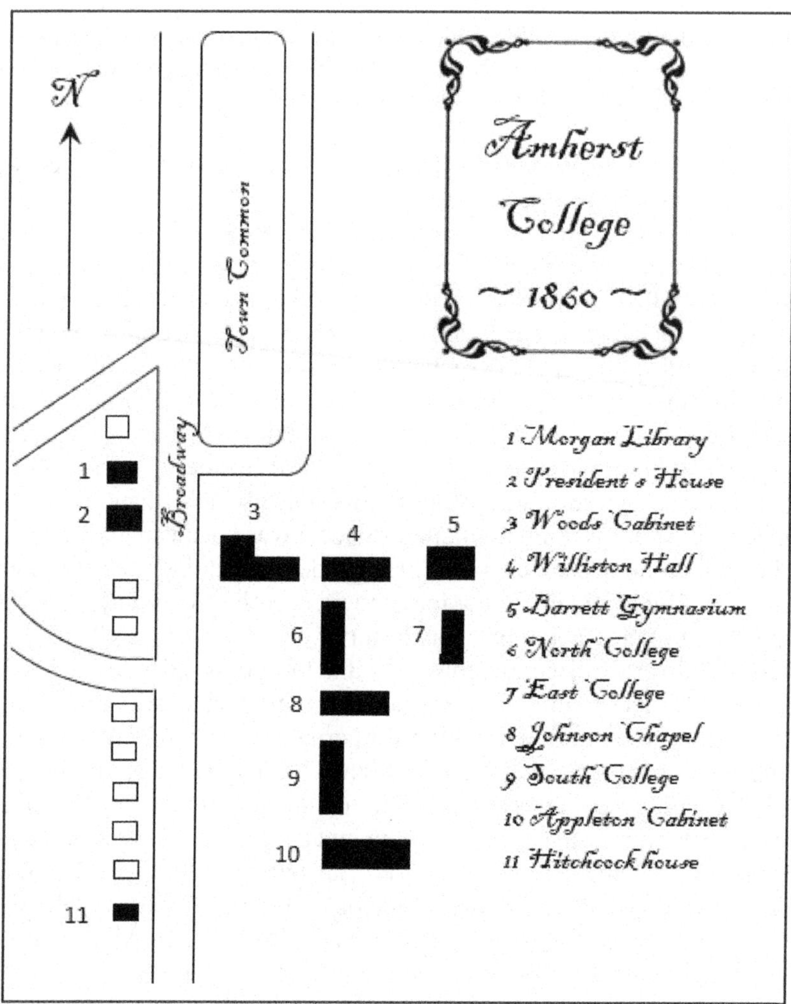

Figure 71. Amherst College in 1860

footmarks and prepared the last of his articles for *Bibliotheca Sacra* that would appear in an 1863 issue. "All these subjects are intensely interesting to me," he recorded in October "and therefore I can pursue them even when suffering severe pain and I think it better for me to make such mental efforts (moderately) than to have the whole time to think of my own suffering and prospects." On the last day of the year he also reported that he had completed *Reminiscences*.

That winter was long and cold in Amherst. By late February Edward's health had deteriorated. Weather provided some convenient analogies for his health:

> The vital monitor still continues to sink lower and lower although it has long seemed as if zero had been reached. My pains and weakness are much greater and the difficulty of outdoor exercise keeps me in the house most of the time. I have never known weather so unfavorable to going abroad as this winter...Would that as life's thermometer is sinking I could see faith's barometer rising as an indication of fair weather. But the index still points far too much to the unsettled and even stormy quarter.

Then in April when winter's worst would normally be done, Orra took sick. "I have lately also had a heavy addition to my trials in the severe sickness of my wife with pneumonia," wrote Edward on April 5, 1863. Pneumonia, he added, was a family scourge.

> My wife's father and mother died of it and so did my father and our first child nearly two years old and four years ago it brought me to the borders of the grave nor from its efforts have I ever recovered. Physicians at the time said I would not live. But God thought otherwise and should my wife recover it will be God's work.

Orra's illness reportedly resulted from going out one wintry evening to attend a religious meeting. "She has been brought very low and for some days I had nearly given up all hope and so had the physician. But the Great Physician now allows us to have some hope that she may recover."

Orra did recover, for a time, but in May she relapsed, this time with consumption. She was gravely ill and in those days there was little to do but pray. On Thursday, May 26, 1863, Edward and all five children were present to say their goodbyes. A few days later in his notes, written in another hand, perhaps of one of his daughters, Edward recorded his thoughts:

> God has spared me to make one more entry in this journal by an amanuensis. The most unexpected and perhaps the most important of all which it contains is the death of my beloved wife who left us Thursday, 26th at 6 o'clock P.M. and so quietly and without suffering did she pass away that it made death rather attractive than repulsive to us all. O, if we could only go as she did, who would not be willing to make the exchange of worlds.

Professor William S. Tyler delivered a touching eulogy to Orra White Hitchcock two days later. He had known Orra and Edward since he first came to Amherst College as a student in 1829. Following his graduation he had served for several years as a tutor during which time he boarded in the Hitchcock household. Tyler was therefore able to speak with equal familiarity of both wife and husband.

Orra was a woman of intellect, of artistic ability, of acute religious sensibilities, said Tyler, a devoted wife, mother, friend, and Christian. Perhaps most important of all for her family was her sense of balance in life.

> She was blessed…with a tranquil temperament, and a calm and even temper. I never saw her,—I doubt if any one ever did,—when the equilibrium of her faculties was disturbed or the evenness of her temper ruffled. Those who knew her most intimately, have often remarked that they never knew such repose and quietness united with so much energy and efficiency.

Without that trait, Tyler suggested, her husband would never have been able to achieve as he had. As to Edward, Tyler added,

> He calculated confidently on her presence to soothe and support him in his own dying hour. But…was it not like her, when her eye grew dim, and her hand feeble, so that she could no longer do for you as she was wont in the affairs of this life, to go home before you, and prepare a way and a place for your speedy coming. She has been teaching you how to live; now she has taught you also how to die.

Figure 72. Reverend William S. Tyler (1810-1897)

Edward Hitchcock, 1863

26 Reminiscences

"I still linger on the shores of time."

Amherst, Early February 1864

Mary and Jane Hitchcock stood in the cold morning air at the depot awaiting the arrival of the train from Springfield. Around them stood tradesmen, railroad workers, and the familiar faces of a few friends and neighbors from Amherst. A round-faced woman in a heavy coat approached them smiling, a thick woven shawl wrapped about her for extra warmth.

"Good morning Mary, Jane."

"Mrs. Adams, how are you?" replied Mary.

"We are all well, thanks be. All except our youngest who has the croup. But he is mending, I am happy to say." Then her voice lowered and she spoke softly: "And you? How is your father? We have been very worried."

"He carries on, ma'am–no better, but no worse. He is so very frail, however. Our sister Kate and her family are expected on the Springfield cars."

"All the way from Cincinnati—oh, my goodness, what a journey. And they have two little ones now as well."

"It will be just Kate and Mr. Storrs," answered Jane. "The journey would have been be too difficult for the children at their age—in winter." She paused. "We were so looking forward to seeing Charlie and little Katharine."

Just then the Springfield train rolled into the station and shuddered to a halt. Soon Kate and Henry Storrs emerged, and all stood on the platform exchanging greetings. With Henry's help John Deignan, handyman to the Hitchcocks, loaded the Storrs's luggage into the carriage as the three sisters climbed aboard.

"How is Father?" asked Kate of her sisters. "Your last letter had us very worried. Is he any stronger?"

"He is very weak, Kate," replied Mary. "He hardly takes any nourishment—he says it will only disagree with him. And he does get confused at times. One moment he will be quite alert, and a few moments later he will ask where he is, or what day it is. Emily absolutely dotes on him—she will be so happy to see you both. And we shall all want to hear about the children."

"And Ed and Charlie—how are they?" inquired Kate.

"They are both fine. And they have been such a help of late. They were bringing in wood when we left."

Finally the carriage passed over College Hill and made the descent toward the Hitchcock home. As they approached they saw some commotion in the yard and heard laughter.

"What in the daylights are those two brothers of ours up to?"

It was Edward, Jr., and Charles, each holding the arm of one of the wicker chairs from the parlor, swinging it about and laughing. In the chair was what appeared to be a pile of coverlets and quilts. As the carriage drew to a halt at the front of the house and the three sisters stepped out onto the snow, a pale face looked out from beneath the coverlets, smiling. It was their father.

The men set the chair down in the snow and Kate knelt in front of it. "Dearest Father, how good it is to see you," she said, her voice cracking with emotion.

"Hello, Catherine my dear," he replied. "Welcome home. And Mr. Storrs, how very good of you both to come."

Then Kate looked up into the smiling faces of her brothers. "Ed, Charlie, what in heaven's name were you two thinking, taking him out into the cold?"

"It was his wish, Katie," replied Edward, Jr. "He insisted—and he would not be denied."

Just then her father spoke up. "Do not be angry with your brothers. I have been in the bed of sickness for an eternity, and I wanted nothing so much as to be outside, to take in some fresh air, to gaze upon God's creation once more." He laughed and everyone joined him until he added, "I only wish your mother could be here to share it with us all."

Once in March of 1840 when his spirits were particularly low, Edward Hitchcock contemplated the possibility of losing his wife: "Oh this is almost the only earthly trial which I cannot think of with calmness! The idea unmans me—yet I can bless God for the glorious hope we cherish of meeting in heaven!"

Now his beloved Orra was indeed gone. Just a few days after her death he wrote, "And now, Lord, what remains for me, but to go? What more, if I remain, can I do for my family, for the College, for the cause of science or religion?" Actually, a good deal, as it turned out. To his great fortune, he still benefitted from the constant attentions of his children. And his mind was as sharp as ever. As to his emotional state, fear of his own decline and death that might have hobbled another were always Edward Hitchcock's strongest motivators.

On the same day that he wrote of Orra's death and the devastation it had wrought on him, he also recorded an important new item of intelligence: the cast of the skeleton of *Megatherium,* the one he and Edward, Jr., had been trying for several years to secure from the British Museum, was finally on its way to Amherst. It would be a magnificent addition to the Appleton Cabinet.

As to writing and publishing, he was still active in those endeavors as well. He reported that he was examining final proofs of "The Law of Nature's Constancy," a paper that would appear in the July issue of *Bibliotheca Sacra.* He had published two articles in that journal in the last two years. In the first, "Exegesis of I Corinthians 15:35-40, as Illustrated by Natural History and Chemistry," he addressed a question frequently raised by skeptics: How is it possible for the dead to be resurrected even after their bodies have been laid in the grave for long periods? Doesn't chemistry teach us that those remains decay and are returned to the earth? Only a tiny portion of the body need survive for that person to be resurrected, Hitchcock argued, just as a seed contains only a tiny portion of a plant from which it was derived, an argument that might have satisfied some believers but not skeptics. In "The Cross in Nature and Nature in the Cross," he argued that the earth was fallen and sinful even before the first man and woman lived in Eden. In "Law of Nature's Constancy Subordinate to the Higher Law of Change," he addressed the greatest challenge to orthodox Christianity of his time, the writings of Charles Darwin. The danger in Darwin's theory according to Hitchcock was the suggestion that the processes of nature are self-sustaining, that no deity need be invoked to bring new lifeforms into existence.

Also about to be published was an important addition to his ichnological research entitled "New Facts and Conclusions respecting the Fossil Footmarks of the Connecticut Valley." It would be his sixty-second and final article to appear in the *American Journal of Science and Arts*. It included new insights he had gained both from a careful examination of new tracks recently added to the Appleton Cabinet as well as from the reexamination of some old tracks. In the article he admitted to doubts about the "ornithic character" of some of the tracks, particularly the thick-toed tracks. Some new evidence had come to light regarding the number of phalanges in the toes and whether they were consistent with birds, at least modern-day birds. In the end he reaffirmed his original conclusion: the thick-toed tracks were bird tracks.

Hitchcock noted another landmark achievement in his notes of early July: "…a publisher has been found for my Reminiscences of Amherst College…The prospect is strong now that ere many months the whole volume of 400 pages will be published." He had submitted his resignation to the Board of Trustees shortly after Orra's death to be effective on Commencement Day, July 9, 1863. The trustees had refused to accept it. Nevertheless, he now felt free to see his book into print:

> The chief remaining objection to the publication of this work, viz., my connection with College, seems to me therefore to be taken out of the way, for although the Trustees did not accept my resignation, I have in fact ceased to have any connection with the operations of the College.

"I still linger on the shores of time, balancing as it were between life & death and suffering intensely," Hitchcock wrote to his friend Benjamin Silliman at Yale in August in a letter delivered by his youngest child, Emily, who was visiting friends in New Haven. He went on to tell Silliman of the completion of *Reminiscences* and to thank him for his letter of condolence after Orra's death.

> I was greatly indebted to you for your last kind letter of sympathy & condolence & intended to answer it but my strength would not allow. Many debts of this kind must remain unpaid till I enter if I ever do the house not made with hands, eternal in the heavens.

That letter may have been the last communication between the two men whose friendship spanned more than four decades.

In his notes of early September Hitchcock reported that he had been examining the final proofs of *Reminiscences.* He was satisfied with them in general, although he did register one complaint about the frontispiece:

> The publishers are of opinion that my portrait, prefixed to the work, would add to its interest with very many. I cannot agree with them in this opinion and had set myself resolutely against any thing of the kind, but I yield the point with as good a grace as I can.

That portrait (see page 329) is a stylized likeness of the man in a high collared shirt and cravat, his hair attractively coiffed, looking youthful and vigorous thanks to the skill of the artist and lithographer. It elicited this interesting reaction from one reviewer in the *Springfield Republican*: "The title-page of the book is faced by an excellent likeness of its venerable author, very properly a lithograph; the rocks of New England can alone aptly reproduce the features of one who has given to their study so large a part of his life."

In October 1863, the labor of two years finally went to press, bearing the all-encompassing title, *Reminiscences of Amherst College, Historical, Scientific, Biographical and Autobiographical: Also, of Other and Wider Life Experiences*. As the title suggests, the work was a history of both the college and of the man—the two were inextricably intertwined.

The first chapter, "Biographical Notices," includes tributes to dozens of men who played important roles in the history of Amherst College, its founders, previous presidents, trustees, friends, and faculty members, the longest and most effusive of which are those for Presidents Moore and Humphrey, Reverend Joseph Vaill, and Samuel Williston. In "Statistical History," Hitchcock enumerates the college's successes in terms of student enrollment, number of faculty, programs, and buildings. The next chapter reviews the history of the college's cabinets, laboratories, and library. The chapter entitled "Financial History" records the college's past "financial embarrassments," probably in more detail than some would have wished to see in print.

In "History of Temperance in the College" Hitchcock notes with satisfaction the development of the temperance movement at Amherst, beginning with the establishment in 1830 of the Antivenenean Society. He then devotes some fifty pages to a subject particularly dear to his heart, the religious history of the college, including revivals and religious instruction. He discusses with pride the greater than one half its graduates to that time who had entered the ministry. He lists and describes individually the sixty-nine graduates who had gone on to serve as missionaries in all corners of the globe. A chapter entitled "Scenery and Geology" then takes the reader on a walking and riding tour of the Connecticut Valley, beginning with College Hill and traveling farther and farther afield, describing mountains, valleys, ravines, lakes, and waterfalls, and including accounts of a number of his mountain excursions.

The eighth and final chapter, "Personal History," is by far the longest. It is a rambling narrative, but it manages to fill in many fascinating details about Hitchcock's life, mostly about his nearly four-decade association with Amherst College. He describes his duties as a faculty member, his ascent to the presidency, and his travels in Virginia and in Europe. He recounts the story of the "Great Almanack Debate" with Edmund Blunt, casting himself as the underdog who ultimately triumphed. He also resurrects two more recent controversies, his role in the founding of the American Association for the Advancement of Science, and his dispute with Dr. James Deane, memories which clearly still rankled his wounded pride.

Humor finds its way into *Reminiscences* more than might be expected, including the story of the fumes emanating from Hitchcock's chemical laboratory that lingered in Dr. Humphrey's class (see page 125). He relates several amusing anecdotes from his mountain excursions such as the ascent of Mount Holyoke during which the party encountered a rattlesnake. When they told a local resident what they had seen, the man was interested: "Probably he wished to obtain some rattlesnake oil, which is reputed to have wonderful virtues, or he wanted to bite through the snake once or twice, which is said to be a specific against toothache. We did not try the experiment." Hitchcock is also willing to make light of himself on occasion, as when he recounts the story of the man in Greenfield who, upon seeing him purchasing slabs of rock at the auction of the collections of Dexter Marsh, commented, "The man who will waste money like that, should have a guardian placed over him."

Tragedy was also a part of the life of the college. Hitchcock writes of the passing of several greatly admired faculty members including Professors Sylvester Hovey, Nathan W. Fiske, and Charles B. Adams. He relates the shocking death of a young graduate, Henry Lyman, who was murdered in Sumatra while serving as a missionary. Perhaps most striking and heart-wrenching is his account of the death of Jonathan D. Torrance, a student from Enfield, the result of a prank by his classmates. That incident received as much attention from the popular press of his time as the rest of the book.

Hitchcock does not hesitate to express his opinions on a range of subjects such as the dangers of debt, the hazards of overeating, and his distaste for certain of the college's buildings. His words regarding the octagonal design he chose for the Woods Cabinet sound a bit defensive: "It is no wonder that it should greatly disturb the ideas of a man whose highest notion of architectural beauty is a right angle and a parallelopiped."

He pays tribute to his wife at several points in *Reminiscences,* citing the 232 plates and 1134 woodcuts she created for his works. "Though pressed by the cares of a numerous family, rarely, if ever, during forty years, she turned a deaf ear to my solicitations for drawings. And without these, my scientific labors would have been meagre enough." He credits daughter Mary for her drawing of the college campus in its early days. He also makes brief mention of both sons, Edward, Jr., and Charles, in relation to the cabinets and the Vermont geological survey.

Inserted at the back of *Reminiscences* is a 10" by 15" map entitled "The Geology Around Amherst College." It offers the reader a geological perspective of the world that surrounded Edward Hitchcock for more than four decades of his life. It includes some interesting geological features such as old riverbeds, old sea beaches, moraines, and deltas. It uses the native names for several of the mountains, names that he himself assigned: Mettawompe, Norwottuck, and Nonotuck.

Figure 73. View of Amherst College, ca 1855

Besides the portrait of the author, the book includes three drawings of the campus. Two, dated 1821 and 1824, were drawn by his daughter Mary from old views of the college. A third depicts the campus in the 1850s, rising like a citadel on a hill, with the Woods Cabinet, Lawrence Observatory, and Appleton Cabinet prominently displayed. The Hitchcock homestead may be seen in the lower right corner including the distinctive "Octagonal Cabinet" that Hitchcock had constructed to house his personal collections.

More than a century and a half has passed since the publication of *Reminiscences,* yet it stands as the most detailed account we have of Edward Hitchcock's life and his work at Amherst College. It is notable for the author's candor regarding the college's troubles, his doubts about his suitability for the presidency, and his bouts with despondency. The litany of successes during his tenure as president might strike a reader as self-serving, but the facts speak for themselves—the college enjoyed a remarkable recovery during those years. We might wish for more details about his early life, his mother, his schooling, his preaching, his brief pastorate in Conway. On the other hand, he seemed more than generous in listing and praising as many figures from the college's past as he could recall.

Hitchcock restrains himself from introducing into the narrative too much mention of his faith, except perhaps for an occasional reference to Divine Providence. There are just two exceptions: a single line at the end of his introduction—"God bless Amherst College, now and in all coming time, with all connected with it, and all its graduates"—and the last paragraph of the work in which he gives full voice to the fundamental principle of his being:

> I testify at the age of threescore and ten, that though I find the powers of life giving way, and a growing indifference to the works of Man, my attachment to the works of Nature has all the ardor and enthusiasm of youth. Hannah More testified that it was so with her at fourscore and two. And why should it not be so with the Christian forever! for though the first and the sweetest song of heaven is, Worthy is the Lamb that was slain, yet the second sounds from the same golden harps, with a rapture scarcely less, great and marvellous are thy works, Lord God, Almighty!

Reminiscences was marketed by the publisher, Bridgman and Childs of Northampton. Advertisements appeared in newspapers in Northampton, Springfield, Boston, Hartford, and New York City. The book was available by mail from the publisher and from book retailers in each city.

Only a few publications offered reviews. One writer noted that *Reminiscences* was,

> …of interest both as a narrative and as a study of human nature…Mixed with some pardonable egotisms, it brings before us a vivid picture of the genuine old New England puritan character, in its energy, its stubborn endurance, and its rigid honesty and integrity, its horror of debt and dependence, and its quiet enthusiasm.

A review in the *American Journal of Science and Arts*, possibly authored by Benjamin Silliman himself, was generous in praise for both book and author:

> The book is a reflex of the man—full of simple, almost childlike, earnestness, concealing nothing, not even personal expenses… What Dr. Hitchcock has done for science in connection with the inception and growth of its various departments in Amherst is here made apparent, not by any boastful or self-laudatory statements, but inferentially from the simple thread of history.

The only extended review of *Reminiscences* by a newspaper appeared in the *Springfield Republican* days after the book was published. The article was generally favorable, but the editors could not resist the opportunity to end the review by grinding away at an old ax:

> We would gladly close the book without a single unfavorable remark, but a notice it contains of the writer's controversy with Dr. Deane of Greenfield cannot be silently passed by. We owe much to the gathered wisdom of a life-time, to the ripe honors won by fruitful years, but we owe more to the truth whose champion has fallen. The old-time readers of The Republican are aware of our well-grounded conviction that, on this subject, justice is with the dead.

With the publication of *Reminiscences,* even the indefatigable Edward Hitchcock seemed to be losing his motivation for life. In his notes of early September he wrote, "…[I]t does seem to me that this must be my last intellectual effort as an author. For although I feel as if I could wish for some object of this kind to which to turn my attention and must think it would be favorable to my health I find my brain of late quite feeble and almost incapable of much mental effort."

Autobiography of Edward Hitchcock, D. D.

REMINISCENCES OF AMHERST COLLEGE.

THIS work of Dr. Hitchcock possesses a peculiar interest, as it was written with the full consciousness on his part, that it was the last of his earthly labors. It is in fact a series of autobiographical sketches, comprising his own life experience, containing a large amount of facts, anecdotes and principles drawn from every day life and from almost all parts of the world, so that general readers will find it of absorbing interest. Twelve mo., 400 pages, with portrait and four engravings. Price $1.50. Copies sent by mail on receipt of price.
33 BRIDGMAN & CHILDS, Publishers, Northampton, Mass.

Figure 74. Advertisement in the *Hampshire Gazette*, March 15, 1864

Despite his increasingly fragile condition, Hitchcock found sufficient energy that fall to pursue several projects that were dear to his heart. Two were unsuccessful. One of these was the establishment of a permanent Professorship of Natural Theology and Geology that would include the duties of curator of the college's cabinets. He had held that position since 1845 and hoped to find funds to ensure it would continue in perpetuity. His son Charles had been appointed Curator of the Cabinets from 1858 to 1863 and was reappointed for the 1864-1865 academic year. The position was, according to Charles, woefully underpaid. Whether Edward lobbied for Charles to receive the appointment is not known. By September it was clear that he had not succeeded: "…[T]he effort has failed and still I say the will of the Lord be done! It has indeed blasted all my hopes as to my professorship and the cabinets when I am gone and prostrated my most cherished plans sought after by 40 years labour but still I say God's will be done."

Another apparently unfruitful project that fall was the completion of an allegory entitled "The Sea of Life." He had hoped it would be published, but in one of his notes he expresses doubts about that possibility:

> Much has been written lying up on my bed with my hand too feeble to hold the pen steady. Had I undertaken this work ten years ago and followed it up it does seem as if a useful little work might have been produced by this time. Whether I have now made it of any consequence others must decide. Oh how strange to be talking at this late date about publishing another book!

"The Sea of Life" survives only as a handwritten manuscript; there is no record that it ever found its way into print, although a hint to its content appears in the last section of the same title in his article, "The Law of Nature's Constancy."

Despite these setbacks, Hitchcock was able to point to one significant achievement in the last months of his life, a new acquisition for the Appleton Cabinet. Thanks to the efforts of Professor Charles U. Shepard, the college had been offered a large collection of European fossils. It was, wrote Hitchcock, an "important desideratum," one that filled a gap in the college's fossil collection. Funds were raised through a petition to the state legislature. The grant was secured in April 1863, but at great personal cost. Three times during the winter of 1862, Edward had traveled to Boston to lobby for the petition, although his condition was so weakened that he had to be accompanied by his wife.

On January 4, 1864, Charles Hitchcock of Deerfield died. Wrote Edward the following day, "Another blow has fallen and I am made brotherless as I was before without sisters. Charles perhaps the most amiable and naturally gentlemanlike of our numbers has fallen at the age of 78 before that dreadful enemy of our family–Pneumonia. There were five of us and I alone am left—the youngest of all." Henry had died three years earlier, Emilia and Charissa almost a decade previously. "I trust the four are now singing the everlasting song. Oh how little prepared I am to take my place at the foot of the choir and yet I do long to join the almost restored brotherhood!"

A month later he recorded the final entry in his notes. The handwriting is uneven and the entry ends mid-sentence. Typically, his thoughts even then were of Amherst College and its future:

> And yet it is still delayed! and I bless God for it although I do earnestly long to be gone yet he has allowed me to be the means of accomplishing some important things for the College the most so is the probable establishment a few years hence of a Professorship of Natural Biblical and Pastoral…

Even in time of great frailty, Hitchcock longed to be active, to be out of doors, to breathe the fresh air. William S. Tyler reports that his friend rode on horseback as long as he could sit up, then by carriage, and finally was borne about on a chair carried by his two sons, "that he might breathe the out-door air which he so much loved and look upon the face of nature, his beloved."

Tyler visited Hitchcock in the last few days of his earthly existence. He had been on the faculty since 1832, and we can imagine that the two had many college matters to discuss. But at length Edward spoke of his undiminished faith in God. When asked if Christ was precious to him, he replied in full voice, "Precious!...he is unspeakably precious…He is more than that—infinitely more. He is everything. He is all in all." He then spoke of wanting to be reunited with loved ones, with pious friends, "…with all the wise and good of all ages."

"The last night of his life," wrote Tyler, "he seems to have been fully aware that the hour of his departure was at hand." His children were all with him and reported that their father was in full possession of his faculties most of the night, although he occasionally spoke to friends who were not there.

At one point he asked one of his sons to arrange the pillows under his head. "Place the cross there," he said. "Father, I thought you had always had the cross near you," replied his son. "Yes, but I have learned its value here, right in this place."

A few minutes later he said, "I am going—I am going—farewell to earth." And he was gone.

Amherst's third meetinghouse

27 Floating Memories

"Blessed are the dead that die in the Lord...that they may rest from their labors, and their works do follow them."

Wednesday, the second day of March 1864, was a sunny but bone-chilling day in Amherst. Although it was a weekday, schools and businesses were closed, mills silenced. Farmers who otherwise would have been occupied all day with their livestock, or collecting sap, or dressing the snow-covered fields, on this day hurried to get their necessary labors finished early.

At one o'clock a single bell tolled dully from the steeple of the village church, summonsing one and all. Across the common and up the hill they poured, some on foot, others on horseback, in wagons, or in carriages. From coaches drawn up along the common, well dressed men and women from Boston, Hartford, Springfield, and Pittsfield, stepped out into the midday sun. These were city folk looking a bit out of place and disoriented as they stood among the hundreds of residents hoping for a seat in the meetinghouse.

The crowd was a most unlikely admixture–old and young, rich and poor, learned and unschooled, farmers, mill workers, housewives, school children, college students, scientists, professors, politicians, theologians—all wishing to be in this town, at this church, on this particular day, to show their respects. The mere fact that such a diverse gathering of humankind all regarded the dearly departed as one of their own spoke volumes about him. For this man was no ordinary man, this man was Edward Hitchcock.

Inside the plain, unadorned meetinghouse every pew was full and, as the hour of the service approached, those who arrived last had to stand along the sides of the sanctuary or in the entryway, while many more gathered outside in the cold, hoping to hear the proceedings if not see them.

At one-thirty dozens of friends gathered with the family outside the Hitchcock home and heard a brief prayer. Shortly before two o'clock, a long, sober procession began to wind its way up the road toward the church. First came the students, several hundred in all, each in a black suit with a mourning badge attached to his lapel. They were followed by the casket, drawn on a wagon pulled by a team of muscular draft horses, black crepe hung from their harnesses. Immediately behind the wagon walked the family members as well as several household workers who had become intimate friends of the family. Behind them followed the Faculty and Board of Trustees of Amherst College.

As the procession approached the village church all heads were bowed in honor of their neighbor and friend. Inside the meetinghouse the casket was placed on a long low bench at the front of the sanctuary. The professor lay there in silent repose in a black suit and starched white shirt, his hands folded together over his coat.

The ceremony began with a choral voluntary followed by a scripture reading and introductory prayer by President Stearns. The choir then sang a hymn:

Servant of God, well done,
Rest from thy loved employ.

When the hymn was finished and the last notes of the pipe organ had echoed from the walls, the sanctuary fell silent. Slowly, a bearded and stooped figure rose from a pew and stepped up to the pulpit. It was Reverend Professor William S. Tyler, one of the senior members of the college faculty, and an old friend of Edward and Orra Hitchcock. Despite his age, his voice rang loudly in the meetinghouse. His discourse, "The Wise Man of the Scriptures," began with the wisest man of all, Solomon. At length it turned to his dear friend who lay just a few feet away. It was a fine eulogy, one that aptly captured the wisdom, the spirit, the character of Edward Hitchcock. After more than two hours, Professor Tyler concluded with words from the book of Revelation:

And I heard a voice from heaven saying unto me,
blessed are the dead that die in the Lord...
that they may rest from their labors,
and their works do follow them.

Reverend Joseph Vaill then gave the final prayer. With the service ended, another procession moved slowly, somberly through the village to the cemetery, the casket carried by six pall bearers, all friends and colleagues of Professor Hitchcock. Many students and townspeople followed. A brief ceremony took place before the granite obelisk marking the family grave that already bore the name Orra W. Hitchcock. Engraved at the base were words that summed up perfectly the life of Edward Hitchcock:

The cross in nature
and nature in the cross

The death of Edward Hitchcock was reported in newspapers across the nation, from New England to Louisiana, New York to Delaware, Kansas to Colorado. It was announced as well in two newspapers in Scotland. In time, notices and tributes also appeared in scholarly journals both in North American and in Europe. An obituary notice in the *American Journal of Science and Arts* noted about Edward Hitchcock,

> Earnest, simple, and sagacious, indefatigable under all discouragements, his clear, firm grasp of truth sustained and raised him above all difficulties and has secured him an honored name in science. And this is not all, for science with him was ever made tributary to Christian truth and effort.

Daniel R. Goodwin, a scientist from Philadelphia, penned a tribute in the *Proceedings of the American Philosophical Society:* "...after all, Dr. Hitchcock was not so much a great genius, or a great savant, as a great and good man." He compared him to two other great men of science:

> ...like Newton, he always held science and religion together, not in antagonism, but in co-ordination and harmony...like Franklin, he combined his scientific pursuits with a steady and zealous devotion to the duties and utilities of practical life...He observed, he studied, he thought, he felt, he acted; but he was no mere observer, no mere student, no mere thinker, no mere sentimentalist, no mere agitator or drudge, no mere fragment of humanity, however sharp, or polished, or brilliant. He was a whole-souled, large-minded, living man, recognizing his practical relations to man and God, as well as his intellectual relations to nature and truth. His highest ambition and most fervent

> prayer undoubtedly were, to be a true man and an earnest Christian, rather than a savan or a philosopher, to have his name written among the wise who shall shine as the brightness of the firmament, rather than emblazoned on the records of human science and learning.

Another tribute appeared in the *Proceedings of the American Academy of Arts and Sciences* several months after his death. It was likely written by William B. Rogers, a prominent American geologist and the founder and first president of the Massachusetts Institute of Technology. Rogers was at the time Corresponding Secretary of the Academy and had known Edward Hitchcock for nearly a quarter century. He made special note of Hitchcock's geological surveys, his writings on surface geology, and his ichnological studies. Of the fossil footmarks he made one particularly striking remark:

> The late Dr. Deane and Mr. Marsh of Greenfield, had, indeed, brought these objects to his notice, and had pronounced them to be the tracks of birds,—for which these gentlemen were entitled to special acknowledgments; but the scientific investigation belonged almost wholly to Professor Hitchcock, and has been, indeed, the most arduous, and perhaps the most important, scientific work of his life.

The comment might have been directed to Deane's friend and eulogist, Thomas T. Bouvé, who was still active in the Academy and may well have been in attendance on that day.

Two additional tributes were delayed because of the war. One by J. P. Lesley entitled "Memoir of Edward Hitchcock" was delivered before the National Academy of Sciences in 1866. Another, "Scientific and Religious Character of Edward Hitchcock," was delivered in the same year by Almira Phelps at the American Association for the Advancement of Science meeting in Buffalo (see page 320).

One curious counterpoint to such words of praise appeared in a short death notice published in the *New York Tribune* just a few days after his death.

> Dr. Hitchcock was a man of lively imagination—more remarkable for his zeal in the pursuit of science than for soundness of judgement—with a tendency to ingenious, and perhaps, fantastic theories—of undoubted probity in purpose and action, but with a sharp vein of cynicism in his manners.

If the allusion to "fantastic theories" had to do with giant creatures walking about in ancient times, that was a theory that may once have been regarded as fantastic, but by 1864 enjoyed wide acceptance. As to his "vein of cynicism," anyone who knew the man—including some of his detractors—would likely have replied that, whatever other faults he may have had, Edward Hitchcock did not have a cynical bone in his body.

The obituaries, the eulogies, and the tributes offered many high-sounding words of praise for Edward Hitchcock, scientist, educator, man of faith. But it was his personal qualities that shone through most brightly in the recollections of three of his former students who, by 1864, had already made their marks in the world, yet found time to reflect on the death of their former professor.

Reverend Denis Wortman, Jr., an 1857 graduate of Amherst College, was by 1864 pastor of a large church in Brooklyn, New York. Writing in the *Christian Intelligencer*, a New York weekly, he recorded "a few floating memories" of his old professor:

> In the hearts of those whose privilege it was to know him, he was singularly dissociated from his position, his honors, and his fame. It was the man himself—the man so sincere, simple and unassuming, so kind, so great, that they revered and loved...

As a preacher, was he eloquent? Not perhaps in the minds of some, wrote Reverend Wortman,

> ...[B]ut if it requires eloquence to hold the breathless attention of an audience of students for an hour, perhaps more, to awaken the deepest emotions of every hearer, and make almost every eye moisten with tears, and send all away convinced of the truth, Dr. Hitchcock was a man of uncommon eloquence.

According to Reverend Wortman, some of his classmates sought to avoid attendance at Sabbath services, but not when Professor Hitchcock was scheduled to preach:

> The students used to calculate the day when it would be the President's turn to preach. There was less sickness on that Sabbath than on any other. The monitors had a lighter task to mark absentees. Paper and pencils were brought into greater requisition by those who took notes, "for we must not lose the sermon today."

On graduating from Amherst in 1836, Reverend Samuel C. Damon served as a missionary in Hawaii for four decades, his ministry including native Hawaiians as well as thousands of seamen who passed through the islands each year. He was also editor of a widely distributed monthly newspaper, *The Friend*, which frequently included reports from his alma mater. Professor Hitchcock, wrote Reverend Damon, was a "distinguished divine, scholar, and philosopher." He was eminent in science, and "...among the noblest and ablest defenders of the cause of Evangelical Christianity." Reverend Damon, too, was particularly affected by Hitchcock's sermons: "As a preacher he was exceedingly admired and beloved. Well do we remember the delightful thrill it imparted to the whole body of students when it devolved upon him to occupy the pulpit upon the

Sabbath." Reverend Damon also testified that Hitchcock was instrumental in leading him to sign the Pledge of Temperance in his freshman year at Amherst.

> More than thirty years have since passed away, and that Pledge is still our Pledge. The benefits of adhering to it in all climates, on sea and land, words fail us fully to describe...and to-day we feel well nigh as hale, healthy, hearty and vigorous as when in the flush of youth and spring-time of life we attached our name to that Pledge.

In 1830 a young man entered Amherst College named Henry Ward Beecher. Even while still a student he rose to eminence as an advocate for the abolition of slavery, a cause also championed by his sister, author Harriet Beecher Stowe. Beecher boarded with the Hitchcocks for several years and so came to know the family well. By 1864 he was editor of *The Independent*, a weekly newspaper he founded in New York City that advocated for the cause of abolition. In his tribute to Professor Hitchcock, Beecher recounted a story that he felt best captured the spirit of the man:

> We shall not soon forget the simple enthusiasm—a kind of dry ecstasy—with which he returned home one day with a new species of flower which he had discovered. Another collector, keen and searching, had been over the same ground, but missed it! "I was about to go up the bank, when I saw the flower across a patch of water and brush. I could not wait to go round. I ran across, and I waded, sure from the first sight that it was new, and the nearer I came the faster I walked, for fear something should get them before I did." His zeal for a flower, without special beauty and of no practical use, made a profound impression upon our mind, and opened up a new idea of the worth of a flower, which is not quite expended yet. His eyes sparkled as he told the simple story, and his white face glowed with charming pleasure.

With both parents now gone and the public events related to their father's death complete, the Hitchcock children began the sad work of settling their parents' affairs. The household and its accumulation of nearly four decades had to be disposed of and the property readied for sale.

Just four months before his death, Edward had written his will, with a few changes added on January 1, 1864. He had already donated to Amherst College several collections of rocks, minerals, fossil footmarks, and dried plants. To those gifts he added three more larger collections of rocks and minerals he wished to bequeath to the college on his death including 3200 specimens from Massachusetts, more than 2000 from elsewhere in the United States, and 600 more from England. These he offered on several conditions: first, that the college expend at least $100 annually on new specimens and books in geology;

second, that "the identity and integrity of these collections be preserved"; third, that all the specimens be kept in glazed cases accessible to visitors; fourth, that the collections "might ever be employed here to illustrate the connection of science and religion." On this last point he did make one exception:

> ...[S]ince my son Charles is almost destitute of property, and has greatly assisted me in making and arranging these collections, should he find them very important in some other place to which he may be called, I feel bound to place them under his control, with the power to remove them if necessary.

By 1868 Charles had been appointed to the geology faculty at Dartmouth where he would remain for half a century. Whether he ever exercised his right to remove the specimens his father donated to Amherst College is not known.

As to the remainder of his property, Edward Hitchcock left it all to his children, including the house, a ten-acre woodlot in Hadley, sixty acres of meadowland in Deerfield, some stock holdings, and a United States Treasury note. Of his published works he listed six that might continue to produce some income, notably *Elementary Geology*, *Religion of Geology*, and *Reminiscences*, although, he added, "of these not much." He then continued, "The rest of my personal property consists of Natural History Collections deposited in Amherst College, a manikin, and other anatomical models, my Library and furniture, a Solar Microscope, a common microscope, a small collection of rocks and minerals at my house, geological drawings, horse, cow, carriage, wagons, etc." He left the house and the woodlot in Hadley to his four daughters, specifying that one or more of them be permitted to live in the house and make use of the woodlot for as long as they wished. Once those properties were finally sold, he wished for the proceeds to be distributed equally among his daughters. He also left six hundred dollars to each daughter as well as some funds for the education of their children.

To Edward, Jr., and Charles he bequeathed the meadowlands in Deerfield. Edward, Jr., was to receive the manikin, anatomical models, and drawings, the silver service that had been given to him by the college, and incomes from four of his books. Charles would receive the income for the other books as well as his instruments:

> ...my aneroid and syphon barometer, my compound and solar microscope, my case of plotting instruments, my pentagraphic delineator; also my small collections of simple minerals and of rocks and fossils with the case containing them at my house.

The value of Edward Hitchcock's estate was estimated at $18,000. Edward, Jr., and Charles were named executors. In a letter to Edward, Jr., written just a

Figure 75.
Emily Hitchcock Terry
(1838-1921)

few days after the funeral, the Reverend Henry M. Storrs, husband of Kate, observed that the will provided nothing for charities or missions, but added that Edward had made contributions to benevolent causes throughout his life. Whatever was left he clearly believed should go to his family. Storrs also wrote, "I am glad the house is likely to remain just so until Catha shall once more have the saddened pleasure of revisiting and reviewing it."

Mary, Jane, and Emily Hitchcock continued to live together in the family homestead for several months following their father's death, with Edward, Jr., and his family nearby. In August 1864, Jane Elizabeth Hitchcock married Granville Putnam, an Amherst graduate. The ceremony took place in the college chapel with President Stearns officiating. After the wedding the Putnams lived in Boston where Granville was principal of a public school. Emily Hitchcock eventually moved to New York City where she enrolled as an art student at Cooper Union. Charles and Martha Hitchcock resided for several years in Andover, Massachusetts, where three of their five children were born. Charles taught for a time at the female seminary in Andover, but also worked as a consultant to mining companies in New York City before he began his career at Dartmouth. Catherine Hitchcock Storrs and her family, by then including three children, lived three more years in Cincinnati before moving to Brooklyn, New York, where Reverend Storrs had accepted a new pastorate.

Following the funeral, life at Amherst College quickly returned to normal. Both the Alexandrian Exhibition and Senior Class Day were held in June, commencement in July. The graduating class of twenty-nine was the smallest in the college's history, due largely to the departure of students for the war effort. But total enrollment that fall was high and would continue to rise, particularly after the war's end. The college continued to pursue its historical mission of preparing young men for the ministry, although the proportion of students going on to the ministry gradually declined.

As to Edward Hitchcock's aspirations for the college he loved, some of them were realized, some were not. He had dreamed of establishing a permanent professorship in Natural Theology and Geology, the post he had held since 1845.

But with his death, that position also passed away. Wrote Tyler, "It was made for him, and he for it, and the Trustees have never been able to find any one to fill his place, although they have sought anxiously for suitable candidates." Edward had also pleaded for the establishment of a permanent curatorship of the cabinets, but that hope would never be fulfilled. Nevertheless the work went on, due in large measure to Edward Hitchcock, Jr., who volunteered to take on many of those duties and went to great lengths over thirty years to expand the cabinets and improve the exhibits.

Figure 76. The Hitchcock monument, West Cemetery, Amherst

Thanks to John Tappan, another of Edward's wishes was realized shortly after his death, establishment of a new professorship in religion. The two friends had discussed the idea, but many details remained to be worked out. In 1866, the trustees accepted a gift of $25,000 from Tappan to establish the Samuel Green Professorship of Biblical History and Interpretation and Pastoral Care, named after the pastor of Tappan's church in Boston.

Edward Hitchcock's dreams for education extended beyond Amherst College. He championed two other institutions nearby. One was the Massachusetts Agricultural College. His interest in "scientific agriculture" went back to his youth. Since 1850 he had served on the committee looking into the formation of a state agricultural college. He had been offered the chairmanship of that commission in 1855 but had declined. The matter languished for years until, on April 29, 1863, legislation was enacted establishing the Massachusetts Agricultural College. In June 1864, the Board of Trustees voted to locate the institution in Amherst. Ironically, the only votes against that choice were those of the members from western Massachusetts. According to one report, their opposition was based on concern that locating the new institution in that town would make it dependent on or pit it against Amherst College. Massachusetts Agricultural College opened its door in Amherst in 1867, thanks in no small measure to the efforts of Edward Hitchcock. Both the agricultural college, known today as the University of Massachusetts, and its neighbor, Amherst College, thrive to this day.

Just a few miles away lay another institution of higher learning that owed much to his devotion and dedication. On Thursday, July 21, 1864, several hundred students, graduates, faculty members, and guests gathered to observe the twenty-seventh anniversary of Mount Holyoke Female Seminary in South Hadley. Among the speakers was a student. On what would normally have been a day of celebration, her words struck a somber note, first regarding the war:

> Three times the flowers have blossomed and faded, since we in our peaceful homes first heard the rumor of war, since brothers, husbands and sons began to go forth at their country's call to conflict and to battle and we cannot number now, the graves, nor the broken home circles. Thousands upon thousands of boyish forms—yours mother and yours father—have gone out from the dear old home and suffered bravely and fought nobly—and died willingly, and their bright young heads are pillowed now in unknown graves, upon southern soil.

She then turned to other losses of the past three years:

> Names too upon the role of Fame have been suddenly stricken off. Science and art have given up their votaries. Painters have dropped the brush, and poets, historians and novelists the pen from their unwilling fingers, and passed away into the eternal silence.

Finally, she spoke of one more loss, a very personal loss for Mount Holyoke, of a few months earlier:

> And how our hearts yearn to give a fitting tribute to one whose name is known over both continents–whom it was our joy and pride to claim as friend and helper and patron, our own loved and honored trustee, the teacher and pastor, professor and president, of Amherst College, the Author Geologist and Naturalist, the man of science and the Christian. Edward Hitchcock.

Edward and Orra Hitchcock had known Mary Lyon for two decades before she founded her seminary. On several occasions they had made their home hers. She had been so encouraged by the Hitchcocks that she asked Edward to take a position on the original Board of Trustees of the seminary in 1837, a post he held for nearly a quarter century. He frequently delivered sermons, lectures, or addresses at the seminary. All four of his daughters attended; both sons taught there on occasion. The Hitchcock family was intimately connected with the extended family of Miss Lyon that was Mount Holyoke Female Seminary, one day to become Mount Holyoke College.

The educational legacy of Edward Hitchcock runs wide and deep in America. Three institutions of higher learning owe their very existence to his dedication to learning. All three have endured the test of time and stand today in some measure as monuments to one man's dedication to the educational enterprise.

RETROSPECTIVE

Sandstone slab with fossil footmarks

28 The Sandstone Bird

"...to leave his trace on earth, too deep for time and fate to wear away."

In 1836, only a few months after the publication of his first paper on the fossil footmarks, scientist and preacher Edward Hitchcock put pen to paper and composed a poem. Just as his scientific imagination had been reinvigorated by thoughts of giant birds stalking the mudflats of the Connecticut Valley in ancient times, so had his poetic muse been enlivened by those same images. The result was "The Sandstone Bird."

The original poem underwent many changes as Hitchcock sought to evoke the Triassic environment and the extraordinary creatures that populated it according to those famous footmarks. In an era when most poetry was romantic or spiritual, it must have surprised readers of a new literary journal, *The Knickerbocker*, to discover that verse about a giant prehistoric bird in the

December 1836 issue. Surely such a creature was a fantasy, the product of some overindulgent imagination anxious to publish a bit of surrealistic poetry. But it was very real to its author, very real indeed:

And up flew swiftly, what a sawyer seem'd,
But prov'd a bird's neck, with a frightful beak.
A huge-shaped body follow'd; stilted high,
As if two mainmasts propp'd it up. The bird
of sandstone fame was truly come again;
And shaking his enormous plumes and wings,
And rolling his broad eye around, amaz'd,
He gave a yell so loud and savage too—

The first stanza of an earlier version of "The Sandstone Bird" seems to attribute a motive to that denizen of the dark and distant past:

Bird, a problem thou has solv'd, Man never has:
to leave his trace on earth,
Too deep for time and fate to wear away.

Curiously, that line was absent from the poem as it appeared in *The Knickerbocker.* Perhaps Hitchcock had decided it was inappropriate to attribute such a motive to a primitive creature. But he must have liked it. In 1841 it appeared, slightly modified, in the concluding section of his *Final Report on the Geology of Massachusetts,* providing a dramatic coda to a lengthy discussion of the fossil footmarks:

> The proudest monuments of human art will moulder down and disappear; but as long as there are eyes to behold them, the sandstone of the Connecticut valley will never cease to remind future generations of the gigantic races that passed over it, when yet in a half formed state.

Birds, a problem ye have solved,
Man never has:—to leave a trace on earth
Too deep for time and fate to wear away.

Three years later, he used the line once again near the conclusion of an article in the *American Journal of Science and Arts*, with one small alteration:

Reptiles and birds, a problem ye have solved,
Man never has:—to leave a trace on earth
Too deep for time and fate to wear away.

The substitution of "Reptiles and Birds" for "Birds" is a clear indication of the evolution of his thinking about the makers of those tracks.

The sentiment expressed in that verse reveals more of the poet than of the giant bird of yore. "To leave a trace on earth too deep for time and fate to wear away" was a motive very much on the mind of Edward Hitchcock throughout his life. In 1813 he addressed the Literary Adelphi of Deerfield on the subjects of immortality and ambition. Aspiring to leave a legacy, proclaimed the twenty-year-old, was not a matter of mere pride or the need for self-aggrandizement, but a fundamental trait of humankind.

> The desire of immortalizing his name is implanted in the soul of perhaps every person on earth...In the breast of every man we perceive a spirit of ambition inciting it to deeds which will lift him high among his fellow men...The soul conscious of its excellence will never rest short of its destined goal. It will never stop beneath the stars, nor circumscribe its vast desires by the narrow limits of earth.

What then are the "enduring traces" of Edward Hitchcock's life that time and fate have not worn away? In the history of geology there are many: his geological survey of Massachusetts that became a standard for many other states to replicate; his role in organizing the first meeting of the Association of American Geologists in 1840; his opinions on such diverse subjects as the Taconic inversion, metamorphism, and riverine geomorphology; and, of course, his views on Agassiz's glacial theory.

It is true that after briefly embracing Agassiz's theory in 1841, Hitchcock rejected it in favor of his glacio-aqueous explanation of drift phenomena. In that opinion he was not alone, for most American geologists of the 1840s and early 1850s shared his doubts about the glacial theory. But when the tide did turn in the 1860s, two geologists who emerged as the most influential advocates for Agassiz's theory were men strongly influenced by the work of Edward Hitchcock. In Britain it was Sir Andrew Ramsay (see page 250). In America it was James Dwight Dana at Yale whose *Manual of Geology*, published in 1862, finally brought Agassiz's once revolutionary glacial theory into the mainstream of American science.

But Hitchcock's most enduring legacy as a scientist surely lies in the field of ichnology. His researches on the fossil footmarks were nothing short of revolutionary for his time. That bird-like creatures existed in "sandstone days," thousands of millennia earlier than anyone had previously imagined, was in itself extraordinary. That the evidence for their existence was widely distributed in the Connecticut Valley and yet largely unrecognized for so long, that too was remarkable. And the idea that so much information could be gleaned from mere tracks in stone was entirely novel.

There were times, particularly early in his researches, when Hitchcock was criticized for his conclusions about the fossil footmarks. But just six years after his first publication on those tracks, his views had gained wide acceptance from such eminent European scientists as William Buckland, Charles Daubeny, and Sir Charles Lyell, as well as many of the most respected American geologists of his time. By the end of his life, particularly after the publication of *Ichnology of New England*, there could be no question that his work and most of his conclusions had been accepted by the scientific community.

The one sticking point was always the fundamental question, Were those the tracks of giant birds? Even some who accepted that they were animal tracks had difficulty with the notion that birds could have existed so far in earth's past, and particularly such immense birds as *O. giganteus* or *O. ingens*. Historians of science, paleontologists, and Hitchcock scholars have often posed the question, Why did Hitchcock insist that the creatures responsible for the fossil footmarks were birds? The simple truth is, he did not *insist* on it—he *favored* it, true enough, but he did not *insist* on it.

Over the course of a quarter century he examined thousands of tracks and described them in minute detail, considering more than thirty characteristics of toe, claw, foot, straddle, and stride. He compared them to the tracks of present-day birds. He favored the "avian hypothesis" simply because the evidence pointed to it. It was not a matter of dogma—it was a matter of induction, a conclusion based on the facts available to him. His conclusion, if we were to apply a modern-day ornithological aphorism, was simply this: "If it looks like a duck and it quacks like a duck, it's probably a duck!"

What he did insist on, what were truly matters of dogma for him, were the principles of empirical science: keeping an open mind, gathering additional data, consulting others more knowledgeable than oneself. And he remained loyal to those principles, for the most part, throughout his life.

From the very beginning Hitchcock acknowledged the difficulties of attributing those tracks to birds. In "Ornithichnology," his first published article on the tracks, he argued that they were likely made by bipedal creatures with feet nearly identical to modern birds: "They could not have been made by any other known biped, except birds," he asserted, but added, "On this point, I am happy to have the opinion of more than one distinguished zoologist." That those doubts remained five years later is clear in his *Final Report* of 1841 where, "in the cautious spirit of true science," he replaced the genus name *Ornithichnites* with *Ornithoidichnites*:

> I have endeavored to take a middle course, by naming in my Final Report, some of these tracks, Ornithoidichnites, or tracks resembling those of birds, and others, Sauroidichnites, or tracks resembling those of Saurians [lizards]. Living analogies lead us to conclude that most of them are the tracks of birds: but there

> is plausibility enough in the opposite conjecture, to justify the use of terms that imply resemblance rather than actual identity.

At the end of that report he once again stated his case for the "ornithic character" of the tracks, but with an important proviso:

> ...[I]n regard to all my conclusions, if it can be shown that I am wrong, most cheerfully will I resign my present opinions. Nor even in such a case, shall I feel that I have labored in vain; since I shall have turned the attention of geologists to a most interesting subject.

In an 1843 article he stated that some of the tracks he had identified as birds might well be reptiles:

> That there may have been animals in the red sandstone period, of a different class, say reptiles, with feet so exactly like our present birds, as some of the tracks on stone seem to be, it is easy to imagine: especially when we learn that there was at least one extinct reptile (the pterodactyle) that walked on two feet.

And in *Ichnology of New England* he once again addressed the question directly:

> I speak of those animals as certainly birds, though doubts sometimes cross one's mind on this point: and I am aware that with some distinguished zoologists these doubts are strong. But I follow what seems to me at present the most probable view.

Just one year before his death, he was still wrestling with the question. In a paper presented before the American Academy of Arts and Sciences in Cambridge in December 1862, he presented new evidence unearthed in a careful reexamination of some of the specimens, evidence regarding the number of phalanges. The results led him to pose this provocative question: "Were any of the animals that made the fossil footmarks birds?" His tentative conclusion:

> The facts, however, do show us that the quadrupeds of sandstone days had strong ornithic characters, and they justify the conclusion, that, if none of the animals that made the tracks were veritable birds, they approached very near them in character.

Then, in a brief postscript dated January 15, 1863, Hitchcock reported on additional information that seemed to favor the avian hypothesis. "I incline to the opinion that it may so turn out, and if so that we may still confidently maintain that these species were birds." Finally, in another postscript dated two months later, he reported succinctly: "It so turns out."

In addition to his oft-stated doubts and deliberations on the bird vs. reptile question, Hitchcock's species lists also reflect his ambivalence. In 1837 he concluded that six of twenty-two species were not birds; he suspected they were four-footed and named five of them *Sauroidichnites,* meaning like a saurian. In 1844 he listed eleven species as *Sauroidichnites,* nineteen as *Ornithoidichnites*. In 1847 he allowed that two or more "biped saurians" might well have been responsible for some of the tracks. In an 1848 article he wrote of these putative quadrupeds, "Yet a large proportion of them bore such a strong resemblance to the tracks of saurian reptiles, that I denominated them Sauroidichnites; intending, however, by the term, merely to convey an intimation that they might prove to be reptilian." Twelve of forty-nine species "were certainly quadrupeds," he wrote in the same article, but then added that of thirty-two bipeds, about ten were either batrachians (i.e., frogs or toads) or lizards. In his *Synopsis* of 1858 he altered his taxonomy to include two groups of birds as well as a group of "ornithoid lizards or batrachians."

Far from insisting on the avian hypothesis, Hitchcock equivocated on the subject throughout the nearly three decades that he studied them. Even in the last year of his life he continued to question his conclusion, ready at any point to accept the reptilian alternative.

Only in the last few years of Hitchcock's life did a clearer picture of the true nature of dinosaurs gradually come into focus. The early reconstructions of fossil remains unearthed by European scientists had dinosaurs looking more like crocodiles, plantigrades with short legs and broad, flat feet, entirely unbirdlike. Richard Owen set these creatures apart from other reptiles, coining the name *Dinosauria*.

Hitchcock's trackmakers, on the other hand, were clearly digitigrades, long legged with feet raised on elongated toes, very much like those of modern birds. Their posture and gait, their digital formulas, even their social organization pointed to the birds of today. Those footmarks bore little resemblance to dinosaurs as they were known in his day. Hence it is no surprise that the Amherst professor saw little to recommend Owen's dinosaurs as makers of the Connecticut Valley tracks.

Owen's early notion of *Dinosauria* began to change in 1858 when two American scientists uncovered the remains of an ancient reptile buried in limestone in New Jersey. *Hadrosaurus* was enormous, at least twenty-five feet long, with large hind legs and short forelegs. It was unquestionably a reptile, but it was digitigrade, had three toes, and walked upright most of the time, much like a giant wingless bird. A similar creature, *Dryptosaurus*, was unearthed nearby in 1866. It too was a very large quadruped with long, powerful hind legs and short forelegs. But if dinosaurs such as *Hadrosaurus* and *Dryptosaurus* were huge and flightless, did they have any connection at all to birds as we know them? In 1861 new evidence was discovered in a quarry in

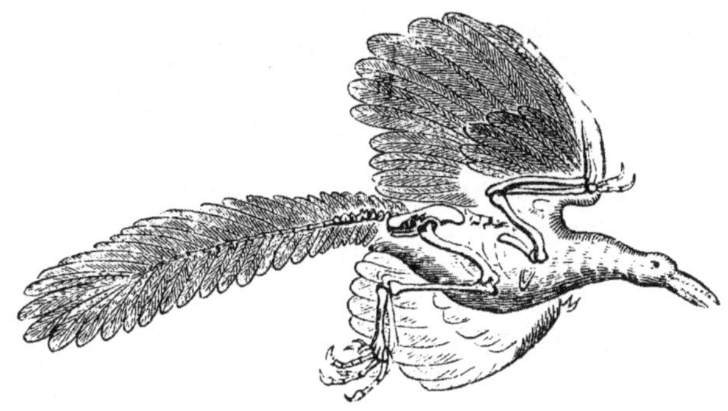

Figure 77. *Archaeopteryx*, an artist's conception, 1871

Germany that would finally answer the question of the ancestry of modern birds. Several small fossils were discovered that appeared to be intermediate between reptile and bird, possessing some of the features of a dinosaur and some of modern-day birds. One was known as *Archaeopteryx,* another as *Compsognathus.* In the minds of many paleontologists then and now, those fossils provided ample evidence for a link between birds, dinosaurs, and reptiles. "The road from Reptiles to Birds is by way of *Dinosauria*," wrote Thomas H. Huxley in 1868.

Edward Hitchcock was quick to use *Archaeopteryx* in support of his avian hypothesis. In his last work on ichnology, *Supplement to the Ichnology of New England,* he devoted ten pages to a discussion of *Archaeopteryx.* It was a bird, he argued, possibly of the type he believed formed the tracks. To many paleontologists, that was a bit of a stretch to say the least. *Archaeopteryx* had four legs and a long, bony tail, entirely different from his bipedal trackmakers. Furthermore, it was a fraction of the size of the creatures that made most of his tracks, and it was found in late Jurassic or Cretaceous rock, millions of years later than the new red sandstone of the Connecticut Valley.

Edward Hitchcock went to his grave knowing that his paleontological work was widely recognized as groundbreaking, notwithstanding the avian versus reptilian question. But for a time in the twentieth century, the notion that those tracks had been made by giant birds was treated with scorn and ridicule by some. Even his skills and credentials were called into question.

Robert Bakker, an eminent American paleontologist and revolutionary thinker on dinosaurs of the present day, wrote of his youth, "The dino books I grew up with dismissed Hitchcock as a bungling footprint specialist who deluded himself into believing that dinosaur tracks in the Connecticut Valley red beds were made by nonexistent Jurassic birds." One of those books was written by Edwin H. Colbert, a distinguished paleontologist affiliated with the American Museum of Natural History, in 1945. Colbert admitted that Hitchcock was a pioneer, but asserted that his conclusions about the character of the trackmakers were wrong:

> Hitchcock may be considered as one of the first collectors on this continent of dinosaurian remains (or at least the evidences as to the existence of dinosaurs), even though he at first did not realize the significance of his finds. Of course Hitchcock's mistake is readily understandable, when it is remembered that in his day dinosaurs were virtually unknown and when it is realized that the tracks he saw, those of two-legged dinosaurs, closely resemble large bird tracks.

Science historian Dennis R. Dean was harsher. In a 1969 article he described Hitchcock as "...the last of the first-rate amateurs," an astonishing demotion for a man who had devoted a quarter century to his fossil footmarks research, published over two dozen peer-reviewed articles as well as a 700-page book on the subject, a man who in his time was considered the foremost authority on and founder of the field of ichnology. Wrote Dean, "Hitchcock is the last significant geological theorist who dabbles, who creates, who imagines, and the grand assurances, the flights of pious imagination, which characterize his works are tragic in their obsolescence."

So much for "leaving a trace on earth too deep for time and fate to wear away." The mild-mannered professor from Amherst, it seemed, had been relegated to the ranks of a dabbler or dilettante—clumsy, inept, as out of date as, well, a dinosaur.

But the story of Edward Hitchcock's legacy does not end there. As recently as the 1960s, dinosaurs were still regarded as big, bumbling, slow moving creatures, a class of animals that never fit in, that never fully adapted to the exigencies of a changing world. Extinction, it was said, was the price the dinosaurs paid for their own ineptitude.

That view began to change, largely as a result of work carried out at Yale University. Yale was an important center of research in paleontology, even in Hitchcock's day, due to the work of James D. Dana and Othniel C. Marsh. In the late nineteenth and early twentieth century, others such as George Wieland and Richard S. Lull continued that tradition, making Yale an important breeding ground for innovative research and visionary thinking in paleontology.

A century after Hitchcock's death, John H. Ostrom of Yale and Robert T. Bakker, then a Harvard graduate student, formulated some revolutionary ideas that overturned many of those stereotypes regarding dinosaurs. Ostrom found some extraordinary fossil remains that suggested that many dinosaurs walked upright on two large hind limbs and may have been warm-blooded. Bakker used a variety of evidence from bone structure to paleoclimate to predator-prey ratios to confirm that many dinosaurs were warm-blooded, fast moving, and large brained.

Figure 78. Photographs of tracks of *Anomoepus* from *Supplement to the Ichnology of New England*, 1865. These were among the first photographs to appear in Hitchcock's published works.

The taxonomic implication soon became clear: birds are direct descendants of the dinosaurs. Bakker wrote, "For those of us who are fond of dinosaurs the new classification has a particularly happy implication: The dinosaurs are not extinct. The colorful and successful diversity of the living birds is a continuing expression of basic dinosaur biology."

Clearly the tides of dinosaur phylogeny were changing in Hitchcock's favor. Harvard paleontologist Adrian Desmond wrote in 1977 that this new view of the relationship between dinosaurs and birds "...perhaps excuses Edward Hitchcock for sticking to his belief that the Connecticut Valley tracks were those of giant birds." Martin Lockley of the University of Colorado agreed: "...[It] means that Hitchcock was right all along: The tracks were indeed those of special types of bird; not creatures identical to modern turkeys, but their ancient theropod ancestors."

In light of these new insights into dinosaur evolution, Bakker in 2005 argued that the reputation of Edward Hitchcock was in need of a "makeover." Hitchcock, he wrote, was the "...earliest and in many ways the best mind in dinosaur science." Of Hitchcock's original paper, "Ornithichnology," Bakker wrote:

> I find Hitchcock's 1836 monograph awe-inspiring. His observations are detailed, his reasoning tight. This one publication made paleoichnology a robust discipline, a window into the grand succession of dominant life forms in the terrestrial sphere.

Hitchcock correctly deduced from his tracks the posture, the gait, the stride, even the digital formula of the creatures that created those tracks. His conclusion was that no reptile or saurian could have formed them—they were in every respect like the tracks of birds. Hitchcock had it right from the start, argued Bakker, "placing birds and dinosaurs in their correct mutual relations...five years before Owen coined his memorable term 'Dinosauria.'"

Hitchcock wrote his *Supplement* in the last few months of his life, and it may fairly be argued that his mind was by then made up, that he had lost all objectivity in his arguments for the avian hypothesis. But if this was a lapse, it was a minor one in the life of a giant of paleontology. Wrote Bakker,

> All of us 21st-century students of the dinosaur-bird relations owe a tip of the hat toward the Reverend Edward Hitchcock. His research program is well worth emulating: study the form and function of every joint, every bone element, put them in an ecological and behavioral context; then, ponder how the forces operating in Deep Time shaped the extinction of great categories and the arrival of new ones.

And while the trackmakers were eventually acknowledged to have been dinosaurs, they were the progenitors of modern birds. "What gave the theropod dinosaurs the advantage?" asked Bakker. "Surely Hitchcock was right here—it was avian feet carried on avian limbs attached to a basic avian body plan."

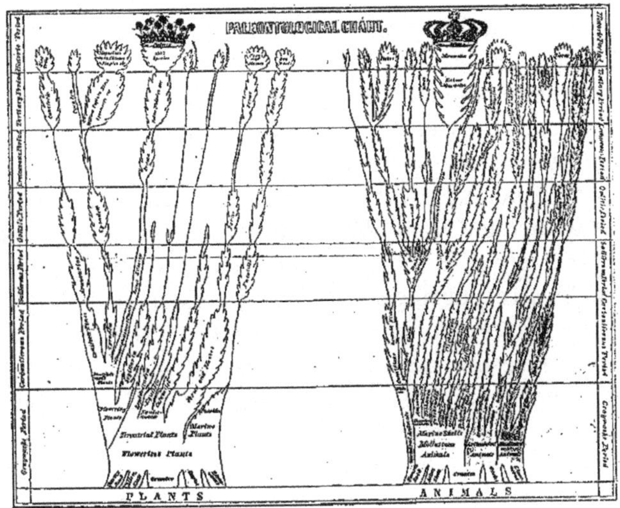

Palaeontological Chart from Elementary Geology, 1840

29 The Tree of Life

"The real question is not whether these hypotheses accord with our religious views, but whether they are true."

In 1840 when Edward Hitchcock published the first edition of his textbook, *Elementary Geology,* a large, hand-colored illustration entitled "Palaeontological Chart" was selected for the frontispiece. Likely drawn by Orra, it received barely a mention by reviewers and critics at the time. But that chart has attracted more attention from science historians in recent times than any other part of *Elementary Geology;* some have dubbed it Hitchcock's "Tree of Life."

The "Palaeontological Chart" consists of two elongated tree-like diagrams displayed side by side, one labeled "Plants," the other "Animals." The vertical axis is a time scale that includes the major geological periods as they were known in Hitchcock's day: Graywacke, Carboniferous, Saliferous, Oolitic, Cretaceous, Tertiary, and Historic. At the base of the diagram of the plants are two groups, the lowest the "Flowerless Plants" with "Flowering Plants" a bit higher. "Flowerless Plants" are divided above into "Terrestrial" and "Marine," "Flowering Plants" into dicots and monocots. Each of these groups is further divided and by the Historic Period are presented in eight groups, the Conifers, the Cycads, the Flowering Plants, the Palms, the Lycopods, the Horsetails, the Ferns and Mosses, and the Seaweeds. An ornate crown rests on the palms, suggesting they represent the epitome of plant life on earth. At the bottom of the diagram of the animals are four groups, "Vertebral Animals," "Molluscus Animals," "Articulated Animals," and "Radiated Animals." These are further divided as one ascends the tree, with seventeen groups at the top, representing the major animal groups on earth including Fishes, Lizards, Birds, Mammals, Corals, Insects, Spiders, and several groups of shelled animals. At the apex of the Mammals is written the word "Man," adorned by his own crown.

It would be tempting to conclude from the "Palaeontological Chart" that Edward Hitchcock was espousing a two-lineage version of evolution, suggesting that all plants were derived from a common plant ancestor and all animals from a common animal ancestor. But that idea was not at all what lay behind this illustration. The French naturalist Jean-Baptiste Lamarck was one of a number of early exponents of the idea of "transmutation," that species of living things have been transformed into other species. Hitchcock disagreed vehemently. All life forms, he argued, were found as fossils in a range of rock formations representing a great span of earth's history. "Hence we learn that the hypothesis of Lamarck is without foundation, which supposes there has been a transmutation of species from less to more perfect, since the beginning of organic life on the globe."

Hitchcock's "Palaeontological Chart," then, was not meant to suggest that lower groups gave rise to or were transmuted into higher groups. It simply illustrated the eras in which those groups were created. Furthermore, he contended, similarities between more recent groups and ancient forms were evidence not of a continuous lineage, but of a common plan or essence existing in the mind of the Almighty. If man resembled other mammals, it was not due to shared ancestry. It was simply a body plan favored by God in His wisdom. What worked for the primates, He must have reasoned, will work also for the human race.

At the very time that Hitchcock's "Palaeontological Chart" first appeared in print, Charles Darwin was constructing his own "Tree of Life," one based on a radically different conception of how life on earth had developed. The similarities among groups of living things, past and present, Darwin posited, were evidence not of the wisdom of the creator, but of common ancestry. Earlier groups gave rise gradually to later groups due entirely to natural forces, although he was still formulating his ideas about the nature of those forces. As early as 1837, Darwin noted the powerful effects of artificial selection in breeding of pigeons, dogs, and livestock. If humans could produce such dramatic changes in species in a few generations, he reasoned, could not some similar processes be operating in nature whereby species were changed, transmuted, over time?

Charles Darwin and Edward Hitchcock had many shared interests—had they ever met, they would no doubt have had much to talk about. Darwin had high praise for Hitchcock's 1841 report (see page 171) as well as his research: "In my opinion these footsteps (with which subject your name is certain to go down to long future posterity) make one of the most curious discoveries of the present century and highly important in its several bearings." But their views of the development of life on earth, while they might appear superficially similar, could not have been more different.

Darwin's "Tree of Life" and his thoughts on the process of natural selection did not appear in print until 1859 in *Origin of Species*. It naturally enraged many religious leaders and authors, the suggestion that all life shared a common ancestor, the implication that man was just another twig on that tree.

The thirty-first edition of *Elementary Geology* coauthored by Edward and Charles H. Hitchcock was published just three years after *Origin of Species*. It contained a sharp critique of Darwin's hypothesis of transmutation of species and natural selection. The authors quoted Agassiz: "The connection of faunas…is not material, but resides in the thought of the Creator." Most tellingly, the "Palaeontological Chart," the frontispiece of thirty editions over two decades, was nowhere to be found. Hitchcock wanted nothing to do with Darwin's irreligious notions.

In July 1863, barely six months before his death, Hitchcock delivered his final published word on science and religion in *Bibliotheca Sacra*. In "Law of Nature's Constancy Subordinate to the Higher Law of Change," he addressed the greatest challenge to orthodox Christianity of his time, the writings of Charles Darwin. Needless to say, he disapproved. He first raised concerns about Darwin's formulations on religious grounds. They made unnecessary the existence of a Deity, they led to the "grossest materialism," they rejected the concept of immortality, and they removed all moral responsibility of man to God.

Then, after enumerating his objections to Darwinism on religious grounds, Hitchcock's offensive pivoted in a new direction: "But after all, the real question is, not whether these hypotheses accord with our religious views, but whether they are true." He proceeded to state his scientific objections to Darwinism. First, if Darwin's ideas were correct, he argued, there should be ample evidence of intermediate or transitional forms. "The most important point in it relates to organic remains. For if the doctrine of transmutation of species be true, we ought to find ten thousand intermediate varieties in the successive formations." And what about man? asked Hitchcock.

> Whence came he? If he is only one of the lower animals metamorphosed, we ought surely to find a multitude of intermediate varieties. But not one has ever

> been brought to light...Man's appearance at so late a period in the earth's history, and so independent of all other species, seems a providential testimony to the absurdity of this hypothesis.

As to the mechanism of transmutation, Hitchcock was not convinced by Darwin's explanation. Natural selection, he seemed to imply, might be capable of causing one species to give rise to another, but only the Creator could set those processes in motion. We might have expected Edward Hitchcock to leave it there, but he did not. In the end he added this tantalizing thought on the idea of transmutation of species:

> The fact that these new creations are repeated at intervals, and seem to form a part of a series of operations, which we know to be natural, makes it quite probable they also are natural. Perhaps this unknown law will by and by be discovered, as many new laws have been to explain phenomena once supposed to be miraculous because anomalous and inexplicable.

Ever the empiricist, the venerable professor from Amherst could not rule out the possibility that species might in fact transmutate, or evolve, into new species. Had he lived long enough to see additional evidence for Darwin's theories, the indefatigable Edward Hitchcock might well have found a way to accept them, to understand them as all a part of God's plan.

The publication of *Origin of Species* was a watershed event with far-reaching consequences for science and its relationship with religion. Until 1859, many scientists professed to be believers in religion with varying approaches to accommodating science. But after the publication of *Origin of Species*, some argue, the relationship between science and religion would never be the same. Science, it is often claimed, became secular, unshackled by and unconcerned with matters of faith.

Some have labeled Edward Hitchcock one of the last of the Christian geologists. But if by that term is meant someone who allows religion to intrude upon and influence science, then it is not a fair assessment of Edward Hitchcock. For Hitchcock found his own way of bridging the gap between science and faith. Reverend Moses Stuart had proposed that science and religion need not be linked, that each should be allowed to go its own way without regard for the other. Edward Hitchcock's paradigm differed only slightly from Stuart's, although it might be argued that the two would produce identical results. Science, when properly understood and thoroughly investigated, would never lead him astray. One way or another, if he was diligent, thoughtful, prayerful,

Figure 79. Charles Darwin (1809-1882) and *On the Origin of Species*

he would find the truth. And one way or another, that truth would confirm his faith: "Scientific truth, rightly understood, is religious truth."

Nearly half a century earlier in "The Moral Telescope," a young Edward Hitchcock had written that if, after careful scrutiny and investigation, a religious doctrine proved contrary to reason, "I am bound not to receive it." He repeated that sentiment in *The Religion of Geology*, albeit with conditions and circumlocutions. But as a practical matter, whenever there was a clear conflict between scientific truth and his religious beliefs, Hitchcock accepted the scientific truth. If it seemed to contradict the Bible, he would not be deterred. For he had full confidence that the truth of the words of revelation would eventually be upheld by science. He recognized that there were some matters of science that seemed incompatible with his faith; perhaps Darwinism and transmutation among them. Of such apparently irreconcilable conflicts he wrote in his notes:

> But when I see Divine Benevolence in ninety-nine out of a hundred of the movements and contrivances of nature I know that their Author must be

> infinitely benevolent and I wait the light of eternity to clear up a few excepted cases.

Hitchcock left an enormous body of work that testifies to his unconstrained pursuit of scientific truth. Granted his faith sometimes made the acceptance of those truths difficult. Perhaps it slowed him along the way, as in his prolonged allegiance to the biblical account of Noah's deluge or his protracted hedging and equivocation on the glacial theory. He clearly had a strong distaste for the notion of transmutation of species which drove him to oppose Darwin's theories. But as he had done so often in the past, he left the door open.

The most accurate assessment of Edward Hitchcock's creed is not that he was conflicted about his faith and his science, but that he never let disagreements between those two realms discourage him from the search for truth. Far from being the last of the Christian geologists, he may have been one of the first of a new breed of scientist, men and women possessed of a strong religious principle while remaining true to science.

Edward Hitchcock's younger son, Charles H. Hitchcock, was a direct descendant of that lineage. For over fifty years he was a leading voice in American geology, particularly in glacial geology. It did not trouble him, so far as his writings and the words of his colleagues reveal, that this was not a matter found in the book of Genesis, or that Noah's flood may have been a minor, regional phenomenon, rather than the singular, world-changing event suggested in the scriptures. Charles may even have been a convert to Darwinism. And yet early in the twentieth century he published a paper in *Bibliotheca Sacra* that presented what he considered a plausible scientific explanation for the parting of the Red Sea.

As with the father, so with the son: science and religion walking comfortably, side by side.

Epilogue

Stephen Jay Gould, one of the twentieth century's most influential evolutionary biologists, authored more than twenty books on Charles Darwin, evolution, and the relationship between science and religion. In *Leonardo's Mountain of Clams and the Diet of Worms*, Gould wrote of the dual role of a worldview in the life of a scientist. He chose as an example James Dwight Dana.

Professor James Dwight Dana of Yale was a friend and colleague of Edward Hitchcock, and an eminent paleontologist of nineteenth century America. Like Hitchcock, Dana was a man of deep religious convictions who was reluctant to give up his faith in the face of scientific evidence. Dana constructed a conceptual framework for the development of life on earth based on "serial creation," the idea that God created living things in many creative events over the millennia. Each creation, Dana believed, was an improvement over the last, each group of species more closely suited to life on earth. From the lowly fishes and reptiles, to the birds and mammals, and finally to man, God endowed earth with a series of lifeforms, each an improvement over the previous, ending, of course, with man. Perfection in animals, asserted Dana, could be judged by the degree of cephalization. The larger the head and the farther forward it was carried on the body, the more nearly perfect the animal. In this system *Homo sapiens* represented the very pinnacle of animal perfection.

His worldview allowed James Dwight Dana to integrate a wide range of knowledge into what he believed was a coherent scheme. But it prevented him from entertaining the notion of transmutation and made him an outspoken opponent of Darwinism for at least fifteen years. And when he finally acceded to the possibility that Darwin had it right, it was a caviling, conditional acceptance. In Gould's terms, Dana's worldview created a "conceptual lock" against new ideas.

Every scientist has a worldview, a paradigm that influences to some degree the ability to consider new evidence, to entertain dramatically different concepts from those that have become long held. James Dwight Dana was beholden to his construct of cephalization; it was his "conceptual lock" against Darwinism. Similarly, French anatomist Georges Cuvier spent most of his career developing his "principle of the correlation of parts," an elaborate theory based on the assumption that a precise relationship existed among the anatomical features of a species. Any change to even a single feature would be destructive to the species; thus transmutation of a species was impossible. So when Darwin promulgated the process of natural selection and suggested that it was responsible for transmutation of species, Cuvier resisted. Louis Agassiz, that lion of American science who was sometimes quick to embrace new, revolutionary concepts, was wedded to his belief that the relationships among species "…resides in the thought of the Creator." He went to his grave opposed to Darwinism.

Did Edward Hitchcock have a "conceptual lock" on new ideas? He certainly had a worldview, and it began with the Holy Scriptures. But coequal with religion in Hitchcock's worldview were the tenets of inductive reasoning, of empiricism. Again and again in his life he first resisted, then eventually accepted new concepts, new paradigms in geology and in paleontology. Even Darwinism was not entirely beyond the pale for him. Whether he would ever have accepted it will never be known, but he gave several hints that he was still open to evidence that might sway him.

Thomas Henry Huxley, perhaps Darwin's greatest promoter and supporter, wrote, "My business is to teach my aspirations to conform themselves to fact, not to try and make facts harmonize with my aspirations." While Edward Hitchcock might not have gone quite that far, in his own way and at his own pace, he was able more successfully than some other eminent scientists of his time to bring his aspirations into conformity with the facts as he saw them.

This then was the most important and enduring legacy of Edward Hitchcock's life: that he allowed science to lead him where it might, without regard for his faith. It seems in retrospect to contradict his oft-expressed belief that science and religion are not in conflict. But of course, Edward Hitchcock did not see it that way. His confidence in the congruity of religion and science, far from shackling him, actually freed him to pursue truth wherever it took him. He was certain, as certain as one can be about anything, that the search for truth would not lead him astray, that all knowledge was derived from God.

The story is told, although the source is unknown, of an incident late in the teaching career of Edward Hitchcock. His senior geology class was meeting for the first time in a newly renovated lecture room on the upper floor of a campus building, a room that had been equipped with a window in the roof to better illuminate the space beneath. Such a window may have been unusual in his day, a modern architectural innovation. The old professor stood before his class gazing up at the new window and smiling as he spoke the words that might be regarded as the guiding principle of his life:

"Young gentlemen, all the light we have here comes from above."

Notes and References

Abbreviations:

AC	Amherst College Archives and Special Collections, Amherst, Mass.
AJS	*American Journal of Science and Arts*
AMM	*American Monthly Magazine and Critical Review*
BR	*Biblical Repository and Quarterly Observer*
BS	*Bibliotheca Sacra (and Biblical Repository)*
EMJH	Edward (Jr.) and Mary Judson Hitchcock Family Papers, 1840-1962 at AC
EOH	Edward & Orra White Hitchcock Papers at AC
FH	*Franklin Herald,* Greenfield, Mass.
HD	Henry N. Flynt Library, Historic Deerfield, Deerfield, Mass.
HFE	*Hampshire and Franklin Express,* Amherst, Mass.
HFP	Hitchcock Family Papers at PVMA
NAR	*North American Review*
PVMA	Pocumtuck Valley Memorial Association, Deerfield, Mass.
SR	*Springfield Republican,* Springfield, Mass.

General References

Bakker, Robert T. "Introduction: Dinosaurs Acting Like Birds, and Vice Versa–An Homage to the Reverend Edward Hitchcock." In *Feathered Dragons: Studies on the Transition from Dinosaurs to Birds*, edited by Philip J. Currie, Eva B. Koppelhus, Martin A. Shugar, and Joanna L. Wright. Bloomington, IN: Indiana University Press, 2004, 1-11.

Carpenter, Edward W., and Charles F. Morehouse. *The History of the Town of Amherst, Massachusetts.* Amherst, Mass.: Carpenter and Morehouse, 1896.

D'Arienzo, Daria. "The 'Union of the Beautiful with the Useful': Through the Eyes of Orra White Hitchcock." *Massachusetts Review* 51 (Summer 2010): 294-336.

Herbert, Robert L. "The Complete Correspondence of Edward Hitchcock and Benjamin Silliman, 1817-1863: The *American Journal of Science* and the Rise of American Geology," transcribed and annotated with an introductory essay," Amherst College Archives and Special Collections, 2020, http://bit.ly/2m6vnxtHitch.

________. "Dr. James Deane of Greenfield: Edward Hitchcock's Rival Discoverer of Dinosaur Tracks," Mount Holyoke College Institutional Digital Archive, 2014, http://hdl.handle.net/10166/3529.

Hitchcock, Edward. "An Attempt to Discriminate and Describe the Animals that Made the Fossil Footmarks of the United States, and Especially of New England." *Memoirs of the American Academy of Arts and Sciences* 3 (1848): 129-256.

________. "Description of Two New Species of Fossil Footmarks." *AJS* 2nd ser. 4 (July 1847): 46-57.

________. Diary and observations notebooks, July-October 1830, EOH, Box 11, Folder 7; October 1830-October 1831, EOH, Box 11, Folder 8; May 1832-January 1833, EOH, Box 11, Folder 9; and May and September-November 1833, EOH, Box 11, Folder 10.

________. *Elementary Geology.* 1st ed. Amherst, Massachusetts: J. S. and C. Adams, 1840; 8th ed. New York: Mark H. Newman and Co., 1847; 31st ed. (co-authored with Charles H. Hitchcock) New York: Ivison and Phinney, 1860.

________. Expenses, notebook, 1830-1833, EOH, Box 11, Folders 12 and 13.

________. *Final Report on the Geology of Mass.* Amherst, Mass.: J. S. and C. Adams, 1841.

________. *Ichnology of New England: A Report on the Sandstone of the Connecticut Valley.* Boston, Mass.: William White, 1858.

________. "The Law of Nature's Constancy Subordinate to the Higher Law of Change." *BS* 20 (July 1863): 489-561.

________. "New Facts and Conclusions Respecting the Fossil Footmarks of the Connecticut Valley." *AJS* 2nd ser. 36 (July 1863): 46-57.

________. "Ornithichnology—Description of the Foot Marks of Birds, (Ornithichnites) on New Red Sandstone in Massachusetts." *AJS* 29 (1836): 307-40.

________. "Private Notes" (3 vols.), 1828-1864, EOH, Box 19, Folders 3-5.

________. *The Religion of Geology and Its Connected Sciences.* Boston, Mass.: Phillips, Sampson, and Company, 1851.

________. *The Religion of Geology and Its Connected Sciences.* 2nd ed. London: James Blackwood, 1859.

________. *Reminiscences of Amherst College, Historical, Scientific, Biographical and Autobiographical.* Northampton, Mass.: Bridgman & Childs, 1863.

________. "Supplement to the Ichnology of New England." *Proceedings of the American Academy of Arts and Sciences* 6 (December 1862): 85-92.

________. *Utility of Natural History, A Discourse.* Pittsfield, Mass.: P. Allen, 1823.

________ and Charles H. Hitchcock. A *Synopsis of the Genera and Species of the Lithichnozoa in the Hitchcock Ichnological Museum of Amherst College.* Amherst, Mass.: Amherst College, undated, probably 1858.

Hitchcock, Edward, Jr. Notebooks A, B, C, and D (Memoirs), EMJH Box 7, Folders 22-32.

[Jackson, Charles T.]. "Professor Hitchcock's Report on the Geology, etc., of Massachusetts." *NAR* 42 (April 1836): 422-48.

King, Stanley. *The Consecrated Eminence: The Story of the Campus and Buildings of Amherst College.* Amherst, Mass.: Amherst College, 1951.

Lesley, J. P. "Memoir of Edward Hitchcock 1793-1864." *Biographical Memoirs, National Academy of Sciences* 1 (1877): 113-134.

McMaster, Robert T. "Edward Hitchcock's Geological Survey of Massachusetts: 1830-1833." *Earth Sciences History* 39(1) (2020): 91-119.

________. "Lord Is It I? The Sermons of Edward Hitchcock." *Historical Journal of Massachusetts* 48 (Summer 2020): 94-123.

Pick, Nancy. *Curious Footprints: Professor Hitchcock's Dinosaur Tracks and Other Natural History Treasures at Amherst College.* Amherst, Mass.: Amherst College Press, 2006.

Root, Martin, 1847-1851, Diary, AC, Amherst College Alumni Biographical Files, 1821-.

Sheldon, George. *A History of Deerfield, Massachusetts.* 2 vols. Greenfield, Mass.: E. A. Hall & Co., 1895.
Silliman, Benjamin, letters to Edward Hitchcock, 1817-1860, EOH, Box 3, Folders 37-40, Box 4, Folders 1-4.
Smith, Beatrice Scheer. *A Painted Herbarium: The Life and Art of Emily Hitchcock Terry, 1838-1921.* Minneapolis, MN: University of Minnesota Press, 1992.
Stearns, Malcolm, Jr., "Epaphras Hoyt, Public Servant: A Topical Biography." 1939. HD.
Tyler, William S. *A Biographical Sketch of Mrs. Orra White Hitchcock.* Springfield, Mass.: Samuel Bowles and Company, 1863.
________. *History of Amherst College During its First Half Century 1821 to 1871.* Springfield, Mass.: Clark W. Bryan and Company, 1873.
________. *A History of Amherst College During the Administrations of its First Five Presidents from 1821 to 1891.* New York: Frederick H. Hitchcock, 1895.
Walker, Alice M. *Historic Homes of Amherst.* Amherst, Mass.: Carpenter & Morehouse, 1905.

Transcriptions

The digital documents listed below are available at www.EdwardHitchcock.com; some or all will also be made available courtesy of the Amherst College Archives and Special Collections at acdc.amherst.edu. Quotations in the text may be located by searching the appropriate transcription. Transcriptions of the letters between Edward Hitchcock and Benjamin Silliman by Robert L. Herbert are listed under "General References" above.

McMaster, Robert T. "Geological Survey Notes of Edward Hitchcock 1830-1835."
________. "Letters of Edward Hitchcock and Family 1819-1864."
________. "Memoirs of Edward Hitchcock, Jr. 1901-1906"
________. "Private Notes of Edward Hitchcock 1829-1864."
________. "Sermons of Edward Hitchcock 1819-1862."
________. "Teaching Notes of Edward Hitchcock 1825-1863."
________. "Unpublished Works of Edward Hitchcock 1809-1850"

Links to Finding Aids:

Edward & Orra White Hitchcock Papers (EOH)
http://asteria.fivecolleges.edu/findaids/amherst/ma27.html
Edward and Mary Judson Hitchcock Family Papers, 1840-1962 (EMJH)
https://asteria.fivecolleges.edu/findaids/amherst/ma2.html
Amherst College Early History Collection, 1815-1891
http://asteria.fivecolleges.edu/findaids/amherst/ma55.html
Amherst College Board of Trustees Records. Meeting Minutes, 1825-2013
http://asteria.fivecolleges.edu/findaids/amherst/maRG001-01.html
Hitchcock Family Papers (HFP)
https://deerfield-ma.org/wp-content/uploads/2013/10/Hitchcock-Family-Papers2-1.pdf

Links for Searching Digitized Material:

Amherst College Archives and Special Collections, https://acdc.amherst.edu/
Henry N. Flynt Library, Historic Deerfield and Pocumtuck Valley Memorial Assoc., https://library.historic-deerfield.org/eg/opac/home
Mount Holyoke College Archives and Special Collections, https://aspace.fivecolleges.edu/

CHAPTER 1: The Hatter of Deerfield

(pp. 11-12) Details of life in Deerfield in the eighteenth century are from Sheldon's *History of Deerfield, Massachusetts.* The theological and political views of Rev. Jonathan Ashley are discussed in that source, in Justin Hitchcock's "Remarks and Observations," and in Miller's *The Reverend Jonathan Ashley House.*

(pp. 16-17) The account of the April 20, 1776, town meeting is from Sheldon's *History of Deerfield, Massachusetts,* 700.

Granville Jubilee, The. Springfield, Mass.: H. S. Taylor, 1845.

Hitchcock, Justin, to David and Silence Hoit, April 3, 1778. HFP, Box 1, Folder 6.

________. "Indenture of Justin Hitchcock, May 5, 1766." HFP, Box 1, Folders 6.

________. "Remarks and Observations by Justin Hitchcock." HFP, Box 1, Folder 6.

________. "The Says of People." HFP, Box 1, Folder 6.

Hoyt, David W. *A Genealogical History of the Hoyt, Haight, and Hight Families.* Providence, RI: Providence Press Co., 1871.

Johnson's New Universal Cyclopaedia. New York: A.J. Johnson, 1881.

Melvoin, Richard I. *New England Outpost: War and Society in Colonial Deerfield.* New York: Norton and Co., 1989.

Miller, Amelia. *The Reverend Jonathan Ashley House.* Deerfield, Mass.: Historic Deerfield, 1962.

CHAPTER 2: Justin and Mercy

(pp. 19-20) An account of the ratification process for the Massachusetts State Constitution in Deerfield appears in Sheldon's *History of Deerfield.*

(p. 21-2) Details of Justin's hatmaking business are found in his Account Book.

(p. 22) Edward's comments on his father's financial difficulties are from *Reminiscences,* 281.

(p. 26) Election as a deacon was so great an honor in that era that it was often inscribed on one's gravestone, as it was for Justin Hitchcock, his son Henry, and his grandson Nathaniel Hitchcock. Justin served for 24 years, Henry for 26 years, Nathaniel for 31 years. Justin's son Charles was also a deacon.

(p. 26) Epaphras and Elihu Hoyt were outspoken anti-masons; for a time in the 1830s Epaphras published the *Franklin Freeman*, an anti-mason newspaper. While many anti-masons objected to Masonry on religious grounds, the content of the *Freeman* was entirely political according to Stearns, "Epaphras Hoyt, Public Servant," 113-25.

(p. 28) Edward Hitchcock's descriptions of his obstinate behavior as a child are from his "Private Notes," entry for November 3, 1855.

Hitchcock, Justin. Account Book, 1783-1800. Account Book Collection, PVMA.

________. "Remarks and Observations." HFP, Box 1, Folder 6.

Sheldon, George. *The Little Brown House on the Albany Road.* Deerfield, Mass.: George Sheldon, 1913.

CHAPTER 3: A New Academy

(pp. 29-30). Records of Edward Hitchcock's enrollment at Deerfield Academy including the date of his first attendance are found in Deerfield Academy Catalogue of Students, 1799-1855. His studies of spherical trigonometry with Epaphras Hoyt in 1811 are mentioned in *Reminiscences*; his early notes on the subject may be found in "Calculation of the Orbit..."

(p. 36) According to Sheldon's *History of Deerfield*, the Literary Adelphi were founded on August 6, 1804. But the title of Hitchcock's address to the group in 1814 indicates it was delivered on August 8 of that year, "at their seventh anniversary."

Cutter, William R. *Families of Western New York.* New York: Lewis Historical Publications, 1912, 345-6.

Deerfield Academy Catalogue of Students, 1799-1855. PVMA.

Herrick, Claudius, to Thomas Lewis, June 28, 1799. HD.

Hitchcock, Edward. "Calculation of the Orbit of the Meteor…," HFP, Box 2, Folder 9.

________. "Poetical Sketch of Democracy in the County of Hampshire," 1809, EOH, Box 22, Folder 41.

Lyman, Joseph. *Advantages and Praises of Wisdom.* Greenfield, Mass.: F. Barker, 1799.

Opal, J. M. *Beyond the Farm: National Ambitions in Rural New England.* Philadelphia, PA: University of Pennsylvania Press, 2008.

Private and Special Statutes of the Commonwealth of Massachusetts, 1780-1805. Boston, Mass.: Manning and Loring, 1805.

CHAPTER 4: The Great Almanack Debate

(pp. 37-9) Edward's tutelage under his uncle, Epaphras Hoyt, is discussed in Sheldon's *History of Deerfield;* an account of their sessions in the elm tree is found in Sheldon's *Little Brown House.*

"Academic Honours," *AMM* 4 (November 1818), 65.

Blunt, Edmund M. Letter to the editors, *AMM* 2 (January 1818): 169-70.

________. Letter to the editors, *AMM* 3 (August 1818): 296.

Hitchcock, Edward. *Country Almanack for the Year of Our Lord 1814.* Greenfield, Mass.: Denio & Phelps, 1814.

________. "Messrs. Editors." *AMM* 2 (February 1818): 248-9.

________. "Messrs. Editors." *AMM* 3 (July 1818): 210-2.

________. "To Astronomers and Navigators." *AMM* 2 (December 1817): 89-90.

Hoyt, Epaphras. *Antiquarian Researches or Indian Wars.* Greenfield, Mass.: Ansel Phelps, 1824.

________. "Astronomical Observations Made Near the Centre of the Village of Deerfield, Mass." *Memoirs of the American Academy of Arts and Sciences* 3 (1815): 305-7.

Marché, Jordan D. II. "Edward Hitchcock's Promising Astronomical Career." *Earth Sciences History* 12 (1993): 180-6.

CHAPTER 5: Bonaparte's Downfall

(p. 49-50) Details of the Literary Adelphi and the Young Ladies' Literary Society are found in Sheldon's *History of Deerfield.* An account of the performance appeared in *FH*, December 6, 1814, 3.

(p. 53-4) Accounts of the meeting of the Washington Benevolent Society appear in Sheldon's *History of Deerfield* and in *FH*, July 13, 1813, 2-3.

Herbert, Robert L., and Daria D'Arienzo. *Orra White Hitchcock: An Amherst Woman of Art and Science.* Hanover, NH: University Press of New England, 2011.

Hitchcock, Edward. "The Appeal," *FH*, August 11, 1812, 2 (signed "The Voice of New England").

________. *Emancipation of Europe, or The Downfall of Bonaparte: A Tragedy.* Greenfield, Mass.: Denio & Phelps, 1815, prologue.

________. *FH*, November 10, 1812, 1.
________. "Genius and Application," Undated (1814?), EOH, Box 22, Folder 26.
________. "On a Separation of the United States," EOH, Box 18, Folder 6.
"Rejoicing Over the Fall of Napoleon," *Boston Globe*, December 20, 1914, 44.

CHAPTER 6: Season of Love

(pp. 59-60) In an entry in his "Private Notes" dated February 8, 1829, Hitchcock writes of a conversation he had with Reverend Willard shortly before departing from Deerfield. One line of dialogue is taken directly from those notes.

(p. 64) In *Reminiscences* Hitchcock states that his preceptorship lasted three years, beginning in fall 1816. But in a letter written to Benjamin Silliman of Yale in January 1819, he writes that his separation from the Academy was "some months back."

(p. 70) For Hitchcock's thoughts on his first sermon see "Notes 1819" from Yale.

Fitch, E. T. *An Inquiry into the Nature of Sin.* New Haven, CT, A.H. Maltby, 1827.
Hitchcock, Edward. "Basaltick Columns." *NAR* 1 (September 1815): 337-8.
________. "Eulogy on J. Dickinson," 1815, EOH, Box 22, Folder 18.
________. Farewell address at Deerfield Academy, 1817, EOH, Box 22, Folder 25.
________. "Moral Telescope," *FH*, January 13, 20, 27, February 3, 10, 24, May 5, 1818.
________. "Notes 1819," EOH, Box 18, Folder 1.
________. "Southampton Lead Mine." *NAR* 1 (September 1815): 335-7.
________ to Benjamin Silliman, January 29, 1819, in Fisher, George P. *Life of Benjamin Silliman M.D.* 2 vols. New York: Charles Scribner and Company, 1866.
Kingsley, William L. *Yale College: A Sketch of Its History.* New York: Holt, 1879.
"Torquetum Astronomical Device," Impressions from a Lost World, https://dinotracksdiscovery.org.
Tuckerman, Frederick. "President Edward Hitchcock." *Amherst Graduates' Quarterly* 10 (November 1920): 2-13.

CHAPTER 7: Preaching in the Wilderness

Much of the material on Hitchcock's sermons in Chapters 7-9 appeared originally in McMaster, "Lord Is It I? The Sermons of Edward Hitchcock" in the *Historical Journal of Massachusetts* (see General References).

(pp. 75-6) Some of the dialogue between Edward and Orra is based on Hitchcock's "Remarks on Fungi Painted 1821."

(pp. 77-8) Details of John Emerson's arrival in Conway and the town's history are from Pease, *History of Conway Massachusetts 1767-1917.*

(p. 84) A specimen list that appears to be a draft of the one sent to John Torrey is part of a series of lists dated 1822 in Edward Hitchcock, "Remarks Upon Fungi Collected & Painted in the Summer of 1821," EOH, Box 20, Folder 31.

Herbert, Robert L. *Fungi Selecti Picti 1821: Watercolors by Orra White Hitchcock (1796-1863).* Northampton, Mass.: Smith College, 2011. The original album is held by Smith College Special Collections.
Hitchcock, Edward. "Description of a New Species of Botrychium." *AJS* 6 (1823): 103-4.
________. "Remarks Upon Fungi Painted 1821," EOH, Box 20, Folder 31.
________. "A Sketch of the Geology, Mineralogy, and Scenery of the Regions Contiguous to the River Connecticut." *AJS* 6 (1823): 1-71, 201-36, and 7 (1824): 1-30.

"Minutes of a Meeting of the Congregational Church of Christ in Conway," May 28, 1821, EOH, Box 1, Folder 11.

Pease, Charles S., ed. *History of Conway Massachusetts 1767-1917.* Springfield, Mass.: Springfield Printing and Binding Company, 1917.

Torrey, John, to George de Schweinitz, May 3, 1822. In Shear, C. L. and Neil E. Stevens, eds. "The Correspondence of Schweinitz and Torrey." *Memoirs of the Torrey Botanical Club* 16 (July 1921): 119-300.

Town and Vital Records of Conway, Massachusetts, 1760-1868, Genealogical Society of Utah, Salt Lake City, UT.

CHAPTER 8: Revivals and Declensions

(pp. 87-8) The sermon quoted is No. 189, "Duties of Children," delivered in October 1823.

(p. 90) Hitchcock's comments on the preaching style of some European ministers are from an entry in his travel diary dated June 30, 1850.

Balmer, Randall, and Lauren F. Winner. *Protestantism in America.* New York: Columbia University Press, 2002.

"Natural history," *FH*, December 2, 1823; *New England Farmer* (Boston, Mass.*)*, December 6, 1823, 5; *New York Statesman*, November 15, 1823; *Pittsfield Sun* (Mass.), November 27, 1823.

Review of *Utility of Natural History* by E. Hitchcock. *NAR* 18 (January 1824): 213-4.

Romer, Robert H. *Slavery in the Connecticut Valley of Massachusetts.* Florence, Mass.: Levellers Press, 2009.

CHAPTER 9: The Sovereignty of God

(pp. 103-4) The Hitchcocks' son died on March 15, 1824. Edward delivered the sermon, "Sovereignty of God, Part 1," the following Sunday. On the cover of the handwritten manuscript, he indicates his choice of hymn number 97 for the morning service. Elsewhere in his sermon notes he mentions the "Hartford Hymnal," probably a reference to *The Hartford Selection of Hymns* (1823). Selection 97 of that volume is the hymn, "As thy days, so shall thy strength be," based on Deuteronomy 33:25.

Hitchcock, Edward. "Extract from a Farewell Discourse." *Christian Spectator* 8 (1826): 120-3.

________. Letter of resignation, 1825, EOH, Box 1, Folder 11.

CHAPTER 10: Silliman's Apprentice

(pp. 111-12) Edward Hitchcock received his official dismissal from his ministerial duties on October 25, 1825. The couple likely departed from Conway soon after that date. Edward's sister, Emilia, and Henry Billings of Conway announced their marriage intentions on December 24, 1825; they were married in Deerfield on January 14, 1826.

Silliman, Benjamin. *Elements of Chemistry, In the Order of the Lectures Given in Yale College.* 2 vols. New Haven, CT: H. Howe, 1830.

CHAPTER 11: A Vast Laboratory

(p. 123) Marino sheep had become a popular breed throughout New England by 1825 according to Russell, *A Long Deep Furrow*, and were abundant in Amherst by 1837 according to Carpenter and Morehouse, *History of the Town of Amherst, Massachusetts*.

(pp. 128-31) Details of the history of the town of Amherst are from Carpenter and Morehouse, *History of the Town of Amherst, Massachusetts*.

Hitchcock, Edward. "Influence of Nervous Disorders Upon Religious Experience." *Christian Spectator* 1 (April 1827): 177-205.

________. "Rarified Air Balloons." *AJS* 12 (1827): 372-3.

Tuckerman, Frederick. *Amherst Academy: A New England School of the Past, 1814-1861*. Amherst, Mass.: Trustees of Amherst College, 1929.

CHAPTER 12: The Balance of the Universe

(p. 133-4) The christening of Edward Hitchcock, Jr., the first to take place in the new chapel, is mentioned in Carpenter and Morehouse, *History of the Town of Amherst, Massachusetts*. President Humphrey was the pastor of the church at that time and would likely have presided. The prayer offered by Edward Hitchcock is from "Consecrating prayer written on the birth of his son," May 24, 1828.

Hitchcock, Edward. *Catalogue of Plants Growing Without Cultivation in the Vicinity of Amherst College*. Amherst, Mass.: J. S. and C. Adams, 1829.

________. "Consecrating prayer on the birth of his son," May 24, 1828, EOH, Box 19, Folder 2.

________. "Notice of the Report on the Geology of North Carolina…by Denison Olmsted." *AJS* 14 (1829): 230-51.

Letter to the editor, *FH*, December 8, 1818, 3.

CHAPTER 13: The Blessings of Temperance

(p. 145-6) By 1834 Stephen West Williams, cousin of Edward Hitchcock, had earned a reputation as both a physician and a scientist, having published many articles in medical journals. Whether Edward ever discussed his health problems with Williams is not known.

(p. 147-8, 150-3) The "Private Notes" of Edward Hitchcock that have been preserved total more than 50,000 words; some 80 pages are missing, either lost or intentionally removed; in the entry dated April 17, 1859, he writes that he has considered removing some pages.

(p. 151) In 1817 Hitchcock and Williams ran a display advertisement in the *Franklin Herald* soliciting rocks and minerals for their collections which they planned to donate to Deerfield Academy. For their efforts the pair were elected honorary members of the Historical Society of New York in 1818.

Burk, C. John. "Evolution of a Flora: Early Connecticut Valley Botanists." *Rhodora* 96 (January 1994), 75-96.

Hitchcock, Edward. "Blessings of Temperance in Food." *American National Preacher* 9 (November 1834): 81-96; "Consequences of Intemperance in Eating." *ANP* 8 (May 1834): 369-380; "Nature of Intemperance in Eating." *ANP* 8 (March 1834): 337-352.

________. *Dyspepsy Forestalled and Resisted*. Amherst, Mass.: J. S. and C. Adams, 1830.

Searcy, Karen B., and Matthew G. Hickler, "The Steven West Williams Herbarium: An early 19th century plant collection from Deerfield, Massachusetts." *Rhodora* 119 (2017): 132–162.

Swedlund, Alan C. *Shadows in the Valley: A Cultural History of Illness, Death, and Loss in New England, 1840-1916.* Amherst, Mass.: University of Massachusetts Press, 2010.

CHAPTER 14: The Diluvial Current

Much of the material in this chapter appeared previously in McMaster, "Edward Hitchcock's Geological Survey of Massachusetts: 1830-1833" in *Earth Sciences History* (see General References).

(pp. 155-6) According to Hitchcock's survey notes and his expense records, Story Hebard (AC 1828) accompanied him on his first geological survey excursion in Summer 1830. Hitchcock observed striae and boulders at many locations across southeastern Massachusetts on that trip. His observations in the town of Troy (known today as Fall River) are recorded in his survey notes for August 6, 1830. Throughout his Geological Survey Notes he made note of the evidence of a "diluvial current," but he often expressed doubts that a flood, however great, could exert enough force over such a wide area and in only one direction.

(p. 157) Hitchcock's commission makes no mention of the title "State Geologist," nor does Hitchcock himself ever make a claim to it, although many sources refer to him with that title. Joseph A. Sinnott, who was appointed State Geologist in 1971, wrote in "History of Geology in Massachusetts," "Historians will have to decide, based on semantics, whether J. A. Sinnott was the first State Geologist in the Commonwealth but to Edward Hitchcock belongs the honor of running the first Geological Survey."

(p. 171) For an example of the "oft-quoted witticism," see "Our Mineral Wealth," *Lowell (Mass.) Daily Citizen and News*, September 22, 1869, 2.

(p. 172-3) For a discussion of Hitchcock's equivocation, see Marché's "Edward Hitchcock, Roderick Murchison, and Rejection of the Alpine Glacial Theory (1840-1845)." R. Silliman examines Lyell's influence on American geological thought in "Agassiz vs. Lyell: Authority in the Assessment of the Diluvium-Drift Problem." Quotations are from E. Hitchcock, *Final Report*, 11a.

"Appointments by the Governor and Council," *Boston Courier*, June 28, 1830, 1.

Copeland, Jennie F. *Every Day But Sunday: The Romantic Age of New England Industry.* 4th ed. Boston, Mass.: Blue Mustang Press, 1936.

"Geology of Massachusetts," *Boston Courier*, December 23, 1833, 1.

Hendrickson, Walter B. "Nineteenth-Century State Geological Surveys: Early Government Support of Science." *Isis* 52 (September 1961): 357-71.

Hitchcock, Charles H. "Edward Hitchcock," *The American Geologist* 16 (September 1895): 133-49.

Hitchcock, Edward. "First Anniversary Address Before the Association of American Geologists." *AJS* 41 (July-September 1841): 232-275.

________. "Remarks on the Geology and Mineralogy of a Section of Massachusetts, on Connecticut River, with a Part of New-Hampshire and Vermont." *AJS* (1818): 105-16.

________. *Report on the Geology, Mineralogy, Botany, and Zoology of Massachusetts.* Amherst, Massachusetts: J. S. and C. Adams, 1833.

[Jackson, Charles T.] "Report of a Geological Survey of Massachusetts." *American Monthly Review* 2 (August 1832): 95-101.

Lincoln, Levi, *Letter from the Late Gov. Lincoln to Gov. Davis: Senate Bill No. 6 1834,* 10.

Lougee, Richard J. "Hanover Submerged." *Dartmouth Alumni Magazine* 27 (May 1935): 5-8.

Marché, Jordan D. II. "Edward Hitchcock, Roderick Murchison, and Rejection of the Alpine Glacial Theory (1840-1845)," *Earth Sciences History* 37 (2018): 380-402.

Merrill, George P. *Contributions to a History of American State Geological and Natural History Surveys.* Washington, D.C.: Government Printing Office, 1920.

________. *Contributions to the History of American Geology.* Washington, D.C.: Government Printing Office, 1906.

Oldale, Robert N. "Seismic investigations on Cape Cod, Martha's Vineyard, and Nantucket, Massachusetts." In *Geological Survey Research 1969: United States Geological Survey Professional Paper 650-B.* Washington, DC: United States Geological Survey, 1969, B122-B127.

"Report on the Geology, Botany and Zoology of Massachusetts," *Vermont Chronicle* (Bellows Falls, VT), January 24, 1834, 14.

Reports of the First, Second, and Third Meetings of the Association of American Geologists and Naturalists. Boston, Mass.: Gould, Kendall, & Lincoln, 1843.

Resolves of the General Court of the Commonwealth of Massachusetts. Boston, Mass.: Dutton and Wentworth, 1831.

[Silliman, Benjamin]. "Professor Hitchcock's Geology of Massachusetts." *AJS* 24 (July 1833): 396-7.

Silliman, Robert D. "Agassiz vs. Lyell: Authority in the Assessment of the Diluvium-Drift Problem." *Earth Sciences History* 13 (1994): 180-6.

Upham, Warren. "Memorial of Charles Henry Hitchcock." *Bulletin of the Geological Society of America* 31 (March 1920): 64-80.

CHAPTER 15: A Wreath for the Tomb

(pp. 177-8) Edward Hitchcock, Jr., writes of this incident in Notebook B, 13.

(p. 181) Some of the descriptions of the Hitchcock home are from Walker's *Historic Homes of Amherst.*

Hitchcock, Edward. Account Book 1828-1864, EOH, Box 2, Folder 13.

________. "The Connection Between Geology and Natural Religion." *BR* 5 (January 1835): 113-38.

________. "The Connection Between Geology and the Mosaic History of the Creation." *BR* 5 (April 1835): 439-51; *BR* 6 (October 1835): 261-332.

________. "The Historical and Geological Deluges Compared." *BR* 9 (January 1837): 78-139; *BR* 10 (October 1837): 328-73; *BR* 11 (January 1838): 1-27.

________. "Notice and Review of *Reliquiae Diluvianae* by William Buckland." *AJS* 8 (1824): 150-168,317-338.

________. "Remarks on Professor Stuart's Examination of Genesis 1 in Reference to Geology." *BR* 7 (April 1836): 448-87.

________. Review of *Reliquiae Diluvianae* by William Buckland. *Christian Spectator* 6 (August 1824): 415-36.

________. *Wreath for the Tomb.* Amherst, Mass.: J. S. and C. Adams, 1839.

"President Hitchcock and His Family." *Amherst Graduates' Quarterly.* 29 (May 1940): 203-4.

Stuart, Moses. "Critical Examination of Some Passages in Gen. 1." *BR* 6 (January 1836): 46-106.

CHAPTER 16: Footmarks in Stone

(pp. 189-90) Dr. Deane's first letter to Edward Hitchcock, dated March 1835, appears in E. Hitchcock, *Ichnology of New England.* In his reply of March 15, 1835, Hitchcock promises to visit Greenfield to examine the specimen. For background on Deane see Herbert, "Dr. James Deane of Greenfield."

(p. 197) An account of the 1841 meeting of the AAG is found in *Reports of the First, Second, and Third Meetings of the Association of American Geologists and Naturalists.* Boston, Mass.: Gould, Kendall, & Lincoln, 1843.

Buckland, William, *The Bridgewater Treatises VI: Geology and Mineralogy Considered with Reference to Natural Theology*. 2 vols. London: William Pickering, 1836.

[Chapin, A. B.] "Ornithichnology." *The Knickerbocker* 7 (June 1836): 578-82.

________. "Ornithichnology Reconsidered." *The Knickerbocker* 8 (October 1836): 456-8.

Daubeny, Charles. *Sketch of the Geology of North America.* Oxford, England: The Ashmolean Society, 1839.

"Description d'Empreintes de Pieds d'Oiseaux dans le Grès Rouge du Massachusett." *Annales des Sciences Naturelles* 2nd ser. 5 (March 1836): 154-79.

Hitchcock, Edward. "An Attempt to Name, Classify, and Describe the Animals that made the Fossil Footmarks of New England." *Proceedings of the Association of American Geologists Sixth Meeting* (April 1845): 23-5.

________. "Ornithichnology Defended." *The Knickerbocker* 8 (Sept. 1836): 289-95.

________. *Report on the Geology, Mineralogy, Botany, and Zoology of Massachusetts.* 2nd ed. Amherst, Mass.: J. S. and C. Adams, 1835.

Lyell, Charles. "On the Fossil Foot-prints of Birds and Impressions of Rain-drops in the Valley of the Connecticut." *Proceedings of the Geological Society of London* 3 (June 1842): 793-796.

Olsen, Paul E., and Emma C. Rainforth. "The Early Jurassic Ornithischian Dinosaurian Ichnogenus *Anomoepus*." In *The Great Rift Valleys of Pangea in Eastern North America, Vol. 2: Sedimentology, Stratigraphy, and Paleontology,* edited by P. M. LeTourneau and P. E. Olsen. Columbia University Press, 2: 314-367.

"Ornithichnology: Description des Impressions de Pieds d'Oiseaux (Ornithichnites), Trouvées sur le Grès Bigarré du Massachusetts." *Bibliothèque Universelle de Genève* n.s. 3 (1836): 189-96.

Review of *Elementary Geology* by Edward Hitchcock. *AJS* 39 (July/September 1840): 391-2.

Review of *Elementary Geology* by Edward Hitchcock. *NAR* 52 (January 1841): 103-9.

Review of *Geology and Mineralogy Considered with Reference to Natural Theology* by Rev. William Buckland. *British Critic* 4th ser. 20 (October 1836): 295-328.

Review of "Ornithichnology" by Edward Hitchcock," Annual Review of Zoology for 1836. *Archiv für Naturgeschichte* 2 (1837): 202-3.

CHAPTER 17: A Terrible Incubus

(pp. 201-2) Details of the decision to offer the presidency to Hitchcock on December 16, 1844, are found in the Board of Trustees Records, Meeting Minutes 1825-2013. Hitchcock recorded his doubts about his suitability for the office in his "Private Notes," entry dated March 1845, and in *Reminiscences*.

(p. 203) In the course of my research I made the surprising discovery of a family connection to the first president of Amherst College. Judah Moore, brother of President Zephaniah Swift Moore, married Mary McMaster, my great-great-great aunt, in 1778.

(p. 203) William S. Tyler, author of *A History of Amherst College*, was a graduate of Amherst and subsequently a member of the faculty. His affiliation with Amherst College spanned nearly seventy years, from 1828 to 1896.

Amherst College Board of Trustees Records, Meeting Minutes 1825-1923, AC.

Amherst College Faculty Records, August 15, 1836, AC.

Anti-Slavery Society, to the faculty, October 21, 1834, Amherst College Early History Manuscripts and Pamphlets Collection, AC.

Barnes, Albert, to Heman Humphrey, October 8, 1844, Amherst College Early History Manuscripts and Pamphlets Collection, AC.
Humphrey, Heman, to the Anti-Slavery Society, February 17, 1835, Amherst College Early History Manuscripts and Pamphlets Collection, AC.
Letters to the editors, *Boston Recorder*, October 1 and 8, 1841, December 9, 1842, and others.
"Troubles in College," *Greenfield (Mass.) Gazette and Mercury*, July 4, 1837, 3.
Vaill, Edward. Report, August 8, 1843. Amherst College Early History Collection 1815-1891, AC.
Wilson, Douglas C. "Crimes of Impropriety: Amherst's Link to the Amistad Story." *Amherst Magazine* (Summer 1998): 15-9.

CHAPTER 18: The Highest Use of Learning

(pp. 213-4) Edward Hitchcock, Jr., refers to this meeting in a letter to his mother, Orra White Hitchcock, on March 4, 1845. In Notebook A he describes Samuel Williston as "susceptible to flattery."

Amherst College Board of Trustees Records, Meeting Minutes 1825-2013, AC.
"Amherst College," *HFE*, April 18, 1845, 1.
Conant, Frank P. *God's Stewards: Samuel and Emily Williston.* Easthampton, Mass.: Williston Northampton School, 1991.
Hitchcock, Edward. *Highest Use of Learning.* Amherst, Mass.: J. S. and C. Adams, 1845.

CHAPTER 19: A New Millennium

(pp. 223-4) The details of that occasion are described in *Reminiscences* as well as in a newspaper account of the event in the *Springfield (Mass.) Republican.*
(p. 227) Arrowroot, a starchy substance obtained from the roots of certain tropical plants, was beneficial for relieving the symptoms of dyspepsia according to Hitchcock. For an amusing account of a modern-day test of that palliative see Pick, "Recipes for Dyspepsia."
(p. 230) Heman Humphrey may have been a bit austere, but he was not entirely lacking in a sense of humor, as attested by one story that received wide publicity. "One morning before recitations, some of the students fastened a living goose in the President's chair. When the President entered the room and discovered the new occupant of his seat, he turned on his heel and coolly observed, 'Gentlemen, I perceive you have a competent instructor, and I will therefore leave you to your studies.'" From the *Alexandria (VA) Gazette*, Friday, July 27, 1838, 2.
(p. 230) John M. Tyler, son of William S. Tyler and himself a graduate of Amherst College, was professor of biology at Amherst from 1879 to 1917.

Amherst College Catalog 1845-1846, AC.
"Amherst College—Religion," *Southern Patriot* (Charleston, SC), May 14, 1846, 2.
Hitchcock, Edward. "Blind Slave in the Mine." Tract #126, *American Tract Society* 4 (1848).
[Hitchcock, Edward], "Mesmeric Meeting of the Senior Class of 1849 in Amherst College," *HFE*, November 9, 1849.
"Letter to the editor [from people of Sunderland]," *HFE,* November 16, 1849, 3.
"Naming Mount Toby Anew," *HFE*, June 22, 1849, 2.
Pick, Nancy. "Recipes for Dyspepsia." *Gastronomica* 5(2) (2005): 19-22.
"Revival in Amherst College," *Christian Observer* (NY), May 1, 1846, 2.
Revival of Religion in Amherst College," *HFE,* April 30, 1846, 1.

Richard Parker Morgan Database, American Antiquarian Society, Worcester, Mass., http://morgan.mwa.org/studentnames/.
[Mt. Holyoke excursion], *SR*, July 13, 1846, 2.
Tyler, John M. "The First Hundred Years of Amherst College." *Amherst Graduates' Quarterly* 10 (August 1921): 217-31.

CHAPTER 20: The Cabinets

(pp. 237-9) The role of Josiah B. Woods in raising funds for the new cabinet is described in Tyler's *A History of Amherst College* (1895). Enfield, Massachusetts, one of the towns inundated by the Quabbin Reservoir in the twentieth century, was visited by Hitchcock several times according to his geological survey notes. A specimen of epidote from Enfield is listed in Hitchcock's *Catalogue of the Massachusetts State Cabinet.*

(p. 240) Sylvester Hovey was the stepson of Edward's sister, Emilia Hitchcock Billings.

(p. 245) Edward Hitchcock, Jr., was also the first to inscribe Root's diary, probably at the time of their graduation, writing "Shall our pleasant college connection be ever forgotten?"

Calhoun, William B. et al. *Addresses at the Dedication of the New Cabinet and Observatory of Amherst College, June 28, 1848.* Amherst, Mass.: J. S. and C. Adams, 1848.
Hoyt, Epaphras, to Proctor Pierce, January 20, 1815, EOH, Box 3, Folder 22.
Maine Cultivator and Hallowell (ME) Gazette, December 9, 1848, p. 1.
Morison, Samuel E. *Three Centuries of Harvard.* Cambridge, Mass.: Harvard University Press, 1936.
Rudolph, Frederick. *The American College and University: A History.* Athens, GA: University of Georgia Press, 1990.

CHAPTER 21: Towards the Rising Sun

(pp. 247-9) Hitchcock describes an encounter with a Scottish countess at Professor Jameson's home in *Reminiscences.* The name Lady Randolph, Countess of Moray, and the dialogue are fictional.

(p. 249-50) Edward recorded dozens of measurements with an aneroid barometer over the first two weeks of their trip, but curiously he never mentions the device thereafter. He also had with him a magnetometer to measure the strength of the magnetic field at a location. He mentions it only twice, both in Edinburgh (July 29-30), where he found rocks that were strongly polar.

(p. 252-3) Late in life, Emily Hitchcock Terry donated that painting and many others to Smith College where they are held today.

(p. 254) Another interesting personal connection came to light from my research on the Hitchcock's European tour. Among the Irish of 1850 desperate to escape the famine by emigrating to America were Hannah McGurk and her four children. They sailed from Ireland to Liverpool in early October, then departed from Liverpool for Boston a few days before the Hitchcocks departed on their return voyage. Hannah McGurk was my great-great-great-grandmother.

(p. 256) The Hitchcocks may have indulged in wine once or twice while on their tour as suggested by Edward in "Notes on European tour 1850," entry dated June 29, and by Orra in "Diaries of European tour," entry dated September 5, 1850.

Herbert, Robert L. *A Woman of Amherst: The Travel Diaries of Orra White Hitchcock, 1847 and 1850.* New York, iUniverse, Inc., 2008.
Hitchcock, Edward. Letters from Edinburgh, *New York Observer*, August 24 and September 14, 1850.

_______. Notebook of European tour 1850 May 15-Aug 9, entry dated July 17, 1850, EOH, Box 19, Folder 6.

_______. "On the Erosions of the Earth's Surface, Especially by Rivers" and "On Terraces and Ancient Sea Beaches." *Report of the 20th Meeting of the British Association for the Advancement of Science.* London: John Murray, 1851, 85-88.

_______. *Report of Commissioners Concerning an Agricultural School.* Boston, Mass.: Massachusetts Commissioners on Establishment of an Agricultural School, 1851.

Hitchcock, Orra White, Diaries of European tour 1850 May-Oct, entry dated July 17, 1850, EOH, Box 26, Folder 24.

CHAPTER 22: The Religion of Geology

(pp. 259-60) The return of the Hitchcocks to Amherst from their European tour is documented in newspaper accounts such as "Return of President Hitchcock," *Hampshire Gazette* (Northampton, Mass.), October 22, 1850. It is also described in Cutting, *Student Life at Amherst College.* The bridge over the Connecticut River at Northampton was notoriously difficult to cross in winter and was frequently unusable due to ice damage.

(p. 262) Christmas, on the other hand, was barely mentioned in Hitchcock family letters and diaries. Modern-day Christmas observance was only just becoming common in the nation by the 1850s, but his sermons suggest that Edward was not sympathetic toward Christmas and regarded its connection to the birth of Jesus as spurious.

(p. 264-5) Martin Root attended Miss Lyon's funeral and provides an account in Root, Martin 1847-1851, AC, Amherst College Alumni Biographical Files, 252-6.

(p. 267) See Bakker, "Dinosaurs Acting Like Birds," page 6, for a discussion of the importance of "serial creationism" both to opponents and advocates of Darwinism.

(p. 269) The pseudonym "Vindex" was employed frequently by eighteenth and nineteenth century writers. While the identity of the author of the series in the *Boston Investigator* is not known, it might have been Horace Seaver, the editor.

(p. 270) Agassiz's quote appears in "The Diversity of Origin of the Human Races."

(p. 270) See Guralnick's "Geology and Religion Before Darwin" for a discussion of Hitchcock's apparent adoption of Moses Stuart's position on science and religion.

Agassiz, Louis. "The Diversity of Origins of the Human Races." *Christian Examiner and Religious Miscellany* 4th ser. 14 (July 1850): 110-145.

Amherst College Faculty Administrative Records, 1825-1827, entry of Oct. 16, 1826.

[Chambers, R.] *Vestiges of the Natural History of Creation.* London: J. Churchill, 1844.

Cutting, George R. *Student Life at Amherst College: Its Organizations, Their Membership and History.* Amherst, Mass.: Hatch and Williams, 1871.

Guralnick, Stanley M. "Geology and Religion Before Darwin: The Case of Edward Hitchcock, Theologian and Geologist (1793-1864)." *Isis* 63 (December 1972): 529-43.

Hitchcock, Edward. "Address on Retiring from the Presidency." In *Discourses and Addresses at the Installation and Inauguration of the Rev. William A. Stearns, D.D.* Amherst, Mass.: J. S. and C. Adams, 1855, 45-71.

________. "On the Geological Age of the Clay Slate of the Connecticut Valley, in Massachusetts and Vermont," 299-300; "On the Separation of Butter from Cream by Catalysis," 195-6; "Brown Coal Deposit in Brandon Vermont," 95-104; "Coal Field of Bristol County and of Rhode Island," 327-36; and "On the Terraces and Sea Beaches That Have Been Formed Since the Drift Period," 264-9; *Proceedings of the American Association for the Advancement of Science, Sixth Meeting, Albany, NY, 1851.* Washington, DC: S. F. Baird.

________. *Outline of the Geology of the Globe.* Boston, Mass.: Phillips, Sampson, and Company, 1853.

________. *The Power of Christian Benevolence Illustrated in the Life and Labors of Mary Lyon.* Northampton, Mass.: Hopkins, Bridgman, and Company, 1851.

________. "The Relations and Consequent Mutual Duties Between the Philosopher and the Theologian." *BS* 10 (January 1853): 166-94.

________. *Report on Certain Points in the Geology of Massachusetts.* Boston, Mass.: White & Potter, 1853.

________. "Special Divine Interpositions in Nature." *BS* 11 (October 1854): 776-800.

Humphrey, Heman. *The Shining Path: A Sermon Preached In South Hadley, At The Funeral Of Miss Mary Lyon, March 8, 1849.* Northampton, Mass.: J. & L. Metcalf, 1849.

Lee, John Stebbins. Review of *The Religion of Geology* by Edward Hitchcock. *Universalist Quarterly* 8 (October 1851): 329-49.

Munemo, Julia. "Unearthing the Future." *Williams Magazine* 109 (Summer 2015): 36.

Review of *Religion of Geology. Daily National Intelligencer* (Washington, DC), October 11, 1851.

Review of *The Power of Christian Benevolence. Christian Register* (Boston, Mass.), June 21, 1851.

Stebbins, Rufus Phineas. Review of *The Religion of Geology* by Edward Hitchcock. *Christian Examiner* 53 (July 1852): 51-66.

Vindex, "The Religion of Geology No. 2," *Boston Investigator*, October 1, 1851, 2.

CHAPTER 23: The Sabbath of Life

(p. 281-2) According to Stanley King, *The Consecrated Eminence,* the Board of Trustees had granted Hitchcock broad authority over the design and construction of the Appleton Cabinet. Henry D. Sykes was the architect hired for the work. A letter from Edward, Sr., to Edward, Jr., indicates that Edward, Jr., and his family were not expected to attend the inauguration of President Stearns. Edward and Orra's first grandchild, named Edward, would have been almost three months old at the time.

(p. 285) In December 1858, Edward and Charles undertook another geological consultancy, this one for a copper mining company located in Flemington, New Jersey, that was more agreeable than the Kanawha project.

(p. 285) And yet this matter of "private history" somehow found its way into at least two local newspapers, *Greenfield (Mass.) Gazette and Courier*, June 4, 1855, 3.

Billings, E. Review of *Report on the Geology of Vermont* by Edward Hitchcock et al. *AJS* 2nd ser. 33 (May 1862): 416-420.

Hitchcock, Charles H. "Impressions (Chiefly Tracks) on Alluvial Clay in Hadley, Mass." *AJS* 2nd ser. 19 (May 1855): 391-6.

Hitchcock, Edward. "Lecturing Tour at the West." *The Congregationalist* (Boston, Mass.), February 29, 1856.

________. "On a New Fossil Fish, and New Fossil Footmarks." *AJS* 2nd ser. 21 (January 1856): 96-100.

________. "Report of Dr. Hitchcock." In *Great Kanawha Estate: Evidence of Value and Title.* No city or publisher stated, ca. 1855, 41-7.

________. *Report of the Geological Survey and Condition of the Hunterdon Copper Company's Property.* Philadelphia, PA: J. B. Chandler, Printer, 1859.

________, Albert D. Hager, Edward Hitchcock, Jr., and Charles H. Hitchcock. *Report on the Geology of Vermont.* 2 vols. Claremont, NH: Claremont Manufacturing Company, 1861.

Hitchcock, Edward, Jr. "Description of a New Species of Clathropteris, Discovered in the Connecticut Valley Sandstone." *AJS* 2nd ser. 20 (July 1855): 22-25.

________. "A New Fossil Shell in the Connecticut River Sandstone." *AJS* 2nd ser. 22 (September 1856): 239-240.

CHAPTER 24: The Aged Warrior

(pp. 295-6) The family outing described is based on an entry in Edward's "Private Notes" dated December 31, 1859, in which he recalled a winter outing with his family one year earlier to enjoy the "remarkable exhibition of frostwork on the trees." Some of the descriptions are taken from Edward's account of a previous family outing mentioned which he described in *Coronation of Winter*.

(p. 306) A few years later, Edward, Jr., was appointed Professor of Hygiene and Physical Education at Amherst College. In that post he did offer one lecture each term on sex dealing mainly with the risks of venereal disease and the importance of purity in young men. Those lectures proved very popular with his students who dubbed them the "smut lectures."

[Agassiz, Louis]. Review of *Elementary Anatomy and Physiology, Boston (Mass.) Evening Courier*, March 3, 1860, 1.

"American Association for the Advancement of Science," *SR*, August 8, 1859, 4.

Boston (Mass.) Recorder, January 27, 1859.

Bouvé, Thomas T. Address to the Society dated July 7, 1858, *Proceedings of the Boston Society of Natural History* 6 (October 1858): 391-4.

Bowditch, Henry I. *An Address on the Life and Character of James Deane, M. D. of Greenfield, Mass.* Greenfield, Mass.: H. D. Mirick and Co.,1858.

Deane, James. "Answer to the 'Rejoinder' of Prof. Hitchcock." *AJS* 47 (July-September 1844): 399-401.

________. "Description of Fossil Footprints in the New Red Sandstone of the Connecticut Valley," *AJS* 48 (October-December 1844): 158-67.

________. "Fossil Footprints of Connecticut River." *Journal of the Academy of Natural Sciences of Philadelphia* 2nd ser. 2 (1850): 71-74, and plates.

________. *Ichnographs from the Sandstone of Connecticut River*. Thomas Bouvé, ed. Boston, Mass.: Little, Brown, 1861.

________. "Illustrations of Fossil Footprints of the Valley of the Connecticut." *Memoirs of the American Academy of Arts and Sciences* n.s. 4 (1849): 209-20.

________. "On the Discovery of Fossil Footmarks." *AJS* 47 (July-September 1844): 381-390.

________. "On the Fossil Footmarks of Turner's Falls, Mass." *AJS* 46 (October-December 1843): 73-7.

________. "On the Sandstone Fossils of Connecticut River." *Journal of the Academy of Natural Sciences of Philadelphia*, 2nd ser. 3 (1856):173-78, and plates.

Duns, John. Review of *Ichnology of New England* by Edward Hitchcock. *North British Review* 32 (February 1860): 133-142.

Hitchcock, Edward, "Descriptions of Five New Species of Fossil Footmarks." *Reports of the First, Second, and Third Meetings of the Association of American Geologists and Naturalists* (1843): 254-64.

________. "Rejoinder to the Preceding Article of Dr. Deane." *AJS* 47 (July-September 1844): 390-399.

________. and Edward Hitchcock, Jr. *Elementary Anatomy and Physiology*. New York: Ivison, Phinney & Company, 1860.

Irmscher, Christoph. *Louis Agassiz, Creator of American Science*. Boston, Mass.: Houghton Mifflin Harcourt, 2013.

Review of *Elementary Anatomy and Physiology* by Edward Hitchcock and Edward Hitchcock, Jr. *Freewill Baptist Quarterly* 8 (April 1860): 236.

Review of *Elementary Anatomy and Physiology* by Edward Hitchcock and Edward Hitchcock, Jr. *Massachusetts Teacher* 13 (May 1860): 200.
Review of *Elementary Anatomy and Physiology* by Edward Hitchcock and Edward Hitchcock, Jr. *Ohio Educational Monthly* 9 (July 1860): 223.
Review of *Ichnology of New England* by Edward Hitchcock. *AJS* 2nd ser. 27 (March 1859): 270-272.
Review of *Ichnology of New England* by Edward Hitchcock. *American Presbyterian Review* 1 (January 1859): 176-80.
Silliman, Benjamin, "Address Before the Association of American Geologists and Naturalists assembled at Boston, April 24, 1842." *AJS* 43 (July-September 1842): 217-50.
________. "Ornithichnites of the Connecticut River Sandstones and the Dinornis of New Zealand." *AJS* 45 (April-June 1843): 177-88.
"Who discovered the bird tracks?" *SR*, May 7, 1859, 2.

CHAPTER 25: Troublous Times

(pp. 315-7) Details of the meeting in Newport including the papers presented appear in *Proceedings*. Some of the comments by Louis Agassiz and William B. Rogers at that meeting were reported in newspaper accounts such as the *Commercial Advertiser (New York),* August 2, 1860, 2, *New York Daily Tribune,* August 4, 1860, 8, *SR,* August 4, 1860, 4, *Charleston (SC) Courier*, August 7, 1860, 2, and *Weekly National Intelligencer* (Washington, DC), August 11, 1860, 2.

(p. 318) Hitchcock does not identify the man he was asked to collaborate with, but he does mention the name Wells in a subsequent letter to Edward, Jr. on the subject. Wells published his own geology text with the same publisher a year later.

(p. 321) The *Megatherium* skeleton arrived at Amherst in summer 1863.

(p. 324) Edward, Sr., lived to seventy years, Edward, Jr., to eighty-two. In addition to his honorary M.A. degree from Yale in 1817, Edward, Sr., he received honorary degrees from Harvard in 1840 (LL.D.) and from Middlebury College in 1846 (D.D.).

"Christening" [Rocky Mountain], *Franklin Democrat (Greenfield, Mass.),* October 17, 1859, 2.
"Excursion of the Senior Class of Amherst College–The Pocumtuck Mountain," *SR*, October 19, 1855, 2.
King, Stanley. *A History of the Endowment of Amherst College.* Amherst, Mass.: Amherst College, 1950.
"Married," *Boston Evening Transcript,* June 21, 1862, 3.
[Mt. Kilburn renaming], *Vermont Phoenix* (Brattleboro, VT), October 4, 1856, 2.
"Nonotuck christening," *Franklin Democrat (Greenfield, Mass.),* June 21, 1858, 3.
Phelps, Almira Hart Lincoln. *Reviews and Essays on Art, Literature, and Science*. Philadelphia, PA: Claxton , Remsen & Haffelfinger, 1873, 276-82.
Proceedings of the AAAS Fourteenth Meeting held at Newport, Rhode Island, August 1860. Cambridge, Mass.: Joseph Lovering, 1861

CHAPTER 26 Reminiscences

(pp. 329-30) In *The Wise Man of the Scriptures*, Tyler describes the occasion a few weeks before Hitchcock's death when, at his own request, his sons carried him out of doors so that he could enjoy winter's beauty.

(p. 335) The three views of the college appear opposite pages 56, 64, and 72 in *Reminiscences*. In the text Hitchcock refers to the 1821 drawing as the frontispiece. That was probably his intention, but the publisher persuaded him to substitute his portrait in that prominent position, moving the drawing to Chapter 2. The third campus view also appears in the college catalogue of 1859-1860.

(p. 337) See *Visitor's Guide to the Public Rooms and Cabinets of Amherst College with a Preliminary Report,* pages 5-7, for Charles H. Hitchcock's comments on the inadequacy of the compensation for the position.

Hitchcock, Edward. "Exegesis of I Corinthians 15: 35-40, as Illustrated by Natural History and Chemistry." *BS* 17 (April 1860): 303-12.

_______. "The Cross in Nature and Nature in the Cross." *BS* 18 (April 1861): 253-84.

_______. "Sea of Life," undated, EOH, Box 21, Folders 19-20, Box OS6, Folder 13.

Review of *Reminiscences. Canadian Naturalist and Geologist* n.s. 1 (October 1864): 337-354.

Review of *Reminiscences* in *SR*, October 31, 1863, 7.

Review of *Reminiscences of Amherst College* by Edward Hitchcock. *AJS* 2nd ser. 37 (January 1864): 148-9.

Tyler, William S. *The Wise Man of the Scriptures: A Discourse Delivered in the Village Church in Amherst, March 2d, 1864, at the Funeral of Rev. Prof. Edward Hitchcock D.D., LL. D.* Springfield, Mass.: Samuel Bowles and Company, 1864.

CHAPTER 27: Floating Memories

(pp. 339-41) The details of Hitchcock's funeral are from an account that appeared in the *Springfield (Mass.) Republican,* March 3, 1864, 2.

Acts and Resolves Passed by the General Court of Massachusetts in the Year 1863. Boston, Mass.: Wright and Potter, 1863.

"Agricultural College at Amherst," *SR,* June 4, 1864, 2.

"Anniversary at South Hadley," *SR,* July 22, 1864, 2.

Beecher, Henry W., "Prof. Edward Hitchcock," *The Independent (NY),* March 3, 1864.

"Copy of the Will of Edward Hitchcock," 1864, EOH, Box 2, Folder 2.

Damon, S. C., "Professor Edward Hitchcock," *Friend (Honolulu, HI),* May 1, 1864.

"Death of President Hitchcock," *New York Tribune*, March 2, 1864, 5.

Goodwin, Daniel R. "Obituary Notice of the Rev. Prof. Edward Hitchcock, D.D., LL.D." *Proceedings of the American Philosophical Society* 9 (November 1864): 443-9.

Hampshire Gazette (Northampton, Mass.), March 8, 1864, 2.

"In Memoriam," author unknown, 1864, EOH, Box 2, Folder 11.

Obituary for Edward Hitchcock. *AJS* 2nd ser. 37 (March 1864): 302-4.

Obituary for Edward Hitchcock. *Proceedings of the American Academy of Arts and Sciences* 6 (May 1862-May 1865). Boston: Welch, Bigelow, and Co., 1866.

Wortman, Dennis, Jr., "Edward Hitchcock," *Christian Intelligencer,* March 17, 1864.

CHAPTER 28: The Sandstone Bird

(p. 355) The article published in the *Proceedings* of the Academy was written in the third person, probably by the recording secretary of the Academy.

(p. 356-60) Further discussion of the re-evaluation of Hitchcock's "avian hypothesis" may be found in Bakker, "Dinosaurs Acting Like Birds" and in Pick, *Curious Footprints* (see General References).

Bakker, Robert T. "Dinosaur Renaissance." *Scientific American* 232 (April 1975): 58-78.

Colbert, Edwin H. *The Dinosaur Book: The Ruling Reptiles and Their Relatives.* New York: McGraw-Hill Book Company, 1945.

Cope, Edward D. "The Fossil Reptiles of New Jersey." *American Naturalist* 1 (March 1867): 23-30.

Dean, Dennis R. "Hitchcock's Dinosaur Tracks." *American Quarterly* 21 (Autumn 1969): 639-44.

Desmond, Adrian J. *The Hot-Blooded Dinosaurs: A Revolution in Palaeontology.* New York: Warner Books, 1977.

Fairchild, Herman L. "Glacial Geology in America." *The American Geologist* 22 (September 1898): 154-93.

Foulke, William Parker. "*Hadrosaurus Foulkii*: a new Saurian from the Cretaceous of New Jersey, related to the Iguanodon." *AJS* 27 2nd ser. (March 1859): 265-276.

Hitchcock, E. "Descriptions of Five New Species of Fossil Footmarks." *Reports of the First, Second, and Third Meetings of the Association of American Geologists and Naturalists* (1843): 254-64.

________. "Fossil Footsteps in Sandstone and Graywacke." *AJS* 32 (July 1837): 174-6.

________. "Immortality," Commonplace Bk. No. 3, November 25, 1813, EOH, Box 18, Folder 6.

________. "The Sandstone Bird," two manuscript drafts, 1836 December, EOH, Box 15, Folder 24.

________. ["The Sandstone Bird"]. *Knickerbocker* 8 (December 1836): 750-2.

________. "Summary of "Report on Ichnolithology or Fossil Footmarks." *AJS* 47 (April-June 1844): 113-114; *AJS* 47 (July-September 1844): 292-322.

Huxley, Thomas Henry, to Ernst Haeckel, January 21, 1868, in Huxley, Leonard, ed. *Life and Letters of Thomas Henry Huxley*. 3 vols. London: Macmillan and Company, 1913, 437.

Lockley, Martin G. *Tracking Dinosaurs: A New Look at an Ancient World.* Cambridge, UK: Cambridge University Press, 1991.

Marché, Jordan D. II. "Edward Hitchcock's Poem, 'The Sandstone Bird' (1836)." *Earth Sciences History* 10 (1991): 5-8.

Ostrom, John H. "The Ancestry of Birds." *Nature* 242: 136.

CHAPTER 29: The Tree of Life

(p. 363) Hitchcock quotes Agassiz in *Elementary Geology*, 31st ed., page 270, in what appears to be his own translation from *Bulletin de la Société des Sciences Naturelles de Nuchatel* 17 (April 1845): 189-90.

Darwin, Charles to Edward Hitchcock, November 6, 1845, EOH, Box 3, Folder 8.

Evans, L. T. "Darwin's Use of the Analogy between Artificial and Natural Selection." *Journal of the History of Biology* 17 (Spring 1984): 113-140.

Hitchcock, Charles H. "The Bible and Recent Science." *BS* 64 (April 1907): 299-313.

[Hitchcock, Edward], "Moral Telescope," *FH,* Feb. 24, 1818.

Lawrence, Philip J. "Edward Hitchcock: The Christian Geologist." *Proceedings of the American Philosophical Society* 116 (February 1972): 21-34.

Youmans, Edward L. ed. "Sketch of Charles Henry Hitchcock." *Popular Science Monthly* 54 (December 1898): 260-8.

Epilogue

(p. 369) The anecdote was reported in many newspapers and periodicals. For example, *The Intelligencer (Anderson, SC),* June 2, 1897, 4; *Current Anecdotes,* October 1903, 14; *Church School Journal,* January 1911, 37.

Gould, Stephen Jay. *Leonardo's Mountain of Clams and the Diet of Worms*. New York: Harmony Books, 1998.

Huxley, Thomas H., to Charles Kingsley, September 23, 1860. In *Life and Letters of Thomas Henry Huxley,* 3 vols., edited by Leonard Huxley. London: Macmillan and Co., 1913, 316.

Switek, Brian. *Written in Stone: Evolution, the Fossil Record, and Our Place in Nature.* New York: Bellevue Literary Press, 2010.

Acknowledgments

I wish to thank the following individuals who have assisted me in this project: Daria D'Arienzo of Meekins Library, Williamsburg, MA, formerly of the Amherst College Archives and Special Collections, Amherst, MA; Margaret R. Dakin, Michael Kelly, Sarah Walden McGowan, and Este Pope of the Amherst College Archives and Special Collections, Amherst, MA; Stephen Fisher of the Mead Art Museum, Amherst College, Amherst, MA; David Bosse and Heather Harrington of the Memorial Libraries, Historic Deerfield and the Pocumtuck Valley Memorial Association, Deerfield, MA; Sarah L. Doyle of the Jurassic Roadshow, Turners Falls, MA; Sarah Williams of the Conway Historical Commission, Conway, MA; Jordan D. Marché II of the University of Wisconsin, Madison, WI; C. John Burk of Smith College, Northampton, MA; Nanci Young of the Smith College Archives, Northampton, MA; Marie Panik of Historic Northampton, Northampton, MA; Sharon Roth of the Greenfield Historical Society, Greenfield, MA; Elise Bernier-Feeley of the Hampshire Room for Local History, Forbes Library, Northampton, MA; Micha Broadnax of the Archives and Special Collections, Mount Holyoke College, South Hadley, MA; Cynthia Harbeson of Special Collections, Jones Library, Amherst, MA; Markes Johnson of Williams College, Williamstown, MA; Alfred Venne and Hayley Singleton of the Beneski Museum of Natural History, Amherst College, Amherst, MA; Quentin Donohue of Holyoke High School, Holyoke, MA; Randy Converse, Madison, WI; Eric B. Schultz; Emma C. Rainforth of Ramapo College of New Jersey, Mahwah, NJ; and Julia W. Logan of the Rauner Special Collections Library, Dartmouth College, Hanover, NH.

I wish to express my appreciation in particular to Daria D'Arienzo, Sarah L. Doyle, Jordan D. Marché II, C. John Burk, Quentin Donohue, and Eric B. Schultz for their reviews of portions of the manuscript. I would be remiss not to make special note of Robert L. Herbert of Mount Holyoke College who passed away just weeks before this book went to press. Dr. Herbert was without doubt the foremost Hitchcock scholar of our time. His works on Edward and Orra White Hitchcock, Benjamin Silliman, and James Deane have been invaluable to me throughout this project.

The following institutions are also acknowledged for their cooperation and assistance: American Antiquarian Society, Worcester, MA; Amherst College Archives and Special Collections, Amherst, MA; Beneski Museum of Natural History, Amherst College, Amherst, MA; Conway Historical Commission, Conway, MA; Forbes Library, Northampton, MA; Greenfield Historical Society, Greenfield, MA; Historic Northampton, Northampton, MA; Jones Library, Amherst, MA; Mead Art Museum, Amherst College, Amherst, MA; Meekins Library, Williamsburg, MA; Memorial Libraries, Historic Deerfield and the Pocumtuck Valley Memorial Association, Deerfield, MA; Mount Holyoke Archives and Special Collections, Mount Holyoke College, South Hadley, MA; and Smith College Special Collections, Smith College, Northampton, MA. The on-line resources provided by the Boston Public Library have been especially valuable to my research.

John A. Diemer, editor of *Earth Sciences History*, and two reviewers provided valuable assistance with my manuscript on Hitchcock's geological survey of Massachusetts which appeared in a recent issue of that journal. I also wish to thank Mara Dodge, editor of the *Historical Journal of Massachusetts*, and two reviewers, for their comments and suggestions on my article on Hitchcock's sermons that appeared in a recent issue of that journal. Their comments and suggestions proved highly beneficial in this project as well.

Finally, I thank my wife, Susan D. Milsom, for her careful editing of multiple early versions of this manuscript as well as her constant encouragement and support throughout this project.

IMAGE CREDITS

Front Cover and Title Page: Steel engraving, in William S. Tyler, *A History of Amherst College* (New York: Frederick H. Hitchcock, 1895), 116.

Page iv (Frontispiece). Track of *O. tetradactylus,* drawing by Orra White Hitchcock, in E. Hitchcock, "Ornithichnology—Description of the Foot Marks of Birds (Ornithichnites) on New Red Sandstone in Massachusetts," *American Journal of Science and Arts* 29 (January 1836): 307-40; excerpt from *The Sandstone Bird* by E. Hitchcock, 1836, an unpublished version, from a letter (EH to BS, March 1, 1836).

Page viii (Introduction). Marble bust of Edward Hitchcock, sculptor Martin Milmore, 1869, courtesy of Mead Art Museum, Amherst College.

Page 9 (I. Deerfield). "Southern view of Deerfield (central part)," wood engraving by John Warner Barber in *Historical Collections* (Worcester, Mass.: Dorr, Howland and Company, 1839), 246.

Page 10 (Figure 1). "The State of Massachusetts from best information 1796," map by Reid, John, Cartographer, Publisher, William Winterbotham, and United States Bureau Of The Census (New York: J. Reid, 1796), https://www.loc.gov/item/2018590106/.

Page 11 (Chapter 1). View of Pocumtuck, in Clifton Johnson, *An Unredeemed Captive* (Holyoke, Mass.: Griffith, Axtell & Cady Company, 1897), 47.

Page 17 (Figure 2). The Hitchcock House, Deerfield, Mass., 2020, photograph by the author.

Page 19 (Chapter 2). "Sugarloaf Mountain, Deerfield" by Orra White Hitchcock in E. Hitchcock, *Plates Illustrating the Geology and Scenery of Massachusetts* (Boston, Mass: Pendleton's Lithography, 1833), Plate 7.

Page 22 (Figure 3). "Winter in Deerfield," in G. Sheldon, *The Little Brown House on the Albany Road* (Deerfield, Mass.: George Sheldon, 1913), cover.

Page 24 (Figure 4). "The Prayer at Valley Forge," oil painting by Henry Brueckner, engraved by John C. McRae ca. 1889, image from https://www.loc.gov/item/96521655/.

Page 26 (Figure 5). Reverend Jonathan Edwards (1703-1758), image from Wikimedia, https://commons.wikimedia.org/wiki/File:Jonathan_Edwards.jpg

Page 27 (Figure 6). Deerfield town historian George Sheldon (1818-1916), steel engraving in *History of the Connecticut Valley in Massachusetts with Illustrations and Biographical Sketches*. 2 vols. Philadelphia, PA: Louis H. Everts, 1879, 616.

Page 29 (Chapter 3). The original Deerfield Academy building, est. 1799, photograph in C. Johnson, *Old-time Schools and School-books* (New York: Macmillan Company, 1904), 148.

Page 31 (Figure 7). Original map of Deerfield village circa 1801, based on property data in G. Sheldon, *A History of Deerfield, Massachusetts* Vol. 1. Greenfield, Mass.: E. A. Hall & Co., 1895.

Page 37 (Chapter 4). "The Comet of 1811," in *Polehampton and Good's Gallery of Nature and Art* (London: R. Wilks, 1818).

Page 39 (Figure 8). Portrait of Major General Epaphras Hoyt (1765-1850), in G. Sheldon, *The Little Brown House on the Albany Road* (Deerfield, Mass.: George Sheldon, 1913), 22.

Page 41 (Figure 9). Cover of 1816 edition of E. Hitchcock, *Country Almanack* (Greenfield, Mass.: Denio and Phelps, 1816).

Page 44 (Figure 10) Astronomical charts from Hitchcock's *Country Almanack 1818* (Deerfield, Mass.: John Wilson, 1818).

Page 47 (Figure 11). Above, portrait of Edmund M. Blunt, in "History of Newburyport Newspaper," by Russell Leigh Jackson, from the Essex Institute Historical Collections, Vol. LXXXVIII, April 1952, courtesy of *The Daily News of Newburyport;* below reward notice, in Blunt, *Nautical Almanac* (New York, Edmund M. Blunt, 1816).

Page 49 (Chapter 5). "The morning of the 19th Brumaire," lithograph of painting by Henri Frédéric Schopin in *The Eclectic Magazine of Foreign Literature, Science, and Art,* January-April 1853, frontispiece.

Page 59 (Chapter 6). "Yale College (New Haven)," steel engraving by W. H. Bartlett, in N. P. Willis, *American Scenery; or, Land, Lake, and River Illustrations of Transatlantic Nature* (London: G. Virtue, 1840), 74.

Page 63 (Figure 12). "Titan's piazza: Mount Holyoke," woodcut in E. Hitchcock, *Final Report on the Geology of Massachusetts* (Northampton, Mass.: J. H. Butler, 1841), 245.

Page 67 (Figure 13). Portrait of Professor Benjamin Silliman (1779-1864), in George P. Fisher, *Life of Benjamin Silliman Vol. 1*, (New York: Charles Scribner, 1866), frontispiece.

Page 73 (II. Conway). "Southern view of Conway," wood engraving by John Warner Barber in *Historical Collections* (Worcester, Mass.: Dorr, Howland and Company, 1839), 245.

Page 75 (Chapter 7). "Residence of J. C. Newhall," lithograph in *History of the Connecticut Valley* in *Massachusetts with Illustrations and Biographical Sketches*. 2 vols. Philadelphia, PA: Louis H. Everts, 1879, 284.

Page 78 (Figure 14). "Ordained," in *Franklin Herald*, July 3, 1821, 3.

Page 79 (Figure 15). Map of Conway circa 1824 based on "Plan of Conway by Arthur W. Hoyt, 1830."

Page 81 (Figure 16). *Hydnum imbricatum*, drawing by Orra White Hitchcock, courtesy of Smith College Archives.

Page 85 (Figure 17). Title page and one page of watercolors from "Fungi, Selecti Picti," by Orra White Hitchcock, photographs by the author.

Page 87 (Chapter 8). "Camp meeting," in B. W. Gorham, *Camp Meeting Manual* (Boston, Mass.: H. D. Vegen, 1854), frontispiece.

Page 91 (Figure 18). *Botrychium simplex*, drawing by Orra White Hitchcock, in E. Hitchcock, "Description of a New Species of *Botrychium*," *American Journal of Science and Arts* 6 (1823), Plate 8.

Page 97 (Figure 19). Edward Hitchcock, *Utility of Natural History: A Discourse* (Pittsfield, Mass.: Phinehas Allen, 1823).

Page 99 (Figure 20). "Diluvial Hillocks," woodcut by Orra White Hitchcock in E. Hitchcock, *Final Report on the Geology of Massachusetts* (Northampton, Mass.: J. H. Butler, 1841), 256.

Page 101 (Figure 21). "State of the Church and People in Conway," a sermon delivered in January 1824, courtesy of Amherst College Archives and Special Collections, Amherst, Mass.

Page 103 (Chapter 9). "The Burial Hill," steel engraving, in William H. Bartlett, *The Pilgrim Fathers* (London: A. Hall, Virtue & Co., 1854), 172.

Page 106 (Figure 22). *Carex hitchcockiana*, drawing by Orra White Hitchcock, in Chester Dewey, "Caricography," *American Journal of Science and Arts* 10 (1826), Plate 2.

Page 109 (Figure 23) "Afflicted Saint, to Christ Draw Near," in The Hartford Selection of Hymns (Hartford, Conn.: Peter B. Gleason and Company, 1821.

Page 110 (Figure 24). Little Edward's grave, Conway, Mass., 2020, photograph by the author.

Page 111 (Chapter 10). "A quadrangular building fitted up for the general purposes of a Chemical Laboratory," wood engraving, in S. Parkes, *Chemical Catechism* (London: Longman et al., 1854), xxxiv.

Page 115 (Figure 25). "Small apparatus for the chemical laboratory," in S. Parkes, *Chemical Catechism* (London: Longman et al., 1834), xxxvi.

Page 118 (Figure 26). Above, simple blow pipe in B. Silliman, *Elements of Chemistry In the Order of the Lectures at Yale College Vol. 1* (New Haven, Conn., Hezekiah Howe, 1833), 128; below, compound blow pipe from *Illustrated Wholesale Catalogue with Prices Current of Chemical & Physical Apparatus and Assay Goods* (New York: Eimer and Amend, 1892), 70.

Page 121 (III. Amherst). "Phoenix Row, 1840," lithograph in Carpenter and Morehouse, *History of the Town of Amherst, Massachusetts* (Amherst, Mass.: Carpenter and Morehouse, 1896), 446.

Page 123 (Chapter 11). "An old wood-cut of Common," in Carpenter and Morehouse, *History of the Town of Amherst, Massachusetts* (Amherst, Mass.: Carpenter and Morehouse, 1896), 296.

Page 130 (Figure 27). A map of Amherst with a view of the college and Mount Pleasant Institution by Alonzo Gray and Charles B. Adams, published by Pendleton's Lithography, 1833.

Page 133 (Chapter 12). "Hitchcock home in Amherst," photograph in Alice M. Walker, *Historic Homes of Amherst* (Amherst, Mass.: Carpenter and Morehouse, 1905), 86.

Page 135 (Figure 28). Reverend Zephaniah Swift Moore (1770-1823), in W. S. Tyler, *A History of Amherst College* (New York: Frederick H. Hitchcock, 1895), 27.

Page 139 (Figure 29). The first page of Edward Hitchcock's lecture notes for geology, ca 1828, courtesy of Amherst College Archives and Special Collections, Amherst, Mass.

Page 141 (Figure 30). Posters by Orra White Hitchcock for use in Edward Hitchcock's classes at Amherst College. Above, "Sectional view of the crust of the earth," 72¼" x 73¼"; below, *Ornithichnites* tracks, 27" x 65½". Dimensions are from R. Herbert and D. D'Arienzo, *Orra White Hitchcock: An Amherst Woman of Art and Science.*

Page 145 (Chapter 13). "View of Amherst in 1835 from Mount Pleasant with the Holyoke Range in the distance," by Henry J. Van Lennep, in E. Hitchcock, *Final Report on the Geology of Massachusetts* (Northampton, Mass.: J. H. Butler, 1841), Plate 6.

Page 148 (Figure 31) Title page, E. Hitchcock, *Dyspepsy Forestalled and Resisted* (Amherst, Mass.: J. S. and C. Adams, 1831).

Page 151 (Figure 32). "Mineralogy," in the *Franklin* (Mass.) *Herald*, September 23, 1817, 3.

Page 154 (Figure 33). "Rocking stone: Fall River," in E. Hitchcock, *Final Report on the Geology of Massachusetts* (Northampton, Mass.: J. H. Butler, 1841), 375.

Page 155 (Chapter 14). "Sketch on Cape Ann," by Henry J. Van Lennep, in E. Hitchcock, *Final Report on the Geology of Massachusetts* (Northampton, Mass.: J. H. Butler, 1841, 270.

Pages 158-9 (Figure 34). Edward Hitchcock's travels for the Massachusetts Geological Survey, 1830-1833

Page 162 (Figure 35). Geological map of Massachusetts, in E. Hitchcock, *Report on the Geology, Mineralogy, Botany, and Zoology of Massachusetts* (Amherst, Mass.: J. S. and C. Adams, 1833), Plate I.

Page 165 (Figure 36) Top, left, a page from Hitchcock's 1830 geological survey notes; top, right, a page from Hitchcock's 1832 notes including a cross section through the Connecticut River, courtesy of Amherst College Archives and Special Collections; below, the same cross section redrawn by Orra White Hitchcock as it appeared in E. Hitchcock, *Report on the Geology, Mineralogy, Botany, and Zoology of Massachusetts* (Amherst, Mass.: J. S. and C. Adams, 1833), 423.

Page 167 (Figure 37). "Confluence of Deerfield and Connecticut Rivers," woodcut by Orra White Hitchcock in E. Hitchcock, *Final Report on the Geology of Massachusetts* (Northampton, Mass.: J. H. Butler, 1841), 263.

Page 173 (Figure 38). Louis Agassiz (1807-1873), photograph by William Shaw Warren, image from Wikimedia, https://commons.wikimedia.org/w/index.php?curid=16445252

Page 176 (Figure 39). "Gay Head," by Orra White Hitchcock, in E. Hitchcock, *Final Report on the Geology of Massachusetts* (Northampton, Mass.: J. H. Butler, 1841), 275.

Page 177 (Chapter 15). "The Return," lithograph of drawing by Orra White Hitchcock, in E. Hitchcock, *A Wreath for the Tomb* (Amherst, Mass.: J. S. and C. Adams, 1839), frontispiece.

Page 180 (Figure 40). A page from the account book of Edward and Orra White Hitchcock, November 1829 to February 1831, courtesy of Amherst College Archives and Special Collections, Amherst, Mass.

Page 183 (Figure 41). Fossilized fern, woodcut by Orra White Hitchcock, *Plates Illustrating the Geology and Scenery of Massachusetts* (Amherst, Mass.: J. S. and C. Adams, 1833), Plate XIII.

Page 184 (Figure 42). "Bashapish falls," woodcut by Orra White Hitchcock in E. Hitchcock, *Final Report on the Geology of Massachusetts* (Northampton, Mass.: J. H. Butler, 1841), 291.

Page 188 (Figure 43). Map of locations of fossil footmarks.

Page 189 (Chapter 16). "A view of the Moody Footmark Quarry…," in E. Hitchcock, *Ichnology of New England* (Boston, Mass.: William White, 1858), frontispiece.

Page 191 (Figure 44). Dr. James Deane (1801-1858), image used with permission of the Historical Society of Greenfield, Greenfield, Mass.

Page 193 (Figure 45). Red sandstone slabs with tracks, in E. Hitchcock, *Ichnology of New England* (Boston, Mass.: William White, 1858), Plate LII.

Page 194 (Figure 46). Hitchcock's first effort at a taxonomy of the fossil footmarks, in E. Hitchcock, "Ornithichnology—Description of the Foot marks of Birds, (Ornithichnites) on new Red Sandstone in Massachusetts," *American Journal of Science and Arts* 29 (1836): 307-40, 316-7.

Page 201 (Chapter 17). "Amherst College 1821," drawing by Mary Hitchcock, lithograph by J. H. Bufford, in E. Hitchcock, *Reminiscences of Amherst College* (Northampton, Mass.: Bridgman & Childs, 1863), 57.

Page 203 (Figure 47). Portrait of Reverend Heman Humphrey (1779-1861), oil painting by Charles Loring Elliott, 1848, gift of Humphrey Doermann, courtesy of Mead Art Museum, Amherst Coll., Amherst, Mass.

Page 204 (Figure 48). "A Whole Hog Abolitionist," *Boston Investigator*, July 22, 1836, 3.

Page 209 (Figure 49). "Samuel Williston," steel engraving in *History of the Connecticut Valley* in *Massachusetts with Illustrations and Biographical Sketches*. 2 vols. Philadelphia, PA: Louis H. Everts, 1879, 284.

Page 211 (IV. President Hitchcock). "The President's House" in W. S. Tyler, *A History of Amherst College* (Frederick H. Hitchcock, New York, 1895), 82.

Page 213 (Chapter 18). "North-western view of Amherst College," wood engraving by John Warner Barber in *Historical Collections* (Worcester, Mass.: Dorr, Howland and Company, 1839), 311.

Pages 220-1 (Figure 50). Edward Hitchcock and Orra White Hitchcock, standing, albumen print *carte de visite*, ca 1863, courtesy of Amherst College Archives and Special Collections, Amherst, Mass.

Page 223 (Chapter 19). "View from Mount Holyoke," wood engraving by John Warner Barber in *Historical Collections* (Worcester, Mass.: Dorr, Howland and Company, 1839), 341.

Page 229 (Figure 51). Map of mountain excursions at Amherst College, 1845-1861.

Page 235 (Figure 52). Edward Hitchcock, T*he Inseparable Trio, A Sermon Delivered Before His Excellency George H. Briggs, Governor, January 24, 1850* (Boston, Mass.: Dutton and Wentworth, 1850.)

Page 236 (Figure 53). "Diluvial grooves in gneiss: Billerica," by Orra White Hitchcock in E. Hitchcock, *Report on the Geology, Mineralogy, Botany, and Zoology of Massachusetts* (Amherst, Mass.: J. S. and C. Adams, 1833), 160.

Page 237 (Chapter 20). "Woods Cabinet and Observatory," pen-and-ink drawing, in W. S. Tyler, *A History of Amherst College* (Frederick H. Hitchcock, New York, 1895), 116.

Page 240 (Figure 54). New telescope in the Lawrence Observatory, 1854, photograph, courtesy of Amherst College Archives and Special Collections, Amherst, Mass.

Page 241 (Figure 55). The collections of Charles U. Shepard as exhibited in Walker Hall, 1868 or later, courtesy of Amherst College Archives and Special Collections, Amherst, Mass.

Page 245 (Figure 56). "Cascade in Leverett," woodcut by Henry J. Van Lennep. in E. Hitchcock, *Final Report on the Geology of Massachusetts* (Northampton, Mass.: J. H. Butler, 1841), 287.

Page 247 (Chapter 21). "The transatlantic steam ship Liverpool," lithograph by H. R. Robinson, image from Library of Congress, Washington, DC. LC-DIG-pga-08080.

Page 251 (Figure 57). Map of the Hitchcocks' European tour, 1850.

Page 259 (Chapter 22). "American railroad," lithograph, in *Eighty Years' Progress of the United States* (New York: New National Publishing House, 1864), 199.

Page 263 (Figure 58). "New library at Amherst," in F. Gleason, *Ballou's Pictorial Drawing-Room Companion* Vol. 8 (Boston, Mass.: M. M. Ballou, 1855), 169.

Page 266 (Figure 59). Cover of *The Religion of Geology and Its Connected Sciences*. 2nd ed. (London: James Blackwood and Company, 1859).

Page 271 (Figure 60). Top, left, advertisement for Ayer's Cherry Pectoral cough remedy, 1891; right, poster for submarine armor with Hitchcock testimonial, 1854, courtesy of Amherst College Archives and Special Collections, Amherst, Mass.; bottom, lightning rod advertisement with Hitchcock testimonial, *Franklin Democrat*, June 19, 1854.

Page 275 (Figure 61). Assyrian relief representing King Ashurnasirpal II from Room H in the Palace of Ashurnasirpal II, from the Nineveh Gallery, gift of Dr. Henry John Lobdell (Class of 1849), courtesy of Mead Art Museum, Amherst College.

Page 279 (V. Retirement). "Appleton Cabinet," in E. Hitchcock, *Ichnology of New England* (Boston, Mass.: William White, 1858), Plate IV.

Page 281 (Chapter 23). Sketch of the interior of the Ichnological Cabinet, in E. Hitchcock, *Ichnology of New England* (Boston, Mass.: William White, 1858), Plate IV.

Page 288 (Figure 62). Left, fern fossil in E. Hitchcock, Jr., "Description of a New Species of Clathropteris, Discovered in the Connecticut Valley Sandstone." *AJS* 2nd ser. 20 (July 1855): 22-25; right, fossil shell in E. Hitchcock, Jr., "A New Fossil Shell in the Connecticut River Sandstone." *AJS* 2nd ser. 22 (September 1856): 239-240.

Page 294 (Figure 63). Ambrotype sketches of three sandstone slabs with tracks, in E. Hitchcock, *Ichnology of New England* (Boston, Mass.: William White, 1858), Plate XLII.

Page 295 (Chapter 24). "Sleigh ride," by C. T. Willis, in *St. Nicholas Magazine* 44 (December 1916), 165

Page 303 (Figure 64). "Turner's Falls," lithograph of drawing by Orra Hitchcock in E. Hitchcock, *Plates Illustrating the Geology and Scenery of Mass.* (Amherst, Mass.: J. S. and C. Adams, 1833), Plate VIII.

Page 307 (Figure 65). Illustrations drawn through the microscope in E. Hitchcock and E. Hitchcock, Jr., *Elementary Anatomy and Physiology* (New York: lvison, Phinney & Company, 1860, 10, 18, 20.

Page 310 (Figure 66). The interior of the Appleton Cabinet, undated photograph courtesy of Amherst College Archives and Special Collections, Amherst, Mass.

Page 315 (Chapter 25). Orra White Hitchcock, head-and-shoulders portrait from *carte de visite*, 1860, photographer J. L. Lovell, courtesy of Amherst College Archives and Special Collections, Amherst, Mass.

Page 320 (Figure 67). Portrait of Reverend William A. Stearns (1810-1884), in A. Van Wagenen, *Genealogy and Memoirs of Isaac Stearns and His Descendants* (Syracuse, N.Y. : Courier Printing Co., 1901), 356.

Page 321 (Figure 68). *Megatherium*, poster on canvas by Orra White Hitchcock, courtesy of Amherst College Archives and Special Collections, Amherst, Mass.

Page 322 (Figure 69). Dr. Edward Hitchcock, Jr., photograph in Amherst College Class Album 1881, courtesy of Amherst College Archives and Special Collections, Amherst, Mass.

Page 323 (Figure 70). Charles H. Hitchcock, photograph in William H. Ballou, "World's Geologists at St. Petersburg," *Appleton's Popular Science Monthly* 51 (1897), 217.

Page 326 (Figure 71). Map of Amherst College circa 1860.

Page 328 (Figure 72). Reverend William S. Tyler (1810-1897), photograph, in Amherst College Class Album 1881, courtesy of Amherst College Archives and Special Collections, Amherst, Mass.

Page 329 (Chapter 26). Portrait of Edward Hitchcock, lithograph, in E. Hitchcock, *Reminiscences of Amherst College* (Northampton, Mass.: Bridgman and Childs, 1863), frontispiece.

Page 335 (Figure 73). View of Amherst College, Amherst College Catalog 1859-1860, courtesy of Amherst College Archives and Special Collections, Amherst, Mass.

Page 337 (Figure 74). Advertisement for *Reminiscences of Amherst College*, in *Hampshire Gazette*, March 15, 1864.

Page 339 (Chapter 27). Amherst's third meetinghouse, in W. S. Tyler, *A History of Amherst College* (Frederick H. Hitchcock, New York, 1895), 204.

Page 346 (Figure 75). Emily Hitchcock Terry, portrait from *carte de visite*, photograph by Hofman, undated, courtesy of Smith College Archives.

Page 347 (Figure 76). The Hitchcock monument, West Cemetery, Amherst, 2020, photograph by the author.

Page 351 (Chapter 28). Ambrotype sketch of slab with tracks of *Grallator cuneatus* and *formosus*, *Argozoum pari-digitatum* and *Brontozoum*, in E. Hitchcock. *Ichnology of New England* (Boston, Mass.: William White, 1858), Plate XXXIX.

Page 357 (Figure 77). *Archaeopteryx,* an artist's conception, in G. Mivart, *On the Genesis of Species* (London: Macmillan and Company, 1871), 132.

Page 359 (Figure 78). Photographs of tracks of *Anomoepus*, in E. Hitchcock, *Supplement to the Ichnology of New England* (Boston, Mass.: Wright and Potter, 1865), Plate XV.

Page 361 (Chapter 29). "Palaeontological Chart," attributed to Orra White Hitchcock, in E. Hitchcock, *Elementary Geology* (New York: Ivison and Phinney, 1840), frontispiece.

Page 365 (Figure 79). Charles Darwin, portrait in watercolor by George Richmond, 1840.

Page 407. Photograph by Michael B. Milsom

Index

About the Author

ROBERT T. MCMASTER's interest in Edward Hitchcock began when he visited the Pratt Museum of Natural History at Amherst College over half a century ago. After completing his undergraduate studies at Clark University in 1970, he attended graduate school at Andover Newton Theological School and Boston College, earning a master's degree in geology and education at B.C. in 1974. He taught middle school science and worked as an administrator for several environmental education organizations over the next fifteen years. Returning to graduate school in 1990, he earned an M.A. in biological sciences at Smith College and a Ph.D. in plant biology at the University of Massachusetts. He taught biology at Holyoke Community College in Holyoke, Massachusetts, from 1994 to 2014. He has authored many articles on botany, conservation biology, and the history of science, and has written three historical novels, *Trolley Days*, *The Dyeing Room*, and *Noah's Raven,* set in New England in the World War I era.

THE TROLLEY DAYS BOOK SERIES
Novels of early 20th century America

The nineteen-teens was a tumultuous era in American history. The pace of social change was dizzying: the rising tide of worker unrest, the battle for women's suffrage, the scourge of discrimination against minorities. New technologies–electricity, the telephone, the automobile–were transforming life. Meanwhile the war raging in Europe was drawing America inexorably into its vortex.

Author Robert T. McMaster transports his readers back in time to early 20th century America in the Trolley Days Series of historical novels. Set in a bustling New England industrial city, these books follow the lives of teenagers Jack Bernard and Tom Wellington through good times and bad, hope and despair, love and loss. Readers young and old will be captivated by the world of their grandparents and great-grandparents, an era seemingly remote that nonetheless speaks to us across the generations.

Trolley Days, ***The Dyeing Room***, and ***Noah's Raven*** are currently available in paperback and in several eBook formats.

For additional information visit
www.TrolleyDays.net

Made in the USA
Columbia, SC
15 August 2021